SLIPPERY ROCK UNIVERSITY
The Legend Behind the Name

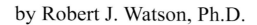

by Robert J. Watson, Ph.D.

Slippery Rock Specialties, Ltd.
100 Watson Glen
Slippery Rock, Pennsylvania 16057

Cover Photo Courtesy of Gordon Ovenshine, Slippery Rock University Office of Public Relations.

Slippery Rock Specialties, Ltd.
100 Watson Glen
Slippery Rock, Pennsylvania 16057

© 2011 by Robert Jay Watson
All rights reserved. Published 2011

Printed in the United States of America

Layout and design by Kari Anne Zeigler

ISBN: 978-0-9847822-0-8
Library of Congress Control Number: 2011940600

Printed by

M ECHLING
BOOKBINDERY
Books...made to order

1124 Oneida Valley Road Rt. 38
Chicora, PA 16025
1-800-941-3735
www.mechlingbooks.com

TABLE OF CONTENTS

Alma Mater
Where the Slippery Rock Creek wanders
With its sparkling falls,
There in stately grace and beauty,
Stand old S. R. Halls.

Chorus
Sing her praises loud resounding,
Speed them on their way;
We'll be true to thee, oh, S. R.
True for aye and aye.

II.
All thy halls the day in dying
Crowns with golden light,
And the morn in waking splendor
Greets thee in thy might.

III.
Long may you, our Alma Mater,
Shed your light abroad,
As your loyal sons and daughters
Live for you and God.

Joan Easley
Adda M. Elliott
1921

FOREWORD

Recently I was asked if I found it difficult to leave Slippery Rock University when so many exciting projects were still underway. Wouldn't it be nice, they suggested, to stay and see them through completion? The obvious answer is "yes." But I told my questioner that all of us first step into the stream of history when we arrive and step out again when we leave; but the stream flowed before us and will continue to flow after us. Rarely is anyone privileged to step in at the headwaters of an institution's history and remain through the entire journey down the stream. We are present only in our time and place. To understand our time and place and to appreciate what adventures might unfold downstream, we should be students of what occurred upstream. And if we are fortunate, we will have a guide that interprets our lessons in ways that enhance our understanding and appreciation for our heritage and gives insight to our future.

We are fortunate to have a history of Slippery Rock University. Historian Rufus Fears argues that human nature never really changes such that similar circumstances will produce similar events. For those of you familiar with the first volume of our history will be stuck by the similar themes that appear in this volume. The lesson is that we should know our history to recognize those themes so that today and tomorrow's leaders and participants would have the wisdom to respond in ways that produce better results. As Professor Fears concludes, the lessons from the past help make decisions in the present and plans for the future.

History is a story and like all stories there are representations of facts and events that come alive in our mind by humanistic interpretations. Good history presents a story that shapes the way we understand the present. The story weaves together dispassionate data to present the genius or folly of decisions and the consequences of events. Even though the prime character in this story is an institution, we know it best through the people who shaped it. Through the narrative we become involved in these lives to learn of their problems and triumphs. A good story tells us of people and how they acted together. If there is anything unique about the Slippery Rock story it is in the drama that often accompanied the university's most significant moments. As noted historian Peter Stearns said, "History helps us understand change and how the society we live in came to be. The past causes the present, and so the future."

Any institution is a product of its past and that is certainly true for Slippery Rock University. When the first volume of this history was completed, the institution was strong and growing both in size and academic reputation. It was taking a different shape from its origins but firmly built on those foundations established more than one hundred and twenty years ago. Now it is a comprehensive university without a singular disciplinary focus. Although teacher preparation is still a significant degree choice among its students, other disciplines have increased their enrollments to shape a new definition for the university. You will also find that technology unimaginable in the history reported in the first volume has played a significant role in shaping the Slippery Rock University of today and will be an even more dominant determinant for the future.

What you will also find in this second volume is the most recent stages of transformation shaped both by outside constraints such as the persistent decline in state allocations and by people such as my predecessors and their compelling visions for the university. Like most public universities across the nation, Slippery Rock University's mission and responsibility to the Commonwealth of Pennsylvania has been that of a public good committed to providing high quality affordable access to those who seek a higher education. In this history you will find that the social contract between the Commonwealth as attended by elected officials and the university has become more one-sided with the university absorbing more of the costs of educating its students from tuition revenue and not from the taxpayers. The consequences of more than two decades of this persistent shift in support have had a profound impact on the directions taken by university leadership and resulted in different demographics represented by today's student population. This is one of many fascinating threads woven in this volume.

One lesson from these historical threads is discovering how Slippery Rock University has become a set of best practices. Here you find examples of an institution that has overcome challenges of finance and enrollment to be models of fiscal management, enrollment and retention strategies, and how the institution has created an environment marked by mutual respect within a community of scholars, educators, staff, and students.

We are fortunate that Dr. Robert Watson has devoted so much time to this second volume of Slippery Rock University history. I doubt anyone is more dedicated to Slippery Rock University or has such an archive of evidence about the university. As a member of a family that can trace every year of existence and five generations as stockholders, trustees, faculty, administrators, and students at this one university, Dr. Watson has lived in the history of the institution his entire life in one capacity or another. As a witness to that history, he could have simply penned a book. Instead, he carefully researched, interviewed, and thoroughly investigated as well as documented this history. The readers as well as the University are in debt to his dedication and contribution.

Robert M. Smith, President
Slippery Rock University
November 1, 2011

PREFACE

"Where the Slippery Rock Creek wanders" today, lies a village home to a premier residential public university. Nearly 125 years ago, the citizens of Centerville, striving to create an educational opportunity for their daughters and sons, gave birth to its beginnings. Founded in 1889, this two-year normal school underwent several stages of metamorphosis – state teachers college, state college, and university. However, perhaps one of the greatest stages has occurred, without the name ever changing. From three barn-type buildings, situated on ten acres of agricultural fields, the Normal School realized a humble origin. As Governor Beaver stated upon the recognition of the Normal School, it was "not so much for what the buildings were but on account of the supreme faith of the people that they were doing something worthy of acceptance." Thus, began a nurturing process that was so personal, the school was destined to be successful. Through the years of change and growth, emerged a university, with so much more than an unusual name. Now, dozens of modern buildings with superb conveniences and outstanding technological infrastructure are situated on more than 650 acres of picturesque landscape. However, perhaps the most important achievement of Slippery Rock University is the ability of its outstanding faculty and staff to deliver unparalleled opportunities to its students, every day. The author wishes the reader enjoyment when perusing these pages, which hopefully give justice to this premier residential public university.

No work of this magnitude could ever be accomplished without considerable assistance. The writer expresses his gratitude for the support given him from so many faculty, staff, alumni, and friends of the University who provided the author with important data included in this study. A large debt of gratitude is due Ms. Claudia Fischer who provided her skills and expertise in the preparation of the endnotes and appendix as well as communicating for the author with faculty and staff. Special recognition is due the Offices of University Archives and University Public Relations for their tireless efforts. Sincere appreciation is given to the following faculty, staff and alumni who gave special attention to providing the author photographs and other documents utilized in this effort. In alphabetical order, they are Ms. Deborah Baker, Mr. Larry Campbell, Mr. Bryan Fuhs, Mr. Jonathon Holtz, Mr. Robert McComas, Mr. Kevin McLatchy, Ms. Tina Moser, Dr. Bruce Orvis, Mr. Gordon Ovenshine, Mr. John Papa, Ms. Kelli Rensel, and Ms. Judith Silva.

Heartfelt appreciation and highest praise is extended to Dr. Richard K. Seckinger who was the author's doctoral advisor and professor, and still today, his personal friend and mentor. It was this man who instilled in the author a love for historical research and the desire to publish it.

Finally, the writer expresses his gratitude to his loving wife, Karen, and daughters, Kate, Laura, and Emily, for their continuous encouragement, understanding and support during this time of research and publication.

The writer will always be indebted for the inspiration and love given him by his parents, John A. and G. Irene Watson.

CHAPTER I

In the Beginning

In 1753, Major George Washington and Christopher Gist made their way through the region in western Pennsylvania later to be known as Slippery Rock township en route to Fort LeBoeuf, some ninety miles north.[1] Some four decades later, in 1796, while Washington was now in his second term as the young nation's president, Zebulon Cooper and his uncle, Nathanial Cooper, arrived along the banks of the Slippery Rock Creek to become the area's first permanent residents.[2]

The majority of early settlers following the Coopers were of Scotch-Irish ancestry and, true to their traditions, recognized the family, church and school to be the most important influences in the lives of their children. Early in the 1800's they established their first school on the Woolford farm about one and one-half miles northeast of Centerville (Slippery Rock). The Kelly School, as it was known, operated for several years with Stephen Cooper, William Parker and Adam Dunn as teachers.[3] Other schools followed and, in the 1820's, a log school house was erected northwest of town. In the following decade, another school house was built to the south of the town.[4] In the town of Centerville, two school buildings were built in 1857; one for youngsters and the other for older pupils. In 1881, a four-room frame school house was built on New Castle Street and served as the town school and community center until it burned in 1900.[5]

The desire for higher education was also present during these early years. From 1848 to 1850, a private school was operated by William Murphy, a chair maker, who was also an able scholar and progressive teacher. Other attempts to establish private schools in the 1850's and '60's were unsuccessful.[6] In the mid 1870's, Alfred D. Lee came to Centerville from Scio College, Ohio, and proposed to establish an academy. By selling lots from a tract of land he supposedly bought on Wolf Creek, he gained sufficient funds to purchase initial materials for the construction of a four-room brick building. The Hemlock Springs College operated somewhat

successfully with the students studying one subject per six-week term; but, because Mr. Lee lacked funds for final payments for all the land and building materials, the school was closed and partially dismantled. No further attempts were made for higher education in the Slippery Rock area until 1887.[7]

During the summer and fall of 1887, the citizens of Centerville, a small western Pennsylvania community in Butler County of less than a thousand inhabitants, were seriously considering establishing an academy.[8] While an elementary school was available, there was no more advanced school to which the young people could go. They were forced to travel to Grove City, Clarion, Greenville or New Wilmington for an advanced education.

In order to measure the depth of interest in the borough, J. T. Bingham called a meeting to be held in the local Presbyterian church on the evening of December 7, 1887.[9] John Reed presided over this meeting with Dr. C. W. Bard, a local physician, recording the discussions.[10] The Reverend Robinson, a local minister, spoke to the group on the civic responsibility of the community toward education.[11] Interest in a school was high, so they quickly turned to consider ways to finance the undertaking. They adopted two subscription plans. One was designed to cover the costs of the principal's salary and general maintenance of the school. Under it, supporters of the school were asked to contribute five dollars a year for the next three years. After three years, they thought the school would be self-sufficient. A second plan was designed with the hope of collecting funds for a school building.[12]

About two weeks later, on December 19, Mr. Bingham called his group together to give the discouraging report that, despite their efforts to raise money on behalf of the academy, only thirty-four subscribers had pledged to pay five dollars for each of the next three years.[13] This amounted to only $510, which was hardly enough to maintain a school. Dr. C. W. Bard reported that $2,475 had been pledged for the school's building fund.[14] Though discouraged, these men, who were determined to have their school at Centerville, began to consider alternatives. Dr. C. W. Bard and J. E. Bard suggested that a normal school might receive more community support than an academy.[15] They were right, for the suggestion generated immediate enthusiasm and J. N. Watson, J. M. Covert, and F. P. Bingham were asked to find out how much it would cost to set up a normal school and what state requirements would have to be met in order to have such a school at Centerville.[16]

Within a week, Dr. A. M. Patterson and J. E. Bard had traveled to Clarion and came back with the sobering news that the cost was much higher than had been expected. At this meeting on January 16, 1888, Mr. Bard then urged that a committee of ten be appointed to solicit additional subscriptions for the maintenance and building funds. J. N. Watson, J. H. Christley, J. C. Kerr, J. P. McQuistion, Neyman Christley, T. S. Coulter, A. J. Bard, William Kaufman, W. H. Wilson and Robert McCoy were named to that second fund raising committee.[17]

Interest increased steadily and for the first time key support from outside the geographic area emerged as Hon. John M. Greer and J. M. Galbreath of Butler, on February 6, 1888, addressed a group of interested individuals.[18] Their stirring words aroused such enthusiasm that "a large amount of money was subscribed before the meeting adjourned."[19]

The committee of ten men, charged with the responsibility of raising at least $15,000, agreed to the following subscription plan by which these new funds were to be collected:

> We, the undersigned, agree to pay the sum opposite our names for the purpose of erecting Normal School buildings in Centerville Borough or vicinity, said subscriptions to be null and void unless the sum of Fifteen Thousand Dollars be subscribed. Said subscription payable as follows: one third when contract is given, one third when buildings are half completed, and balance three months from date of second payment; said subscriptions to be considered as shares at One Hundred Dollars each—each share representing one vote.[20]

The women of Centerville also rose to the occasion and established the Ladies Normal School Fund which greatly assisted the subscription committee.[21] Together, the women and men of the town of Centerville persevered and through such events as the "double up" meeting of February 24, 1888, at which many subscribers doubled their original subscriptions, sufficient funds were raised to establish a permanent organization, The Slippery Rock State Normal School Association.[22]

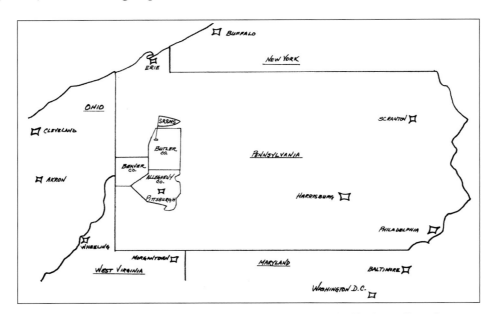

Eleventh Normal School District, Butler, Beaver and Allegheny Counties

In March of 1888, the stockholders of the Slippery Rock State Normal School Association held an organizational meeting. John N. Watson, A. M. Patterson, and J. C. Kerr drafted an agenda which included the following questions:

> What shall be the name of our Association
> Who are legal voters in this Association
> How shall we vote
> Who shall be our Chairman
> Who shall be our Vice President
> Who shall be our Secretary
> Who shall be our Treasurer
> Who shall be our Collector
> Who shall be our Notifier
> Shall the Trustees select the location or shall it be decided by the Association
> Shall all committees be appointed by Chairman or voted by Association[23]

Later that evening, the Association reconvened to hear an address by Hon. John M. Greer, State Senator from Butler. They also agreed to limit the capital stock of the Association to $40,000—four hundred shares at one hundred dollars per share.[24] Thirteen members of the Association were elected to serve on the Board of Turstees: George Maxwell, T. F. Patton, Neyman Christley, J. C. Kerr, Benjamin Pearson, Lewis Patterson, T. S. Coulter, A. M. Patterson, W. H. Wilson, J. E. Bard, H. P. Griffith, C. W. Bard, and William Kaufman.[25]

A week later, the Board of Trustees met and elected the following officers: President—George Maxwell; Vice-President—J. C. Kerr; Secretary—C. W. Bard; Treasurer—W. H. Wilson.[26] The stockholders, meeting separately at the same time, adopted a constitution of the Association prepared by G. L. Snyder, J. M. Greer, and T. S. Coulter.[27] With the newly-elected officers leading the Trustees, such decisions would be made regarding the location of the school site, cost, style, and construction of the buildings, selection of the curriculum, and employment of the first faculty and principal.

Lewis Patterson, a member of the Board, suggested that they consider his in-town property as the site for the normal school. On March 19, 1888, the Board visited the property and after some discussion, unanimously accepted his proposal.[28] The details of this offer were later set forth by Mr. Patterson:

> I, Lewis Patterson, will sell the ten acres bounded as follows On the South by Mel. Dites lot and four rod on Kiester Station road North and East by land of Lewis Patterson West by Cartwright Hilgar and others at two hundred dollars per acre ($200.) I will subscribe fifteen hundred dollars ($1500.) I will retain five hundred dollars in stock ($500) of subscription and give the balance of subscription – one thousand dollars ($1000.) in stock to whom I may choose and the balance or five hundred dollars ($500.) a bond is given payable when the state receives [sic] said property or if the state does not receive [sic] it I exchange the bond for that amount of stock to be given to whom I choose.[29]

Throughout the month of March, the building committee of the Trustees, chaired by George Maxwell, discussed with architects building designs and costs. They decided to ask Mr. S. W. Foulke, architect of New Castle, Pennsylvania, to make preliminary sketches for three buildings and give an estimate of the construction costs. One building was to serve as a chapel, classroom building and office building and the two others were to be the dormitories for men and women.[30] Satisfied with Mr. Foulke's work, the Trustees employed him as the architect and instructed him to construct plans and specifications for these buildings.[31]

After nearly a month of discussion of the building plans, the Board of Trustees invited contractors to submit construction bids. Early in May, the Trustees unanimously elected to award the $25,000 building contract to J. M. Vance of New Castle, Pennsylvania;[32] however, five days later, the Trustees withdrew its offer to Mr. Vance and, with one dissenting vote, decided to award the building contract to Joseph F. Gorely, also of New Castle.[33]

During these months of planning for the construction of the campus, the Centerville community rallied in support of the normal school. An indication of the variety of such support is seen in the following account of the efforts of the "young ladies" of the community to raise money for the proposed school.

> Not to be outdone by the older people, the young ladies pledged $1,500 for the building fund and proceeded to earn and pay this pledge.

One of their most popular activities was the conducting of an "ice cream parlor" two or three nights a week in any available store. All of the ice cream and cake not only was "home-made" but was donated. The girls drove with horse and buggy for miles about the countryside collecting the cream and eggs for this confection. Their efforts must have been appreciated when factory ice cream was unknown, but best of all the pledge was paid in full.[34]

Mr. T. S. Coulter, chairman of the subscription committee, was able to report that on May 3, 1888, $17,325.00 had been subscribed for the school.[35] This figure did not include "doubtful" subscriptions. This was an impressively large sum of money pledged by local citizens for a school whose future was in no way certain. State approval for a normal school was absolutely essential and this, of course, would not be forthcoming until the community had demonstrated its firm commitment toward such a school.

Construction continued throughout the summer and fall of 1888. The Trustees, stockholders and townspeople all assisted in the work on the buildings whenever time would permit.

According to an early account, the people in the community

worked with a will and with one ultimate aim, the construction of something that would benefit the surrounding country. If any could be given more credit than others, the credit for unselfish effort must be given to George Maxwell and to Lewis Patterson who gave ungrudgingly of their time and efforts though neither had children to reap the benefits of the school. Mr. Maxwell gave his entire time during the summer of 1888 to overseeing the construction of the buildings.[36]

Another Trustee, A. M. Patterson, hauled stones from the school grounds and with them constructed a road.[37] The Ladies Normal Fund Association sewed all the carpets for the dormitory rooms and made all the necessary bedding.[38] A group of young women donated the pulpit Bible for the Chapel.[39] In November of 1888, the Trustees took the official step of filing with the state their application for a normal school.[40]

As construction drew to a close in the middle of a severe winter, the townspeople could begin to see completion drawing nearer. John Greer, aided by J. E. Bard and John Kerr, sent out invitations to those who would participate in the inspection of the Slippery Rock

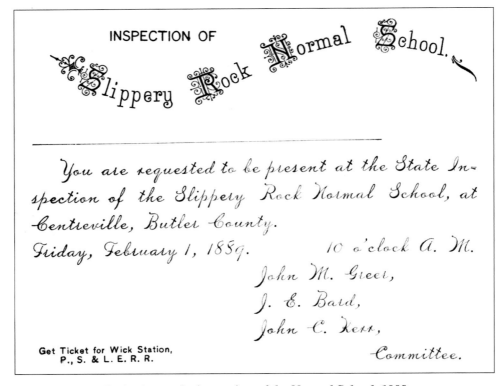

INSPECTION OF
Slippery Rock Normal School.

You are requested to be present at the State Inspection of the Slippery Rock Normal School, at Centreville, Butler County.

Friday, February 1, 1889.   10 o'clock A. M.

John M. Greer,

J. E. Bard,

John C. Kerr,

Committee.

Get Ticket for Wick Station,
P., S. & L. E. R. R.

Invitation to the inspection of the Normal School, 1889

4

Normal School, to be held at ten o'clock a.m. on Friday, February 1, 1889.[41] The stage had been readied and the scene had been set for one of the most dramatic events in the history of the Slippery Rock area. Local citizens had given thousands of hours of their time in preparation for this great event.

As that Friday, February 1, 1889, dawned, the buildings stood magnificently amidst a flawless white background of fresh-fallen snow, as if Mother Nature also had been awaiting that day.[42] From the Wick Station, some three miles east of town, the members of the inspection committee, appointed by Governor Beaver, were shuttled over the snowy countryside in sleighs and sleds. The Hon. S. H. Miller of Mercer, as Chairman, led the inspection committee, composed of Dr. E. E. Higby, State Superintendent of Public Instruction, and other dignitaries, eight of whom were school superintendents from Western Pennsylvania.[43]

After a most thorough inspection of all the buildings, the Trustees, inspection committee and invited guests sat down, at noon, to a dinner in the campus dining hall prepared by the women of the town.[44] The crowd later assembled in the new chapel to hear several speeches. Finally, the Hon. S. H. Miller, speaking for the inspection committee, told the trustees and friends of the proposed school that they would recommend to Governor Beaver that the campus and buildings be accepted as a site for a state normal school.[45] The happy celebrations which followed that evening included a party in the new dining hall open to all townspeople. Governor Beaver quickly accepted the recommendation of his committee, explaining that he favored the recognition of the school "not so much for what the buildings were but on account of the supreme faith of the people that they were doing something worthy of acceptance."[46]

Shortly after the state approved the application for recognition as a state normal school, E. E. Higby, State Superintendent, appointed the following six Trustees to represent the state: John F. Dravo and J. Sharp Wilson from Beaver County; R. B. Scandrett and R. D. McGonnigle from Allegheny County; and John M. Greer and Thomas Robinson from Butler County.[47] The six Trustees representing the state joined the thirteen Trustees originally elected by the stockholders, and these nineteen formed the first Board of Trustees of Slippery Rock State Normal School.[48] Upon formation, the Board elected the following officers: George Maxwell, President; Dr. C. W. Bard, Secretary; and H. W. Wilson, Treasurer.[49]

Fulfilling one of their first responsibilities, the Trustees appointed James E. Morrow to be principal of the school. Born in West Virginia in 1837, he received his first academic degree from Jefferson College in 1856 at the age of 19. He began teaching and, through part-time study, he earned his license in law in December, 1859.

James E. Morrow,
Principal, 1889-1890

Practicing law when the Civil War began, he enlisted as a Private and advanced to the rank of Captain in 1863, in Company F of the first Virginia volunteer infantry. Following the war, he returned to education rather than law. He married Clara J. Johnson of Cumberland, Maryland, in 1867, and raised five boys and three girls: Fred, Earle, Ralph, Jay, Dwight, and Agnes, Alice and Hilda. One son, Dwight, gained fame as a lawyer, legislator and American ambassador, while Dwight's daughter, Anne Morrow Lindbergh, also brought fame to the Morrow name. In 1875, he earned the Master of Arts degree from Jefferson College and three years later began teaching mathematics in the Old Central High School in Pittsburgh.

In 1880, he was appointed principal of what is now the Conroy school in Pittsburgh. At the time of his appointment as principal and also as professor of psychology and history of education at Slippery Rock's new Normal School, he was completing his Doctor of Philosophy degree at Jefferson College.[50]

The Trustees appointed the following six teachers to the school's first faculty:

I. M. McClymonds, M. E.,
     School Management, Methods and Algebra.
I. N. Moore, A. B.,
     Ancient Languages and Natural Science.
John C. Ricketts,
     Arithmetic, History and Civil Government.
W. A. Beer, B. E.,
     Grammar, Rhetoric and Literature.
Maude C. Bingham, M. E.,
     Geometry, Geography and Drawing.
Lizzie A. Marshall,
     Instrumental Music.[51]

With the faculty appointed, Principal Morrow now could give attention to the task of developing a program of studies for the students who were soon to enter the school. They were undoubtedly guided by the school's philosophy: "The ultimate object of the Normal School is to make the Normal student, as far as possible, an educator."

Following the Governor's approval of the Normal School, announcements went out inviting students to apply for admission for the spring term starting on March 26 and ending on June 28, 1889. By the time the Normal School first opened its doors late in March of 1889, 168 students had been admitted. Over two-thirds of the students (116) came from Butler County with neighboring counties accounting essentially for the rest of the student body. Nineteen were from Mercer County; 18 from Lawrence; 7 from Allegheny; 5 from Beaver and 2 from Armstrong. One out-of-state student came from Mahoning County, Ohio. In the very first class, 94 students were women and 74 were men.[52]

So that the graduate would be qualified to teach in Pennsylvania's common schools, a two-year program designed to prepare the student to pass the examinations administered by the State Board of Examiners and to receive the teaching certificate from the state was developed.[53]

The Elementary Program included a Junior and Senior course of study. The Junior course of study included five divisions, E, D, C, B, and A, and a student was placed in the appropriate division based upon admission examinations. In 1889, the course work required in each of the five divisions of the Junior course of study was as follows:

Work of Division E.
     Arithmetic-Practical work through fractions.
     Grammar, with Composition and Spelling.
     Geography of United States and Europe.
     Writing.
     Drawing.
Work of Division D.
     Arithmetic-Practical work, at least to percentage.
     Chemistry.
     Composition, with Spelling.
     Drawing.
     Grammar.
     Political Geography.
     Reading, Voice Culture, Elementary Sounds, etc.
     United States History to the Civil War.
     Writing.
Work of Division C.
     Arithmetic-Practical work—last half of book.
     Algebra-First third of the subject.
     Book-keeping.
     Composition.
     Drawing.
     Elocution.
     Latin-Begun.
     Physiology.
     Civil Government.
Work of Division B.
     Arithmetic-First half completed.
     Algebra-Second third.
     Composition.
     Elocution.
     Grammar.
     History-Civil War and Reconstruction.
     Latin Reader.
     School Economy.
Work of Division A.
     Arithmetic-Last half completed.
     Algebra-Completed.
     Arithmetic-Last half completed.
     Algebra-Completed.
     Composition
     Grammar-Completed.[54]

Upon successful completion of Division A, the most difficult division of the Junior course, and with the recommendation of the faculty, a student was eligible to take the Junior course examination, offered annually by the State Board of Examiners. Upon passing the Junior course examination, a student received a certificate awarded by the Department of Public Instruction entitling the student to admission to the Senior course of study at any State Normal School of Pennsylvania.[55]

The single most important requirement of the Senior course at the Normal School was the model school practice teaching, since as the catalog explained "...

FACULTY.
JAS. E. MORROW, Principal.
I. N. Moore.
John C Ricketts.

FACULTY.
I. M. McClymonds.
W. A. Beer.
Maud Bingham.

Slippery Rock State Normal School.

· · ELEVENTH DISTRICT. · ·

ALLEGHENY, BEAVER AND BUTLER COUNTIES.

Announcement.

The attention of School officers, teachers, and others interested in improving our public instruction, is respectfully invited to our new State Normal School, that they may introduce to its advantages such young teachers of promise as aspire to more thorough preparation for their work.

Spring Term begins Tuesday, March 26, and ends Friday, June 28, 1889.

Expenses: *Tuition, per term,* - *Fourteen Dollars.*
Board, room rent, fuel and light, *Thirty-Two Dollars.*
One-half payable in advance, the balance at middle of the term.
Transportation of student and baggage from Kiesters, *Twenty-Five Cents.*

The State allowance will lessen the cost in some cases.

Location: *3½ miles from Kiesters, on Pittsburgh, Shenango & Lake Erie R. R.; 60 miles from Pittsburgh: 17 miles from Butler; 14 miles from Mercer; and 17 miles from New Castle.*

Special Advantages: *Healthfulness; convenience; noted honesty, hospitality, and religious character of community; new, commodious buildings, thoroughly warmed and ventilated; Presbyterian, United Presbyterian, Reformed Presbyterian and Methodist Episcopal Churches conveniently near.*

The boarding department is under the supervision of the Principal, who resides in the house and boards with the students.

Fall Term, Sixteen Weeks: September 3 to December 20, 1889.

For further information apply to

JAS. E. MORROW, Principal.

Slippery Rock, Pa., March 9, 1889.

Announcement of first term of the Normal School

Early domestic and maintenance staff

no one will be graduated who has not acquired a good degree of skill and success as a teacher." The required course work for the Senior course of study included the following:

First Term.
    Psychology.
    Plane Geometry.
    Physics-First half.
    Rhetoric and Composition.
    Methods.
    Practice and Criticism.
Second Term.
    Methods.
    Plane Geometry.
    Physics—Last half.
    Caesar.
    General History.
    Classics with Essays.
    Practice and Criticism.
Third Term.

    Botany.
    History of Education.
    Methods.
    Practice with Criticism.[56]

Upon successful completion of this program, the student was awarded a Bachelor of the Elements diploma.

Those who successfully completed the two-year, Elementary course of study, and who continued their studies for two additional years, and successfully taught two full terms in the Pennsylvania common schools, were awarded a second diploma, the Master of the Elements. Graduates of a State Normal School in Pennsylvania, who agreed to teach a minimum of two years in the state's common schools, were awarded the sum of fifty dollars.[57]

The schedule of classes for the three terms of the first complete school year, beginning the Fall of 1889, were as follows:

The activities enjoyed by those first Slippery Rock State Normal School students were lawn tennis, croquet,

RECITATIONS—PROGRAM FOR FALL TERM.

DIVISIONS	8:00		9:00	9:45	10:30	11:15		1:15	2:00	2:45	3:30
			FORENOON.					AFTERNOON.			
SENIOR.	Psychology	C H A P E L E X E R C I S E S	Geometry Practice	Pract.	Pract.	Pract.	I N T E R M I S S I O N	Pract.	Pract.	Comp. & Rhetoric	Pract.
JUNIOR A.			Arith.	Phys. Geog.	Alg.	Composition			Grammar		Elocution
JUNIOR B.	S. Economy			Alg.	Grammar	Comp. Hist.		Arith.	Latin Reader		Elocution
JUNIOR C.	Elocution & Bk'kpg.		Alg.	Geog.	Grammar	Writing		Arith. Beg. Lat.	Hist.	Phys. Dwg.	Comp.
JUNIOR D.				Geog.	Arith. Chem.	Writing		Grammar	Dwg.		Comp.
JUNIOR E.			Grammar	Eloc.	Writ.					Arith.	Geog.
SPECIAL	Caesar		Beg. Greek			Dwg.		Beg. Lat.	Latin Reader		
SPECIAL	Higher Algebra		Gen. Hist.	Bk'kpg.							

RECITATIONS—PROGRAM FOR SPRING AND SUMMER TERM.

DIVISIONS	8:00		9:00	9:45	10:30	11:15		1:15	2:00	2:45	3:30
			FORENOON.					AFTERNOON.			
SENIOR.	Elocution	C H A P E L E X E R C I S E S	Pract. Geometry	Pract. Botany	Pract.	Lit. & Comp.	I N T E R M I S S I O N	Pract.	Pract.	Pract.	Meth. & Hist. of Ed.
JUNIOR A.	Psychology		Arith.		Alg.	Composition		Physical Geog.	Grammar		Elocution
JUNIOR B.	School Economy			Alg.	Grammar	Composition		Arith.	History		Elocution
JUNIOR C.	Bk'kpg.		Alg. Bk'kpg.	Geog.	Grammar	Beg. Lat. Writing		Arith.	Elocution	Phys. Drawing	Composition
JUNIOR D.				Geog.	Arith. Chem.	Writing		Grammar	Eloc. Drawing	History	Composition
JUNIOR E.			Grammar	Elocution	Writing					Arith.	Geog.
SPECIAL	Latin		Caesar		Drawing	Beg. Latin			Greek		Civil Gov't.
SPECIAL			General History	Bk'kpg.							

RECITATIONS—PROGRAM FOR WINTER TERM.

DIVISIONS	FORENOON.						AFTERNOON.			
	8:00	C H A P E L E X E R C I S E S	9:00	9:45	10:30	11:15	1:15	2:00	2:45	3:30
SENIOR.	Caesar		Geometry Practice	Pract.	Pract.	Pract. Physics	Pract.	Pract.	Lit. & Comp.	Meth.
JUNIOR A.			Arith.	Phys. Geog.	Alg.	Compo-sition		Grammar	School Economy	Elocu-tion
JUNIOR B.	S. Economy			Alg.	Gram-mar	Compo-sition	Arith.	History		Civil Gov't.
JUNIOR C.	Bk'kpg.		Algebra Bk'kpg.	Geog.	Gram-mar	Writing	Arith.	Elocu-tion	Phys. Drawing	Compo-sition
JUNIOR D.				Geog.	Arith. Chem.	Writing	Grammar	Eloc. Dwg.	History	Compo-sition
JUNIOR E.			Grammar	Elocu-tion	Writing			Arith.		Geog.
SPECIAL			Latin				Latin Reader	Greek		Dwg.
SPECIAL			General History	Bk'kpg.						

baseball, and weekly socials on Saturdays from 7:30 p.m. until 9:00 p.m.[59] The students paid $32.50 the first spring term, which included room, board, and student fees or tuition.[60]

When the first students arrived on campus, they found a campus consisting of three buildings, as described in the first catalog:

There are three buildings, two dormitories and a main school building. They are situated on a commanding eminence. The two dormitories are each 40 x 232 feet, and three stories in height. They contain 150 rooms besides a reception room, dining hall, 40 x 75 kitchen, store rooms, etc. The main building is situated between the two dormitories. It is 60 x 100 feet. The first floor is devoted to recitation rooms, and the second floor is an assembly room. It is 60 x 85 feet; contains 800 opera chairs and a gallery 25 x 60, with 200 additional seats. The buildings are all heated by steam and lighted with natural gas. The buildings are supplied with pure, soft water.

Arrangements have already been made for many improvements during the summer vacation, viz: stone walks, bath rooms, laundry, ornamentation of grounds, and equipment of model school.[61]

In a remarkably short period of time, the citizens of Slippery Rock had created for the young people of the region a normal school. By their own efforts, they had acquired the land, erected buildings, appointed an administrator and approved a faculty. A curriculum which offered to students the ancient languages, the liberal arts and sciences, and a teacher-training program was organized. The foundation was well laid, upon which the future development of the school would proceed.

Three original buildings, North Hall, Chapel, South Hall, 1889

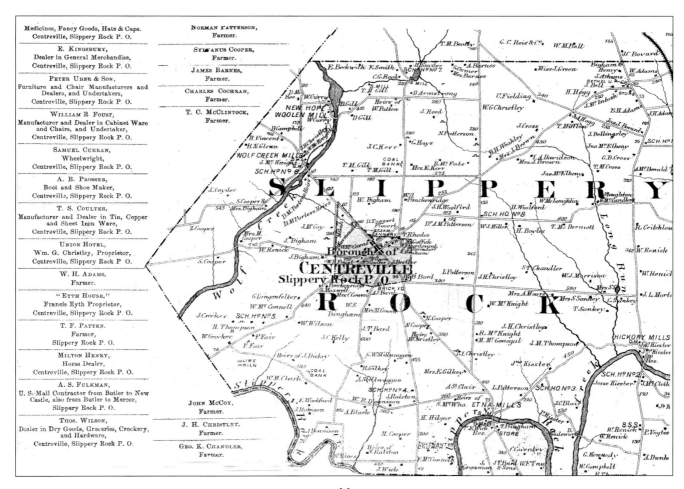

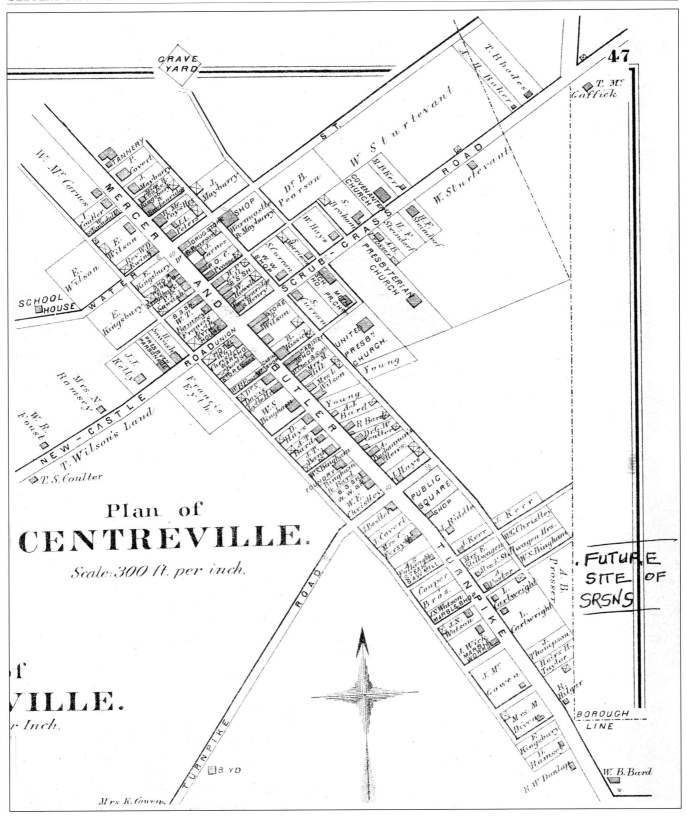

CHAPTER II

Early Years at the Normal School 1890-1916

In the fall of 1889, students flocked to Slippery Rock's Normal School to enter the first full academic year of study. Before the year was over, almost three hundred students were attending the school.[62] This rapid growth was to continue and in three short years the enrollment had doubled. By 1893, the school had over six hundred students in attendance.[63] With this remarkable expansion came many challenges to this young school.

In July of 1890, Dr. Morrow shocked the Board of Trustees with the announcement that he was resigning as principal. A search for his successor began immediately and, by September, Dr. Albert E. Maltby had been selected to head the school.

Dr. Maltby came to Slippery Rock from the Millersville State Normal School in eastern Pennsylvania where he directed the training school. By training, experience, and temperament, he appeared to be well qualified to lead the Slippery Rock State Normal School.[64] A native of New York state, Dr. Maltby attended Cornell University where he studied under Goodwin Smith, the outstanding Canadian scholar.[65] After graduating in civil engineering from Cornell, with honors, in 1876, he taught for two years at the Ury School in Philadelphia.[66] In the late 1870's, he assisted in the surveying of the disputed boundary between Mexico and Guatemala.[67] He then taught mathematics and astronomy at Saint Lawrence University and engaged in doctoral study.[68] After receiving his doctorate in 1884, he joined the faculty of the newly-established Indiana State Normal School where he taught the natural sciences. In 1889, he was appointed superintendent of the Training School at Millersville where he stayed for one year before coming to Slippery Rock.[69]

What Dr. Maltby found when he arrived on the campus of the Slippery Rock Normal School was a row of four frame buildings on the edge of cultivated fields, a rapidly expanding student body and a curriculum hard pressed to satisfy the newer educational demands of a changing society.

Albert E. Maltby, Principal, 1890-1916

13

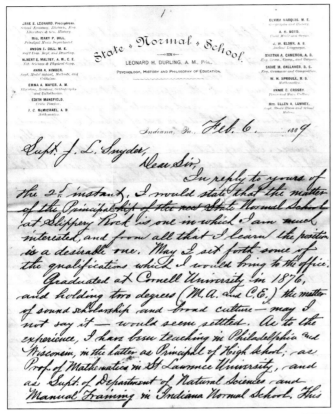

Indiana, Pa., Feb. 6 1889

Supt. J. L. Snyder,

Dear Sir,

In reply to yours of the 2d instant, I would state that the matter of the Principalship of the new State Normal School at Slippery Rock is one in which I am much interested, and from all that I learn the position is a desirable one. May I set forth some of the qualifications which I would bring to the office.

Graduated at Cornell University in 1876, and holding two degrees (M. A. and C. E.) the matter of sound scholarship and broad culture — may I not say it — would seem settled. As to the experience, I have been teaching in Philadelphia and Wisconsin, in the latter as Principal of High School; as Prof. of Mathematics in St. Lawrence University, and as Supt. of Department of Natural Sciences and Manual Training in Indiana Normal School. This

is my fifth year in my present position (I. S. N. S.) and the matter of retention of this position is assured by the most hearty support of the trustees, and by popularity with scholars and townspeople. I could bring to my work the experience of twelve successful years of teaching, and records as graduate from two Schools of Methods, in one of which I afterward became a teacher. This in addition to my college courses. My reputation in this part of the state is of the best, and seems growing year by year. Called to eight County Institutes, and successful in all; such is the record for this year. The Indiana Board has decided to utilize the splendid training which I have had in that department, and has placed me in charge of the Manual Training Dept. recently established here. It is no self-praise to say that my reputation in Mtl. Moulding, Apparatus, Etc. extends far beyond the state. Col. Parker has already offered me a position in the Cook Co. Normal School at a high salary, and speaks of me as one of the best teachers.

My practical experience five years as one of the principal teachers in a prominent Normal School of the State would seem to fit me for the work, while ability to teach thoroughly all the branches from Mathematics to the Languages, must add to the recommendation.

In regard to my Church relations, I am

Indiana, Pa., ... 188

a member of the Episcopal Church, but on account of the absence of any facilities for attending the services of my own church I have attended the Methodist Episcopal in town. Chapel services at Indiana Normal School are conducted by the teachers in turn, and so the extempore prayer has become habitual to me. You will see then that I am not one who believes that all good is to be found in one Church, but who does the work which he finds to do whether in prayer-meeting or in congregation.

In regard to terms, I should want a fair salary suitable to my work and ability, and a cordial call to the work of the Principalship. Considerable power must be given into the hands of the man who undertakes such a work, and trustees and teachers must pull as a team. I am a married man, 38 years of age, in good health, five feet six inches high, and a "pusher", so they say. I don't

want the position without the friendship of all the Board and their "live" and "active" support from the start. Col. Parker says, "One thing which impresses me with the success which you have attained as a teacher is the perfect enthusiasm of your pupils". I have no cause to blush for my reputation in Western Pennsylvania or elsewhere.

Should it seem advisable, I could obtain an opportunity to visit Slippery Rock and present matters to the various members of the Board more in detail. It seems hardly right to put all this laudation into writing, but it is necessary for the better understanding on all sides. Among the persons to whom I unhesitatingly refer are Dr. Shaffer of Kutztown, Principal Johnson of Philadelphia (High School). Prof. Oliver of Cornell, Van Velzer of Madison Univ. (Wisconsin) Dr. Higbee, and Henry Houck and J. L. Stewart of the State Dept. and J. L. Snyder, Reading, Pa. Hoping that you will pardon this self-laudation I remain

Yours Most Truly

Albert E. Maltby

Natural Sciences & Training

I. S. N. S.

In my letter to him I asked him to state frankly, and fairly all reasons why he should be able for such a position. This accounts for him writing in such glowing terms of himself. J. L. Snyder

Dr. Maltby's original letter of application - note date as he had applied for the first principalship when Dr. Morrow was hired

14

State Normal School,
ALBERT E. MALTBY, Ph. D., Principal.

Slippery Rock, Pa., Sept 12 1893

Miss Luella Mohr,

My Dear Lady

I am very glad to hear from you, and hope that you will enjoy your work during the year. The number is somewhat large for one teacher, but I have the utmost confidence that you will be able to carry the school forward with credit to yourself and this school. We begin this fall term with a large attendance, and

---

2 *State Normal School,*
ALBERT E. MALTBY, Ph. D., Principal.

Slippery Rock, Pa., 189

We are making some very great changes in the appearance of the buildings. The Ladies' Dormitory is entirely remodelled and an addition will be made, entirely changing the outlook of the "barns." You know that Rome was not built in a day, and it will take a few years for me to have wrought to my purposes the materials for this school, but the pupils hereafter will have no occasion to blush for the appearance of Slippery Rock. Her reputation as a school

A letter from Dr. Maltby to an alumna describing the campus in 1893

State Normal School,
ALBERT E. MALTBY, Ph. D., Principal.

Slippery Rock, Pa., 189

for complete work is already of the best. Few graduating classes hold records for obtaining better positions than '93 has secured, and we hope to keep you informed of any good opportunities going. Many thanks for the name and success to you in the work. Remember me to my pupil M. Dickson,

Very truly yours

Albert E. Maltby

North Hall after re-design with brick veneer, about 1895

15

To meet the critical need for more classroom facilities and increased space for the campus library, Dr. Maltby put in motion a plan calling for the construction of a large, brick, multi-purpose building, which, in addition to housing recitation rooms and the library, would contain laboratories, rooms for literary societies and a gymnasium.[70] Mr. S. W. Foulke drew up the architectural plans for this building which the Board of Trustees approved.[71] Construction of the $75,000 structure began in 1891 and it was ready for use in 1893.[72] Trimmed in Ohio sandstone, this majestic red brick building, appropriately called Main Building, quickly became the center of life on the Slippery Rock campus.[73] Dr. Maltby set up his administrative office on the first floor of this structure.[74] The library was located on the second floor with the gymnasium on the third.[75]

Construction of Old Main in 1892

The Main Building, 1895

16

Reading Room in Old Main

Boardwalk, Old Main and North Hall, 1898

Chemistry Class - note third student from right with skull

As enrollment soared well past 600 in 1894, existing dormitories were unable to accommodate all of the students; so Dr. Maltby directed the enlarging and remodeling of North Hall, a women's dormitory.[76] By changing the L-shaped building into one resembling an E and by adding a Norman, a Gothic and a Turkish tower, the hall now had 148 rooms which could house 300 students.[77] Early in his administration, key acquisitions of land were made which unified the campus and gave the school direct access to Main Street.[78] The Long Walk which permitted easy access from the heart of the campus to Main Street, first constructed of plank boards, was later rebuilt of cement.[79] Dr. Maltby, a civil engineer, did much of the surveying of the land which the school acquired.[80]

Sewing Class

Though the curricula of the normal schools in Pennsylvania were principally designed to meet the requirements for the state's teaching certificate, Slippery Rock's academic program began to reflect the educational philosophy of its new principal, Dr. Maltby. In the first catalog published in his administration, the school dedicated itself to provide for the "scholastic training of our students" and "to make skilled teachers of our students."[81]

The basic two-year Elementary Program continued to be the one most students followed. Now, during Dr. Maltby's first year as principal, they were able to elect a course in trigonometry, surveying and typewriting. The music offerings now included instruction in vocal and instrumental music.[82] The Form Study and Drawing course was expanded to four periods per week for the entire year.[83]

18

For the students who had completed the Elementary course, the following course was available:

JUNIOR YEAR:
Fall and Winter Sessions—Moral Philosophy, Four Orations of Cicero, Plane and Analytical Trigonometry, Analytical Geometry, Higher Algebra, Chemistry, General History.
Summer Session—Logic, One Book of Vergil's Aeneid, Surveying, Solid Geometry, Spherical Geometry and Trigonometry, Zoology.

SENIOR YEAR.
Fall and Winter Sessions—Philosophy of Education, Five Books of Vergil's Aeneid, Differential and Integral Calculus, Mechanics, Geology, Astronomy, English Literature.
Summer Session—Course of Professional Reading, Germania of Tacitus, Mechanics, Integral Calculus, Higher Physics, American Literature.[84]

In 1891, Dr. Maltby joined his fellow principals in Pennsylvania's Normal Schools in adopting a one-year, post graduate course which included work in mathematics, Latin, pedagogy, natural science, history and literature.[85] With the exception of the unit in Pedagogy, most of the courses in the post-graduate course were offered at Slippery Rock in its Scientific course.[86]

The year 1893 saw the beginning of Slippery Rock's long and distinguished tradition in the field of physical education. In the new physical culture program, students were exposed to gymnastics, marching, Delsarte movements, and exercises with wands, bells and clubs.[87]

Two literary societies—the "Bryant" and the "Netrophian"—were first established at Slippery Rock under Dr. Morrow's administration.[88] The "Netrophian" gave way to the "Philomathian" in 1893 and, together with the "Bryant," continued to be quite popular with the students during Dr. Maltby's term of office.[89] The students were strongly encouraged to participate in one of the societies as the following announcement in the 1893 Catalog reveals:

Among the attractions of the school are two flourishing Literary Socities, [sic]

conducted by the students—the "Bryant" and the "Philomathian." They hold weekly meetings. Any student may become a member of either of these societies by paying a small initiation fee. The training given in these socities [sic] is of such great value that students cannot afford to neglect the opportunities furnished for literary and oratorical culture.[90]

Other extra-curricular activities popular with students were lawn tennis, baseball and croquet. Saturday evening socials helped also to interrupt an otherwise busy academic week centered around academics, library work and culturally-related activities.

The supervision of students was strict at this time, as evidenced by these "Regulations for Students" which appeared in the school catalogs throughout most of Dr. Maltby's administration:

REGULATIONS FOR STUDENTS
The discipline of the school is made as simple as possible. Self-control is the ideal sought. Students are expected to do without compulsion what is required and to refrain voluntarily from all improprieties of conduct. The intelligent conception of duty and a quickened conscience will generally result in a cheerful voluntary obedience. That government is best that seems to govern least.

Nothing less than regular attendance, good behavior, and hearty allegiance to all the interests of the school will be accepted as the conditions of membership.

1. Study hours will be published at the commencement of each session, and the bell will be rung to give notice of them. Students must devote these hours exclusively to study and recitation.

2. All students are required to be present at all devotional and general exercises in the chapel, unless excused. Attendance on religious worship during the Sabbath is required.

3. A record of scholarship will be kept, which will be open to inspection by the students and the public.

4. No student may indulge in the use of tobacco in any of its forms in or about the building, or of intoxicating drinks.

5. Gentlemen not connected with the school will not be permitted to call upon lady students without permission.

6. Students whose sense of honor and propriety cannot be trusted will be summarily dismissed. They will also be sent away whenever in the opinion of the Faculty it is evident that they are pursuing a course of conduct detrimental to themselves and the institution.[91]

The cost of attending Slippery Rock in 1890 was low, as the list of tuition, boarding and special charges outlined in the school catalog reveals:

REGULAR CHARGES—Tuition and boarding, including heat, light, furnished room, and use of Text Books, for the Fall Term of 16 weeks, $60; for the Winter Term of 12 weeks, $45; for the Spring Term of 14 weeks, $55; for any time less than a full term, $4 a week.

Tuition without boarding, for the Fall Term, $18; for the Winter Term, $14; for the Spring Term, $16; for a less time during any term, $1.25 a week.

The State aid of 50 cents a week is deducted from the bills of students who comply with the conditions stated under the heading, "State Appropriations to Students," thus making the total cost for tuition and boarding, for the Fall Term, $52; for the Winter Term, $39; for the Spring Term, $48; for the entire year, $139. During the Senior year the cost for tuition and boarding reduces to $89 if the pupil graduates. Tuition alone, for Fall Term, $10; for Winter Term, $8; for Spring Term, $9.

SPECIAL CHARGES—Boarding, including heat, light, etc. during the vacations will be $3 a week. Transient board will be $4 a week; by the day, 75 cents.

The hack hire between Keister's and Slippery Rock is 25¢.

INSTRUMENTAL MUSIC—The charges for instrumental music, two lessons a week and two practice periods a day, will be, for the Fall term, $16; for the Winter Term, $12; for the Spring Term, $14; for any time less than a term, $1.20 per week.

Students under 17 years of age are granted by the school reductions similar to those received by teachers through the State appropriation.[92]

The first five years of Dr. Maltby's leadership at Slippery Rock were ones marked by impressive growth in the life of the school. But, at the close of his fifth

North Main Street, Slippery Rock at turn of century

Keister Railway Station, transfer point to Slippery Rock, turn of century

year, in 1895, the school began to experience a series of disasters which challenged in a different way his skills as an administrator. Just before dawn, on May 13, 1895, a fire broke out in South Hall—the school's only men's dormitory—and within an hour had destroyed the structure leaving over a hundred male students without housing accommodations.[93] Dangerously close to the flames stood the chapel and, next to it, North Hall, the women's dormitory—both of wooden construction. Only prompt action by the town's firefighters kept the fire from spreading and destroying literally the entire Slippery Rock campus. Fortunately, no one was injured in the fire, though there were some tense moments. Several students were temporarily trapped in their rooms. Others climbed down escape ladders constructed of rope and many fled through windows with all the personal belongings they could carry. Professor Hamm and his wife lost everything, including a library valued at one thousand dollars.[94] The townspeople responded immediately to the crisis by opening their homes to the 7 roomless students. By noon, all of the young men had a place to stay. The property loss in the South Hall fire was placed at $25,000. Twelve thousand dollars of property insurance went to the

mortgages and $3,000 of additional insurance to cover losses of furniture and books.[95] Immediately, Dr. Maltby directed the planning of a new South Hall and, with the full support of the Board of Trustees, construction began in the summer of 1895. By the following year, the new brick, U-shaped, three-story dormitory was completed.[96] A tower held a bell which signaled meal times and other campus activities.[97]

In June of 1896, as Slippery Rock was recovering from the South Hall fire, the school's wooden chapel caught fire and was destroyed.[98] Again the school acted promptly and within a year, a new stone chapel of Norman-French architecture with stain-glass windows was built.[99] The auditorium, which could seat a thousand persons, had a full stage, dressing and storage rooms, and an organ.[100] This was a beautiful building, constructed at a cost of $47,000 and quickly replaced Main Hall as the center of student activity.[101]

In 1900, still another fire destroyed a building used by the Normal School.[102] This time it was the model school on New Castle Street where Slippery Rock carried on many of its practice teaching programs.[103] Originally built as the town's public school in 1881, the Trustees

If in these colors you believe,
Put this emblem, on cap or sleeve.

at the Normal School purchased it in 1889 for $4,000.[104] Within the year, a two-story buff brick building, trimmed in sandstone, was built on the campus facing Main Street at a cost of $27,000.[105] This new Model School housed both the elementary training school and the Normal Science Department.[106] With the completion of the Model School, the Slippery Rock campus contained five modern buildings, architecturally positioned across a landscaped campus. Only North Hall remained of the Normal School's original buildings which Dr. Maltby found when he first arrived at Slippery Rock a decade before.

In the academic year of the South Hall Fire, in 1895, enrollment at Slippery Rock stood at 634.[107] There were 388 women and 246 men representing sixteen Pennsylvania counties and five other states.[108] This enrollment pattern remained fairly constant over the next twenty years. In most years, there were twice as many women as men at Slippery Rock.

In 1894, a major study of curricular programs in the normal schools in the state of Pennsylvania was completed, resulting in a number of important changes in the academic programs at Slippery Rock. Since entering students were bringing widely different scholastic backgrounds to their normal school studies, the State created a separate "Preparatory Studies" course for those deficient in the primary subjects.[109] In it students studied reading and orthography; physiology and hygiene; political and physical geography; and penmanship.[110] A normal school could require other studies

in arithmetic, English grammar, algebra, etc., if it desired; but the "final" examination in these "added branches" would be deferred until the end of the junior year.[111] Basically, this program included the requirements of the former divisions E and D. The junior year was now to include the work covered I the former C, B, and A divisions.[112] Studies included English grammar and Latin, arithmetic and algebra; botany; civil government; drawing, bookkeeping and vocal music; physical culture; and pedagogics, which included school management and methods of teaching the common branches.[113] This change in the two-year teacher certification program in the normal schools in the state meant that only the better prepared students would actually be able to complete the course in two years.

Normal School advertisement featuring the new model school, 1900

The Model School, also known as West Hall

The principals of the normal school in Pennsylvania also agreed in 1894 to completely revise the post-graduate area of advanced pedagogics in an effort to gain increased recognition in the field of higher education.[114] They adopted three advanced courses of study called the Regular Normal Course, the Scientific Course and an Advanced Normal Course, each described in detail in the following excerpt from Slippery Rock's catalog.

REGULAR NORMAL COURSE, Three years
(This Course includes the studies of the Elementary Course, and the following branches: A full equivalent will be accepted for any of the textbooks named in this Course.)
PEGAGOGICS: Advanced Psychology; Moral Science; Philosophy of Education; Methods of Teaching; Practice of Teaching; Pedagogical Works; Froebel, Education of Man, Quick, Educational Reformers; Fitch, Lectures on Teaching; School Supervision, School Apparatus; Discussion of Manual Training, Physical Culture, etc.
MATHEMATICS: Solid Geometry; Plane and Analytical Trigonometry; Surveying.
LANGUAGE: Latin, Caesar, 3 books; Vergil's Aeneid, 8 books; Cicero, 3 orations.

NATURAL SCIENCE: Chemistry, including Chemistry of Soils; Zoology, including Entomology; and Geology.
LITERATURE: Higher Literature, English and American, including a study of at least four classics
SCIENTIFIC COURSE, Four Years
(This Course includes the studies of the Regular Normal course and the following branches:)
PEDAGOGICS: Logic; Course of Professional Reading selected from Regular or advanced Normal Course; a Thesis on a professional subject.
LANGUAGE: Latin; 3 books of Vergil's Aeneid, 3 orations of Cicero, or a full equivalent; (an equivalent of Greek, German or French will be accepted for any of the following studies: Vergil, Cicero, Higher Algebra, Spherical Trigonometry, Surveying, Analytical Geometry, Calculus, Mathematical Natural Philosophy and Mathematical Astronomy, and an equivalent of Latin and advanced work in Natural Science for any of the foregoing mathematical studies.)
MATHEMATICS: Higher Algebra; Spherical Trigonometry and Surveying, with

Physical culture on Normal School Campus, early 1900's

A game of tennis at the Normal School, 1905

use of instruments; Analytical Geometry; Differential and Integral Calculus.

NATURAL SCIENCE: Higher Natural Philosophy; Astronomy, Descriptive and Mathematical.

HISTORICAL SCIENCE: English History; Grecian History; Roman History.

ADVANCED NORMAL COURSE, Five Years

(This course includes the studies of the Scientific Course, and one year's additional work in Pedagogics, as follows: A full equivalent will be accepted for any of the textbooks in the Course.)

PSYCHOLOGY: James. Advanced Course.

Laurie's Institutes of Education; Rein's Outline of Pedagogy; Herbart's Science of Education; Spencer's Education; Rosmini's Method in Education; Davidson's Education of the Greek People.

Discussion of Methods and Objects of Leading Educators: Froebel, Pestalozzi, Dr. Arnold, Horace Mann and others.

Discussion of Educational Theories.

Education in the United States: Education in Pennsylvania (Wickersham); General Survey of History of Public Education in Germany, France and England.

Advanced work in Language, Mathematics, Natural Science, etc., may be taken at the option of the student.[115]

As this program in Advanced Pedagogics was organized, each advanced course was built upon an earlier one; so, for example, if a student wished to take the five-year Advanced Normal Course, he would have to successfully complete the two-year Elementary Course, another year in the Regular Normal Course and still another year in the Scientific Course, in that order.

In 1895, students at Slippery Rock were given the opportunity to take courses which prepared them to teach in the newer kindergartens which were becoming popular in Pennsylvania's more educationally-minded communities.[116] Seniors and post-graduate students received their practice teaching in a local kindergarten. A few years later, in 1897, Nature Study was added to the curriculum and the following year, a Sunday afternoon Bible Study course taught by Rev. Dr. George Hamm offered students the opportunity to engage in "a special study of the life of Christ."[117]

In 1900, another major reorganization of the programs of study in Pennsylvania's normal schools was made by the directors of these schools. Now the basic elementary program was expanded to a three-year course of study.[118] Essentially, a new Senior Year was constructed which incorporated much of the course work which had been offered in the old post-graduate "Regular Normal course."[119] It is to be recalled that this was the year of post-graduate study which had followed the two-year course under the former curricular plan. The old Junior Year remained basically the same, with methods of teaching placed in the new middle year. Reflecting a diminishing interest in Latin in American schools, the new program allowed students to substitute "modern" courses like chemistry, astronomy, ethics, logic and English history for studies of the books of Caesar, Cicero and Vergil.[120]

The post-graduate programs in Advanced Pedagogics were replaced with a one year "Supplementary Course" leading to the Bachelor of Pedagogics degree. Normal School graduates of the Regular Course, who had two years of teaching experience, could now earn the Master of Pedagogics degree.[121] Unlike the earlier post-graduate program, which included courses in the sciences and the humanities, the prescribed courses in both of these supplementary programs were designed to meet the specific pedagogical needs of the classroom teacher.[122]

The appearance, in 1904, of a listing of academic departments at Slippery Rock reflected a growing academic maturity at the school. Departments recognized at this time were Language, Mathematics, Natural Science, Drawing and Manual Training, School Teacher Elocution, Physical Culture, Kindergarten and Music.[123]

The high importance which the school placed on athletics in student life was clearly explained in this statement which appeared in 1904:

Athletic sports are encouraged as a means of pleasant recreation, for their value in developing the body, as a source of social and ethical culture, and as cultivating the spirit of co-operative enterprise so essential to individuals throughout life When athletics are so managed as to cultivate determination, courage, self-reliance, control, obedience and quickness of decision, there is much to be urged in their favor Tennis, basket-ball, base-ball, and foot-ball are the games most in use. There are numerous good tennis courts on the campus. The Athletic field recently laid out is one of the finest grounds in the State for base-ball and foot-ball. It is well graded, and will soon be placed in so sown with lawn-grass For the other games ample provision will be made. The gymnasium is open for exercise at certain hours under suitable restrictions, to all who are enrolled as students.[124]

In 1906, the West Gymnasium was built providing a facility for basketball and a variety of other physical activities.[125] Constructed of yellow brick, the Gymnasium was faced with a rounded portico and huge round limestone pillars which would soon be flanked by an impressive pair of stone lions to be donated by the class of 1908.[126] Several years later, woman at Slippery Rock

were encouraged to be active in the various athletic programs, as the *Catalog* of 1910 explained:

Athletics are not confined to boys only, as is the case in so many schools, but the girls are encouraged to participate in all girls' sports and have the advantage of the coaching and direction of the directors.[127]

As athletic participation was encouraged, so was attendance at the various lecture series given on campus. Fresh "opportunities for culture," it was felt, would enable Slippery Rock students "to become stronger intellectually through mental contact with the strong minds of the country."[128]

Construction of new Gymnasium and Music Hall on corner of Main Street and Keister Road
John N. Watson, Chairman of Building Committee with other members at lower right

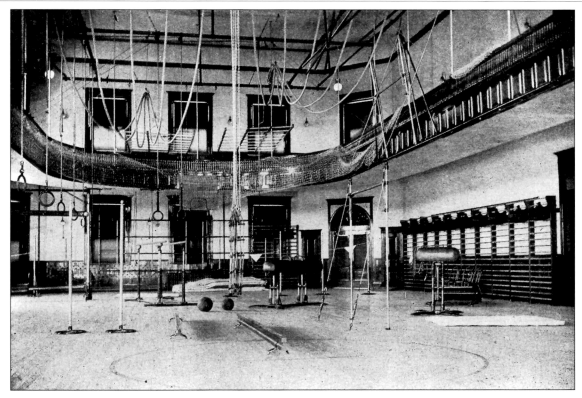

Inside new Gymnasium, 1912

Men's Basketball team with a young coach, N. Kerr Thompson, right, 1915

On the gridiron

Undefeated Championship Football Team, 1907

28

A Baseball game, 1907

Normal School Baseball Team, 1907

Regulations governing student behavior were relaxed a bit in 1904. Instead of carefully regulating a student's life on campus, these rules were designed to maintain good order on the campus:

Disorderly conduct in the buildings is prohibited. Each student will be held accountable for any disturbance or damage in his room.

Students are required to take up enough studies to keep them, in the judgment of the Principal, sufficiently employed, but not to take up more than they can study with profit.

Each student of instrumental music will have regular hours assigned for practice, during which time no spectator must be present to interrupt the exercises or divert the attention.[129]

Fashions in student dress of this time were recalled by a 1907 alumnus:

The girls of that time wore the exact opposite of the present minis. The skirts were so long that a girl was considered bold if her skirt happened to pull enough to show her legs half way to her knees. When the put up their long hair they used a rat (a hank of used hair) that was combed over in front. Occasionally if the girl wasn't careful the "rat" would show. Over their "derrière" and below the belt they wore a "bustle." I never got close enough in my shy way, but I imagine some of the flat chested ones wore "falsies."[130]

During the next decade, dress styles changed, as another student remembers:

Our clothes also were different but the fashion of the times. The girls wore ankle-length dresses on all occasions, daily or formal; the classroom uniform (except at dinner) was a white middy with blue collar adorned with a red silk triangular tie; other styles were frizzy hair with huge bows of ribbon, long bulky blue or red sweaters, blue serge bloomers for gym,

Lawn performance by Old Main, early 1900's

Slippery Rock Band, 1908

lace-trimmed "study caps," and crepe-de-chine blouses for Sunday wear.

The boys attended class mostly in dark serge suite, white shirts, high still collars, dark ties, pressed trousers, high-topped shoes, caps with peaks or skull-caps, white or green football sweaters; occasionally spats were sported on Sunday."[131]

In 1910, the normal school directors in Pennsylvania adopted a new curriculum which now required students to complete a four-year program of studies at their schools.[132] The first three years of the new curriculum at Slippery Rock were virtually the same as in the earlier General Course.[133] The added fourth year offered courses in English grammar, arithmetic, natural sciences, history of education, practice teaching, culturally-related courses, manual training or domestic science, and physical training.[134] For the first time, all of the classes were organized in 45 or 60 minute periods with the state stipulating how many times each class should meet each year.[135]

Students graduating from the new four-year program received a certificate which entitled them to teach in Pennsylvania's public schools, without examination, for two years.[136] Those successful teachers who continued their studies for two more years were awarded a permanent certificate.[137] The post-graduate Supplementary Course remained intact, though now students had to successfully complete the four-year program before engaging in post-graduate study.[138]

Good Roads Day, 1916

The Chapel, 1899

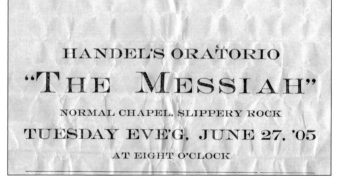

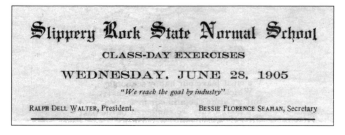

Campus Events, 1904, 1905, 1907

Chapel Auditorium, 1908

Class of '95 with Principal Maltby

A patriotic day, ladies of North Hall with Dr. Maltby, early 1900's

The Normal School Family, in front of North Hall, 1909

Ladies Dorm, North Hall, 1907

In North Hall, turn of the century

An important change in admission procedures was made in 1910, when for the first time, a student's class placement in the normal school program depended upon the rating which the student's high school received from the state. Students graduating from "a first grade and city high school" were automatically admitted to the third year of the new four-year course; students from high schools classified as "second-grade" entered the second year of study; and graduates from "third-grade" high school entered the first year.[139] The "Carnegie Unit," which represented a year's study in any subject or approximately one fourth of a student's course work in high school, was used by admission offices in the state's normal schools for the first time in 1910.[140]

In 1912, the increasingly dysfunctional post-graduate Supplementary Program was no longer available at Slippery Rock.[141] The following year, the programs in music and public speaking were expanded.[142]

In 1915, Dr. Maltby celebrated his twenty-fifth year as Slippery Rock's chief administrator. During this quarter of a century, the school had become one of Pennsylvania's major centers for the preparation of teachers in the western region.

The Board of Trustees, which had faithfully served the Normal School during this crucial period of early development, believed that the time had come to explore the possibilities of having Slippery Rock join the growing number of normal schools which were casting

SRSN Alumni Association invitation and banquet, early 1900's

The Slippery Rock S. N. Alumni Association
of Butler County
will hold their second Annual Banquet
in the Parlors of the Second Presbyterian Church,
Butler, Penn'a.,
Friday evening, March 22, 1907. 8 o'clock
Graduates, former Students and Friends are invited.

Notify the Secretary of the Number of Plates you wish
reserved before March 8, '07.

$1.25 per plate.

J. G. Bingham, Pres.

Pearl McMarlin, Sec.
803 Center Ave., Butler, Pa.

Long walk and campus scene, about 1910

their destinies with the State. On September 27, 1915, a meeting of the stockholders was called to discuss this course of action.[143] The owners of 168 ½ shares of the 197 ¾ outstanding shares were in attendance and all voted for the transfer of the Normal School to the State.[144] Judge A. E. Reiber, on February 19, 196, during a brief court sessions, handed down a decree authorizing the Trustees of the Slippery Rock State Normal School Association "...to make a deed of conveyance of the property and other appurtenances of the school to the Commonwealth."[145] In transferring the Normal School to the State, the shareholders received $100 for each share of stock they owned—precisely the price paid twenty-eight years ago.[146] In giving up the ownership of the school, the former shareholders lost their twelve seats on the Board of Trustees. Under state control, the Board of Trustees was reduced in size from eighteen to nine members, all of whom were now appointed by the Governor of Pennsylvania. In looking back over the history of the Normal School which the local citizens of Slippery Rock had founded and nurtured for two and a half decades, an observer at the time noted that it had been a "great influence for good," not only in the town, but also in the adjoining counties.[147] Its influence in education was increasingly being felt, since by 1916, the majority of teachers in Butler County were either graduates of the Normal School or had taken courses there.

A few months after Slippery Rock joined the State, Dr. Maltby, who had directed the Normal School since 1890, retired.[148] Certainly his firm and dedicated leadership throughout the school's formative years helps to explain, in part, its early success and sustained progress.

Recollections by alumni present interesting insights into the many facets of the personality of this able educational administrator.

Old grads recall him presiding over the chapel exercises, "squinting" out over the top of his "nose pincher" spectacles at the student body. There are those, too, who mention the day the good doctor completely forget the Lord's prayer while presiding over the devotional exercises. But one little trick of Dr. Maltby's that is remembered with more glee than any other, was his habit of visiting Professor Ricketts' mathematics classroom. He used to pick a time when the Professor was engaged in helping some pupil with a difficult problem, then, unobserved by the Instructor, he would quietly dart in the open door, make a few ludicrous and sometimes risque alterations in drawings on the blackboard, and then, amid a burst of hilarity, depart as quickly as he had come. The embarrassed Professor would look up just in time to see Dr. Maltby's coat-tails disappearing into the hall.

Sometimes when the attention in his own classes was not what he desired, he would rouse the somnolent students with a story. But he had a way of fooling them, much to their consternation. For just as the climax was near, and the attention keen, he would discontinue his tale—never to resume it—with the remark: "That is the way you should pay attention all the time." Alumni and former students remember Dr. Maltby as a friend who was always generous with his time. Students found him available for consultation or conversation at all times, whether in his office or at his home. When former students returned to the campus they found him ever ready to greet them with a warm and sincere welcome.

Though generally of a kindly nature, he, nevertheless, possessed a fiery temper which those who knew him best tried to avoid arousing. It was said that he had indulged somewhat in the fistic arts at Cornell; a fact which some recalcitrant students and town ruffians learned

Slippery Rock's skating pond, about 1910

Chapel, South Hall, West Gym/Music Hall, 1907

Main Street, Model School at right, 1914

to their sorrow. Especially when the latter group attempted to raid the regular Saturday night sessions of the literary societies in Old Main.[149]

A class friend of Dr. Maltby's offered this assessment of his contributions to the history of Slippery Rock:

Dr. Maltby assumed charge of the school when he had reached middle life and a full attainment of his mental and physical powers; when his poise and balance were stabilized by mature judgment; and when his leadership was also perfected by travel and by experience in the classrooms of other Pennsylvania State Normal Schools. It is indeed fortunate for the school that fifteen months after opening its doors, it could attract to it a leader so young, so capable, and so endowed with a vision as was Dr. Maltby. Here was just the opportunity for a vigorous personality to exercise its powers in molding an embryo institution. In 1890 he found it a row of frame buildings on the edge of cultivated fields; in 1916 he left its walls of brick and stone, circling on a beautiful campus set with trees, shrubs, and flowers. These marks of his mathematical, architectural, and artistic skills are augmented by the far-reaching impression made upon the young men and women who went out from the school to carry the message of fidelity, honesty, perseverance, and scholarship to the childhood of the world. Let us leave the further spread of his tribute of praise to them, as they labor to perpetuate his memory by the imitation of his worthy example.[150]

The year 1916 was an important turning point in the life of Slippery Rock's Normal School. By now, familiar patterns of leadership and control were ending and new ones were about to be tried. The way in which the school would adjust to these new circumstances would determine, in a fundamental way, the character of the institution for decades to come.

39

Birds eye view of S.R.S.N. buildings, 1910

Campus Buildings, 1908

40

Campus Scenes, 1900-1916

Students at the drinking fountain beside Chapel

Tempting the Lion, donated by class of 1908

Around the sun dial near South Hall

"Right is Might" or "The Hand of God" Play

"RIGHT IS MIGHT" or "The Hand of God"

PRESENTED BY

SLIPPERY ROCK VOLUNTEER FIRE COMPANY

Under the Direction of D. C. McLAUGHLIN

Tuesday, May 30, 1916, at Normal Chapel

CAST OF CHARACTERS

Col. George Horton, commandant at the fort_____Arthur Heyl
Lieut. Arthur Donaldson } officers at the fort _____ { William Barron
Capt. Harry Bates { Roy Grubb
Corporal Dennis Hennessy, a stuttering Irishman _____Hugh Cooper
Prof. Obadiah Fakus, a quack doctor with facial nervous affection
Eugene Vanatta
Dr. Hugh Dickson, regimental surgeon_____James Kiester
Fighting Wolf, chief of the Yuquis_____Erle Watson
Jimmie, a camp follower_____Walter Winner
Rev. John Crosby, a missionary to the Mexicans and Indians
Clarence Moore
Captain Dongo Sangario, a Mexican officer of Villa's staff, James Kiester
Allene Horton, the Colonel's daughter_____Rebecca Bingham
Juanita, Fighting Wolf's daughter_____Ruth Taylor
Patrica Mulligan, Irish maid with passion for grand opera__Leila Watson
Mrs. Hazel Beatrix Winslow, a temerance reformer____ Frances Clutton
Soldiers at the fort—
George McQuiston, Henry Dickson, Walter Winner, William Schaer,
Leason Doutt.

Ready for Gym Class/Physical Culture

Fountain in front of North Hall

Drinking from one of the many campus springs

Spoon Holder, one of the 3 stone benches donated by class of 1911

North Hall dining room set for a meal

Patriotic dining room, North Hall

44

Athletes, 1907-1913

Football Team, 1907

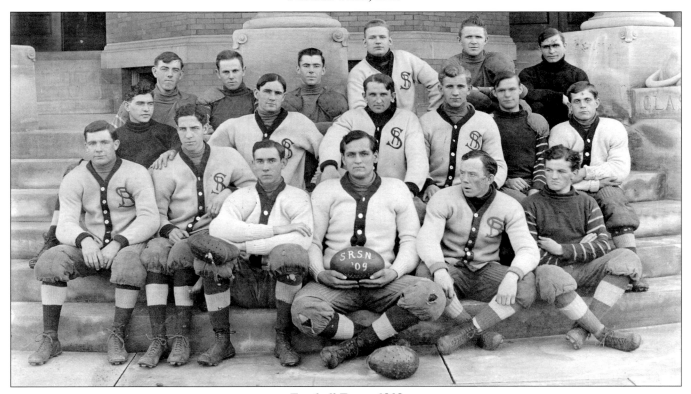

Football Team, 1909

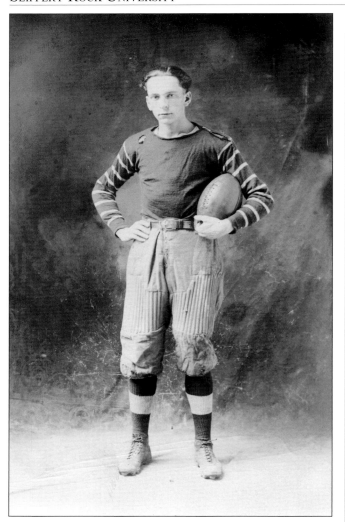

I. M. Stoops, 1912

Dressed for the game, 1910

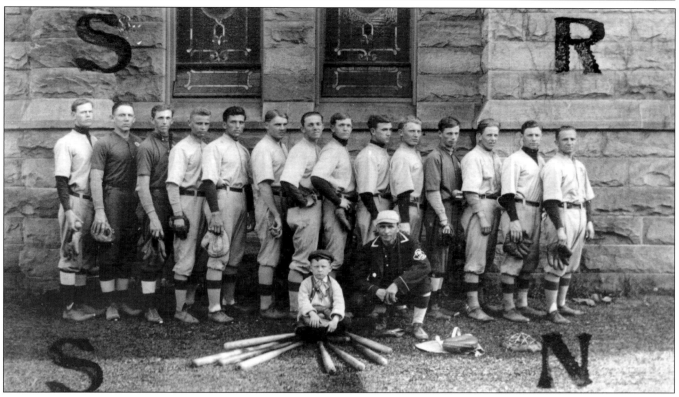

Baseball Team in front of Chapel, 1913

Baseball, 1908

Baseball, 1911

Early Girls Basketball Team, 1913

Basketball, 1910

48

In and Around the Village of Slippery Rock
1895-1916

The Great Auto Race, April 1909
Model School in background

On the Slippery Rock Creek

A hack returning from Keister Rail Station at intersection of Main St. and Keister Road
West Gym in background

Gus Clutton, second from right, and classmates waiting for the train at the Stone House, near Halston

50

Crazy Snake, First Prize in the July 4, 1909 parade

The Slippery Rock Train Wreck, near Branchton, April 26, 1916

*Frances Clutton with Howard McMullen and
the new automobile, 1914*

Post Office on Main Street

Main Street

Delivering the Saturday Evening Post in town

John N. Watson, left one of the founders, stockholders and early trustees or SRSNS with partner C. C. Williams in front of their general store, 126 S. Main Street

Slippery Rock Livery and Blacksmith, near campus

Frances Clutton with her Ralston School class on an outing

Students relaxing on campus

Some of the prized poltry and rabbits on campus

Written Documents, 1909-1912

Slippery Rock State Normal School

REPORT OF M

Senior Class,   Term Ending **Mar. 26th,** 190 9

	Term Work	Grade		Term Work	Grade
SPELLING			CÆSAR		
WRITING			CICERO		
READING			VERGIL	95	96
ELOCUTION			RHETORIC		
COMPOSITION			CLASSICS		
GRAMMAR			LITERATURE	90	90
POLIT. GEOGRAPHY			HIST. EDUCATION		
PHYS. GEOGRAPHY			ARITHMETIC		
DRAWING			MENTAL ARITHMETIC		
BOOK-KEEPING			ALGEBRA		
CIVIL GOVERNMENT			GEOMETRY		
U. S. HISTORY			TRIGONOMETRY	96	96
SCHOOL ECONOMY			SURVEYING		
JUNIOR LATIN			PHYSIOLOGY		
VOCAL MUSIC			BOTANY		
INST. MUSIC			ZOOLOGY		
METHODS	90	87	CHEMISTRY	92	92
PRACTICE	96 95m		GEOLOGY		
PSYCHOLOGY			ASTRONOMY		
MANUAL TRAINING			PHYSICS	95	94
GENERAL HISTORY			LOGIC		
ENGLISH HISTORY			ETHICS		
FRENCH			PHYSICAL CULTURE		
GERMAN			CONDUCT		100

Passing grade in studies is 80 per cent.
Any grade below 100 in conduct is unsatisfactory.

Albert E. Maltby

Principal.

Report card listing all classes required by Normal School
Passing grade is 80%

SLIPPERY ROCK STATE NORMAL SCHOOL
ALBERT E. MALTBY, Principal

Frances Clutton

Chapel Excuse

Monday | Tuesday | Wednesday | Thursday | Friday | Saturday

Until Dec 18, 1912

Albert E. Maltby

A rare Chapel excuse

Slippery Rock, Pa............. 3/31 ....190 9
STATE NORMAL SCHOOL

Mr _Augustus Clutton_   _Spring_ Term
Grade............

CLASS	TEACHER	TIME	ROOM	BOOK NO.
Chemistry	Adv.	11:15	130	
Hist. of Ed.		7:45	7:45	
Eng. History		10:30	1:15	
Surveying		10:30		
Methods		3:30		
Vergil		9:45		
Gram		8:45	11:15	

Albert E. Maltby
PRINCIPAL

Spring class schedule, 1909

Established 1889   **Eleventh District**

The Slippery Rock State Normal School

J. E. BARD, PRESIDENT
J. N. WATSON, SECRETARY
H. R. SMITH, TREASURER
BENJ. PEARSON, SUPERINTENDENT

Slippery Rock, Pa.,   *191*

Buildings in order of Erection

Name	When Built	Cost
Main Bldg	1891 – 93	$ 75.000 00
Ladies Dorm	1889 – 1894 Remodled & enlarged	58.000 00
Boys Dorm	1895 – 96	45.000 00
Chapel	1896 – 97	40.000 00
Model School	1900	30.000 00
Mus Hall (?) Gym	1906 – 07	65.000 00
Laundry	1903	5.000 00
Boiler House	1910	6.000 00
		$ 324.000 00

Value of other property   36.130 00

"   " grounds & Bldgs $ 360.130 00

Value of furniture &c $ 24.249.19

Value of Library   9.664.95

Value of Musical Instruments   2569 78

Value of Apparatus   3 455 33

                                  39.939.25

Total value of Bldgs grounds equipments $ 400.069.25

Amt of debt at this date

" " judgment or mortgage   none

" " floating debt   "

Board of Trustees tabulation of value of campus buildings and contents, about 1911

CHAPTER III

Slippery Rock Becomes
a State Teachers College
1916-1934

For a year after the retirement of Dr. Maltby, Slippery Rock searched for his successor. During the interim, Professor Isaac Newton Moore, the Vice Principal, was asked to serve as Acting Principal of the school. A member of the original faculty of the Normal School in 1889, Principal Moore had been affiliated, as teacher or administrator, with Slippery Rock for almost a quarter of a century.[151] This was a good choice for, in the words of one observer, "Professor Moore's years of experience, his keen insight, and his quiet,

J. Linwood Eisenberg, President, 1917-1934

dignified manner made it possible for him to conduct the school successfully through this difficult period of its history.[152]

In July of 1917, the search for a permanent top administrator at Slippery Rock was over. Dr. J. Lindwood Eisenberg, Superintendent of Schools of Chester County, had been selected.[153] Dr. Eienberg brought impressive educational credentials and a rich background of professional experiences to Slippery Rock. He earned a Bachelor of Education degree (1895), a Bachelor of Arts degree (1906), and a Master of Arts degree (1908), from Ursinus College and a Doctor of Philosophy degree (1913) from the University of Pennsylvania.[154] He had served as a classroom teacher, a grade school principal, a supervising principal (Royersford, Pennsylvania), a part-time college teacher (Ursinus College and the University of Delaware), a faculty member of a normal school (West Chester State), a director of a demonstration school (Wittenberg College), and a superintendent of schools (Chester County, Pennsylvania).[155]

When Dr. Eisenberg took office as Principal of the new state-owned Normal School, the United States was rapidly increasing its involvement in World War I. School enrollment dropped from 500 students in 1917 to 433 in 1918, as more and more men were entering the nation's armed forces.[156] Only 89 men were on campus at this time.[157]

Though the nation was at war, Dr. Eisenberg quickly gave notice that it was not his intention to simply wait until hostilities were over before initiating changes at Slippery Rock. Within a year after he arrived, the basic program of studies was expanded with three important additions. The first and, in terms of the future development of the curriculum of Slipper Rock, the most important was the new three-year physical education program.[158] This

57

Morrow Way to Chapel, about 1920

program offered students work in anatomy, kinesiology, vocal expression, English, educational gym, physiology, playground training, rhetoric, psychology and child study, hygiene and school sanitation, pedagogy of physical training and dramatic art.[159]

The second curricular development was the creation of a commercial department with three programs in book-keeping, shorthand, and teacher training for commercial teachers.[160] The purpose of this department was:

> to train young men and women in the forms, customs and laws of business; to cultivate in them habits of neatness, accuracy and thoroughness; to familiarize them with practical business problems, and in every way possible prepare them to become commercial teachers, or for successful business careers.[161]

The third curricular innovation was a two-year course designed for those who planned to teach in Pennsylvania's rural schools, but who were unable to take the regular normal school course.[162] Students who graduated from the eighth grade in communities where there were no high schools could be admitted to the first year of this program upon presentation of a certificate of graduation.[163] Students without graduation certificates could be admitted by examination.[164] While similar to the regular normal school course, this program for rural school teachers carried a heavy emphasis on pedagogy.[165] During that same year, the music program was expanded to include a supervisor's course.[166] Up to this time, the department of music was one of the most active departments at the school with constant efforts being made to improve their program.

In the 1919 *Catalog*, the following announcement appeared:

DEMAND FOR TEACHERS

The demand for trained teachers is far beyond the possible supply. At the present time every one who has an inclination toward teaching and who possesses time and talent should secure Normal School training to be prepared for teaching. Those now in service should prepare for better positions and more efficient service.[167]

This announcement not only reveals the serious-ness of the teacher shortage following World War I, but also tells much about Dr. Eisenberg's educational philosophy.

In that same year, 1919, a Department of Household Science and Art was established to meet the following needs:

If the house is to be an attractive institution, the woman must have time which she may spend in exercising physically or mentally. This is termed leisure. In order to have this time, her household duties must be accomplished in a practical and economical way. Not practicality and economy measured in dollars and cents alone, but that measured in conservation of time and energy also. This conservation results in the raising of standards and qualities, for it is only when one knows how to do a thing well, and knows when it is well done, that the best results are obtained.[168]

The courses required within this two-year program were divided into two areas of household science, "cookery" and "sewing."[169]

Beginning with the 1920-21 academic year, the Slippery Rock State Normal School switched from a three-term year (not including summer school), to a two-semester year; and credit for courses offered within the Normal School were no longer computed in clock hours, but instead on a semester hour basis.[170] With this move, Slippery Rock drew closer to four-year institutions, a goal toward which Dr. Eisenberg was working. A uniformity within the Normal School was now established.

Also, in 1920, new requirements for admission were adopted at Slippery Rock. The requirements directed that graduates of approved secondary schools who could present evidence of earning fifteen units of high school course work would be admitted as regular state normal school students.[171] The particular units required for admission were as follows:

English	3 units
Mathematics	1 unit
Science	1 unit
Social Studies	1 unit
	– After Sept., 1923, 2 units
Elective	9 units
	– After Sept., 1923, 8 units[172]

In addition, Slippery Rock, along with the other normal schools in Pennsylvania, was to provide secondary schooling for those students who needed it. As the regulation explained:

…the normal schools shall, when necessary, conduct a secondary department of first class high school grade for those students who do not have similar high school facilities available in their home communities.[173]

Three courses of study were available within the secondary department: academic, commercial, and vocational, all requiring the completion of 16 Carnegie Units for graduation.[174]

Drawing of Slippery Rock State Normal School Campus, around 1915

Students, faculty and staff, Slippery Rock State Normal School, April 29, 1924

Slippery Rock, by 1920, along with these new changes in the curriculum, had altered completely its two-year, four-semester program. The first semester was the same for all students, after which they chose one of five curricula designed for a specific teaching field.[175] The four basic areas of the curriculum were outlined in the 1920 *Catalog*:

THE FOUR CURRICULA

Group I.   Kindergarten-Primary—for teachers of Kindergarten and grades 1, 2 and 3.

Group II.   Intermediate grades—for teachers of grades 4, 5 and 6.

Group III. Grammar Grades and Junior High School—for teachers of grades 7, 8 and 9.

Group IV. Rural—for teachers of rural schools.

1ST SEMESTER

GROUP I (Kindergarten and Grades 1, 2, 3)	Per.	S.H.	GROUP II (Grades 4, 5, 6)	Per.	S.H.	GROUP III (Grades 7, 8, 9)	Per.	S.H.	GROUP IV (Rural)	Per.	S.H.
Introduction to Teaching	4	3	Introduction to Teaching	4	3	Introduction to Teaching	4	3	Introduction to Teaching	4	3
English Fundamentals	3	3	English Fundamentals	3	3	English Fundamentals	3	3	English Fundamentals	3	3
Eng. Composition	2	2	Eng. Composition	2	2	Eng. Composition	2	2	Eng. Composition	2	2
Nature Study	3	2	Nature Study	3	2	Nature Study	3	2	Nature Study	3	2
Art	4	2	Art	4	2	Art	4	2	Art	4	2
Handwriting	2	1	Handwriting	2	1	Handwriting	2	1	Handwriting	2	1
Personal & Sch. Hygiene	2	2	Personal & Sch. Hygiene	2	2	Personal & Sch. Hygiene	2	2	Personal & Sch. Hygiene	2	2
Health Education	3	1½	Health Education	3	1½	Health Education	3	1½	Health Education	3	1½
Elective	3	3	Elective	3	3	Elective	3	3	Elective	3	3
	26	19½		26	19½		26	19½		26	19½

2ND SEMESTER

GROUP I (Kindergarten and Grades 1, 2, 3)	Per.	S.H.	GROUP II (Grades 4, 5, 6)	Per.	S.H.	GROUP III (Grades 7, 8, 9)	Per.	S.H.	GROUP IV (Rural)	Per.	S.H.
Psy. & Child Study	3	3	Psy. & Child Study	3	3	Psy. & Child Study	3	3	Psy. & Child Study	3	3
Kindergarten Theory	2	2	Oral Expression	2	2	Oral Expression	2	2	Oral Expression	2	2
Oral Expression	2	2	English Composition	2	2	English Composition	2	2	English Composition	2	2
English Composition	2	2	The Teaching of Arithmetic	3	3	The Teaching of Math	3	3	The Teaching of Math	3	3
The Teaching of Number	2	2	The Teaching of Geog.	3	3	The Teaching of Geog.	3	3	The Teaching of Geog.	3	3
The Teaching of History	1	1	Health Education	3	1½	Health Education	3	1½	Health Education	3	1½
Industrial Arts	4	2	Elective	3	3	Elective	3	3	Elective	3	3
Health Habits	1	1									
Health Education	3	1½									
Elective	3	3									
	24	20½		22	20½		22	20½		22	20½

3RD SEMESTER

GROUP I (Kindergarten and Grades 1, 2, 3)	Per.	S.H.	GROUP II (Grades 4, 5, 6)	Per.	S.H.	GROUP III (Grades 7, 8, 9)	Per.	S.H.	GROUP IV (Rural)	Per.	S.H.
Student Teaching	10	10	Student Teaching	10	10	Student Teaching	10	10	Student Teaching	10	10
School Efficiency	3	3	School Efficiency	3	3	School Efficiency	3	3	Primary Methods	3	3
The Teaching of Primary Reading	3	3	The Teaching of Oral & Written Composition	2	2	Health Education	3	1½	The Teaching of Oral & Silent Reading	3	3
Health Education	3	1½	Sewing	2	1	Elective	6	6	Health Education	3	1½
Elective	3	3	Health Education	3	1½				Elective	3	3
			Elective	3	3						
	22	20½		23	20½		22	20½		22	20½

61

4TH SEMESTER

GROUP I (Kindergarten and Grades 1, 2, 3)			GROUP II (Grades 4, 5, 6)			GROUP III (Grades 7, 8, 9)			GROUP IV (Rural)		
	Per.	S.H.		Per.	S.H.		Per.	S.H.		Per.	S.H.
Hist. & Prin. of Education	4	4	Hist. & Prin. of Education	4	4	Hist. & Prin. of Education	4	4	Hist. & Prin. of Education	4	4
Children's Lit. & Story Telling	3	2	Juvenile Lit & Silent Reading	3	2	Juvenile Lit & Silent Reading	3	2	Rural School Problems	3	3
Citizenship	2	2	Citizenship	2	2	Citizenship	2	2	Citizenship	2	2
Industrial Arts	4	2	Music	4	2	Music	4	2	Rural Sociology	2	2
Music	4	2	Prevocational Ed.	3	3	Health Education	3	1½	Music	4	2
Health Education	3	1½	Health Education	3	1½	Elective	9	9	Health Education	3	1½
Elective	6	6	Elective	6	6				Elective	3	3
	26	19½		25	20½		25	20½		24	20½

| Total | 98 | 80 | Total | 96 | 81 | Total | 95 | 81 | Total | 94 | 81 |

First column—Number of sixty minute periods per week.   Second column—Number of semester hours of credit.[26]

Upon completion of groups I, II, III or IV, the student was issued a certificate to teach within the grade areas in which he specialized. This certificate was valid for two years, which, if the holder completed two years of successful teaching, was made permanent. Those students not wishing to enroll in one of these four groups had one additional choice, because effective September 6, 1920, Slippery Rock State Normal School had been designated by the Department of Public Instruction in Harrisburg to offer a three year program in Health Education.[177] The program was designed to prepare students to teach and supervise health education in the public schools of Pennsylvania, in athletic associations, and in Y. M. and Y. W. C. A.'s.[178]

The program of studies for this new major in Health Education, as outlined in the *Catalog*, offered an intensive set of courses in the field of health and physical education:

FIRST YEAR

First Semester			Second Semester		
	Per.	S.H.		Per.	S.H.
Educational Gymnastics	8	4	English Composition	2	2
English Composition	2	2	Educational Gymnastics	8	4
Piano	4	2	Psy. & Child Study	3	3
Anatomy	3	3	Oral Expression	2	2
Physiology	4	4	Piano	4	2
Swedish Gymnastics	2	2	Anatomy	1	2
Elective	3	3	Hygiene	2	2
			Elective	3	3
	26	20		25	20

62

SECOND YEAR

First Semester	Per.	S.H.
Educational Gymnastics	8	4
Voice	4	2
History of Hea. Educ.	1	1
First Aid	1	1
Playground Handwork	4	2
Kinesiology	2	2
Physiology of Exercise	2	2
Anthropometry	1	1
Games	1	1
Elective	3	3
	27	19

Second Semester	Per.	S.H.
Educational Gymnastics	8	4
Physiological Psych.	3	3
Massage and Corrective Gymnastics	2	2
Theory of Play Equipment Construction Organization and Pageantry	2	2
Pediatrics	1	1
Elective	3	3
Practice with observation & participation	6	5
	25	20

THIRD YEAR

First Semester	Per.	S.H.
Educational Gymnastics	8	4
History & Principles of Education	4	4
Massage and Corrective Gymnastics	2	2
Histology	2	2
Elective	3	3
Practice	5	5
	24	20

Second Semester	Per.	S.H.
Educational Gymnastics	8	4
Sociology	3	3
General Health Topics	3	3
Bacteriology	3	3
Elective	3	3
Practice	5	5
	25	21

S.R.S.N.S Alumnus, Hayden Nichols, back left, with his class, 1924

Another change occurring in 1920 which pleased the students was the abolishment of the required yearly examinations given by the State Board of Examiners.

State regulations governing the award of the permanent standard certificate for teachers were altered in 1923, so that now four successful years of teaching were required instead of two.[180]

Slippery Rock's summer school program, which began in 1917, expanded as more and more students took advantage of the opportunity to continue their education through the summer months. In 1925, a new summer camp program was offered.[181] Its purpose was to train "by direct contact with nature students entering or attending normal school and colleges, students of the health education department of Slippery Rock State Normal School or similar schools, and teachers who need credits, or wish to broaden their knowledge of Nature Study or Scout Craft." The specific aims of the program were as follows:

1. To present a comprehensive outline of the names and distribution of plants and animals with which we associate.
2. To develop a greater appreciation of nature.
3. To show the living world a series of successive and parallel life histories of plants and animals.
4. To relate the principles of chemistry and physics to those of biology.
5. To present a general discussion together with practice in the art of organizing, setting up and managing all matters relating to camp work.
6. To instruct in the detailed technique of scout craft.
7. To cover the general details of scout organization and administration.
8. To study the relation of mass games to camp activities.
9. To instruct, both in theory and practice, in all matters relating to general water craft.[182]

The camp was located two miles from the main campus along the banks of Slippery Rock Creek. The camp program attracted students not only from Slippery Rock, but from other normal schools as well. It was soon to be named Camp Conawasco.[183]

Starting in 1925, a series of events taking place locally and in Harrisburg were to have enormous significance for the future of the Normal School at Slippery Rock. The Pennsylvania State Board of Normal School Principals adopted for all of the state's normal schools a new set of admission requirements which clearly brought them closer to the academic standards of the nation's four-year colleges. The new requirements were:

1. The State Normal Schools shall admit to the first year class all graduates of four-year high schools, who present (a) At least 15 Carnegie units of credit, or (b) Not fewer than 12 Carnegie units of credit completed in the tenth, eleventh, and twelfth grades (senior high school).
2. Graduates of two-year high schools shall be given not more than 8 Carnegie units of credit, and graduates of three-year high schools not more than 12 Carnegie units of credit, toward the standard admission requirement; provided, however, that such students may take examinations prescribed by the pre-professional bureau of the State Department of Public Instruction in subjects other than those credited by the State Normal Schools and shall be given such additional credit as the bureau may assign as a result of such examination.
3. Credentials of all students entering the State Normal Schools shall be received and evaluated by the normal schools and kept on file for inspection by the State Department of Public Instruction.
4. Until September, 1927, the holders of permanent and professional certificates will be given one credit toward admission as regular students in the State Normal Schools for each subject of high school grade written on the certificate.
5. Advanced credit will be given for equivalent courses in approved teacher-training institutions but no student may obtain a normal school certificate without a minimum residence of one year. Teachers who are granted credit for experience may finish with a minimum residence of one-half year.[184]

Classroom in Old Main, 1925

Along with these higher requirements for admission came action from Harrisburg which, by offering to all of the state's normal schools the opportunity to set up four-year programs of study leading to a baccalaureate degree, would grant to these schools the opportunity to achieve full collegiate status.[185] Slippery Rock State Normal School responded quickly and submitted a petition to the State Council of Education requesting permission to confer degrees to those students who successfully completed four-year academic courses of study.[186] On June 4, 1926, the State Council of Education approved Slippery Rock's request.[187] Francis B. Haas, President of the State Council of Education, sent the following official notice of the Council's action to the school's Board of Trustees:

To the Board of Trustees of the State Normal School at Slippery Rock:

Petition of the State Normal School located at Slippery Rock, Pennsylvania, for power to confer degrees, having been duly heard and considered by the State Council of Education, this council finds:

First. That the course of instruction and standard of admission to said institution, and the composition of the faculty appear to be sufficient.

Second. That the educational needs of the particular locality in which the proposed institution is to be situated and of the commonwealth at large are likely to be met by the granting of said application.

Wherefore. The said council at its meeting held in Harrisburg, Pennsylvania, on June 4, 1926, passed a resolution authorizing the State Normal School at Slippery Rock to confer degrees as follows: The degree of Bachelor of Science in Education to graduates in courses of the following four-year curriculum: elementary education, junior high school work. The degree of Bachelor of Science in Health Education to graduates in courses of the four-year curriculum in health and education.

Wherefore, finally, the State Council of Education by virtue of the authority given to it by the Act of June 26, 1895, P. L. 327 and the amendments thereto, having considered the merits of the application from an educational standpoint hereby grants to the State Normal School at Slippery Rock the power to confer degrees upon the conditions herein stated.

Given under my seal this fourth day of June, nineteen hundred and twenty-six.

Francis B. Haas, President State Council of Education, Department of Public Instruction, Commonwealth of Pennsylvania.

Attest: James N. Rule, Secretary State Council of Education.[188]

This decree assured that, in addition to pre-existing programs, the Normal School was eligible to award two baccalaureate degrees in the three areas of elementary education, the junior high school, and health education. All three areas required 136 semester hours for graduation. Slippery Rock retained the two-year programs for kindergarten-primary, intermediate, and rural school teachers.[189] An advanced two-year program for normal school graduates leading to the Bachelor of Science degree in Education was also created.[190]

The 1926 *Catalog* outlined the program of studies for the three 4-year programs leading to a bachelor's degree:

Requirements for Graduation and Credential

FOUR-YEAR CURRICULUM IN ELEMENTARY EDUCATION FOR CLASSROOM TEACHERS

First Semester

Educational Biology	3	3
Introduction to Teaching	3	3
English	3	3
Oral Expression	2	2
Art (1)	4	2
Music (1)	4	2
Handwriting	2	1
Physical Education (1)	3	1
	24	17

Second Semester

Psychology & Child Study	3	3
English (2)	3	3
Art (2)	3	1½
Music (2)	3	1½
Nature Study	2	2
Teaching of Prim. Reading	3	3
Teaching of Number	2	2
Physical Education (2)	3	1
	22	17

Third Semester

Educational Psychology	3	3
Teaching of Arithmetic	3	3
Teaching of Geography	3	3
Economic Biology	4	3
American Literature	2	2
Nutrition	4	3
Physical Education (3)	3	1
	22	18

Fourth Semester

Teaching of English	3	3
Descriptive Astronomy	3	3
Educ. Measurements	3	3
Economics	3	3
Teaching of Primary Subjects—	4	4
Geography	1	1
Social Studies	1	1
Spelling and Language	2	2
Physical Education (4)	3	1
	19	17

Fifth Semester

Educational Sociology	3	3
Children's Lit & Story Telling	3	3
Health & Hygiene in Elem. Sch.	3	3
Teaching of Social Studies	3	3
American Government	3	3
Elective	2	2
	17	17

Sixth Semester

History of Education	3	3
Physiography	3	3
Teaching & Supervision of Arithmetic in Elementary Schools	3	3
Advanced Composition	2	2
English Literature	2	2
Civic Education in Elem. Sch.	3	3
	16	16

Seventh Semester

Student Teaching & Conf.	13	10
Technique of Teaching	2	2
Principles of Human Geog.	3	3
Kindergarten-Primary Theory	2	2
	20	17

Eighth Semester

History & Appreciation of Art	4	2
History & Appreciation of Music	4	2
History & Organization of Educ. in Penna.	2	2
Practical School Contacts	4	4
Supervision & Administration of Elementary School	3	3
Principles of Education	3	3
	20	16

Requirements for Graduation and Credential

The completion of the foregoing curriculum of 136 semester hours entitles a person to the degree of B.S. in Education which, after two years of successful teaching experience, becomes a life license to teach, supervise, or serve as principal in the elementary field.

FOUR-YEAR CURRICULUM FOR THE PREPARATION OF JUNIOR HIGH SCHOOL TEACHERS

First Semester

Educational Biology	3	3
English (1)	3	3
Oral Expression	2	2
Social and Industrial U. S. History	3	3
Human Geography	3	3
Appreciation & Application of Art	4	2
Physical Education (1)	3	1
	21	17

Second Semester

Introduction to Teaching	3	3
English (2)	3	3
Everyday Science	3	3
Economics	3	3
Handwriting	3	1
World Problems in Geog.	2	3
Physical Education (2)	3	1
	22	17

Fifth Semester

Purpose, Org. & Development of Jr. High School	3	3
Advanced Composition	3	3
Guidance	3	3
First Elective Field	3	3
Second Elective Field	3	3
Free Elective	2	2
	17	17

Sixth Semester

History of Education	3	3
Educational Measurements	3	3
First Elective Field	3	3
Second Elective Field	3	3
Dramatic English	3	3
History & Organization of Educ. in Penna.	2	2
	17	17

Third Semester

Psychology & Adolescence	3	3
English Literature	2	2
First Elective Field	3	3
Second Elective Field	3	3
American Government	3	3
Physical Education (3)	3	1
Free Elective	2	2
	19	17

Fourth Semester

Educational Psychology	3	3
American Literature	2	2
First Elective Field	3	3
Second Elective Field	3	3
Educational Sociology	3	3
Physical Education (4)	3	1
History & Appreciation of Music	4	2
	21	17

Seventh Semester

Student Teaching, Conf., & School Contacts	18	14
Technique of Teaching	2	2
	20	16

Eighth Semester

Principles of Education	3	3
Health & Hygiene in Jr. High School	3	3
First Elective Field	6	6
Second Elective Field	6	6
	18	18

Requirements for Graduation and Credential

The Credential to be awarded on the completion of the 136 semester hours of the foregoing curriculum is a B.S. in Education which entitles the holder to teach in any public school any subject in which he has earned 18 or more semester hours of credit. After two years of successful teaching, a life license in the foregoing field is awarded.

Credentials to be awarded upon the completion of 136 semester hours of the foregoing curriculum is B. S. in Health Education, which entitles the holder to teach and supervise in any public school the subjects of health education and any other subject in which he ha earned eighteen or more semester hours of credit. After two years of successful teaching, a life license in the foregoing field is awarded.[191]

FOUR-YEAR CURRICULUM IN HEALTH EDUCATION

First Semester		
Biology	4	3
Hygiene (1)	3	3
English (1)	3	3
Oral Expression	2	2
Music (Rhythmics)	2	2
Gymnasium	3	1½
Athletics (1)	3	1½
	20	16

Second Semester		
Chemistry	4	3
Anatomy (1)	3	3
English (2)	3	3
Psychology and Child Study	3	3
Hist. of Phys. Educ.	2	2
Gymnasium (2)	3	1½
Athletics (2)	3	1½
	21	17

Third Semester		
Physiological Chem	4	3
Physiology	3	3
English (3)	3	3
Play & Playgrounds	3	3
Playground & Practice	2	1
First Aid	1	1
Gymnasium (3)	3	1½
Athletics (3)	3	1½
	22	17

Sixth Semester		
Individual Gymnastics	3	3
Phys. Educ. in Elem. & Secondary Schools	2	2
Student Teach. & Conf.	6	3
Elective	3	3
Scouting	2	1
Swimming	2	1
Gymnasium (6)	3	1½
Athletics (6)	3	1½
Dancing (2)	2	1
	26	17

Fourth Semester		
Chemistry of Nutrition	4	3
Hygiene (2)	2	2
Anatomy (2)	2	2
Physiology of Exercise	2	2
Elective	5	5
Gymnasium (4)	3	1½
Athletics (4)	3	1½
	21	17

Seventh Semester		
Guidance	3	3
Administration & Supervision	3	3
Student Teach. & Conf. Senior High School	5	2½
Diseases of Children	2	2
Elective	4	4
Antagonistic Exercises	2	1
Gymnasium (7)	3	1½
Dancing (3)	2	1
	24	18

Fifth Semester		
Educational Sociology	3	3
Theory and Methods of Physical Education	4	4
Student Teach & Conf.	6	3
Elective	3	3
Gymnasium (5)	3	1½
Athletics (5)	3	1½
Dancing (1)	2	1
	24	17

Eighth Semester		
Principles of Education	3	3
Principles & Methods of Coaching	2	2
Student Teach. & Conf. Senior High School	5	2½
Phys. Diagnosis & Anthropometry	2	2
Elective	4	4
Festivals and Pageants	1	1
Gymnasium (8)	3	3½
Dancing (4)	2	1
	22	19

Requirements for Graduation and Credential

Credentials to be awarded upon the completion of 136 semester hours of the foregoing curriculum is B.S. in Health Education, which entitles the holder to teach and supervise in any public school the subjects of health education and any other subject in which he has earned eighteen or more semester hours of credit. After two years of successful teaching, a life license in the foregoing field is awarded.[41]

Though the school was no longer just a normal school, it could not change its name to affect its newly won collegiate status until it graduated a student with a bachelor's degree. Miss Marie McKay, the school's Registrar, recalls this somewhat frustrating moment in the school's history:

> It seems there was a technical difficulty— that is, one person had to be graduated in a four-year course before the name of the school could be changed. The registrar worked hard to graduate the first four year student, Merle R. Young, and so legally changed the name from normal school to college.[192]

Merle Young graduated in 1927 with a Bachelor of Science degree in Health Education, and in August of that year, the State Council of Education changed the name to the State Teachers College at Slippery Rock.[193] The summer catalog for 1928 was the first catalog to bear the new name.[194]

In 1926, the faculty adopted a new system of grading, along with stricter requirements for graduation:

1. Point system as follows:
   Each credit hour with a grade of E counts for three points.
   Each credit hour with a grade of G counts two points.
   Each credit hour with a grade of S counts one point.
   Only those students shall be deemed worthy of graduation whose total points equal in number the credit hours required for graduation. This insures that a student in order to graduate must have an average standing for his whole course of not less than S.
2. All students who, at the end of the first semester of the first year of the course, receive as many a two-thirds of the number of hours on their program with a grade of U or C, shall be automatically suspended from the privileges of the school, such students, however, being permitted to return not earlier than a year from their first registration and that they are to repeat the work of the semester with the exception of the subjects in which they received a grade of E, G, or S.

The above is based upon the marking system
   as follows:
     E—excellent
     G—good
     S—satisfactory
     C—credit
     U—unsatisfactory
No percentage value has been attached to these
   letters.[195]

The admission requirements were also revised in 1926 so that now graduation from an "…approved four-year high school, or equivalent training in an approved private secondary school" was required.[196] Non-traditional students seeking admission could take special examinations, request to have their transcripts evaluated by the Credentials Bureau of the Department of Public Instruction, and, if deserving, receive advanced credit for work completed at other schools.[197] In the early 1930's, all students seeking admission to the College were required to take an English proficiency examination and to have a personal interview.[198]

The curriculum was expanded, in 1932, so that now students could earn a Bachelor of Science in Education degree in Kindergarten-Primary grades (K, 1, 2 and 3), Intermediate grades (4, 5 and 6), Secondary Education (grades 7 through 12), and Rural School Teaching as well as a Bachelor of Science degree in Health Education.[199] The following year, the venerable two-year Normal School Certificate program in elementary education, which, for over forty years, had been the backbone of Slippery Rocks curriculum, was ended.[200] The graduation requirement was reduced from 136 semester hours to 128 in 1934.[201]

As the curriculum expanded, at Slippery Rock, so did the student enrollment. The student body increased from 533 (402 women and 131 men) in 1923 to 852 (657 women and 195 men) by the end of the decade.[202]

The following analysis of enrollment by counties gives some indication of the extent to which the College was attracting students from beyond the immediate Slippery Rock area:

Enrollment by Counties	1923	1929
Allegheny	82	288
Armstrong	12	33
Beaver	31	36
Bedford	1	2
Blair	0	3

Enrollment by Counties	1923	1929
Butler	216	174
Cambria	0	4
Cameron	0	1
Clarion	2	3
Clearfield	0	0
Crawford	5	10
Elk	0	1
Erie	2	5
Fayette	1	6
Forest	0	1
Franklin	0	2
Greene	0	1
Huntington	0	1
Indiana	4	9
Jefferson	5	1
Lackawanna	1	0
Lawrence	53	100
Lehigh	0	3
Lycoming	0	5
Mercer	65	68
Mifflin	0	0
McKean	1	2
Northhampton	0	0
Perry	0	1
Potter	0	0
Somerset	0	0
Venango	23	21
Warren	0	3
Washington	4	17
Westmoreland	17	48
Out of State	8	4
	533	853[203]

The summer school continued to attract large numbers of teachers who wished to improve their teaching competencies. In the 1926 Summer Term, for example, 430 of the students enrolled had at least one year of teaching experience, and 28 had spent more than a decade in the classroom.[204]

By 1931, enrollment at the College had climbed to over a thousand. An analysis of these students by class and academic program presents this picture:

Seniors	(Four-Year	78	
	(Two-Year	202	280
Juniors	(Jr. H. S.	51	
	(Health Ed.	55	
	(Elementary	9	115

Sophomores	(Jr. H. S.		43
	(Health Ed.	82	
	(Elementary	4	129
Freshman	(Jr. H. S.		82
	(Health Ed.	129	
	(Elementary	38	
	(Two-Year	195	444
Part-time Campus Students			64
Total			1032[205]

Here it is seen that nearly forty percent of all the full-time students were enrolled in two-year programs, with the Health Education program being the most popular among the four-year programs. For many years, Slippery Rock was recognized as a center for the study of health and physical education school.

In the mid-1920's, the cost of attending Slippery Rock for one semester was about $150. The following chart lists the various expenses students incurred:

First Semester
Boarding, including furnished room,
    heat, light, plain laundry—all
    departments $126.00
Tuition, Secondary Department   45.00

Semester Fee—all departments	10.00
Special registration for special music students	1.00
*Special Music Fees:	
One lesson per week (1/2 hr.)	18.00
Two lessons per week (1/2 hr.)	36.00
Use of Piano:	
One practice period per day	3.00
Two practice periods per day	6.00
Use of Pipe Organ (1 period a day)	18.00
Harmony	15.00
History of Music	4.50
Special Fees:	
Domestic Science	5.00
Advanced Sewing	3.00
Dressmaking	3.00
Manual Training	1.50
Typewriting	5.00
Chemistry Laboratory	5.00
Physics Laboratory	5.00
Agriculture	1.00
Nature Study	1.00

All expenses for semester are due at the time of registration.[206]

South Hall, about 1920

*The Victory Bell
hanging in South Hall*

In order to keep pace with the expanding academic programs and enrollments, Slippery Rock had to enlarge its campus and its physical facilities. Land purchases of 1923, 1925 and 1929 brought the total acreage of the campus to 150 acres. In 1926, the eve of Slippery Rock's ascension to collegiate status, the following enumeration of campus buildings and their value was included in the school's application for four-year status:

Main Building	Office, Library, Instruction	120,000
North Hall	Dining Room & Dorm.	100,000
South Hall	Dormitory	125,000
Chapel	Assembly	100,000
Training School	Training School	60,000
Gym. & Music Hall	Gym. & Practice Rooms	150,000
Boiler House	Boiler & Engine Room	15,000
Laundry & Assorting Rm.	Laundry	5,000
Bake Shop	Bakery	2,000
"The Elms"	Housing Help	4,000
"The Pines"	Students	4,000
"The Maples"	Students	4,000
"The Murphy"	Students	2,500
Garage	Housing Autos	2,500
3 Pump Houses	Wells	500
3 Stables	Horses & Machinery	150
Stevenson	Housing Help	1,800
1 Greenhouse		1,000
(Coal Frame)		200
	Total	697,650,207

In 1929, Dr. Eisenberg launched a major building program. With steady increases in student enrollment, the College was desperately in need of a new teacher training facility. Construction of the Elementary Laboratory School began in 1929, when the Board of Trustees approved contracts for the building amounting to $127,870.[208]

Constructed of brick, the new Elementary Laboratory School was well designed to serve as the setting for the training of future elementary school teachers. Along with the individual classrooms to accommodate all levels from kindergarten through sixth grade, there were other rooms designed for demonstration of special teaching techniques and displaying projects. There were also special rooms designed for observation of class routine without interrupting the learning process.[209] The Director of the Laboratory School was provided an office on the first floor, an educational clinic composed of psychological, reading and speech clinics was on the second floor.[210] Here various types of clinical materials and equipment for mental testing, checking eye disability, discovering faulty reading habits, measuring hearing disability, checking physical health, and ascertaining speech defects were available.[211]

In 1930, President Eisenberg persuaded the Board of Trustees to approve the construction of a new $100,000 East Gymnasium.[212] This new building was attached to the existing gymnasium and was built of matching yellow brick. Now, students could play two basketball or volleyball games simultaneously on one of the largest facilities in the district.[213] The indoor swimming pool, 20' x 60', was placed between the two gymnasiums, with a girls' locker room and shower facilities located in the basement of the East Gymnasium.[214] The two gymnasiums housed not only the offices of the health education instructors, but also would serve as the site for some of the social dances.[215]

At the insistence of President Eisenberg, the Hut was added to the list of building projects.[216] Its chestnut beams and paneling, surrounding the large stone fireplace in the main room, came from lumber taken from the College woods.[217] On the first floor behind the main recreational room, were the game room and living quarters for the directors of the Hut.[218] The basement housed three bowling alleys, ping-pong tables and tables for billiards and pool which were available to students at scheduled times of the week.[219] With such facilities, it quickly became the recreational and social center of the College.

One of the most visible additions to the campus came in 1929 as a gift from the graduating class of that year.[220] The four clock faces in the tower of Old Main were installed that year by Mr. H. Clyde McLaine, through a contract with Marvin Electric Company of New Castle, Pennsylvania.[221] Mr. McLaine installed the clock mechanisms in approximately two months.[222] Since the tall steeple was so narrow inside, a pulley mechanism was put into use to lift the pie-shaped pieces of the clock's faces into position.[223] Mr. McLaine was not unknown to Slippery Rock as he had installed the campus

Elementary Laboratory School cornerstone ceremonies, May 25, 1929

electric plant in 1919 in cooperation with Frederick Wilkes of Westinghouse Electric Company of Pittsburgh, Pennsylvania.[224]

At the close of the decade, Slippery Rock had become a far more diversified and complex institution than it was in the early 1920's, as this organizational chart reveals:

With the inclusion of structured and organized academic departments came extra-curricular activities related to these disciplines. The Music Department introduced a host of music related organizations which included: the first choir, composed of mixed voices which provided music for the Sunday morning chapel service; two girls' glee clubs and a boys' glee club; a baton club which studied the directing of ensemble singing and playing; and the orchestra.[226] The English Department also provided several extra-curricular opportunities for interested students. The Press Club was responsible for the weekly publication entitled "The Slippery Rocket."[227] The Literary Club or the "Ledra Club," a Debating Club, and a Dramatic Club were other extra-curricular activities supported by the Department of English.[228]

The Saxigena, meaning rock development, was first produced in 1912 as a student yearbook by a committee of juniors elected by the entire school.[229]

A variety of organizations sprang up reflecting student interest in other area. The Open Road Club was enjoyed by those interested in nature study and the Science Club was limited to senior honorary students.[230] For the purpose of development of the social and ethnical dimensions in life, the women on campus organized this club.[231] An Art Club attracted those with aesthetic interests. The Student Council helped develop the idea of self-government among the student body.[232]

Many types of athletic activities were available to all students, including a variety of varsity sports. The following regulations governed varsity athletics in 1919:

BOARD OF TRUSTEES
Appointed by Governor—School, Fiscal and Administrative Codes define responsibilities and relations with State Superintendent and State Agencies

PRESIDENT
Executive Officer for Board— Member Board of Presidents— School, Fiscal and Administrative Codes define responsibilities and relations with State Superintendent and State Agencies

DEAN OF INSTRUCTION	DEAN OF SOCIAL ACTIVITIES	DIRECTOR OF TRAINING SCHOOL	BURSAR	SUPT. OF BUILDINGS AND GROUNDS	CHIEF ENGINEER	STEWARD OR DIETITIAN
Instructional Activities Supervision Credentials Records Programs Schedules, etc.	Supervision General Social Life Student Government Boarding regulations Personal records Social calendar	Campus Sch. Cooperative classes Records Programs etc.	Collections Purchases Accounts RETAIL STORE STORES POST OFFICE RECEIVING CLERK	Ground maintenance Building const. Building maint. (other than power serv.) Custodial Service	Plant Service Maintenance Heat Current Water Plumbing	Food Services Maintenance Dining Room Kitchen Bakery Food Selection
LIBRARY SPECIAL CURRICULA	INFIRMARY	PLACEMENT		LAUNDRY	POWER HOUSE	FOOD STORE[75]

Normal School Concert Band, 1921

The following conditions must be met in order to become a member of any athletic team:

The student must be doing passing work in at least four subjects.

The student's general deportment must be in keeping with the regulations of the school.

The student must be governed by the true spirit of sportsmanship in all athletic contests.

The student must observe the training regulations of the coach and physical director.

The following conditions govern the awarding of letters and medals:

Medals shall be awarded to any student who has played during at least fifty per cent of the actual playing time in any individual sport in a series of not less than six games.

Letters shall be awarded to any student who has played the equivalent of three full games in any athletic contest of the school.

All athletic contests which shall be taken into consideration in the awarding of either medals or letters shall be played with teams representing educational institutions.

Any question involving dispute in regard to the interpretation of any one of these rules shall be referred to the athletic committee for final adjustment.[233]

The justification for the expansion of extra-curricular activities at Slippery Rock, both during the normal school and teachers college eras, is best explained in the following statement of intent: "The extra-curricular activities at Slippery Rock have been organized with an ultimate purpose in view—that of developing leadership in school and community life and of employing leisure time in profitable recreation."[234]

May Day celebration, 1920

Theatrical production in Chapel, 1923

Professor Hamm and his Bible Class, 1921

S.R.S.N.S Christmas Vespers

The Literary Societies compete

Bryant Literary Society, 1921

Philomathean Literary Society, 1921

Undefeated Normal School football team with Coach N. K. Thompson, right, 1924

Men's Basketball Team, 1919

Baseball team, 1930

At the tennis courts, late teens

77

Women's basketball outside South Hall, 1919

Women's basketball team, 1921

The Leaders Class, about 1915

A Varsity athletics outing, mid teens

Interestingly enough, while religious denominationalism was barred at such a state school as Slippery Rock, numerous religious activities were sponsored by the school. As an active Christian, President Eisenberg, in his own way, encouraged religious activities on campus. The Y. M. C. A. and Y. W. C. A., two of the most active religious organizations, were formed in 1918, just one year after Dr. Eisenberg's arrival.[235] They held regular Wednesday evening devotional meetings at 6:15 p.m. and a joint religious service each Sabbath evening at 6:15 p.m. in the Chapel.[236] According to one contemporary observer, "most of the young people in the school have identified with these organizations."[237] The School Bible Class, formed by Dr. Hamm, was very popular during the early years of Dr. Maltby's administration. When in 1922, increasing stress was placed "upon the student's participation in the regular organized church schools of the community," the class was discontinued.[238] Students had the opportunity to attend vesper services in the Chapel every Sabbath evening.[239] All students, regardless of faith, were encouraged to attend.

During this time, graduating classes established memorials in the form of scholarships, tablets, fountains, benches, bulletin boards, etc.[240] The classes of 1925 and 1926 began a loan fund available to all students attending

The Slippery Rocket with J. Linwood Eisenberg and William Jennings Bryan, April 27, 1923

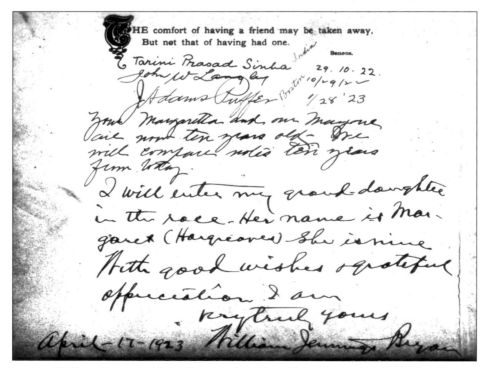

William Jennings Bryan's remarks in President Eisenberg's guest book

the school.[241] The class of 1924, wishing to honor Dr. D. C. Murphy, a long-time professor at the School, created the Murphy Memorial History Library.[242] In that same year, the Alumni Association[243] established the Maltby Memorial Scholarship Fund to assist students at Slippery Rock.[244]

Slippery Rock's popular lecture series, which brought to the campus in the 1920's such renown figures as the Hon. William Jennings Bryan, offered a wide variety of cultural experiences to the School and the community.[245]

Slippery Rock's school colors—green and white—were the choice of the first class that entered in 1889.[246] Succeeding classes would select their own specific colors, and on class day "there was great rivalry between juniors and seniors to see who could keep his colors on South Hall, Chapel, or Main Building as the case might be."[247] In the mid 1920's a color committee developed a quadrangle of colors—red and white, yellow and white, purple and white, and blue and white—from which the School's class would select their class colors.[248]

After serving as chief administrator of the College for seventeen years, Dr. Eisenberg offered his resignation from the presidency to the Board of Trustees early in January of 1934; and Mrs. Emma Guffey Miller offered

John Entz, J. Linwood Eisenberg and Poet Edwin Markam, 1932

the motion that the Board accept it.[249] In 1917, when he first arrived on campus, Slippery Rock was a small normal school which offered two-year certificate programs to some 500 students. When he left, Slippery Rock had achieved collegiate status, offering four-year degree programs to over 1,000 students. That the institution had come of age was a reflection of the many years of dedicated service which its now departing president had given it.

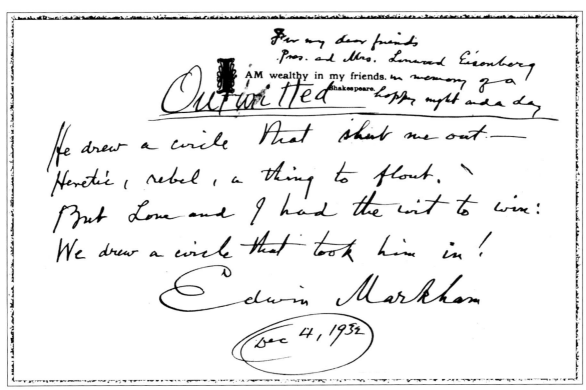

Edward Markham's remarks in President Eisenberg's guest book

Class of 1917

STUDENT'S REPORT	Slippery Rock State Normal School		
Report of............	Period Ending *Mar 19* 19 *20*		

FIRST YEAR	SECOND YEAR	THIRD YEAR	FOURTH YEAR	
Algebra	Plane Geometry	Psychology	Practice Teaching	
School Management	Rhet., Comp., Classics	English Literature	History of Education	*S*
School Law	Botany	American Literature	Agriculture	*u*
Orthography	Zoology	Geography & Methods	Nature Study	
Reading	Civics	U. S. Hist. & Methods	Arithmetic and Methods	*E* *a. gm*
Public Speaking	Modern History	Physiology & School Sanit'n	Grammar and Methods	
Anc. & Med. History	English History	Chemistry	Public Speaking	*S*
Physical Geography	General Methods	Physical Education	Physics	*y*
Arithmetic	Drawing	*Cicero*	Drawing	
Grammar	Physical Education	*German*	Manual Training	
Vocal Music	*Caesar*	*French*	Domestic Education	
Physical Education	*French*	*Spanish*	Physical Training	*y*
Manual Training	*German*	Economics	*Virgil*	*y*
Domestic Science	*Spanish*	Geology	*German*	
Latin		Astronomy	*French*	
French		Solid Geometry	*Spanish*	
German		Trigonometry	Ethics	*S*
Spanish			Sociology	
	Harmony II *E*		Rural School Problems	
	Instrumental Music *E*		Surveying	
	Library Work		*Primary Meth*	*S+*
	Voice *E*			

Passing grade in studies 70 per cent.
Final passing marks for a subject recorded in red ink.
Students will be required to make satisfactory arrangements for all final marks below 70, either by repeating the subject or arranging for special examination.

Form 25-35c-19   *Linwood Eisenberg*   Principal

Student's report card, showing all 4 years required for Normal Certificate, 1920
Note passing grade is 70%

Physical Activities and Athletics, 1920-1930

Second Annual Athletic Dinner program, June 12, 1920

Women's Basketball

New Basketball Uniforms

Women Fencing

Early Gymnastics, 1926

Baseball Team, 1921
Coach N. Kerr Thompson first from left, Coach A. P. Vincent, second from right, back row

Area Scenes, 1924-1934

Heasley's Restaurant, a favorite of the students, north side, Main Street and New Castle Street

Wilson's Service Station, north side, Main Street and Franklin Street

Dr. Eisenberg in front of North Hall

Roaring 20's

Main Street, 1924

*Perhaps first view book for prospective students to consider attending the new
Slippery Rock State Teaches College, about 1927*

Grover C. Watson, back left, 1913 alumnus, Principal of high school near Portersville

Slippery Rock High School in front of Chapel
A. P. Vincent, front row, center, Gus Clutton, front row, fifth from left, mid 1920's

President Eisenberg on the long walk

The water tower and one of the campus ponds

CHAPTER IV

A Period of Expansion 1934-1940

During the middle of the 1930's, Slippery Rock State College was not only struggling to cope with the problems created by the Great Depression; she was also searching for a new president. By July of 1934, the Board of Trustees had narrowed the field of candidates to six: Dr. Carroll, Cr. Fausold, Professor Jones, Dr. Kriner, Dr. Charles Miller, and Dr. Werner.[250] At their July 16th meeting, the Board selected Dr. Miller to serve as the fourth president at Slippery Rock.[251]

Charles S. Miller, President, 1934-1940

Dr. Charles Miller, born in North Lima, Ohio, in 1891, the son of a Methodist minister whose parents were both of Pennsylvania Dutch extraction.[252] His boyhood years were spent in Western Pennsylvania. He received elementary education in Pittsburgh, Leechburg and McKeesport, and his secondary education at South Brownsville High School and the Pittsburgh Academy.[253] With educators on both sides of his family, it is not surprising that he too, decided upon a career in teaching. He entered Allegheny College and, in 1913, received a Bachelor of Arts degree.[254] During his first teaching position at the Edgewood High School, Dr. Miller studied part time at the University of Pittsburgh earning, in 1915, a Master of Arts degree.[255]

In 1916, he was appointed principal of the Clairton High School and, in 1918, principal of the Latrobe High School. Two years later, he was elected to serve as Superintendent of Schools in Latrobe.[256] In 1929, he became Superintendent of Schools at Lansdowne, a suburb of Philadelphia. While there he began graduate study at New York University and, in 1931, received the Doctor of Philosophy degree.[257]

Upon becoming president, Dr. Miller began assessing the needs of Slippery Rock State Teachers College. He found the physical facilities to be particularly inadequate. Unfortunately, the nation was still in the grip of the depression and little money was available for improvement of the school's physical plant. By 1936, however, economic conditions had brightened, enabling Dr. Miller and the Board of Trustees to give specific attention to Slippery Rock's building needs.

Botanical Gardens, 1934

At a fall meeting in 1936, the Board of Trustees conducted a careful examination of the status of the College's physical facilities.[258] They discussed the plight of the many students, who, because of a shortage of campus dormitories, were unable to live on campus. Long lists of student names waiting for campus housing graphically illustrated the seriousness of this problem.[259] The Trustees learned that one wing of North Hall, being of frame construction, was a fire hazard. This unsafe section of North Hall was housing over sixty women.[260] The Library, which had greatly increased the size, and weight, of its collection over the years, was still located on the third floor of Old Main. This was also described as a hazard. The Department of Science was finding it increasingly difficult to carry on the work of its expanding program down in the cramped basement of Old Main.[261]

The Trustees unanimously agreed to send a letter to the Department of Public Instruction at Harrisburg informing them of the seriousness of these problems.[262] They also called for an immediate and thorough examination of all the school's physical facilities.[263]

The survey was completed by the beginning of the new year and, in February, the Board of Trustees conducted another wide-ranging discussion of Slippery Rock's needs for new and renovated campus facilities.[264] Special attention was given to the desperate housing situation which was creating such problems for students.[265] The rising cost of operating the college-owned coal mine, which was located just a few hundred yards east of the powerhouse, caused the Trustees to wonder if it might not be cheaper to purchase coal from a private supplier than extracting it from their own mine.[266]

Chapel and North Hall, left and South Hall, right, 1938

The Long Walk leading to the Chapel, 1934

Graduation procession to Chapel, 1935

Aware that by Pennsylvania Authority Act of 1935, sixty-four million dollars for building construction at state-owned institutions could be made available if the Federal Public Works Administration approved, the Board authorized President Miller to submit to the state authorities a request for $905,000 of building funds for Slippery Rock State Teachers College.[267] The funds were to be allocated for the following building proejcts:

$100,000	Library
$225,000	Arts and Science Building
$175,000	Secondary Training School
$ 35,000	President's Residence
$150,000	Power Plant
$220,000	North Hall Wing Removal[268]

It was the hope of the Board that work could begin at the earliest possible date, with the removal of the hazardous wooden wing of North Hall to receive top priority.

Throughout the spring the Board of Trustees gave intense attention to matters relating to the building program. In May of 1937, President Miller announced that the state of Pennsylvania had tentatively approved Slippery Rock's request for funds under the State Authority Act.[269] By late summer, *The Slippery Rock Signal* was able to report to its readers in bold headlines: 5 NEW BUILDINGS AT SLIPPERY ROCK TO COST $842,000.[270] A three-story Women's Dormitory ($220,000), a Library ($97,000) and President's Residence ($27,165) were to be built from these funds.

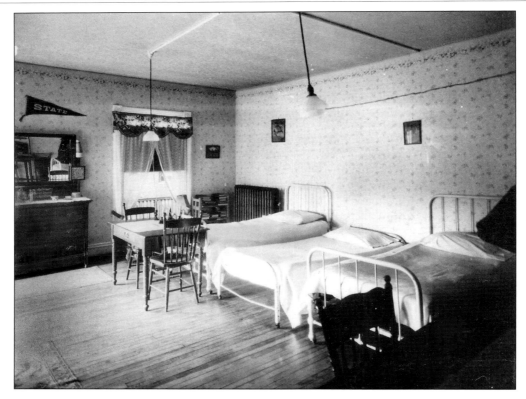

Dormitory room, North Hall, 1935

Dining area in North Hall, 1936

94

Sequential scenes of North Hall fire, October 16, 1937

Improvements to the power plant would cost $33,524.[271] According to *The Slippery Rock Signal*, this grant to Slippery Rock was the largest the state ever made to any of its teachers colleges.[272] Mrs. Emma Guffey Miller, college trustee and member of the State Council of Education, was cited as one who was influential in getting the state assistance which was so necessary for Slippery Rock "to carry out a complete expansion program necessary to its growing educational needs."[273]

Throughout the summer of 1937, officials at the College continued their campus planning. The Board of Trustees announced that the new library would be named Maltby Library, in honor of Dr. Albert E. Maltby, second principal of Slippery Rock.[274] With the presentation in September of the final set of architectural plans by the W. G. Eckles Company of New Castle, all appeared in readiness for Slippery Rock to launch the greatest building program in its history.[275] But it was not to happen this way, for during a beautiful fall homecoming weekend, on October 16, as Slippery Rock was looking ahead to its annual football battle with Westminster College, a fire broke out in the kitchen area of North Hall, the women's dormitory.[276] John Boyd and Horace Hutcheson, on duty at the powerhouse, first noticed the flames at about five o'clock in the morning.[277] Both College and town alarms were sounded and immediately the one hundred and sixty-seven women and faculty began fleeing the dormitory. All escaped safely, but North Hall was almost totally destroyed, despite the efforts of the local firemen, townspeople, and school personnel. Fortunately, their efforts kept the blaze from spreading to adjacent buildings. Damage estimates were placed at $350,000 to North Hall and $150,000 to furnishings and personal belongings.[278] President Miller, who was away in Pittsburgh at the time of the fire, lost most of his personal library and belongings when his North Hall apartment was totally destroyed.[279] Quick action by students saved a few of his things from the fire.

On the night of the fire, while a benefit dance and movie were being offered to students, College officials were making plans for the housing of the women of North Hall.[280] The Presbyterian Church offered its dining facilities to the students.[281] The majority of the women returned to their homes while new housing arrangements were being made. Within less than a week, all of the women from North Hall were relocated in South Hall or the gymnasium.[282] Most of the men of South Hall were provided accommodations in nearby private homes. President Miller and his family moved into the large Stillwagon house across campus and resident faculty went to South Hall.[283]

By the middle of November, $2,175.13 had been collected to help cover the cost of student books lost in the fire.[284] A temporary dining hall, located between the Chapel and South Hall, was to be constructed at a cost of fifteen thousand dollars.[285]

Though the College was now forced to include in its building plans a replacement for North Hall, the Trustees were determined to proceed with its original intentions to build a library, a science building, a secondary training school and a president's residence.[286]

On January 19, 1938, a ground-breaking ceremony was held on campus officially launching Slippery Rock's bold new building program.[287] Over one hundred and sixty guests gathered in the temporary dining hall for a luncheon.[288] Late that afternoon they went to the Chapel where they, and members of the College and community, listened to Mrs. Emma Guffey Miller, member of the State Council of Education and Chairman of the Building Committee of the Board of Trustees at Slippery Rock, describe "The Place of the Teachers College in the

The aftermath of the North Hall fire, 1937

State Program in Education;" to Dr. Henry Klonower, director of Teacher Education and Certification of the Pennsylvania Department of Public Instruction outline the characteristics of "A Modern Professional School for Teaching;" and to Mr. F. Clair Ross, Pennsylvania State Treasurer and member of the General State Authority, present an overview of the "Pennsylvania General State Authority Program."[289]

A special issue of *The Rocket*, the student newspaper, was printed under the headlines BREAK GROUND TODAY FOR FIVE NEW BUILDINGS.[290] Contracting bids for the library, the science building, the secondary training school, and the president's residence were announced.[291] The community had forgotten the disastrous fire of three months ago and was alive with visions of a bright future. By March of 1938, plans for the replacement of North Hall were completed and the Board of Trustees announced the contracting bids which totaled over a half million dollars.[292] This brought the full cost of the five new buildings planned or under construction at 1.2 million.[293] In October, President Miller announced that the General State Authority had approved the use of one hundred thousand dollars for improvements in the power plant.[294] By the close of the year, construction had moved so quickly that the contractors were predicting that some of the buildings would be ready for occupancy early in 1939.[295]

The Maltby Library was formally opened on January 30, 1939.[296] A contemporary publication offers the following description[297] of this beautiful building:

It is located on the site of the former college garden between Maltby Avenue and the east end of Old Main. Rectangular in shape and consisting of a main floor and basement, it was erected at a cost of $100,000. There are many large windows, allowing for the greatest possible illumination of the reading and reference rooms during the daylight hours. The front of the library is one hundred and sixteen feet long with a colonial doorway exactly in the center. A lead coated cupola tops the peak of the slate roof.

Maltby Library is both beautiful and practical in its interior design. On either side of lobby are the large 45 ft. by 36 ft. reading rooms with their round arched ceilings for better reflection of the indirect lighting. Around the walls of these reading rooms are a series of built-in bookcases, readily accessible to the students. In the left reading room are the bound periodicals and in the right reading room are the education, art, and music books. A special reference room containing the encyclopedias and similar general reference books is located to the rear of the left reading room. Tables seating four students are scattered throughout these various rooms, and the pleasant though bookish atmosphere is conducive to better study habits.

Directly behind the lobby desk are located the stacks with their readily adjustable shelves on both the main floor and the balcony above it. Here may be found the other books of the library on history, biography, literature, science, psychology, fiction, and other subjects. Special lights make these books easily recognized on dark days or in the evenings. Other rooms on the main floor consist of two seminar rooms, a workroom, room for newspapers and the office of the librarian. All these rooms are readily accessible to the students during library hours.

Professor I. N. Moore at laying of
Maltby Library cornerstone, 1938

A new speech laboratory and auditorium with its sloping floor has available space for an audience of two hundred and fifty persons. A thirty-six foot stage allows ample space for the production of the smaller plays. In connection with the stage are several rooms used as the dressing rooms, costume storage room and work room.

An extra stack room in the basement in addition to other stacks and bookshelves on the main floor, will accommodate between 40,000 and 50,000 volumes. At the present time at least 22,000 volumes are catalogued in the Maltby Library. Many new books can be added to the present available supply, thus making our library one of the most up-to-date college libraries in Pennsylvania.

By the end of the year, the science building, the secondary training school, the president's residence, and North Hall dormitory were completed. Designed in Georgian and early colonial architectural styles, these buildings gave to the Slippery Rock campus the quiet, dignified appearance of many of the colleges of the East.[298]

These buildings did more, of course, than just improve the looks of the campus; for, as the descriptions appearing in the fiftieth anniversary book, *Thru Fifty Years*,[299] made clear. Consider, for example, what expanded opportunities for research, teaching and learning the new Science Hall, erected at a cost of $222,000, offered the College's faculty and students.

All the science classes of the future will be held in this building; thus the classroom, laboratories, and offices in the basement of Old Main will be moved to the new building.

The physical and chemical science departments will be located on the main floor of Science Hall. Two physics laboratories are located on the north end of the building with a preparation and storage room in between and accessible to both laboratories. Equipped with the latest physical science equipment, it will be possible for the local physicist to delve into many unknown physical problems. A separate laboratory for the advanced physics students is also included in the physical science department. These students will continue the spectrographic

Science Hall, 1940

analysis of matter now being carried on by the advanced physicists of Slippery Rock.

In the opposite end of the main floor are the organic chemistry laboratory and the general chemistry laboratory separated by the storage and preparation room which is accessible to both. In the front of this floor and next to the chemistry laboratory will be the balance room. Two classrooms and a private laboratory are also located in rooms across the front of Science Hall. When these laboratories are fully equipped, they will provide greatly improved possibilities for accurate chemical analysis.

Possibly the outstanding feature of the Science Hall is the large general lecture room located in the rear of the main floor. It is a greatly needed addition to our science facilities. This lecture room with its raised seats will enable all the students in the room to observe the demonstrations being carried on by the instructors at the large demonstration table at the front of the room. A long room behind the lecture room will allow the faculty or visiting lecturers to prepare for their demonstrations and lectures without being molested.

Upon the second floor of the Science Hall are the separate laboratories for bacteriology and physiology on the north end of the building and the biology laboratories on the south end. Storage rooms for science materials are located between the laboratories. An advanced biology laboratory is also located on the second floor. Two classrooms and an office are in the front of the building, besides the science library for scientific reference materials. These separate laboratories will be welcomed by the biological science students who have formerly had inadequate facilities for the proper work.

In the rear of the second floor are three rooms used for various biological materials. An herbarium for herbaceous plants, the museum for stuffed animals, skeletons, fossils, rocks and other specimens, and the animal room are added facilities. A greenhouse is located on the rear roof of the building for growing living plants. A roof beside the greenhouse as well as the main roof in the front of the building, can be used by the astronomy classes for observation

of the constellations, planets, or other heavenly phenomena.

In the basement of the Science Hall are located several additional rooms as well as the main electrical control board. There is a dark room for developing and printing of films and plates. A specially designed acid storage room will safely house the supply of acids. Other rooms in the basement will be used as a repair shop, storage rooms, and rooms for other purposes that may arise. The college laundry will also be housed in the basement of the Science Building.

And with the construction of a $200,000 Secondary Laboratory School, students planning to teach in high school now had a modern, comprehensive facility in which to prepare for their academic careers. As was explained in *Thru Fifty Years*, this makes a complete laboratory school unit from the kindergarten through the twelfth grade.

It consists of a ground floor and two other floors which connect with the corridors of the elementary school division. The high school administration, teachers, and pupils will move into this addition from the old Model School Building.

On the ground floor of the addition are two general classrooms, and two special new auditorium similar in construction to the auditorium in the Maltby Library. The auditorium with its sloping tile floor is 56 ft. long and has a stage 26 ft. wide. It is a great improvement over the present high school assembly room with its noisy seats and creaking floors. In a wing to the rear of the building is a new gymnasium, 60 ft. by 35 ft. in dimensions. The boys' and girls' locker and shower rooms are connected either with the gymnasium or the corridor leading to it.

A library with built-in wall bookcases is located on the first floor of the high school addition. Special classrooms for the vocational and home economic pupils, and several general classrooms are also located on the first floor. Each classroom in the building has a private office for the class instructor. The walls of the library and all other rooms are painted and the rooms illuminated in the most scientific manner of lighting without glare.

The science rooms and the art room are on the second floor. A newly equipped science laboratory with a storage room for chemicals is located in the rear of the second floor. A stairway is located on the west side of the building, allowing for the rapid exit of the high school pupils in case of fire.

The beautiful, half-million dollar, three story brick North Hall with its Georgian and Colonial design was certainly going to improve the quality of student life of those women who would be occupying it. The authors of *Thru Fifty Years* were obviously impressed with this new dormitory.

The beautiful and practical interior of North Hall is an asset to our college campus. When entering the dormitory through the front portico, the main stairway rises from a side hall to the right of the reception hall. By the stairway will be placed the old long-case clock which was saved from the girls' former dormitory by our college firemen. A doorway to the court opens from the beautiful slate floored reception hall inside the main entrance. A small office for the Dean of Women and a room available for telephone service are located off the reception hall on each side of the entrance.

To the right of the reception hall at the southwest corner of the main floor is the dining room. This room is 108 ft. long by 36 ft. wide on the south side and 72 ft. long and 36 ft. wide on the west side. A beautiful star design is carried out in plastics on the ceiling of the dining room. A similar design is also carried out in the beautiful inlaid tile floor, thus matching perfectly the ceiling and floors of the dining room. The furniture consists of mahogany finish oblong tables with leather upholstered chairs to match. A men's coat room is located off the south side of the dining room with an outside entrance for the men students.

In close connection to the dining room are the serving room and the large kitchen. This modern kitchen will be fully equipped to prepare the quantities of food necessary to keep Slippery Rock's student body alive. The food will be moved into the serving room from the kitchen, and from there it can be served quickly to the students. A small office for the school dietitian is located to the side of the kitchen.

The main lounge with light green ceiling and walls is located directly off the reception hall to the north. It is furnished with comfortable chairs and divans of various colors, arranged in groups to allow freer social life. The long windows are covered by Venetian blinds and attractive heavy draperies. One of the features of the lounge is the large fireplace located in the inside wall. A small library room with comfortable chairs and divan is located just off the lounge.

A large hallway leads to the music room in the northwest corner of North Hall. Here the aesthetic nature of our music appreciation students can feel in harmony. A grand piano is in the offset formed by the bay window of this room. The pleasantly decorated surroundings, the comfortable chairs and divans arranged around the room, as well as the piano and radio, will make the music room a center of dormitory social life.

Also located on the first floor are the apartments of the Dean of Women, the Nurse, Matron, Dietitian, the mail room, and the college infirmary. The college infirmary is one of the most complete units to be installed on our campus. There are separate wards on opposite sides of the rear hallway for men and women students, fully equipped for hospital care. A doctor's waiting room and office are also provided for in this wing of the building. An isolation ward for students having contagious diseases or needing complete privacy is separated from the other rooms. The main room for diagnosis and treatment could be readily used for operating purposes if necessary, and has the proper sterilization equipment needed by the nurse. Because of its location, the infirmary has access to the diet kitchen of the dormitory.

Student rooms are located on all three floors and are furnished with maple furniture. Included are the metal beds with springs and mattresses, dressers and mirrors, chests of drawers and double or single desks with book shelves and desk lamps. The corner rooms of the dormitory have private baths, while those students in the other rooms use the general baths and showers. Hair dryers have been installed in the washrooms for the convenience of the students. Ample closet space is also provided with each dormitory room. One of the other features of the upper two floors of the dormitory are the lounges with kitchenettes, which are located on the west side of these floors. They are comfortably furnished for the use of the girls on each floor.

This new dormitory is a decided improvement to the Slippery Rock College campus. It will provide the finest accommodations for all the women students of the college. If environment plays a part in stimulating a desire for knowledge, then the women of Slippery Rock College should make great strides in education in the years to come.

And finally the President's Residence now provided a spacious and comfortable home for the school's top administrator and his family.

A new residence for the President of Slippery Rock College has been finished, and is being occupied by Dr. C. S. Miller and his family. It is located behind the Maltby Library on the property below the athletic field on the hill and next to the Headland residence. Its typical colonial architecture harmonizes with the other buildings erected on our campus. A sloping slate roof with dormer windows, chimneys at opposite ends of the house, windows with shutters, and a central doorway and hall are distinctively colonial. A driveway leads around the left side of the residence to the two car brick garage at the rear.

Our President's residence consists of three floors and a basement, and contains all the provisions of a modern home. The dining room is located to the left of the central hall with the modernly equipped kitchen directly behind it. To the right of the hall is the living room, with the library located to the rear. Fireplaces add to the comfort of both the library and the living room. The sun room is a one story extension to the right of the living room with a flat roof ornately surrounded by stone coping and grill work.

Four bedrooms with two available baths on the second floor and two bedrooms with a bath on the third floor, allow ample sleeping facilities. Available closets and storage space may be found on these two floors as well as on the main floor. In the basement are located a laundry, a game room with a fire place, the fruit cellar, and the heating and ventilating equipment. The entire residence has been equipped with Venetian blinds and beautifully furnished.

Though much energy had gone into Slippery Rock's building program during the early years of President Miller's administration, other dimensions of collegiate life also received careful attention. High academic standards for students and faculty were constant goals for Dr. Miller, since he believed that Slippery Rock should serve as the educational "lighthouse" for its service area, "furnishing service to its schools and teachers" and leading in "research and demonstration of modern methods and thought."[300]

In 1934, these new requirements for all students appeared in the Catalog:

1. All entering students are required to take, without credit, ten lessons on "using the Library."
2. All students are required to take part, without credit, in one extra curricular activity one semester each year.
3. All students, before receiving a final grade in English or arithmetic, must equal eight grade standards of achievement in these subjects.[301]

As in the past, graduates of the elementary, secondary, or health education programs were awarded the Provisional College Certificate, and with three years of successful teaching and six additional semester hours of credit, were entitled to the Permanent College Certificate.[302] During President Miller's administration, the post-baccalaureate student began to receive increasing attention. Graduates with degrees that had prepared them to teach in secondary schools could receive state certification in elementary education by completing thirty hours of approved elementary courses, including six hours of elementary school teaching.[303]

In 1937, important curricular changes were made in the elementary and secondary education programs. Now all students in these two areas were required to take the following basic liberal arts curriculum in their first two years at the College.

First Semester	Clock Hrs.	Sem Hrs.
English, including		
Library Science	4	3
Speech	3	3
Biological Science	4	3
Health Education, including Phys. Educ. & Personal Hygiene	4	2
Place & Purpose of Educ. in the Social Order, including school visitation	3	2
Appreciation of Music	3	2
	21	15

Second Semester		
English	3	3
Principles of Geog.	3	3
History of Civilization	4	4
Biological Science	4	3
Health Education, including Phys. Educ. U Personal Hygiene	4	2
Appreciation of Art	3	2
	21	17

Third Semester		
Literature I	3	3
Economic Geography	3	3
General Psychology	3	3
Physical Science	4	3
Elective	4	4
	17	16

Fourth Semester		
Literature II	3	3
Educational Psychology	3	3
Principles of Sociology or Principles of Economics	2	2
Physical Science	4	3
Elective	6	6
	18	17[304]

The majors in secondary education, who were now required to complete at least 18 semester hours in two fields of certification, followed this curriculum their last two years of study:

Fifth Semester	Clock Hrs.	Sem Hrs.
American Government	3	3
School Law	1	1
Educ. Measurements	2	2
Electives	10	10
	16	16

Sixth Semester		
Adolescent Psychology	2	2
Problems of Junior-Senior High School	2	2
Electives	10	10
	16	16

Seventh Semester		
Educ. Measurements	2	2
Curriculum in Elementary Science	4	3
Visual Education	2	1
Children's Literature & Story Telling	3	3
Evolution of American Public School	2	2
Philosophy of Education	2	2
Elective	3	3
	18	16

Eight Semester		
Student Teach. & Conf.	15	12
Curriculum Materials, Selection & Adaption	4	3
	19	15[306]

John A. Watson, Slippery Rock Rockets varsity tennis player, 1938 and alumnus, 1940

102

In their last two years, the elementary education students took the following specialized courses which prepared them for their professional roles as teachers.

Fifth Semester	Clock Hrs.	Sem Hrs.
American Government	3	3
Teaching of Reading	3	3
Music I	4	2
Art I	4	2
Curriculum in Arith.	3	2
School Law	1	1
Elective	3	3
	21	16

Sixth Semester		
Child Psychology	3	3
Teaching of English	4	3
Music II	3	1 ½
Art II	3	1 ½
Teaching of Health	3	2
U.S. History to 1865	3	3
Elective	3	3
	22	17

Seventh Semester		
Evolution of American Public School	2	2
Visual Education	2	1
Guidance	2	2
Philosophy of Education	2	2
Electives	9	9
	17	16

Eighth Semester		
Student Teach. & Conf	15	12
Curriculum Materials, Selection & Adaptation	4	3
	19	15[305]

Recognizing the rapid development of speech programs in the state's public school system and the importance of speech in the socialized curriculum, Slippery Rock, in 1937, initiated a new certification program in this area.[307] The program included special emphasis in the two areas of dramatic training and speech science.[308]

The student majoring in Health Education did not follow this split academic organization, but, instead, integrated both the liberal arts and the specialized courses throughout the four-year curriculum.[309]

First Semester	Clock Hrs.	Sem Hrs.
English	3	3
Biological Science	4	3
Chemistry	4	3
Personal Hygiene	3	3
Appreciation of Music	3	2
Physical Education Activities	9	3
Totals	26	17

Second Semester		
English	3	3
Biological Science	4	3
Chemistry of Nutrition	4	3
Appreciation of Art	3	2
Place and Purpose of Ed. in the Social Order	2	2
Intro to Phys. Educ.	1	1
Physical Education Activities	9	3
Totals	26	17

Third Semester		
Literature I	3	3
Physiology I	3	3
History of Civilization	2	2
General Psychology	3	3
Phys. Ed. Activities	6	2
Elective	3	3
Totals	20	16

Fourth Semester		
Hygiene (Community)	3	3
Physiology II	3	3
History of Civilization	2	2
Descriptive Anatomy	3	3
Phys. Ed. Activities	6	2
Elective	3	3
Totals	20	16

Fifth Semester

Speech	3	3
Economics or Economic Geography	3	3
Mechanical Analysis of Activities	2	2
Phys. Ed. Activities	9	3
Elective	4	4
Totals	21	15

Sixth Semester

Phys. Education Tests	3	3
American Government	3	3
Mechanical-Anatomical Analysis of Activities	2	2
Principles of Sociology	2	2
Phys. Ed. Activities	9	3
Elective	3	3
Totals	22	16

Seventh Semester

Philosophy of Education	2	2
Leadership in Protective Procedures	2	2
Nature and function of Play	2	2
festivals and Pageants	2	2
Organization & Adm. of Physical Ed.	4	4
Visual Education	2	1
Phys. Ed. Activities	6	2
Totals	20	15

Eighth Semester

Student Teach. & Conf.	18	12
Curriculum Materials	4	4
Totals	22	16[310]

The following year, a secondary education major was required to complete one field of certification requiring a minimum of 24 semester hours and at least one other field of certification requiring a minimum of 18 semester hours, thus utilizing additional electives in certification courses.[311] The secondary education major could seek certification in English, Social Studies, Geography, Mathematics, Physics, Chemistry, Biology, General Science, Science, and Speech.[312]

In 1938, a three-stage professional integration program,[313] combining the theory practice of teaching, was structured to offer the students, (1) courses giving the student perspective in the general field of education, (2) observation of classroom learning experiences directed by master teachers, and (3) actual teaching under professional guidance.[314] These integrative professional experiences were viewed as another effort of the College to improve its academic programs.

The requirements for admission to Slippery Rock during President Miller's administration were based upon four principles: general scholarship, character and personality, health and physical vigor, and a personal interview.[315] The *Catalog* carefully detailed the following four general requirements all candidates for admission had to satisfy.

1. General scholarship as evidenced by graduation from an approved four-year high school or institution of equivalent grade or equivalent preparation as determined by the Credentials Division of the Department of Public Instruction, and ranking in the upper half of the class at graduation. Candidates for admission who lack this rank at graduation will be required to present further evidence of fitness.

a. Applicants ranking in the upper half of their graduating class in high school will be admitted on certificate without further evidence of general scholarship.

b. Applicants who do not rank in the upper half of the graduating class may be admitted on probation, provided:

(1) They are recommended by their high school principal as being able to do creditable work, and

(2) Appraisal of the detailed high school record indicates to admission authorities of the college that the candidate can do satisfactory college work, and

(3) A rating satisfactory to the institution is made on a scholastic aptitude test administered at the college.

Applicants satisfactorily meeting requirements 1, 2 and 3 above will be admitted for one semester on probation. At the end of the probationary period such students will be required to withdraw from the college unless they meet the required standard of scholarship in at least nine (9) semester hours of work.

2. Integrity and appropriate personality as shown by an estimate by secondary school officials of the candidate's trustworthiness, initiative, industry, social adaptability, personal appearance, and sympathy.

3. Health, physical vigor, emotional stability, absence of physical defects that would interfere with the successful performance of the duties of a teacher and absence of pre-disposition toward ill health as determined by a medical examination at the college.

a. All students for admission shall present a certificate of examination signed by a physician legally qualified to practice medicine in the Commonwealth of Pennsylvania. Forms for this examination will be checked by the examining physician at the college and students may be required to undergo a complete reexamination.

b. Applicants may be rejected for the following reasons:

(1) Incurable defects or diseases as of the heart, lungs, kidneys, digestive system, nervous system, including hysteria, epilepsy, nervous instability, skin, organs of the special senses, thyroid;

(2) Defective vision of marked degree;

(3) Permanently impaired hearing;

(4) Marked speech defects;

(5) Unsightly deformities;

(6) Marked obesity.

Students with remedial defects will be accepted on conditions that immediate treatment will be under taken for the removal of these defects.

4. A personal interview with particular attention to personality, speech habits, social presence, expressed interests of the applicant and promise of professional development.

a. The personal interview is to serve two purposes:

(1) It is to give the examining committee of the college an opportunity to select form the applicants for admission those persons who give promise of becoming desirable teachers;

(2) It is to take an inventory of the personal characteristics of the applicants who are admitted, making this inventory available to instructors and officers concerned with personnel work done in the college.

b. The interview will be conducted at the college or at other places and at times designated by the President of the College.[316]

Enrollment at Slippery Rock during President Miller's administration fluctuated, reflecting the economic and political uncertainties of the day. In his first year, 1934-35, there were 671 students enrolled, with the four classes distributed among the three curricula[317] as follows:

Seniors	(Secondary	48	
	(Health Ed.	63	
	(Elementary	8	119
Juniors	(Secondary	39	
	(Health Ed.	35	
	(Elementary	28	102
Sophomores	(Secondary	48	
	(Health Ed.	44	
	(Elementary	8	
	(Two-year	132	232
Freshman	(Secondary	61	
	(Health Ed.	48	
	(Elementary	100	218

Three years later, in 1937-38, enrollment had dropped almost twenty percent to 547 students.[318] An analysis of the classes and curricular majors[319] at this time yields the following information:

Seniors	(Secondary	36	
	(Health Ed.	31	
	(Elementary	27	94
Juniors	(Secondary	31	
	(Health Ed.	33	
	(Elementary	27	92
Sophomores	(Secondary	35	
	(Health Ed.	41	
	(Elementary	144	220
Freshman	(Secondary	28	
	(Health Ed.	43	
	(Elementary	70	141

Of these students, all but three were Pennsylvania residents. Twenty-six Pennsylvania counties were represented, with Allegheny and Butler counties sending more students than other counties.[320] By 1940, the enrollment had climbed to 591, with no appreciable change in the geographical representation of the students.[321]

Student fees at this time were: included a student activity fee of $6 per semester, a contingent fee of $18 per semester, a housing fee of $63 per semester (if one desired a room with running water an additional charge of $9 per semester was assumed), an infirmary fee of $1 per day after three days, an isolation fee of $10 per week, not to include a trained nurse, a tuition fee for out-of-state students of $105 per semester, a private instruction fee of $24 per semester, a degree fee of $5, a transcript fee of $1 for the second and each transcript thereafter, and finally a delinquent accounts fee.[322] By 1940, it cost a student between $162 to $180 to attend Slippery Rock for one semester, surprisingly similar to the 1934 semester fee total.[323]

From the outset of his presidency, Dr. Miller gave strong leadership in the area of student affairs. The "Social Calendar" for 1934-35[324] suggests the range and frequency of campus activities offered at Slippery Rock during his first year.

September 15 – Saturday
    Faculty Reception
September 22 – Saturday
    Campus Party
September 29 – Saturday
    Y.W.C.A. and Y.M.C.A. Party
October 5 – Friday
    Allegheny County Social
October 6 – Saturday
    "Y" Play
October 12 – Friday
    Beaver, Lawrence, Mercer
    Counties Social
October 13 – Saturday
    Regional Conference
    Demonstration Day
    Homecoming Day
    Football – Grove City College
October 19 – Friday
    Butler County Social
October 20 – Saturday
    Parents' Day
    Football – Glenville S.T.C.
    Motion Picture

October 26 – Friday
    Westmoreland and
    Other Counties Social
October 27 – Saturday
    Dance
October 31 – Wednesday
    Halloween Party
November 3 – Saturday
    Lecture Course Number
November 10 – Saturday
    Football-Edinboro S.T.C.
    Senior Party
    Motion Picture
November 12 – Monday
    W.S.G.A. Tea Dance
    Motion Picture
November 17 – Saturday
    Sophomore Play
November 24 – Saturday
    Dance
December 8 – Saturday
    Y.W.C.A. Bazaar
December 15 – Saturday
    Lecture Course Number
December 16 – Sunday
    Christmas Vespers
December 21 – Friday
    Old English Christmas
January 5 - Saturday
    Junior Party
    Motion Picture
January 12 - Saturday
    Dance
January 26 - Saturday
    Basketball
February 2 - Saturday
    Junior Play
February 9 - Saturday
    Basketball Game
February 16 - Saturday
    Sophomore Party
    Motion Picture
February 22 - Friday
    Y.W.C.A. Tea Dance
    Senior Play
February 23 - Saturday
    Basketball Game

March 2 - Saturday
Freshman Party
Motion Picture
March 9 - Saturday
Dance
March 16 - Saturday
Motion Picture
March 23 - Saturday
Lecture Course Number
March 30 - Saturday
Freshmen Play
April 6 - Saturday
Dance
April 13 - Saturday
W.A.A. Party
April 27 - Saturday
Lecture Course Number
May 4 - Saturday
Motion Picture
May 10 - Friday
Senior Day
Senior Reception by Dean of Women
May 11 - Saturday
Pre-Alumni Dinner and Dance
Motion Picture
May 18 - Saturday
Dance
May 25 - Saturday
Alumni Day
May 26 – Sunday
Baccalaureate Sermon
May 27 – Monday
Senior Class Day
May 28 – Tuesday
Commencement

Many of these social activities involved the School's religious, musical, or student organizations. The religious activities included chapel attendance, vesper services, the Young Women's and Men's Christian Associations.[325] The mixed choir, women's chorus, men's glee club, orchestra and band were the most active musical organizations.[326]

Other extra-curricular activities which were organized for the purpose of developing leadership in school and community life, and worthwhile employment of leisure time and recreation[327] were carried on by such organizations as the French Club, Baton Club, Travel Club, Dramatic Club, Open Road Club, Debating Club, What-To-Do Club, Georgraphy Club, Literature Club, Current Problems Club, and Science Club.[328] The most popular sports on campus were tennis, hockey, baseball, basketball and football.[329]

Dr. Miller felt there was room for significant improvement in the area of student affairs and throughout his administration he attempted to utilize student government, extra curricular activities, religious groups and other organizations for the betterment of student life.

In 1939, a Student Life Division was established on campus. The broad purposes of this important new administrative unit were set forth in the following announcement:

> The program of the modern college must extend its activities beyond what is generally known as the curricular. Every phase of life is educative, and can be made conducive to the development of a balanced, wholesome, integrated personality. Particularly in a professional school for teachers must this be evident in the entire college program. The

The first **Rocket***, printed October 8, 1934*

teachers college needs to take into account the entire individual in guiding this development. Classroom and extra-class activities constitute an integral part of the prospective teacher's education. The former aims at the development and enrichment of personality through study or intellectual achievement, and the acquisition of necessary accompanying skills, while the latter has the same broad objective of the personality growth but attains this end by less formally

Women's Swimming Team, East Gymnasium Pool, 1937

Undefeated Championship Football Team, 1939, Coach N. Kerr Thompson, standing second from left

108

directed situations than the academic work of the classroom.

The student life division has a broad scope of activity including:
1. Guidance, both personal and professional
2. Co-curricular activities
3. Social life
4. Student health
5. Religious activities[330]

To assist first semester freshmen in adjusting to college life, the staff of this new division held weekly orientation and guidance sessions for them.[331] Faculty and upperclassmen offered counseling services for freshmen throughout the year.[332]

So that all students would take advantage of the many opportunities available in the extra-curricular program, the College made it mandatory that they participate, without credit, in at least one co-curricular activity for one semester each year.[333] With official recognition now given to the Student Council in 1937, this organization became a much more important group on campus.[334]

Students also had the opportunity of membership in the following organizations: Demosthenian Debating Club, Literature Club, Press Club, Current Problems Club, Elementary Council,[335] Honor Science Club, Nature Guide Club, Open Road Club, Scientific Society, Student Grange, Women's Athletic Association, Varsity Club, Camera Club,[336] Pi Gamma Mu or the national honorary social science society, Phi Sigma Pi, a national honorary fraternity, Gamma Theta Upsilon, the national professional organization in the field of geography, Kappa Gamma, the forensic arts fraternity,[337] Alpha Psi Omega, the national honorary dramatic fraternity, Sigma Tau Delta, the honorary English fraternity, Phi Delta Pi, the national professional physical education fraternity for women, Mu Epsilon Theta, music fraternity, and Kappa Delta Pi, the Honor Society in Education.[338]

Students were given the opportunity of attending Tuesday and Thursday after-dinner dances in the Hut, along with the fall formal reception and a variety of parties and gatherings throughout the school year.[339]

Just as the College was looking back with justifiable pride upon a decade of growth under President Miller's leadership, an unfortunate scandal over the operation of the Bursar's Office developed, casting a shadow over the campus.[340] After an investigation, the Board of Trustees, in February of 1939, suspended the College Bursar because of irregularities in his office.[341] A proud, dedicated and sensitive President Miller was deeply shaken by these disclosures and the unfortunate publicity it brought to the College. By the end of the year, he reached the decision that this incident had impaired his ability to lead the school and in January, 1940, he submitted this letter of resignation to Dr. John Adams, President of the Board of Trustees:

I hereby present my resignation as President of Slippery Rock State Teachers College, effective at the discretion of the Board of Trustees.

No one regrets more keenly than I the unpleasant experience through which I have passed, nor the unfortunate publicity which accompanied it. I am thankful that at no time has my personal integrity been questions, for I have discharged my duties with sincerity of purpose and with one thought in mind, that of advancing the interests of Slippery Rock.

The period during which I have served as President has been one of stress. The problems growing out of the destruction of North Hall by fire, and the planning and directing of the building program placed an almost unbelievable burden upon me beyond that normally required. However, there is a satisfaction in seeing the new physical plant of which Slippery Rock may well be proud.

The academic standing of our faculty has been steadily advanced until today it ranks first in Pennsylvania, and in the upper ten per cent of the teachers colleges of the United States.

Our student body today likewise represents a higher academic standard, and the general tone of the college work done is such that it meets the most rigid collegiate standards.

No one can truly understand the regret with which I sever my connections with Slippery Rock. I have given five and a half of the best years of my life to its advancement. My whole thought is for its continued success, and I shall always watch its achievements with a real personal pride.

I want to thank the Board of Trustees for their aid and support during my entire administration. Without it nothing could have been accomplished, and we can share together the satisfaction that comes with achievement.[342]

The Board accepted his resignation on January 17, 1940.[343]

Following the resignation of Dr. Miller, Dr. Lewis H. Wagenhorst, former director of the Laboratory School and professor of education at the College, agreed to serve as acting president.[344] One of the notable events that took place during his short tenure was the visit to Slippery Rock State Teachers college of the distinguished poet and scholar of Harvard University, Mr. Robert Frost, on April 3, 1940.[345]

In June, the Board of Trustees began in earnest the search for a new president for the school.[346] They urged all who were interested in the position to file an application by the 20th of June.[347] Early in July, they invited several candidates to the campus for interviews.[348] They reached quick unanimous agreement on one candidate. On July 23, 1940, after receiving approval from Harrisburg, the Board formally elected Mr. Dale McMaster to the presidency of the College.[349]

Mr. McMaster came to Slippery Rock from the position of School Superintendent at Johnstown, Pennsylvania.[350] He was born in Adamsville, Pennsylvania and received his public education in the local Crawford County Schools.[351] In 1908, he completed his bachelor degree requirements at Grove City College, and accepted a teaching position in a one-room school at Ogletown, in Somerset County, Pennsylvania.[352] From the Ogletown position, he became affiliated with the Johnstown public schools, where he held various principalships, including Johnstown High School in 1929.[353] After five years as head principal, he assumed the responsibilities of Superintendent of Schools for Johnstown. He served as Superintendent for six years before coming to Slippery Rock.[354] He did graduate study at Teachers College, Columbia University and the Pennsylvania State University. He received his Master of Arts degree from the University of Pittsburgh in 1929.[355] In 1932, he passed his preliminary examination for the Doctor of Education degree.[356] In June, 1940, he was awarded an honorary

Dale McMaster, President, 1940-1941

Doctor of Laws degree from Grove City College at their commencement exercises.[357] Mr. McMaster had held past presidencies of the Pennsylvania High School Principals Organization and the Department of Secondary Education, Pennsylvania State Education Association.[358]

While the Board of Trustees was searching for the College's next president, the Allied Forces were suffering disastrous defeats in Europe. This escalation of World War II would soon be affecting the life of the nation and, of course, Slippery Rock State Teachers College. The school would be looking for steady leadership from President Dale McMaster during this period of grave uncertainty.

William Gary Cunningham, Boston sportswriter at the Boston University game, 1937
This game started Slippery Rock's national notoriety

Game Day Official Program
October 9, 1937

Assistant Coach A.P. Vincent and Coach N. Kerr Thompson at
S.R.S.T.C. vs. Boston University game at Fenway Park, 1937

Aerial view of campus showing the College's largest construction program. Five buildings- North Hall, Library, Science Building, President's Residence and Secondary Education Wing on Laboratory School, 1939

U.S. Senate Chamber Pass signed by Sen. Joseph Guffey, brother of Emma Guffey Miller, 1935

Swimming in Slippery Rock Creek, below Daugherty's Bridge, Rt. 173 south of Campus

The swimming pool at Saul Stoughton's Beach

1938 SRSTC Rifle Team outside the Chapel
A. P. Vincent, coach standing first row, fourth from right

Golden Anniversary Pagent Program, May 26, 1939, celebrating the college's first fifty years

Alumni Day, 1938

114

CHAPTER V

Years of War and Peace
1940-1956

In the fall of 1940, President Dale McMaster identified himself to the incoming students with these humble words: "I'm Slippery Rock's number one freshman."[359] Because of the war, enrollment in his freshman class was smaller than usual and the total number of students on campus was 553, a seven percent drop from the previous year.[360] Within the year, enrollment would drop another twenty percent to 445.[361]

The growing impact of World War II upon Slippery Rock is seen in the action of the Board of Trustees, when, in February, 1941, they granted the first military leave of absence to Mr. Herbert Rasche, Laboratory School Teacher and Assistant Dean of Men.[362] Reflecting the nation's need for more education in the field of science, Slippery Rock introduced in its secondary education curriculum an area of concentration in the sciences.[363]

In Harrisburg, the House of Representatives was considering Bill Number 460, whose purpose was to close the State Teachers Colleges as such, and open them for vocational training in defense work. The Board of Trustees at their February meeting in 1941 vigorously opposed this proposal which would alter fundamentally the character of the state's teachers college. President McMaster, concerned over this most serious challenge to teacher education, reasserted in his commencement address to the 1941 graduating class[364] his belief that well-educated teachers were important for the survival of our nation's way of life.

> "Teaching is a noble profession. The fact that you have spent four years in preparation to become efficient teachers in our American public schools shows ambition. In order to realize this aspiration, you must have, in addition to your training, within you the ability to think clearly on all problems, and a desire to serve society in making sure for your pupils a continuance of the American way of life."[365]

In November of 1941, a short fifteen months after President McMaster became head of Slippery Rock, the entire college community was stunned with the news of his death by suicide.[366] The Butler Eagle reported the tragedy with the headlines COLLEGE HEAD FOUND DEAD IN HIS HOME.[367] According to the newspaper account, President McMaster had breakfast with his wife on the morning of November 4, after which he retired to his study. His wife heard a shot at a quarter past nine. Rushing to the study, she found her husband "... on the floor with a .32 calibre revolver lying nearby."[368] Coroner J. Charles Riengler said President McMaster apparently shot and killed himself and gave a verdict of "probable suicide."[369] After a brief investigation, the coroner reported that he could learn of no motive that would prompt the act, "except possible overwork in connection with school activities."[370]

The keen loss felt by the members of the Board of Trustees after the death of President McMaster was expressed in their following resolution:

> The members of the Board of Trustees of the Slippery Rock State Teachers College desire to express to you our deep sympathy in your hour of sorrow. The death of Dr. McMaster is an irreparable loss to this institution. During the fifteen months that he served as president, he demonstrated his high qualifications for the exacting duties of the office.
>
> His sterling character, his ability as an administrator, the sincerity and kindliness of

his personality, his ability to express himself in public, and many other fine qualities, endeared him to all with whom he came in contact.

We also desire to express our appreciation of the efficient and gracious manner in which you and your two lovely children assisted Dr. McMaster while he was president of the Slippery Rock State Teachers College.[371]

Dr. John A. Entz, Dean of Men and Professor of Mathematics, was named by the Board at a mid-November meeting to serve as Acting President "until a permanent president is elected by the Board."[372] The Board further stipulated that Dr. Entz was not to be "a candidate for the office of President."[373]

The Board established the following criteria to guide them in the search for a new president:

1. Age – Not over 50, preferably younger.
2. Candidate should hold an earned Doctor's degree.
3. Candidate should show evidence of sound physical health as indicated by a report of physical examination conducted by a physician approved by the Board.
4. Satisfactory administrative experience in the field of education, and specific knowledge of the field of teacher training.
5. Evidence of sound moral and religious philosophy and practice.
6. Freedom from political entanglements.
7. Not necessarily an orator of distinction, but a pleasing and effective public speaker to be in demand for commencements and other public occasions.[374]

In early December of 1941, the Board of Trustees held a special executive session to discuss the some twenty candidates who had applied for the presidency.[375] Acting President Entz was not present at the meeting. One thing which was agreed upon at the meeting was that Dr. Entz was doing a very fine job as acting president.[376] Some of the Trustees felt that the Board might therefore move much more slowly in its search for a president.[377] Interviews were held and, on January 10, 1942, the Board, contrary to its earlier decision not to consider Acting President Entz nor anyone over fifty, nominated 62-year-old Dr. Entz.[378] Approval from Harrisburg was

John A. Entz, President, 1941-1946

swift and, on January 16, John A. Entz became Slippery Rock's president.[379]

Dr. Entz was born in 1880 near Williamsport, Pennsylvania, where his father was a local school teacher.[380] After attending Lock Haven State Normal School, he received his bachelor's degree from Albright College.[381] His teaching experience began in Coudersport Schools, and after several years of teaching, and graduate work at the New York University, he became a school administrator at Coudersport.[382] He earned the Master's degree and did advanced work toward the doctorate at the New York University.[383] In 1920, he accepted the presidency of the California State Normal School.[384] He left California in 1929 to become Dean of Instruction at Slippery Rock State Teachers College, under Dr. J. Linwood Eisenberg.[385]

116

Three of Dr. Entz's expressions most remembered by his associates suggest a bit about the man: "We do not do so well, but that we could not do better," "There are three sides to every question: your side, my side, and the right side," and "I wish to make an announcement."[386]

The Saxigena offered the following description of President Entz:

> Every campus has some noteworthy person to whom everyone instinctively turns for guidance. This personality is one who sets the pace for College Activities and is an example to others in the college world. On Slippery Rock's campus Dr. John A. Entz, the president of our college, is such a leader.[387]

During this period the United States underwent the shock of the attack on Pearl Harbor and its direct involvement in World War II in both Europe and Asia. As men and women across the country entered the Armed Services, enrollment at colleges and universities continued to decline. At Slippery Rock the decline was precipitous with almost 25% fewer students on campus in 1943-43 (338) than the previous year.[388] By fall of 1943, only 189 enrolled, which approached the size of the school's student body when it first opened in 1889.[389]

Faced with ever decreasing utilization of its academic facilities, Slippery Rock decided to explore ways in which its educational resources could be used to promote the nation's war effort. In the fall of 1942, two Army Lieutenants surveyed the college to determine if it would be suitable for a training center for Army flight students.[390] The survey demonstrated it was and the College was recommended as a training site for approximately 500 men to the Committee of War Manpower Commission headed by President Edward Elliott of Purdue University.[391] On March 31, 1943, the cadets arrived on campus.[392]

Their arrival to Slippery Rock was quite dramatic with college students, faculty, townspeople and the high school band all out to greet them.[393] The cadets, with representation from nearly every state in the nation, were directed by Captain Carl B. Nusbaum.[394] They were quartered in South and West Halls. The student residents in these halls were moved into renovated quarters in the West Gymnasium, the Hut, and several homes in the town.[395] This first group of cadets was made up of a "…present backlog of Air Corps Enlisted Reserves (Air Crew); qualified Army enlisted men; and civilians of ages 18-26, qualified by the AAF for such training, who may volunteer for induction under the program."[396]

Actual photo of first Air Mail pickup,
Dickey Field, north of Slippery Rock village

Postal envelope commemorating first Air Mail pickup service in
Slippery Rock, July 14, 1941

PROP WASH

Word has been received that Lucian Gastineau, former Air Crew Student of the 329th C.T.D., has been sent directly from classification at Nashville, Tenn., to twin engine advanced flying school at George Field, Vincennes, Ill.

Before entering the U.S. Army Air Corps, Cadet Gastineau served a year in the R.C.A.F. He has 400 hours in the twin engine Anson bomber. When the United States plunged into the war, "Luke" as most of his friends know him, decided his place was in the service of his own nation and fighting with his friends. Giving up all his hard work and the name he had made for himself in the R.C.A.F.

FLYIN' RAPIER

Vol. 2   Slippery Rock, Pa., Oct. 19, 1943   No. 2.

"A"ces Leave For Nashville

Graduating Class Says Farewell

The sixth graduating class of the 329th C. T. D., has left this farewell note to the men and friends they are leaving. The old "A" Squadron asked us to publish this in our next issue of the "Flyin' Rapier":

"We, the men of the sixth graduating class of the 329th A.A.F.

The Flyin' Rapier was published by the Army Air Cadets stationed at S.R.S.T.C., 1943

Air Cadets entertained in East Gymnasium, 1944

Pilot Ted Meding in front of Chapel, 1944

Dear old Bill! —

#19 **Victory Bell**

JUNE 16 1943

Dear friend with the colors :

When your last V.B. was written it told you about the unusual wet weather we had had in Slippery Rock--the truth of the matter is, we then dident know that the same kind of weather would continue for almost a month longer, with rains almost every day, with overcast skies, with the campus grass so long that they finally had to use sickles and scythes, and as this is now being written a crew of men are out forking piles of hay in trucks - that would remind you of a hay field. Now they are able to use the power mowers and the old campus is again looking like itself, altho there is still much to be done yet. Few gardens were plowed until a week ago, and thus a late crop of garden stuff is expected. Floods in the middle west inundated square miles and that will have its effect on foods also. Well, another commencement has come and gone at S.R.--the quietest one that we ever did see, and no Alumni Day for you know why. Inclosed is a copy of the Program which will doubtless be of interest to you. The men of the class who left college during the last semester were, due to a ruling by State Supt. Haas, graduated in absentia--their mothers or fathers being there to receive the diploma, for the sons who were in this mans Army, Navy or Marine Corps. Present in the chapel was Tim Ehlies now a 1st Lieutenant, was home on leave for a little while having been bowled over by the concussion of a Jap shell exploding back of him in Guadacanal--his back muscles were slightly injured-hospitalized him for three months--now as good as ever. Tim was here also for Class Day exercises in the chapel a few days before graduation and he made a nice appropriate response when called upon to receive the 1943 SAXIGENA year book -which, was dedicated to YOU fellows and Girls also with the colors---and a hearty CONGRATULATION --it could not have been better dedicated !!!! It is an interesting and well illustrated volume and if you havent seen it, I think you will some day. And so the regular college year has ended, a short vacation has come and gone for most of us, as now the Pre-Session has started and so we are once again teaching college classes. Of course the regular Army Cadet program goes on indipendent of college classes just the same, with the added pep and zest that this body has added to the campus. They now have their own band, and their ochestra plays for dances. Since the last V.B. has gone out the great victory of Bizerti and Cap Bon has taken place , when thousands of the "Supermen" (pardon the giggle) came in surrendering and wondering what it was all about!!! JUST NOW the world is momentarily watching where OUR next move will be--and would-Hitler like to know!!! I am most keen that these letters reach you fellows especially in combat--they may be days reaching you, and if and when you can find the time to answer, please stretch a point and do so for we will have you in mind every hour--from none would word be more welcome, both to us here at your old college, and to your folks back at home...and may the great portecting hand of Providence watch over you every minute. Be Strong--we know you are Brave ! And just a little word here that we mentioned away earlier in one of the VBs that came out months ago-----Be sure you make a great number of friends in your outfits the same as you did here at college--no telling when these friendships may play a very decided part in your service life. And these friendships you make with your outfit men are also LASTING friendships (just last week the Millers had dinner with a pal and his wife in Pittsburgh-a pal made in World War I-over 20 years ago) and you will be doing the same thing 20 years hence with friends you

The Victory Bell newsletter went to GI's in 1943

During basic training at an Army Air Force Technical Center, the cadets were given a battery of exams which determined the types and numbers of courses they would take during their five month training period at Slippery Rock.[397] Together with college officials, Captain Nusbaum, Lieutenant Charles Cliff and other Army personnel planned a schedule of classes for the cadets in modern history, English, geography, trigonometry, and physics. The Army personnel were responsible for providing instruction in military drill, discipline, customs of the service, and physical education.[398] While at Slippery Rock, the cadets did not receive any flight instruction; but, as they completed their academic training at Slippery Rock, they were transferred to another location for flight instruction.[399]

In addition to contributing to the war effort, the Slippery Rock air cadet program temporarily stabilized conditions on campus. Faculty and staff who might otherwise have been relieved of their duties because of the low enrollment were now involved in the cadet program.

The emphasis on science education continued during Dr. Entz's administration, as students majoring in science in secondary education could now select biology, chemistry, physics, and general science as primary fields of study.[400] Great flexibility in choosing areas of concentration led to the practice of declaring major and minor areas of academic emphasis. Spanish was soon made available to students in the secondary education program.[401]

During the fall of 1943, Slippery Rock sought accreditation from the Middle States Association of Colleges and Secondary Schools.[402] An evaluation of the school was held in mid-term and, in November, Dr. Tillinghost, Secretary of the Commission on Institutions

President Entz (center) and faculty, early 1940's

of Higher Education of the Association, informed the College that it had been awarded full accreditation status.[403] In his letter, Dr. Tillinghost wrote: "It was a pleasure to learn of the good work which is being done at Slippery Rock State Teachers College, and we wish for you a continuation of this success."[404]

The new year brought the news to President Entz that the Air Cadet Program was being phased out at Slippery Rock.[405] In February, 1944, two hundred cadets left the campus with the others slated to leave upon completion of their program.[406] Dr. Entz, fully realizing the impact of the termination of the cadet program on the College, sent a letter to the faculty on February 16 explaining the consequences of this development on summer and fall enrollments.[407] In the meantime, he attempted to find another military training program in which Slippery Rock could become involved, but with no success.[408]

The summer enrollment was down and in the fall of 1944, only 185 women and two men were on campus for full-time study.[409] Slippery Rock, like schools everywhere, found itself overstaffed. Dr. Francis B. Haas, State Superintendent of Public Instruction, wrote to the state's teachers colleges explaining that in light of sharply reduced enrollments "administrative courage must be exercised by the presidents and trustees in the matter of reducing the faculty personnel wherever necessary."[410] Dr. Entz surveyed his faculty and informed the Board of Trustees that the Departments of English, Science and Social Studies were overstaffed and recommended that one instructor in each department could be "temporarily relieved" of teaching responsibilities.[411] Subsequently, one faculty member was retired, another was reassigned and third terminated.[412]

When the war in Europe was over in 1945, the enrollment picture at Slippery Rock began to improve.[413]

Aerial view of campus, mid 1940's

Publication recruiting prospective students to attend SRSTC, 1943

College freshmen observe a fourth grade Lab. School class, 1943

The modern instrumentation in the Lab. School psychological clinic, 1943

The Laboratory School, 1943

Student Managers, Assistant Coach "Pop" Storer, Coach N. Kerr Thompson and Mascot, "Spot," 1942

In September of 1945, the College became a center for a government sponsored training program for cadet nurses.[414] Fifty five student nurses from Butler County Memorial Hospital[415] immediately began their academic studies in such courses as Anatomy and Physiology, Chemistry, Sociology, Psychology, Dietics, Microbiology and Professional Adjustments and Orientation to Nursing Art.[416] These student nurses, who were to complete their academic training at Slippery Rock[417] prior to hospital duty, were all female high school graduates from the Butler area, or nearby communities, who had passed rigid examinations before entering the program.[418] The nurses were housed in North Hall and under the supervision of Mrs. Elizabeth Nisley, the coordinator of the program.[419]

With the war in the Pacific over in August of 1945, the future at Slippery Rock and the nation brightened considerably. Enrollment at Slippery Rock jumped from

187 students to 284, and these figures did not include the fifty five student nurses.[420]

While some student activities had been curtailed during the war, there were those like Coach N. Kerr Thompson, long-time athletic leader of the College, who refused to see Slippery Rock withdraw from intercollegiate competition. Once, in October of 1944, he informed the Board of Trustees that even though there were only ten men on campus, there would be a basketball team, since nine of them were "somewhat athletically inclined" and had "the desire" to play the game.[421]

Expectedly, there were student organizations that devoted a good deal of their time in support of the United States troops overseas. An advertisement in the student newspaper, *The Rocket*, STAMP OUT HITLER (10¢ A STAMP) indicates one of the ways the students backed the war effort.[422]

123

Just as Slippery Rock State Teachers College appeared to be well on its way to a return to normalcy, Dr. Entz shocked the campus with the news of his decision to resign as president.[423] Everyone had expected this man who had so skillfully led the College through some of its most difficult times to enjoy directing it in better years which lay just ahead.[424] His letter to Dr. Clyde C. Green, President of the Board of Trustees, explained the reasons for his decision.

My dear Doctor Green:

I hereby tender my resignation as President of State Teachers College, Slippery Rock, to become effective at such time as may be agreed upon by the Board of Trustees and myself. I am hopeful however, that a President will be selected toward the close of the present semester.

I sincerely regret such decision, but feel that at this time it is wise to yield the post to a younger and more vigorous man. The postwar era of education with the many problems involved will call for outstanding leadership in teacher education. If Mrs. Entz and I are to enjoy a period of retirement, then at our age we must retire from active work.

My administration of four years has been the war period. There were some discouragements. Enrollments took a terrific drop. The faculty had to be reduced. But after all Slippery Rock fared well due to the Civilian Pilot Training program and also the Aircrew program. The college rendered a distinct war-time service of which we can be justly proud.

Yesterday's enrollment of teacher-college students showed an increase of nearly 50% over that of a year ago. In addition there are fifty-five student nurses on the campus from Butler County Memorial Hospital, making a college population of well over three hundred students. This definite up-swing is most gratifying.

I should be very remiss indeed if I neglected to express my sincere appreciation of your confidence in electing me to serve as your President. I shall always consider it a privilege and an honor to have served you. I have endeavored to the best of my ability faithfully to execute the duties of my office.[425]

The Board of Trustees, wishing to give expression to their appreciation of the fine contribution Dr. Entz had made to Slippery Rock[426] honored him with the following tribute:

Doctor John A Entz was a member of the Faculty of Slippery Rock State Teachers College for 17 years and President for four years.

The Board of Trustees is highly appreciative of his efficient work as President of the College. He was a capable administrator, had fine judgment, which was characterized by vision and clear thinking. We know that Doctor Entz had the complete confidence of the Student Body and Faculty. Though seemingly mild in his manner, those of us who know him best realize that he had the courage of his convictions and the firmness necessary to accomplish his purposes.

The service of Doctor Entz needs no special tribute from this corner. The great esteem and respect which all his associates and friends have for him has increased with the passage of time. Inasmuch as his loftiness of purpose, his outstanding personality and character, and his determination for an unselfish career of service, will be reflected to us, and thus it will be said that Slippery Rock State Teachers College is better for his having lived and worked here.

We, the Board of Trustees, were loath, indeed, to have Doctor Entz terminate his work at the College. We did, however, accede to his wishes in the matter. The fact that a job has been well done is undoubtedly a great personal satisfaction. We hope there are many happy, pleasant, and enjoyable days ahead for Doctor and Mrs. Entz. That his retirement, we hope, will bring for him and his wife years of delightful relaxation well earned after a career to which he gave his best.

Once again the College community found itself in search for a new leader. Through September and October of 1945, the Board of Trustees went quietly about the business of finding a successor to Dr. Entz.[427] At the end of November, they announced that Dr. Dale W. Houk, former assistant superintendent of schools of Allegheny County, was selected to head the College.[428] His was the challenge to help Slippery Rock seize the many opportunities for academic service which the post-war period would offer.

Dale W. Houk, President, 1946-1956

Dr. Houk was born in 1903 in the small community of Bruin in Butler County, Pennsylvania.[429] His father was a Presbyterian minister. After attending public elementary and secondary school, he entered Slippery Rock when it was still a normal school in 1919.[430] Following his one year at Slippery Rock, he went to Washington and Jefferson College, Waynesboro College, and Park College in Parkville, Missouri, where, in 1922, he finally received his baccalaureate degree.[431] He returned to Western Pennsylvania to teach and to pursue his graduate study at the University of Pittsburgh.[432] After receiving his master's and doctoral degrees, he went to the Forest Hills school system, near Pittsburgh, where he was supervising principal from 1930 to 1940.[433] In the next five years, he served as Assistant Superintendent of Schools in Allegheny County.[434] While there, he became president of the Southwestern County Superintendents Association of Pennsylvania and president of the Doctoral Association of Educators at the University of Pittsburgh.[435]

When Dr. Houk took office as President in January of 1946, Slippery Rock, along with all of the nation's colleges and universities, was bracing for the largest invasion of students ever experienced in the history of

Basketball Team with Coach N. Kerr Thompson and Coach E. B. Cottrell, 1947

American higher education. Twelve million Americans had served in the Armed Forces during World War II and many of them were now planning to go to college. Tuition and subsistence benefits under Congress's "G.I. Bill" made for many a veteran the dream of a college education a distinct reality.

There were only 284 students on the Slippery Rock campus when Dr. Houk arrived and of the group, only 54 were men.[436] In the next academic year, 1946-47, enrollment soared to 587, a two-fold increase over the previous one.[437] The number of men at the College skyrocketed to 324, which was six times the number enrolled the year before.[438]

Pennsylvania State College, in central Pennsylvania, was experiencing an ever greater flood of students and, as a temporary solution, called upon the various State Teachers Colleges to accept some 1,500 incoming freshmen for one year.[439] Dr. Houk pledged the support of Slippery Rock in this cooperative endeavor and, in the 1946 winter term, accepted about one hundred Penn State freshmen who took basic courses in the lower division of the liberal arts program, in engineering, and

in mineral industries at the College.[440] This cooperative program continued at Slippery Rock until 1950, when Penn State was finally able to accommodate all of its own students.[441] In 1950, with the total enrollment standing at 867, Slippery Rock had grown three times its size during the five years since the war ended in 1945.[442]

Old Main damaged by tornado, 1946

Slippery Rock women of the 1940's

Eligibility for admission to Slippery Rock during the post-war period was determined by a student's general scholarship, character and personality, health and physical vigor, command of the English language and performance on a series of psychological tests.[443]

Minor changes in the College's curriculum took place during the early years of President Houk's administration. A program to train teachers for the growing number of driver education classes in Pennsylvania's high schools was offered.[444] The first courses were held in the summer of 1948 and were well received by the students. Reflecting the decline in the study of Latin in high school, the College, in 1950, no longer offered it as an area of specialization for secondary education majors.[445]

In 1950, the Board of Presidents of the Pennsylvania State Teachers Colleges adopted some important curricular changes for their schools which were to go into effect in the fall of 1951.[446] Students majoring in elementary education would now be permitted to complete fourteen credits of work in the areas of specialization in early childhood education, intermediate education, or "upper-grade" education.[447] The areas of specialization designed to prepare teachers for positions in the upper grades of the elementary school replaced the one which trained teachers for work in the rural schools.[448] In 1952, the number of elective courses available to elementary education majors increased, thus making it possible for them to acquire the competencies required in the new areas of specialization.[449] Upon receiving the baccalaureate degree, the student who had majored in elementary education at Slippery Rock was granted a Provisional College Teaching Certificate from the state of Pennsylvania which enabled the teacher to teach in grades one through six or one through eight depending upon the organization of schools in the local school district.[450]

Under the new curricular program of 1951, students planning to teach in the secondary schools were required to have at least thirty semester hours of credit in the fields of biological science, physical science, general science, history, social science and English.[451] Majors in aeronautics, foreign language, geography, chemistry, physics, mathematics, and speech now were required to have at least twenty-four hours of credit in their respective fields.[452] For a minor field of specialization, a student took the minimum number of credit hours of

The Nature Trail, late 1940's

course work required for state certification. Students majoring in health and physical education could now be certified in recreational leadership by taking twenty-five credit hours of electives distributed throughout their four-year program.[453]

In 1952, a new degree program designed to prepare public school nurses was introduced.[454] In it, licensed, registered nurses, who had satisfactorily completed a three year training course in an approved school of nursing would take forty-five hours of credit distributed in two broad areas of study. One area of study offered courses in public school nursing and organization, community health, nutrition and family casework. The other included academic work in educational psychology, professional education, communications, audio-visual education, and the social sciences. A degree program for dental hygienists was also instituted the same year.[455] Licensed dental hygienists, who had satisfactorily completed an approved two-year curriculum, would engage in two years of study—sixty four credit hours—in the liberal arts and in professional education. The cooperative nurses training program which had been arranged earlier with the Butler County Memorial Hospital was expanded during President Houk's first year in office to include nurses in training at the Oil City Hospital.[456]

In the 1950's, the Pittsburgh Educational Television Station, WQED, began to offer courses for college students.[457] Slippery Rock agreed to cooperate with the

The Model School (West Hall), late 1940's

Morrow Way to the Chapel, early 1950's

station by allowing its students to earn credit for such courses taken over television.[458]

America's involvement in the war in Korea was expanding in the early 1950's, so once again the nation's youth were called upon to serve in the armed forces. This development, occurring at the time that many World War II veterans were completing their course of studies at Slippery Rock, resulted, predictably, in a drop in enrollment at the school. From a post-war high of 867 in 1949-50, enrollment dropped to 761 in 1952-53.[459] The number of men on campus dropped about one hundred and fifty during this same period.[460] When the war ended,

enrollments increased again; so that by 1955-56, there were 920 students at Slippery Rock.[461]

By the middle of the 1950's, Slippery Rock once again found its campus facilities inadequate to serve her expanding student body. In 1955, President Houk, in a report to the Board of Trustees, cited the school's building needs.[462] In the same year, the Chapel had to be closed because of its weakened floors and ceilings.[463] One of the few construction projects undertaken in President Houk's term began in 1955 and committed the school and the Borough of Slippery Rock to the building of a joint sewage plant.[464]

In May of 1956, Dr. Houk informed the Board of Trustees of his decision to resign from the presidency of Slippery Rock in order to join the Pittsburgh Educational Television, WQED, as its Director of Community Relations.[465] In his letter of resignation, he explained that though he had not planned to retire for several more years, he was so interested in this opportunity in educational television that he decided to modify his retirement plans.[466] He offered the following description of his ten-year association with the Board:

My associations in my work with the Board of Trustees have been most pleasant. It has been a privilege to work for you professionally and I trust that our personal associations may continue. I am most appreciative of your confidence in me during my term as President of this College.

On June 9, 1956, the day Dr. Houk's retirement became effective, the Board, after considering Dr. Norman Weisenfluh, Director of Personnel, and Dr. Leonard Duncan, Dean of Instruction, selected Dr. Weisenfluh to serve as acting president.[467]

Slippery Rock's years of uncertainty and dislocation during World War II and the Korean War were over. The College had met well the challenge of this period and, though she did not know it, stood upon the threshold of a dramatic new era of growth.

Old Main through the trees, early 1950's

130

Scenes in the Hut, early 1950's

The Hut, student center, early 1950's

131

The musical group, The Rockettes, performing at a dance, 1937

*Ted Stevenson, Peg Conormine, and
BooBoo Dunlap on Campus, 1940*

*The College Power House, 1952
(Where Weisenfluh Dining Hall parking lot is now)*

132

West Hall Barracks   STATE TEACHERS COLLEGE   Slippery Rock, Pennsylvania

Administration Building   STATE TEACHERS COLLEGE   Slippery Rock, Pennsylvania

133

Maltby Library   STATE TEACHERS COLLEGE   Slippery Rock, Pennsylvania

Interior of Maltby Library   STATE TEACHERS COLLEGE   Slippery Rock, Pennsylvania

Interior of Dining Commons   STATE TEACHERS COLLEGE   Slippery Rock, Pennsylvania

College Chapel   STATE TEACHERS COLLEGE   Slippery Rock, Pennsylvania

South Hall Barracks   STATE TEACHERS COLLEGE   Slippery Rock, Pennsylvania

Lounging Room in Y Hut   STATE TEACHERS COLLEGE   Slippery Rock, Pennsylvania

Science Building   STATE TEACHERS COLLEGE   Slippery Rock, Pennsylvania

East and West Gymnasiums   STATE TEACHERS COLLEGE   Slippery Rock, Pennsylvania

North Hall, Housing Girls' Dormitory
Dining Commons and Infirmary
STATE TEACHERS COLLEGE
Slippery Rock, Pennsylvania

CHAPTER VI

Developing a Multi-Purpose State College 1956-1965

After serving as acting president for just three months, Dr. Weisenfluh was selected by the Board of Trustees, in August of 1956, to be Slippery Rock's ninth president.[468] A native of Old Forge, Pennsylvania, where he received his early education, later a student of East Stroudsburg State Normal School and a graduate of Dickinson College, he came to Slippery Rock in 1929.[469] He received his Doctor of Philosophy degree from the University of Pittsburgh in 1935.[470] During his twenty-seven years at Slippery Rock, he served as an instructor in psychology, director of the laboratory school, assistant dean of men, chairman of the personnel committee, and director of student personnel.[471]

Upon taking office, Dr. Weisenfluh knew that the problem at Slippery Rock which demanded immediate attention was its deteriorating physical facilities. There had not been any major construction work at the College since the late 1930's and he was determined to do something about it. Efforts over the past year to get the state to help Slippery Rock meet its serious building needs were successfully concluded in July, 1956, just one month after his initial appointment as "acting" president. The state agreed to appropriate $1,200,000 for a new men's dormitory and $600,000 for an auditorium.[472] He also reported that the state had been asked to conduct a thorough inspection of Slippery Rock's building needs.

At the request of the College, an inspection team visited the campus in August and bluntly told officials at the school, "you're really in bad shape here at Slippery Rock!"[473] Though this report surprised none, it gave Dr. Weisenfluh an added reason to push vigorously for a major commitment by the College to improve its school plant.

Norman N. Weisenfluh, President, 1956-1964

Under President Weisenfluh's leadership, a comprehensive study of Slippery Rock's physical plant was made by Pennsylvania's General State Authority, the Department of Public Instruction and school officials.[474] In their final report of March, 1957, they called for a massive building program on the campus.[475] In addition to the men's dormitory and auditorium, for which state monies had already been allocated, eight new buildings were to be constructed.[476] Specifically, they recommended that Slippery Rock be provided with a new classroom building, one women's dormitory, one, perhaps two, men's dormitories, a field house and gymnasium, a student community center, an addition to the library, a new administration building, a new dining hall and kitchen, a new maintenance building, and expanded parking areas.[477] Of the existing buildings, the science building, the training school, North Hall (women's dormitory), the gymnasium and the President's residence were to continue to be used.[478] The buildings to be razed were the Chapel, the men's dormitory and the administration and classroom building.[479]

The Board of Trustees immediately approved this Comprehensive Study of Campus and, looking ahead to campus expansion, requested the Department of Public

Opening faculty meeting, fall, 1958

140

Instruction to purchase the 225 acre Gerlach farm, located east of campus, and the Leonard Duncan home on Maltby Avenue, north of the campus.[480] By the end of the year, arrangements had been made to acquire these properties and the D. C. Porter home on East Cooper Street.[481] The General State Authority appropriated $75,000 for architectural plans for a new field house expected to cost over a million dollars.[482] Test borings for the new men's

dormitory and auditorium were going on and plans for the conversion of the industrial arts shop to a cafeteria were being made.[483]

Concern over the fate of the Chapel, which had been condemned and padlocked for several years, mounted during this period of campus planning.[484] Finally, in August, 1957, an alumni committee composed of Ray Haynes, Archie Hillard, Ford Dilworth, Frank Brittan

and Albert McClister met with the Board of Trustees and requested permission to raise money from alumni donations to make necessary repairs to the roof and windows of the Chapel.[485] The Board asked the committee to seek approval from the Department of Property and Supply before making any further plans to repair the building.[486] Sharing a similar concern over the Chapel, the Board appointed a committee of its members to meet with the president of the alumni association and this alumni committee to determine what next steps should be taken.[487] The Board did agree that funds should be requested from the General State Authority for its restoration.[488]

In the fall of 1958, when the cornerstone of the men's dormitory was laid, a ceremony was held marking the occasion.[489] Dr. Andrew M. Bradley, Secretary of Pennsylvania's Department of Property and Supply, spoke, a copper box containing articles of student life was sealed in the stone, and Mrs. Emma Guffey Miller, President of the Board of Trustees, applied the final bit of mortar to the cornerstone.[490] Finally, after two years of planning, Slippery Rock's building program was getting underway.

The year before Dr. Weisenfluh became president in 1956, the Middle States Association for Colleges and Secondary Schools conducted an evaluation at Slippery Rock and found weaknesses in the College.[491] President Weisenfluh, obviously anxious to return Slippery Rock to full accreditation status, invited the executive secretary of the Association to the campus in December, 1956, to discuss plans for the reevaluation of the school.[492] Arrangements were made for a team from the Association to revisit Slippery Rock in the spring of 1957.[493] To everyone's pleasure at the College, the subsequent evaluation was a success and the school became, once again, fully accredited by the Middle States Association.[494]

After spending more than two years in the president's office, Dr. Weisenfluh decided that if Slippery Rock was to fulfill its destiny in higher education, it was necessary for it to establish a set of goals toward which all should strive in the years ahead.[495] In December, 1958, he announced his Ten Year Plan in which he set forth the following eleven major goals he believed the College should be striving to accomplish in the coming decade:

(1) A possible enrollment of over 2,000.
(2) Eighty percent of the students to be taken from the upper two-fifths of their high school classes.
(3) A faculty of the first quality. A selection of new faculty members who have advanced preparation in their fields.
(4) A state college offering a larger number of curricula for the college in addition to teacher education.
(5) A graduate program which will allow for graduate study up to the master's degree.
(6) The use of closed circuit television in teaching.
(7) Financial aid for the bright and needy student.
(8) A service center having psychological, speech, and reading clinics.
(9) Adequate school facilities and buildings to meet the expansion.
(10) A stronger alumni association.
(11) A laboratory school for observation, experimentation, and elementary student teaching which will be administered and supported by the College.[496]

Here was a bold vision of what Slippery Rock might become. It was to be committed to high standards of excellence, both among faculty and students. It would offer a diversified curriculum embracing the various disciplines of the liberal arts, while continuing her long tradition in teacher education. It would expand into graduate education with programs of study leading to the master's degree. With more students attracted to these new programs, it could anticipate enrollment to nearly double, so, by 1968, two thousand students would be on campus.

Several months after the presentation of his Ten Year Plan, President Weisenfluh recommended to the Board of Trustees that the name of the school be changed to Slippery Rock State College.[497] The dropping of the "Teachers" from the name was, he felt, in keeping with the wider academic functions now being defined for Slippery Rock and sister state colleges in Pennsylvania.[498] On January 8, 1960, the change was officially made.[499]

A dramatic example of the spirit of change at Slippery Rock was the cooperative arrangement which the College made with the famous Mayo Clinic in Rochester, Minnesota.[500] Under this program, a student in health education with an interest in becoming a physical therapist would, upon three years of study at Slippery Rock, go, if accepted, to the School of Physical Therapy at Mayo Clinic for a two-year work study program.[501] While there, the student would receive a maintenance stipend and tuition-free instruction.[502] Upon returning to Slippery Rock and completing student teaching requirements, the student would receive a Bachelor of Science degree in Health Education and a certificate in Physical Therapy from the Mayo Clinic.[503] This innovative program, approved by the Board of Presidents of the State Teachers College and the State Superintendent of Public Instruction, began in the fall of 1959.[504]

Important changes were made in the three basic curricular programs at Slippery Rock in 1960, as the role of all of Pennsylvania's state colleges was being expanded. Now all entering freshmen in Slippery Rock's elementary, secondary and the health and physical education program of studies were to take at least sixty credits of academic study in General Education.[505] This meant that every student would be devoting almost half of his four-year program in teacher education to liberal arts courses, in the natural sciences and mathematics, the social sciences, art and humanities. Approximately thirty credits were to be taken in the area of "professional education," which included student teaching, educational psychology, audio-visual education and educational methods and evaluation.[506] Specialized and elective courses completed this revamped curriculum.[507] For students planning to teach in the secondary schools, from twenty-four to thirty-six semester hours of course work were required in the major area of specialization.[508]

In May, 1962, the State Council of Education gave approval to Slippery Rock to offer courses leading to the Bachelor of Arts degree in the Humanities, Social Sciences and Natural Sciences, effective September, 1962.[509] Under the leadership of the acting director of this new liberal arts program, Dr. Albert E. Schmittlein, the following program objectives[510] were developed:

To develop the ability of students to think clearly and to act independently, and to express themselves freely and effectively.

To enable students to achieve personal growth as they prepare to contribute to the making of a better society.

To help students develop social attitudes that employ: (1) Consideration for the viewpoint of others, with freedom from racial, religious, or other social prejudices; (2) Willingness to apply the standards by which we evaluate others to our own abilities and achievements; (3) Concern for the spiritual, intellectual, and creative phases of human life.

To give students a broad background in the arts and sciences so that they will be able to see in perspective the place man has in his own society, in the society of nations, and in the universe, so that they will have first-hand experience with the application of scientific method.

To give students opportunity for depth in at least one field of knowledge.

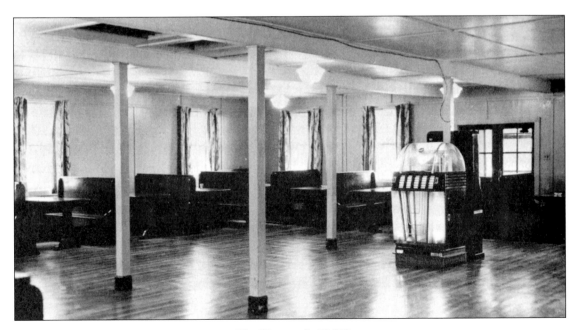

The Hut, early 1960's

143

In each of the three program areas of the Humanities, Social Sciences and Natural Sciences, students were required to take the sixty credit program in general education and to select a first and second field of study.[511] Originally, students could choose from four areas in humanities: speech, English, modern foreign language, and fine arts; seven areas in social sciences: anthropology, economics, geography, political science, history, psychology, and sociology; and four areas in natural sciences: biology, chemistry, physics and mathematics.[512]

At the same time, after the evaluation of the College by a Middle States Association of Colleges and Secondary Schools Committee, the State Council on Education gave approval to Slippery Rock to offer graduate studies in secondary education English, social studies, and health and physical education, leading to the Master of Education degree.[513] The graduate council developed the following objectives[514] for the program:

1. To further the teacher's knowledge and understanding of subject matter in his special area of teaching.
2. To broaden the teacher's interests and to help him to pursue the interests in subjects other than his field of specialization.
3. To provide an opportunity to extend the professional knowledge and skills essential to the development of a "master teacher."
4. To attain greater skill in doing research and in the ability to evaluate and use educational studies and other appropriate source materials.
5. To enable teachers to develop their potentialities for leadership in the profession.

Miss Beverly J. Corll received the first Master of Education degree in Health and Physical Education at the commencement exercises in August, 1964.[515]

A new program in special education was initiated on Slippery Rock's campus in the fall of 1963, by Dr. Jack Dinger, former Coordinator of Programs for Exceptional Children of the Pennsylvania Department of Public Instruction.[516] This important new program was designed to train teachers in special education so that the schools of the state could better meet the needs of those children "who differ from the 'average child' in terms of being: mentally retarded, mentally gifted, physically handicapped, blind, deaf, speech handicapped,

or emotionally disturbed."[517] The program, requiring 18 semester hours of credit in special education courses, led to a Comprehensive College Certificate in Elementary or Secondary or Health and Physical Education and Special Education, the mentally retarded (Educable and Trainable).[518]

A certification program for elementary school librarians, consisting of twelve semester hours, was approved by the State Council on Education in June, 1961.[519] The certification was an endorsement program requiring the student to complete credits in cataloging, classification, instructional materials, children's literature, reference materials, and library organization and administration.[520] Because of the popularity of the endorsement program, the College established, several years later, a separate major program in library science leading to certification of school librarians at either the elementary or secondary level.[521]

Slippery Rock began to reach out of its traditional college community to non-degree students. Representatives from business, education, and industry requested Slippery Rock to offer courses in social sciences, English, psychology and education, to be taught in Butler, Pennsylvania, 20 miles south of Slippery Rock.[522] This action, which took place in September of 1960, was the beginning of Slippery Rock course offerings at an off-campus setting.

During Dr. Weisenfluh's early years as President, there were 900 students enrolled at Slippery Rock.[523] The school was well on its way to reaching its goal of 2,000 students by 1968. While enrollment was rising at Slippery Rock, so were admission standards. Of the freshman class of 1960, approximately 80% of all entering freshmen were in the upper 2/3 of their high school class.[524]

Along with new commitments to expanded curricular offerings for these increasing numbers of students, Slippery Rock maintained its concern for the quality of their extra curricular activities as well. As the 1957 *Catalog explained:*

No less important is the determination of the College to prepare young men and women for an adult life that will be rich in experience and service in a democratic country. The College recognizes the value of spiritual, intellectual, physical and social growth as the foundation for professional teaching competence. Further, the College attempts to foster responsible student participation in as many areas of College operation as practicality permits. Such student participation has been both gratifying and valuable to all concerned.[525]

There were many clubs and activities, some old and some new, coordinated by the Student Government Association which were available to the students. These were:

Student Council, Madrigal Club, Men's Glee Club, College Choir, Vocal Ensembles, College Bank, College Orchestra, Mu Kappa Gamma, The Inter-Varsity Christian Fellowship, Young Men's Christian Association, Young Women's Christian Association, Lutheran Student Association, Newman Club, Dramatic Club, Alpha Psi Omega, Demosthenean Debating Club, Kappa Gamma, Press Club, Saxigena Staff, Varsity Club, Women's Athletic Association, Delta Psi Kappa, Archery Club, Bowling Club, Official's Club, Rocket Ripplers, Kappa Delta Pi, Alpha Phi Omega, Gamma Theta Upsilon, Sigma Tau Delta, A.C.E. Club, Future Teachers of America, Trigcalana, Social Studies Society, International Relations Club, Psychology Club, Commuters Club and Camera Club.[526]

A full athletic program, including football, soccer, cross-country, field hockey, basketball, swimming, gymnastics, tennis, golf, track and field, and baseball, offered many opportunities for wholesome physical activity for students.[527]

Slippery Rock's comprehensive guidance program[528] was designed to meet the following needs:

1. Selection of able incoming students.
2. Orientation of freshmen to the college and to teaching as a career.
3. Discovery by the faculty of the needs, interests, and abilities of students, through:
   (a) The freshmen testing program.
   (b) The freshman orientation program.
   (c) Participation of students in classroom and campus activities.
   (d) Observations of how students conduct themselves or assisting in the campus laboratory school.

4. Attempts to satisfy the needs of students through individual or group instruction, planned experiences or activities, counseling by students or faculty advisers, and various adjustment procedures. Early in the freshman year each student is assigned to a faculty adviser.
5. Discovery and release of talent.
6. Guidance of certain students out of teaching as a career because of lack of interest or ability in the field.
7. Self-development through a program of guided, well-integrated classroom and campus activities designed to produce well-rounded, well-adjusted personalities, acceptable scholastic achievement, and general development with attention to special talents.
8. The meeting of standards for promotion to Junior Standing.
9. Adequate preparation in major and minor fields of specialization.
10. Student teaching and preparation for adjustments to problems of in-service teaching.
11. Placement and follow-up.

Incoming freshmen participated in an orientation program sponsored by the Junior Class which included receptions, dinners, dances, religious activities and athletic events.[529]

As the pulse of student life quickened, students began to press for the right to have social fraternities and sororities. In 1959, the Board rejected the students' appeal, explaining that Slippery Rock's small enrollment made social fraternities and sororities impossible.[530] Only when student enrollment reached at least 1,650 and two thirds of the students and student government approved would the Board permit such social organizations at Slippery Rock.[531]

As more and more students were coming to Slippery Rock, pressure on her physical facilities continued to mount. In the fall of 1959, men were residing in their new Patterson Hall.[532] This dormitory was named after Lewis Patterson who donated the land on which the original buildings were built.[533] The new auditorium was named after Emma Guffey Miller for her long-time support of the College. She was currently president of the Board of Trustees.[534]

South Hall, the oldest dormitory on campus, was considered too old to renovate, so plans were made to raze it as soon as additional facilities were available.[535]

In the fall of 1960, the United States Office of Civil Defense allocated $40,000 for a fall-out shelter to be built under the College's science building.[536] It was designed to offer protection for approximately two hundred persons.[537] Expansion of the library, which had been planned back in 1957, was finally accomplished late in 1960.[538]

Looking a year ahead to the fall of 1961, Slippery Rock administrators were expecting to see 1,500 students on campus.[539] In twenty years they predicted that there would be as many as 4,800 students at the College.[540] Such spectacular growth would be contingent, of course, upon the School's ability to steadily expand its campus facilities.

In the summer of 1961, a new campus plan was designed for 3,600 dormitory students and 2,000 commuting students.[541] The plan called for construction on the old Gerlach farm of academic buildings, health education playing areas, a nine hole golf course and a ten-acre lake.[542] A new football stadium was to be built on the hill overlooking the farm.[543] The science hall was to be converted to a regular classroom building and a new science building and planetarium was to be constructed.[544]

In November, 1961, Slippery Rock received from Mrs. Emma Guffey Miller a forty-two acre tract of land two miles west of town along beautiful Wolf Creek.[545] Located in this tract was a large sugar maple grove which had provided fine syrup and sugar since the days when Indians lived in the area.[546]

In March of 1962, the Board of Trustees, faced with a mounting crisis in student housing, agreed to house, if necessary, from fifty to one hundred students in the Williard Hotel in Butler located some twenty miles south of the campus.[547] By fall of that year, some private dormitory facilities were available for students and tentative agreements were soon made for still another private dormitory to be ready for occupancy by September, 1963.[548]

Construction of the new field house, to be named after James E. Morrow, first president of Slippery Rock, was completed late in 1962.[549] The special education complex, also completed at this time, was named after George M. Leader, former governor of Pennsylvania, whose administration made the funds available for this building.[550]

Emma Guffey Miller and Eleanor Roosevelt, on campus

Mrs. Emma Guffey Miller's invitation, John F. Kennedy reception, 1955

Construction of Morrow Field House, 1962

The Chapel, which had received attention from concerned alumni in 1957, continued to wait for the funds required to carry out the necessary reconstruction. In 1959, the "Save The Chapel Committee" was able to both get permission and a little money to make a few minor repairs on the structure.[551] In the same year, a report on the future of the Chapel suggested that it be used as a music, art and conference center.[552] Estimated costs of such a reconstruction were placed at about $200,000.[553] The Board of Trustees unanimously approved of these plans.[554] Alumni petitioned the Board for action and in June it requested the General State Authority, the State Board of Instruction, Governor David Lawrence "or others who may have power to act on this matter" to restore the Chapel to usefulness.[555] After almost another year of waiting, the Board received the disheartening report from the architects of the W. G. Eckles Company in April of 1960 that the Chapel would have to be gutted and reconstructed at the cost of some $400,000—a figure twice the size of an earlier estimate.[556] Once again, action on the Chapel would be delayed.

In 1962, the Board of Trustees submitted to Pennsylvania's State Planning Board a comprehensive building program calling for the expenditure of almost twelve million dollars at Slippery Rock.[557] The State Planning Board was willing to recommend only three and one half million dollars of this construction.[558] Because of

the Planning Board's policy of cautious expansion based on short-term growth expectancy, it would not approve Slippery Rock's request for a new men's and a new women's dormitory.[559] Nor would it approve of the plan to build a Student Community and Study Center and certain road construction projects.[560] These decisions meant that at least five million dollars of construction projects were removed from the College's original proposal.[561] The Planning Board did approve plans for a science center and electronics laboratory, a modest world culture building, an athletic field, parking lots, the razing of South Hall, various maintenance projects, and, last but not least, the conversion of the Chapel (at a cost of $650,000) to an art and music building.[562]

Rhoads Hall, a woman's dormitory named in honor of Dr. Maragaret V. Rhoads for her thirty-three years of service to the College, was to be ready for occupancy in September, 1963.[563] Weisenfluh Hall, as the new cafeteria and kitchen was called, was dedicated that summer.[564]

Throughout the Weisenfluh era, change in the academic life of Slippery Rock kept pace with its building program. More and more the College came to understand that its commitment to liberal education was as great as its historic one to teacher education. This twin goal was clearly set forth in the following mission statement for the school: [565]

Slippery Rock State College has a two-fold purpose. The first and primary purpose is to prepare teachers for service in the Commonwealth of Pennsylvania. The second purpose is to provide an educational program in the arts and sciences. The specific objectives of these programs are:

1. To develop the ability of students to think clearly, accurately, and independently, and to express their thoughts freely and effectively.
2. To enable students to achieve personal growth and to contribute to the making of a better society.
3. To help students develop socially constructive attitudes such as: (1) Consideration for the viewpoints of others, with freedom from racial, religious, or other social prejudices; (b) Willingness to apply the standards by which we evaluate others to our own abilities and achievement; (c) Concern for the spiritual, intellectual, and creative phases of human life.
4. To give students a broad background so that they will be able to see in perspective the place of man in his own society, in the society of nations, and in the universe; so that they will grow in their understanding and appreciation of the esthetic areas of their own and other cultures; so that they will have first-hand experience with the application of scientific method.
5. To give students opportunity for depth in at least one field of knowledge.

Construction of Spotts World Cultures building, left, Vincent Science Hall, center and Bard Hall, right, 1964

As part of the program for teacher education, the college provides a foundation for a thorough professional and specialized education which recognizes the value of personal, emotional, spiritual, intellectual, academic, physical, and social maturity as basic to professional teaching competence.

Slippery Rock's historic service function to teachers and schools in the western Pennsylvania area continued to receive high priority, as this 1963 announcement attests:

The College also aims to help provide for the needs of the teachers of the area: graduate programs leading to the Master of Education degree are offered; library facilities are made available; evening classes are organized; twelve weeks of summer school provide an opportunity for professional study; workshops in health science, and education are held; professional education groups are encouraged to visit and hold meetings on the campus; faculty members offer their services and leadership in promoting educational opportunities in the surrounding areas.[566]

Earlier opposition to social fraternities and sororities by the Board of Trustees ended and by 1963, Slippery Rock had five national fraternities (Alpha Chi Rho, Sigma Pi, Sigma Tau Gamma, Tau Kappa Epsilon and Theta Chi), one national sorority (Sigma Sigma Sigma), and five local sororities (Alpha Sigma Delta, Beta Chi Gamma, Delta Sigma, Phi Kappa Chi and Sigma Lamda Chi).[567] The Inter-Fraternity and the Pan Hellenic Councils served as coordinating committees for these social organizations.[568]

At this same time, a separate Office of Student Personnel Services was established with the responsibility of assisting in the operation of the many and diverse programs in student health, guidance, athletics, student organizations, religious life, counseling and co-curricular and social activities.[569] Slippery Rock now had fifty active student organizations——twenty-one honorary and social fraternities and sororities, five religious organizations, three music groups, three campus publications, and eighteen special interest clubs.[570]

Slippery Rock's intercollegiate athletic program was very successful in the early 1960's. In 1962, its football squad won the Pennsylvania State College Athletic Conference Title and, in 1961 and 1963, the Western Conference Division Title. In 1960, the track team captured the State Conference Title. The Golf Team won the State Conference Title in 1962 and, in 1963, the cross country and basketball teams earned the same honors.

The years from 1956 to 1963 had been hectic ones for President Weisenfluh. He was now sixty-five years old and, wishing to have time for research and

The Pittsburgh Steelers hold pre-season camp at S.R.S.C., August 1961

study, went on sabbatical leave in January, 1964.[571] It was granted for the period from January through May of 1964.[572] Dr. John B. Edwards, Jr., Dean of Students, was appointed to serve as acting president during his absence.[573]

While Dr. Weisenfluh was on his leave, the Board of Trustees suggested that he retire from the College in September, 1964.[574] This he agreed to do, ending thirty-five years of service to the College.[575] As President since 1956, he had administered Slippery Rock through its change from a single purpose to a multi-purpose institution of higher learning. A grateful College community wished him well as he entered upon his well-deserved retirement.

State Conference Basketball Champions with Coach Bairel and staff, 1962-1963

President Weisenfluh, front row, right with some members of the Board of Trustees
Emma Guffey Miller, front, center,
N. Kerr Thompson, second from right, back row, about 1963

Emma Guffey Miller with President Weisenfluh laying Patterson Hall cornerstone, 1958

South Main Street, 1963

Peggy's Eat Shoppe, 1963

Mrs. Wilson's Service Station, 1963

152

The Roxy Theatre and other businesses on South Main Street, 1963

Looking East on Franklin Street, 1963

153

Sugar Maple time, 1958

Coach Meise with his football captains, 1958

154

Paying for your books in the basement of Old Main Bookstore, 1958

Freshman pranks in front of North Hall, 1958

155

A new freshman moving into Patterson Hall getting advice from Hall Advisor, 1958

Homecoming Queen, Nancy Double, receives congratulations, 1958

Roommates moving into North Hall, 1958

CHAPTER VII

Through a Time of Unrest in the 1960's and 1970's

For a year, Slippery Rock searched for a new president, finally deciding, in March of 1965, upon Dr. Robert S. Carter.[576] A native of Olyphant, Pennsylvania, with two degrees from Bucknell University and a Doctor of Philosophy degree from New York University, he had taught at Westminster College and at Denison University where he was a professor of psychology, the director of vocational service and chairman of the Department of Education.[577]

President Carter perceived Slippery Rock's primary task to be that of improving the quality of its rapidly

Robert S. Carter, President, 1965-1968

expanding academic programs. As he was to explain later: "There is no need at the present time to add more schools. Our need is to spend the next several years strengthening what we now have."[578]

Early in 1966, President Carter announced the creation of the new departments of biological science and physical science.[579] He explained that if capable faculty were available in the fields of sociology and economics, departments would also be formed there.[580] His decision at this time not to renew contracts for some faculty members indicated his growing concern for having a quality faculty at Slippery Rock.[581]

Enrollments continued to climb with 2,767 students on campus during President Carter's first year in office.[582] This student body would swell to 3,575 during the 1967-68 term.[583] Needless to say, pressures on the school's physical facilities increased as well.

Harner Hall, named after Dean Lois V. Harner, was ready for occupancy in the fall, 1965.[584] During this period, privately-owned dormitories helped to solve some of the school's student housing problems.[585] By spring of 1966, five buildings were under construction on the campus—a science building, a world cultures center, a women's dormitory and two privately-financed dormitories.[586]

Amidst this construction, and one year after his appointment, a formal inauguration ceremony for President Carter was held on April 13, 1966.[587] A large number of representatives from colleges and universities from across the state and nation, from the local community, and from Harrisburg attended this impressive event. Dr. Arthur Blair Knopp, President of Denison University, presented the major address entitled "New Beginnings."[588]

Save the planet, outside Weisenfluh Dining Hall, late 1960's

Student demonstration outside the Hut, late 1960's

President Knopp's sense of "new beginnings" astir at Slipper Rock proved amazingly prophetic for, within a month's time after Dr. Carter's inauguration, on May 2, hundreds of students began a protest demonstration in front of the President's Residence demanding a new day for students' rights at Slippery Rock.[589] Students were particularly outraged when detectives President Carter had hired from a Pittsburgh agency to replace campus security personnel appeared on campus in plain clothes and began asking students to show their identification cards.[590] They charged that these detectives had been hired to spy on them.[591] President Carter met with some of the students in his home and explained that he had acted "primarily to cope with security problems at the rapidly growing institution."[592] Later, after reflecting upon the demonstration, he remarked, "I think it's spring."[593]

The next day more students, perhaps as many as half the student body, boycotted classes.[594] Five hundred or more marched around Old Main, singing freedom songs and carrying posters describing their oppression at Slippery Rock.[595] The students demanded an end to the dress codes and unreasonable searches, the introduction of a class cut system and the recognition of the right of women over twenty-one to live off campus.[596] They defended their demonstration because they felt that there was too little time left in the semester for their grievance to be handled through normal channels.[597]

On Wednesday, the students continued to demonstrate and this time before the cameras of two of Pittsburgh's television stations.[598] They were now demanding that they have increased representation on the school committee which dealt with student discipline and that they be allowed to withdraw from courses early in the semester without penalty.[599] President Carter met with over fifteen hundred students and urged them to return to class.[600] He pledged that the College's established procedures for dealing with grievances would be available for everyone at Slippery Rock and asked the students to follow them.[601] Satisfied that their demands would receive administrative attention, the students called off their demonstration and returned to class on Thursday.

Curricular expansion continued at Slippery Rock during the middle 60's. Reflecting national concern over ecological problems and space exploration, the College created a new certification program in Earth and Space Science for undergraduates.[602] This was an interdisciplinary program involving academic study in physics, geology and geography. Students in elementary education now were able to receive a Master's degree in their field.[603] President Carter was particularly anxious

The busy Main Street bus stop on Friday afternoon, late 1960's

159

that graduate students at Slippery Rock be able to receive the Masters of Arts and Master of Science degrees, as well as the Master of Education degree, since, he explained, "our current Graduate program is too strong for the degrees we are forced to confer."[604]

In 1966, the Department of Special Education expanded its certification programs so that now students could be trained to work with the mentally retarded, the physically handicapped, and the socially and emotionally maladjusted.[605] At the same time the Department of Modern Languages offered students the opportunity to study Russian.[606] The following year Slippery Rock developed a cooperative engineering program with the Pennsylvania State University.[607] Upon completing three years of study at the College and two years at the University, a student could earn a Bachelor of Arts degree in the natural sciences from Slippery Rock and a Bachelor of Science degree in any one of seven areas of engineering from Pennsylvania State University.[608] Graduate programs were available now in physical science, and in guidance and counseling.[609] The dental hygienist program, which had been offered at Slippery Rock since 1952 was dropped from curriculum.[610]

The College Library, keeping pace with Slippery Rock's growth, increased its total holdings from 58,000 volumes in 1965 to 108,000 in 1967.[611]

The "Save the Chapel" committee, was dismayed to learn that the Executive Director of the General State Authority had suggested to the Superintendent of Public Instruction that it would make good sense "to tear this old building down and replace it with a new one within the same allocation."[612] Mrs. Emma Guffey Miller and Mrs. Leila Vincent attempted to persuade the Board of Trustees that the Chapel could be saved if it were reconstructed as a fine arts center.[613] They failed and, once again, the Chapel question remained unsolved.[614]

After serving less than three years as Slippery Rock's president, Dr. Carter tendered his resignation to the Board of Trustees.[615] Because of mixed feelings among Board members, no immediate action was taken on his request.[616] One member, springing to the defense of President Carter's busy and at times controversial administration, announced, "Particularly I want it known that Dr. Carter has brought this school so far in such a short time."[617] It was not until March that the Board officially accepted his resignation, but stipulated that it

Frosh sporting dinks and signs, late 1960's

Maltby Library, 1966

would not become effective until June.[618] At this same meeting, the Board upheld President Carter's request that his administrative assistant be relived of his duties and that the chairman of the Department of English not have his contract renewed.[619] Three days later, on March 9, 1968, President Carter asked to be placed on detached service.[620] This was done and the Board appointed Mr. Robert A. Lowry, Director of Admissions, to be Slippery Rock's Chief Administrative Officer until September, 1968.[621] His title was later changed to Acting president.[622]

A native of Kittanning, Pennsylvania and graduate of Slippery Rock in 1948, Mr. Lowry had served as Slippery Rock's first Director of Admissions since 1957.[623] Upon hearing of his appointment, the Slippery Rock faculty sent the following resolution of support for him to the Board of Trustees:[624]

WHEREAS: The Board of Trustees of Slippery Rock State College, in selecting Robert

A. Lowry as temporary head of this institution, have chosen one of unquestionable integrity and good repute; and

WHEREAS: Acting President Lowry's long and selfless devotion to his Alma Mater gives him a special claim upon our affection and support; therefore be it

RESOLVED: that the Board of Trustees be wholeheartedly commended for their excellent judgment; and be it further

RESOLVED: that we pledge to Acting President Lowry our undivided loyalty, our commitment beyond the normal burden of our employment, and our enthusiastic best wishes in the arduous task he has undertaken.

While little of great consequence rarely transpires at a college during the term of an "acting" president, this was not to be the case for Mr. Lowry. As the search for his permanent successor was going on, he found himself centrally involved in the College's desperate effort to halt the deterioration of its reputation and standing in the academic community resulting from the circumstances surrounding the recent changeover in its administration. The seriousness of Slippery Rock's plight became known on May 9, 1968, when the Middle States Association of Colleges and Secondary Schools informed the College that unless changes were made at the school, it would be dropped from the list of accredited institutions on June 30, 1968.[625] The Association felt that the recent behavior of the central administration and the Board of Trustees constituted a serious threat to the well-being of the College and that it had an obligation to see that the situation be improved.[626] The Association further stipulated that if the College could offer evidence that it was seriously addressing itself to these problems and was making progress toward their solution, then it would remain on the accredited list.[627] However, by October 1, 1970, Slippery Rock would have to submit a complete report covering the areas of school governance, faculty, goals, curricula and library.[628]

Mr. Lowry arranged a meeting with Mr. F. Taylor Jones, Executive Secretary of the Association's Commission on Institutions of Higher Education, in order to explore with him the next steps the College should take.[629] It was agreed that the Commission should schedule an immediate on-site inspection to appraise first-hand conditions at the College.[630] On June 1 and 2, 1968, a five-member team of representatives from the Commission carried out an intensive examination and, seeing evidence of improvement, gave to the College an additional four months, until November 1, 1968, to improve even further conditions at the school.[631]

While Slippery Rock was desperately striving to retain its accreditation status, the search for a president went on at a furious pace. The Board of Trustees, anxious to have the members of the faculty assist in the selection process, invited them to appoint their own search committee.[632] The screening of the candidates went on throughout the month of May and, on June 3, 1968, one day after the committee of the Middle States Associations' Commission on Institutions of Higher Education had left, the Board of Trustees announced that both they and the faculty had agreed that Dr. Albert A. Watrel was their choice to be the College's next president.[633]

In gratitude for the outstanding leadership Mr. Lowry had given to the College during its most difficult period of transition, Mr. Peter Bender, President of the Board of Trustees, wrote a letter commending him for his "dedication to education and more important, to Slippery Rock State College by assuming the duties of acting president and fulfilling those obligations with competence. Your intimate knowledge of this institution and the intricacies of the administration, faculty, and students was instrumental in providing the cohesiveness necessary during the change in administration."[634]

On the 28th of June, 1968, Dr. Albert A. Watrel assumed the presidency of Slippery Rock State College.[635] He had been the Associate Vice President for Academic Affairs and the Chairman of the Department of Chemistry at the State University College at Cortland, New York. During the past year, he was an administrative intern at San Jose State College in California.[636] This program was directed by the American Council on Education and supported with grants from the Ford Foundation.[637] Born in New York, Dr. Watrel earned a Bachelor of Science, a Master of Science and a Doctor of Philosophy degree in biological chemistry from Syracuse University.[638] During his sixteen years in teaching and administration, he had

Albert A. Watrel, President, 1968-1976

received numerous grants from the National Science Foundation, the Atomic Energy Commission and the New York State Department of Education.[639]

The overriding problem which the new president faced when he arrived at Slippery Rock was that of accreditation. With assistance from the consultant appointed by the Middle States Association, President Kenneth C. McKay of Union College, President Watrel, along with the entire college community, began an all-out effort to improve the operation of the school.[640]

By September, 1968, the College had improved its faculty by increasing the number of teachers holding doctor's degrees by nine per cent; the administration had developed a planning document for the school; the faculty had approved a resolution of support and cooperation; and the Board of Trustees had adopted a set of by-laws.[641] Pleased with the progress, the Middle States Association gave Slippery Rock another four months, until March 1, 1969, to demonstrate its continued ability to put the affairs of the College in order.[642] The School was also informed that a full evaluation would be held in October of 1970.[643]

Problems over accreditation, however, were not the only ones which Slippery Rock faced in 1968. This year which witnessed the tragic assassinations of Martin Luther King and Robert Kennedy brought shock and anguish to the American people. College campuses across the country shook with unparalleled disorder as students expressed their frustration and concern over these events.

During this period of social upheaval, there was a heightened interest in providing broader opportunities in higher education for minority groups, and especially for Black Americans, at colleges like Slippery Rock. An Equal Education Opportunity Program, under the direction of Dr. James Unterwagner, was established at the College for those students "who are highly motivated to achieve a college degree but because of cultural deprivation did not achieve good high school grades or college board scores."[644] With the arrival of thirty-two students, thirty of whom were Black, in the fall of 1969, the program got underway.[645]

The upward spiral of enrollment continued in 1968, pushing Slippery Rock's student body to nearly four thousand.[646] Alarmed over the shortages of facilities at the College, President Watrel told the Board of Trustees that "we must get a dormitory for next year or the freshman class will be cut from 1,100 to 600 students."[647] Agreements were reached with a private company and construction began in the spring for an apartment complex slated to be finished in time for the 1969 fall term.[648] In the summer of 1969, a new library, another world culture building and a student union were under construction.[649]

Curricular expansion kept pace with the building program at Slippery Rock. Early in 1969, the College approved two new programs in biology, one leading to the Master of Science degree and the other to the Master of Education degree.[650] For graduate students preparing to work with the mentally retarded, physically handicapped, brain injured and emotionally disturbed, a new master's program in Special Education was now available.[651] As the programs in health and physical education continued to attract more and more students, the College decided to elevate this department to the status of a school in December, 1969.[652] In this new School of Health, Physical Education and Recreation, students were able to study in the newer areas of public health, pre-physical therapy, health technology, outdoor education, school nursing, and conservation, as well as the traditional fields.[653]

With budgeted costs outstripping income, Dr. Watrel recommended that for the 1969-70 spring semester, student fees, which included tuition, be increased "$50.00 to $225.00, in order to survive the academic year."[654] Though the Student Government, led by President Daniel LaPorte, objected vigorously, the Board of Trustees approved the increase.[655] Though Mr. LaPorte lost this fight, he did gain non-voting membership on the Board of Trustees by action of Governor Raymond Shafer.[656]

As Slippery Rock wrestled with problems of rising academic needs with limited resources, it occurred to Dr. James Roberts, Vice President for Academic Affairs, that some other schools were facing similar difficulties, perhaps intercollegiate academic cooperation might be a solution. He discussed with St. Fidelis College, a private Catholic college twenty-five miles from Slippery Rock, the possibility of mutually sharing faculty, students and facilities.[657] Agreements were rather quickly reached and Slippery Rock became the first state college in Pennsylvania and, perhaps in the country, to enter into such a consortium with a private institution of higher learning.[658]

Sensing the need for greater flexibility at a state-owned college like Slippery Rock, President Watrel suggested that an educational foundation be established for the school.[659] As envisioned by him, such a foundation's initial capital could come from "existing monies and funds which are held by the College, and which

The Rocklettes made half-time special, 1972

Coach Block and his 1969 Tennis Team

are not required to be deposited to the state as part of augmentation."[660] In addition, he explained that income could come from "grants, fees for the management of the monies therein, profits from conferences and other continuing education activities, gifts…"[661] By summer of 1970, the basic agreements on what was to be called The Slippery Rock Foundation were reached and, on July 23, a set of bylaws was adopted.[662] Dr. Watrel was to serve as President of the Board of Directors, assisted by Vice President, Dr. James Roberts, and Secretary-Treasurer, Dr. Donald Thompson.[663]

With the passage of House Bills 999 and 1000, in February, 1970, the Pennsylvania legislature granted to its State Colleges and University more autonomy in administering their academic affairs.[664] A Board of State Colleges and University Directors was created with broad powers to establish fiscal, personnel and educational policies.[665]

In the same month, Slippery Rock received the sad news of the death of its oldest and most dedicated supporter—Mrs. Emma Guffey Miller.[666] Long-time member and president of the Board of Trustees, and "Grand Old Lady" of the Democratic Party, who, at 95, had been the

oldest member of the Democratic National Committee, Mrs. Miller had given over the many years of her life valuable assistance to Slippery Rock.[667] Appropriately, the College paused in appreciation of her life-long service to the school.

Slippery Rock's alumni, anxious to promote the College's athletic fortunes, established in September, 1970, the N. Kerr Thompson Scholarship Fund for athletes.[668] Members of the College's Board of Trustees were offered associated memberships in the fund.[669] Several months later the Alumni Association invited the Board of Trustees to send representatives to their Board of Directors meetings.[670] The Board accepted the invitation and appointed four of its members to represent them at these meetings.[671] Later, in March, 1970, the Board of Trustees extended non-voting membership to representatives from Slippery Rock's faculty and alumni,[672] Dr. Robert Lowry, former acting president of the College, not surprisingly was selected by the faculty to serve them in this capacity.[673]

The long-awaited visitation of the representatives from the Middle States Association of Colleges and

Secondary Schools was held on October 25-28, 1970.[674] The evaluators held extensive meetings with the administration, faculty and Board of Trustees, as they examined the many facets of Slippery Rock's operation. It was not until the following April, 1971, that President Watrel received the good news from the Association that Slippery Rock's accreditation was reaffirmed.[675]

During President Watrel's term of office, which spanned the most violent years of student unrest on America's college campuses, relations between students and the central administration at Slippery Rock were relatively good. One incident which took place in the 1970-71 school year, however, shattered the otherwise normal calm at the College. Angered by what he thought was the irresponsible way the student newspaper staff were managing The Rocket, President Watrel stopped its publication and ordered that, beginning with the second semester, all funds from the College's cooperative activity fund be withheld.[676] He set down four conditions[677] which the student staff would have to meet before The Rocket resumed publication:

1. Select a faculty adviser who meets with President Watrel's approval.
2. Allow all students at the newspaper to freely elect the editor.
3. Define the qualifications for editor and process by which he is elected.
4. Establish educational objectives for the newspaper and indicate how these may be attained.

President Watrel explained that he had "no desire to violate the basic concept of freedom of the press, but rather to cultivate the concept of responsible journalism in our student newspaper staff."[678] The students agreed to meet his conditions and The Rocket soon appeared again on campus.

The Rocket in front of Vincent Science Hall, early 1970's

The use of drugs on campus was a continuing concern for students and administrators alike.[679] The Student Government, Office of Student Affairs, President Watrel and the Board of Trustees all gave their attention to this problem.[680] In addition to local campus controls, outside professionals were utilized in the effort to curb the use of drugs.[681]

In the early 1970's, pressure from the students for open-house dormitories grew. Finally, in June, 1971, the administration agreed to allow open-house privileges for all dormitory residents, with the exception of freshman women, for a trial period of six months.[682] By November, the administration was so pleased with the satisfactory way these new arrangements were working that they were made permanent.[683]

So that faculty and students in the Department of Biology would have the opportunity of having increased practical field experience, Slippery Rock arranged with Pennsylvania's Department of Forests and Waters to build a Biological Field Station on Lake Arthur in Moraine State Park in 1970.[684] Initially, Mr. Murray Shellgren coordinated the efforts of the scientists who were involved in a study to determine what aquatic life could exist in this man-made lake.[685] A lease, which called for an annual payment of one dollar, gave Slippery Rock the use of the Lake Arthur site for five years.[686]

The College also received permission at this time from the Western Pennsylvania Conservancy, to use the Jennings Nature Reserve.[687] This 300-acre reserve located just five miles south of the campus and contiguous with Moraine State Park was an important educational and recreational center. The Slippery Rock Foundation agreed to pay the annual rent of seven thousand dollars.[688] It was the aim of the College to offer guided tours of the grounds, to provide access to the interpretive center and provide lectures, films, and other educationally oriented programs to both students and the public.[689] Later in 1974, Slippery Rock, along with Clarion, California, and Edinboro State Colleges and Indiana University, became a member of the Penn Soil Conservation Education Center, which was to be changed to the Ivan McKeever Environmental Learning Consortium.[690] Slippery Rock's role in the consortium was to offer leadership in environmental education in Western Pennsylvania, as well as coordinating the work being done at the McKeever Center and the Jennings Nature Reserve.[691]

Growth in Slippery Rock's undergraduate and graduate programs in the Arts and Sciences continued under President Watrel's leadership. In 1971, the administration of these many academic departments was placed under three new separate schools.[692] The School of Natural Sciences and Mathematics now housed the departments of biology, chemistry, geology, mathematics, psychology and physics; the School of Social and Behavioral Sciences, the departments of geography, economics and business, history, sociology and anthropology and political science; and the School of Fine Arts and Humanities, the departments of art, English, modern languages, speech and theatre, music and philosophy.[693]

Even though greater emphasis was being given to studies in the liberal arts, 80% of the students at Slippery Rock were still involved in some form of teacher education.[694] So, when the National Council for the Accreditation of Teacher Education announced its plans to evaluate the College in October, 1971, President Watrel began intensive preparation for this visit.[695] Dr. Leland Moon of the University of Evansville assisted as an NCATE consultant in the preparation of a three-volume self-study document.[696] The evaluation team in October was led by Dr. Glenn G. Brooks of Wisconsin State University of Platteville.[697] The following spring, NCATE informed the College that its baccalaureate programs in elementary and secondary education were re-accredited and that initial accreditation was awarded to the master's degree programs for elementary teachers, guidance counselors, reading supervisors, physical education and special education teachers.[698] By this time, Slippery Rock was conferring annually over 180 masters' degrees.[699]

In the fall of 1971, Slippery Rock established an off-campus continuing education center in New Castle and began a ten-year long range plan which identified future roles for the faculty, students, alumni and administration in this center.[700]

An Army Reserve Officers Training Corps was established at Slippery Rock through a system of cross enrollment with the University of Pittsburgh.[701] In September, 1972, there were five undergraduate men and five women enrolled.[702] Under this program, students received full tuition and in their junior and senior years, one hundred dollars per month.[703]

The Alumni Association, which had fought so desperately to save Slippery Rock's historic Chapel, received the dreadful news, early in March, 1971, that the Board of Trustees had approved the demolition of the building.[704] The alumni, hoping to preserve the memory of the Chapel, asked President Watrel to consider using the Chapel windows and/or stone to construct a meditation room in a future building and to preserve "all cornerstones, contents thereof, and date stones" from the Chapel as memorial items.[705] They also suggested that stones from the building could be used for landscaping.[706] The Alumni Association also agreed to furnish a Chapel memorial plaque.[707] The Board of Trustees, sympathetic to the wishes of the alumni, requested President Watrel to do all he could to meet their requests.[708]

In the fall of 1971, the faculty of all fourteen of Pennsylvania's state colleges participated in an election to determine whether or not they wanted a collective bargaining agent to represent them in their negotiations with the Commonwealth.[709] If they wished such an agent, they had the option of choosing the Association of Pennsylvania State College and University Faculty/ Pennsylvania Association for Higher Education, the American Federation of Teachers or the American Association of University Professors.[710] The faculties supported this new development in faculty-administration relations and elected APSCUF/PAHE to be their agent.[711]

As the nation was giving more and more concern to the rights of minority groups in education, employment, etc., Slippery Rock, like colleges everywhere, established an Affirmative Action Program.[712] In 1972, the College sent numerous representatives to conferences in Harrisburg in order to learn how to implement such programs.[713] The Pennsylvania Human Relations Commission publication, Affirmative Action Recommendations for Pennsylvania State-Owned Institutions of Higher Education, offered guidelines which the College considered.[714] Slippery Rock's Progress Review Report indicated what the school was doing to achieve equality of educational opportunity on its campus.[715] In March, 1973, an Affirmative Action Officer was appointed.[716] At the end of the year, the College received a $10,000 grant from Harrisburg to assist in its implementation of the Equal Education Opportunity Program.[717] With such grants and by adjusting fees and granting deferments to needy students in the program, Slippery Rock attempted to meet its responsibilities toward its minority students.[718] The Black Action Committee, which was formed later in the year, gave Black students an organization committed to dealing with their special needs and through which they could convey their concerns to the wider college community.

Main Street, about 1975

167

With the passage in Washington of the Family Educational Rights and Privacy Act (commonly known as the Buckley Amendment) in 1974, students at colleges like Slippery Rock were guaranteed access to their academic and health records.[719] The students also had the right to challenge anything in their record which they considered inaccurate or misleading. In addition, records could be released only with the written consent of the student. Mr. Joseph Marks, Registrar, developed a set of policies and procedures following the guidelines contained in the Act and apprised all of the students of their rights under this new federal legislation.

In an effort to control the rapid proliferation of academic offerings at Pennsylvania's state colleges and university, Harrisburg established a moratorium of all new programs.[720] When, in 1973, the ban was lifted, an undergraduate teacher education major in communication was introduced at Slippery Rock, along with eight new graduate programs—Master of Arts degree in English and Social Studies (History); Master of Science degree in Physical Science and Health and Physical Education; and Master of Education degree in Biology, English, Physical Science and Social Studies.[721]

As a result of a mandate from the State Department of Education to each state college and university to create a State College Planning Commission, Slippery Rock invited students, faculty, administrators and towns-people to form such a Commission.[722] The Commission, organized in September, 1973, was charged with the responsibility of developing short and long range plans for the College.[723] The following year, all fourteen state institutions of higher learning held a planning confer-ence.[724] Slippery Rock identified its curricular missions in the future to lie in the areas of business administration, social welfare, rural and urban studies, fine arts, nursing education, and administration..[725] Within two years, the College had gained approval to offer programs in public administration, computer science, early childhood, rural and urban studies, environmental studies and critical languages.[726]

When the federal government agreed to give aid to Slippery Rock's efforts to create an innovative program leading to the Bachelor of Science degree in Nursing, the College embarked on an intensive planning schedule for this new degree program.[727] Dr. Diana Ney, a nursing educator at Slippery Rock, coordinated the planning effort which involved representatives from hospitals, health agencies, community leaders, and educators.[728]

By fall, 1974, the new nursing program was approved and available to students.[729]

By the middle of the decade there were over five thousand students at Slippery Rock. The 1975-76 enrollment stood at 5,329, with 2,376 males and 2,953 females.[730] In that year, 1,079 baccalaureate degrees were awarded and 209 master's degrees.[731]

Student activities at the College kept pace with the rising enrollment. There were increased responsibilities for the traditional governing organizations—Student Government, House Council, Associated Residence Hall Students and the Interfraternal and Panhellenic Councils.[732] The various musical groups—chamber orchestra, college choir, string ensemble, concert band, chamber singers, brass ensemble, women's glee club, stage band and the Rocket Marching Band—offered rich opportunities for learning and enjoyment in this area of artistic expression.[733] The Rocket Marching Band received nationwide recognition when it performed during "half-time" at a Baltimore Colts football game in Maryland in the fall of 1969.[734] The following list[735] suggests the enormous variety of "special interest" clubs which Slippery Rock students supported:

American Chemical Society, A.C.E.I., Bushido Karate Association, Council on International Relations and United Nations Affairs, Health and Physical Education Majors Club, Jigoro Kano Judo Club, Reader's Theatre, Officials Club, Psychology Club, Student Pennsylvania State Education Association, Society for the Preservation of Idle Fingers and Minds, Veterans Club, Rocklettes, Orchesis, Ski Club, Society of Physics Students, Students for Free Expression, Women's Recreation Association, Young Democratic Club, Varsity Club, Spanish Club, Philosophy Club, Intercollegiate Conference on Government, Geology Club, Debate Society, French Club, Black Action Society, Cheerleaders, Association for Women's Rights and Council for Exceptional Children.

During the 70's, national Greek letter organizations flourished on campus. These social fraternities—Alpha Chi Rho, Alpha Sigma Phi, Lambda Chi Alpha, Phi Mu Delta, Sigma Pi, Tau Kappa Epsilon, Theta Chi, and Theta Xi—and these social sororities—Alpha Omicron

Pi, Alpha Sigma Alpha, Alpha Sigma Tau, Alpha Xi Delta, Delta Zeta, Kappa Delta, Sigma Sigma Sigma, and Zeta Tau Alpha—had chapters at Slippery Rock.[736]

The Inter-Varsity Christian Fellowship, Newman Center, Young Women's Christian Association, and the Christian Science Organization offered students opportunities for religious fellowship and service while at Slippery Rock.[737]

The Rocket, Ginger Hill, The Saxigena, and the WNFT radio station continued to keep students informed of the happenings at the College.[738]

In 1975 the character of the College's student body began to change a bit as "senior" citizens began to take advantage of a state law which allowed them to enroll in college courses free of charge.[739] The Pennsylvania legislature thought that this was one way the state could recognize "the debt we owe to our senior citizens for their many significant contributions to the Commonwealth through the years."[740]

Intercollegiate athletics continued its winning ways at Slippery Rock. During the 1971-72 year, its teams won conference titles in track, golf, and cross country, and the basketball team won divisional honors.[741] The following year, the basketball team, coached by Mel Hankinson and Cliff Wettig, finished fourth in the NAIA National Basketball Tournament in Kansas City, and the football team, under Coach Bob DiSpirito, won the state conference championship.[742] In 1973 the football team once again won the state conference championship and traveled to Tacoma, Washington, to play in a game with the University of Puget Sound.[743] Again state champions the following year, the team played Ithaca State College in NCAA-sponsored post season play.[744] In recognition of their fine work on the gridiron, Pennsylvania's Lieutenant Governor Ernest Kline presented the team with a trophy.[745]

Though the N. Kerr Thompson Stadium had been built several years earlier, its playing field and running

Style of the early 1970's

College Choir, Washington, D.C., 1976

Pennsylvania Conference Football Champions, 1972

*Margaret Thompson, widow of Coach N. Kerr Thompson
with President Watrel at the Stadium dedication, 1974*

track were not able to be used until 1974.[746] At the dedication of this 10,000 seat stadium, the thirty-two years of service the legendary N. Kerr Thompson had given Slippery Rock as coach, professor and administrator were recalled.[747]

Women's athletic programs at Slippery Rock were beginning to keep pace with the men's, and, in 1974, the women's field hockey team and the tennis squad had exceptionally fine seasons.[748] The men's soccer team won the Pennsylvania state conference title that year.[749]

The Wall Street Journal, taking note of the College's fine football team, published on the front page of its September 11, 1975 edition an article entitled: "Go Slippery Rock! Brunt of All the Jokes Longs for Last Laugh."[750]

The team was also featured in an NCAA television special "Saturday's Heroes," which was broadcast over the ABC network.[751]

The purpose[752] of this busy and diverse athletic program, which, by 1975, had included nineteen men's and women's intercollegiate sports, as well as a variety of intramural sports for both men and women, was explained in the College's Catalog:

Basketball Team, On to Kansas City, 1973

Rock Cross Country -vs- California, Homecoming, 1971

171

Football team's flight to New Orleans to play Nichols State, 1972

The honorable K. Leroy Irvis,
Commencement speaker, 1976

The primary purpose of the athletic program at Slippery Rock State College is to provide increased opportunities for the development of each participating individual physically, mentally, emotionally, morally and socially. The program is so conducted as to assure the wholesome use of leisure time, to provide a healthy focal point for group spirit, and to provide laboratory experiences for prospective teachers and/or coaches.

By the middle of the 70's, the faculty at Slippery Rock consisted of approximately 350 members. Because of a continuing leveling off of appropriations from Harrisburg to its state colleges, there were, from time to time, ominous reports of faculty retrenchment at Slippery Rock. While the College was forced, in 1975, to reduce by seventeen and a half, the number of its teaching positions, it was not necessary, because of retirements and careful budgeting, to carry out any actual retrenchment of faculty personnel.[753]

As Slippery Rock continued to expand throughout the Watrel administration, so did the budgets necessary to support such growth. By the mid-seventies, the College was experiencing difficulty in balancing its budget and for the 1976-77 fiscal year, it faced a $1.4 million deficit.[754]

Though an unbalanced budget was an indicator in 1975 of deepening difficulties for the College, few could have imagined what a storm of trouble lay just ahead for the school. It all began with explosive suddenness on the morning of June 11, 1976, when President Watrel removed Dr. James Roberts from his position as Vice President for Academic Affairs.[755] Pennsylvania Governor Milton Shapp, on the advice of his Secretary of Education, John C. Pittenger, immediately fired President Watrel.[756] Secretary Pittenger, obviously upset over President Watrel's actions, called his firing of Dr. Roberts "arbitrary and without reason."[757] In defense of Governor Shapp's decision to fire President Watrel, Secretary Pittenger announced that his Department of Education had been investigating for a considerable period of time "the deteriorating situation at Slippery Rock." As a result of his investigation, the Secretary charged President Watrel with having:

- Attempted to falsify recommendations of the academic vice president for faculty promotions in 1974.
- Attempted to provide inappropriate financial assistance to athletes.
- Permitted the food service program to operate at a deficit "approaching $250,000 this year in spite of a directive from the DE."
- Allowed poor management practices at the book store which resulted in the indictment of the former manager for embezzlement.
- Authorized the questionable use of state funds to construct an "elaborate press box," at the football stadium.
- Attempted to coerce the editors and staff of the student newspaper to adopt a more favorable view of his administration.[758]

Governor Shapp appointed Dr. James Roberts Acting President of Slippery Rock and ordered Dr. Watrel "to cooperate with Dr. Roberts in every possible way."[759] On the afternoon of June 11, three Pennsylvania state troopers arrived at Old Main to escort Dr. Watrel from his office.[760] These troopers were there not to arrest Dr. Watrel, but rather to insure the safety of all the records important in the investigation of his administration.[761] To this end, the locks to the president's office and to all the file cabinets were changed under police supervision.[762]

Local newspapers and others around the state headlined the story of Governor Shapp's firing of President Watrel and offered readers detailed accounts of this dramatic turn of events at Slippery Rock.[763] A week later The Rocket devoted its special summer edition to the dramatic events of June 11th.[764] In it a lead editorial appeared under the heading "Shapp's Action Supported."[765]

The Board of Trustees held a special meeting on Sunday, June 13, in Miller Auditorium, to discuss the firing of President Watrel.[766] A large number of faculty, staff and students were present. Both Dr. Watrel and Dr. Roberts had been invited to this meeting, as well as the state's Secretary of Education, John C. Pittenger.[767]

Dr. Watrel spoke to the assembly and vigorously denied the allegations of his wrong doing made by Secretary Pittenger and circulated by the media.[768] In his closing remarks, he offered this personal view of

Lawrence Park, 1977-1979

173

his administration: "During the past eight years, we have been proud of what we have accomplished at Slippery Rock State College, and I have always kept the welfare of the College foremost."[769]

In Dr. Robert's opening comment, he said:

I accept Governor Shapp's appointment as Acting President of Slippery Rock State College, I appreciate his confidence and that of Secretary Pittenger in selecting me to carry on the responsibilities of governing the institution by directing its affairs at this crucial time.[770]

He then outlined his goals for the school and asked all of the members of the College community to join him in working for the best interest of the school.

Let us transcend individual interests and alliance in favor of the common good. Let us join together rather than divide. Let us strive toward uniting the various elements and interests within our community for the sake of a common advancement in which we can all take pride.[771]

Secretary Pittenger, whose statement was the longest of the three, expanded upon his allegations which appeared in the media.[772] In closing, he expressed his deep concern for Slippery Rock, as well as for the entire state college and university system.[773]

Re-pointing brickwork of Old Main, 1978

Mr. Blase Scarnati, directing practice, 1977

With Dr. Watrel gone, Dr. Roberts in the president's office, and the search committee of the Board of Trustees looking for a permanent president, things at Slippery Rock returned to some degree of normalcy. Dr. Roberts, who had served as Vice President at the College since 1966, was interested in giving a steady administrative hand to Slippery Rock, as it sought to look, not backward, but forward to meeting the tasks which lay ahead.

Because of the way in which he was conducting the affairs of the school, many at the College expected Dr. Roberts to be appointed as the "permanent" president. Indeed, when, in May, 1977, the Board of Trustees submitted their presidential nominations to Pennsylvania's Board of State College and University Directors, they ranked Dr. Roberts first choice among four candidates.[774]

In over three months, there was no news form Harrisburg. Then, in August, the Board of Trustees was informed that Governor Shapp had appointed Dr. Lawrence Park to be Interim President at Slippery Rock for a term of two years.[775] Dr. Park had been president of Mansfield State College for nine years before coming to Slippery Rock.[776] A native of Newburgh, New York, he received a baccalaureate from the State University of New York at New Paltz and master's and doctor's degrees from New York University.[777] He had served in various administrative positions in the public schools, at the Pennsylvania State University and at the State University of New York at Geneseo.[778]

Six months later, in February 1978, the Board of Trustees began another presidential search which, it was anticipated, would last for one year.[779] It was the Board's plan to have President Park's successor take office on July 1, 1979.[780]

In the period since 1976, changes continued to take place at Slippery Rock. Eight new programs were added to the curriculum in the 1976-77 academic year. Six led to Bachelor of Science degrees in computer science, economics and business, music therapy, public administration, social welfare, and rural and urban studies.[781] At the graduate level new certification programs in school supervision and early childhood education were introduced.[782] In the 1976 summer term, advanced high school students were invited to take college courses for credit.[783] An intensive set of workshop experiences were also offered that summer.

In the fall of 1977, a Master Planning Council was formed with the responsibility of making "a

Evolution of the Marching Rockets

175

comprehensive study of plans and goals for the College."[784] So that all segments of the College would be represented on this important Council, members of the faculty, administration, student body and the non-instructional staff were asked to serve on this Council, along with the Director of Institutional Research.[785]

A fine arts building, estimated to cost nearly $2 million, was under construction and scheduled to be completed in 1979.[786] For the first time, in 1978, students could earn a Bachelor of Fine Arts degree in art.[787]

In the late 1970's, enrollment at Slippery Rock, as at other colleges and universities across the nation, began to drop. This was a reflection of the fact that there were smaller numbers of men and women of traditional college age available for higher education. There were 5,244 students at Slippery Rock in the fall of 1976; in 1978, the enrollment was 4,756—a drop of about 10%.[788]

The College's athletic teams continued to bring honor to the school[789] as the football and soccer squads earned the western division conference titles in 1976 and the track and baseball teams won state conference titles in 1978.[790] In this same year, the basketball team won the western division title.[791]

Computer Center, early 1970's

As the decade of the 1970's was drawing to a close, America's colleges were emerging from one of the most turbulent periods in the history of American higher education. Slippery Rock had met well the many challenges this era had brought and was looking ahead with renewed confidence to the opportunities the 1980's would bring.

The Marching Rockets, in front of Old Main, 1978

176

Male Athletes, 1960's and 1970's

Gymnast, Willie Stringer in good form,
high above his trampoline, 1966

Mens Baseball coaches Wally Rose, left and
Ed Walsh talk strategy, 1974

Coach Wally Rose, left, with All-American Gymnasts
Tom Horne and John Daller, mid 1960's

Olympic medalist Stan Dziedzic, 1972 alumnus, on the mat

Coach Jim Egli holding trophy and the 1974 undefeated championship Men's Soccer Team

Women Athletes, 1960's and 1970's

Coach Wilma Cavill, front, left and the Women's Swimming Team

Coach Martha Haverstick, back, left and the Women's Tennis Team

Coach Pat Zimmerman, upper right, with 1975 Women's Field Hockey Team

Coach Marie Wheaton, far left, with 1975 Women's Volleyball Team

Women's Lacrosse

Women's Softball

Coach Ann Griffiths, back, left and the Womens Basketball Team

181

Artist Lecture Series, 1973

Vincent Price

Marcel Marceau

Dan Rather

Arthur C. Clarke

182

CHAPTER VIII

New Challenges, New Opportunities

For over a year, the presidential search committee was busy at work looking for a new leader for Slippery Rock State College. Formed in February, 1978, with representatives from the alumni, students, faculty, staff, administration and community, its specific responsibility was to present the names of six candidates to the College's Board of Trustees.[792] A year later, the committee recommended to the Board that Drs. Edward F. Cook, Joseph P. Guisti, Carrol Krause, Herb. F. Reinhard, James N. Roberts and Joseph T. Sandefur be considered for the presidency.[793] After lengthy deliberation, the Board agreed to submit without preference the candidacies of Drs. Cook, Guisti and Roberts to the Board of State College and University Directors in Harrisburg.[794]

Unknown to the Board, Dr. Lawrence Park, interim president at the College, at the insistence of the officials in the Department of Education, released the names of all six of the candidates to the Department without informing the College's Board of Trustees.[795] Infuriated with such a breach of procedure, the Trustees warned that they would initiate legal action against the Board of State College and University Directors if their three candidates, and only these three, were not forwarded to Governor Thornburgh.[796]

Concerned with the intense feelings developing in the Slippery Rock community over the presidential selection process, the Department of Education, hoping to reduce anxiety, invited all six of the candidates to Harrisburg for interviews.[797] Held in late February, the interviews were conducted by Dr. Robert Scanlon, Secretary of Education, Dr. Clayton L. Sommers, Commissioner of Higher Education or his representative, and three members of the Board of State College and University Directors.[798] Dr. Krause was prevented from going to Harrisburg by a snowstorm in his home state of South Dakota and Dr. Sandefur had withdrawn his

application for the position.[799] The recommendations of this group in Harrisburg, along with those of the College's Board of Trustees, were sent to the Governor's office for review.

Herb. F. Reinhard, Jr., President, 1979-1984

Several weeks later, the editors of the campus newspaper, The Rocket, surprised everyone with the announcement that they had learned from informed sources that Governor Thornburgh had been urged by Secretary Scanlon and the Board of State College and University Directors to appoint Dr. Reinhard as Slippery Rock's next president.[800] The Executive Secretary of the Board of State College and University Directors did acknowledge that one name had been sent to the Governor but refused to disclose the name.[801] Several months passed with no news from Harrisburg. Finally, late in April, Governor Thornburgh startled the Slippery Rock community with his announcement that he was rejecting the three candidates submitted by the College's Board of Trustees and requested that three additional nominations be forwarded to him.[802] Again, Harrisburg was ominously quiet. Then, suddenly, on May 17, 1979, at a press conference in Mercer, Secretary Scanlon disclosed that Dr. Herb. F. Reinhard was appointed by Governor Thornburgh to be the president of Slippery Rock State College.[803] The Slippery Rock community was delighted to get this long-awaited news. Secretary Scanlon spent the next two days at Slippery Rock and learned first-hand how pleased those at the College and the community were with the decision.[804] Indeed, with the selection of Dr. Reinhard as its president, the college community experienced a collective sigh of relief as it now, for the first time in three years, put behind it the bitterness and acrimony created in the wake of the firing of its president back in 1976. This long struggle had attracted national attention as newspapers and journals kept the public informed of this agonizing period in the College's history. Now, all eyes were focused upon the future.[805]

Dr. Reinhard quickly reassured the College that his vision of the school's future was bright with promise. "I believe very strongly that Slippery Rock State College has tremendous potential for the future," he wrote to the chairperson of the Board of Trustees.[806] He also explained that "all of us—faculty, staff, students, Trustees, and residents of the Slippery Rock community will need to work together in a spirit of mutual trust, respect and cooperation in order to reach that potential."[807] At a meeting of college faculty and administrators in August, 1979, Dr. Reinhard's address was greeted with a standing ovation. His words to the Board of Trustees that "Slippery Rock is a fine institution that collectively we can make even finer" caught the imagination of the campus and was later to be adopted by the Alumni Association as the theme of their membership campaign.[808] The Association would present him with a banner displaying his words of confidence.

Dr. Herb. F. Reinhard was born in Covington, Kentucky, on September 12, 1930. He was educated in elementary and secondary schools of his hometown, Cincinnati, Ohio, and Hollywood, Florida. He earned a B.S. in Psychology and M.S. in Guidance and Counseling from Florida State University and a doctor's degree in Higher Education Administration and Student Personnel from Indiana University. Prior to his coming to Slippery Rock, Dr. Reinhard served as Assistant to the President of Florida A. and M. University in Tallahassee, Florida for five years. He had also held positions in Academic Affairs and Student Affairs at the University of Tennessee, Western Carolina University, Florida State University, Indiana University and Auburn University. In addition, he served four years as a neuro-psychiatric technician in the United States Navy and as Director of Research and Chief of College and University Affiliations for the State Department of Health and Rehabilitation Services in Florida. In 1955, he married Nancy Warner. They have four children, Herb. III, Don, Mark and Ann. In addition to his extensive educational experience, Dr. Reinhard has also played professional baseball with the Brooklyn Dodger Farm System and has been a professional entertainer.

When Dr. Reinhard picked up the reins of the presidency of the College, he faced a projected deficit in the 1979-80 operating budget of almost a million and a half dollars. Immediately, he set to work correcting this threatened fiscal imbalance and, within three months, had produced a budget that was balanced.[809] His achievement is particularly remarkable at this time, for it is something which seven of the fourteen state colleges and university in Pennsylvania were unable to do.[810]

President Reinhard's opening months were extraordinarily busy ones, as he initiated a number of new activities on campus, e.g., an orientation program for faculty and staff, a President's Advisory Committee, a Student Organization Leadership Conference, an All-College Academic Convocation, a Cost-Reduction Ideas Committee, a Pressbox Committee, Clerical and Management team seminars, an all-college family picnic and a Legislative, Public Officials and Community Days.[811] He set up a Staff Center where faculty and staff could meet for breakfast and lunch. He also made the President's House available for entertainment, recruitment, and receptions for faculty, staff, students and guests of the College. An Athletic Task Force of students, faculty and staff was created for the purpose of examining the various areas of the athletic programs at the College.[812]

In the fall of 1979, the College honored a number of people who had served Slippery Rock with dedication by giving their names to campus buildings. The following chart identifies the building and the honored individuals:

Building	To Be Designated As
1. Behavioral Science Building	Strain Behavioral Science Building
2. Dining Hall	Boozel Dining Hall
3. Education Building	McKay Education Building
4. Hi-Rise I	Dodds Hall
5. Hi-Rise II	Founders Hall
6. Infirmary	McLachlan Student Health Center
7. Library	Bailey Library
8. Music Building	Swope Music Building
9. World Culture Building	Spotts World Culture Building

In Honor Of	Former Position
1. Dr. Warren T. Strain	Geography faculty member
2. George D. Boozel	Dining hall employee
3. Miss Maree McKay	Registrar
4. Mr. Archie Dodds	Athletic Director
5. Founders of the College	
6. Richard McLachlan, M.D.	College Physician
7. Dr. Matilda Bailey	English faculty member
8. Dr. M. Clair Swope	Music faculty member
9. Dr. Carle B. Spotts	English faculty member[813]

Capitalizing on Slippery Rock's unique sounding name and athletic history, President Reinhard promoted the establishment of the Slippery Rock National Athletic Fan Club. By April of 1980, nearly eleven hundred people from approximately thirty-five states had joined, contributing eleven thousand dollars toward an athletic scholarship fund.[814] A Dollars for Scholars program was also created, with the first academic scholarships granted to students in the fall of 1980.[815]

President Reinhard established the first office of Alumni Affairs and Development in the school's history. Two alumni chapters were quickly established in Allegheny and Erie counties and, by spring, there were three more chapters in Washington, D.C., Florida, and California.[816]

The need for a new student dormitory on campus was recognized by President Reinhard and he worked closely with the Board of Trustees in search of a solution. For the past few years, the student occupancy rate in the campus dormitories was running over 100 per cent. A new dormitory project for Slippery Rock had actually been approved by Harrisburg some years earlier, but the funds for it had been frozen by the State Department of Education and Office of Administration.[817] Early in 1980, the College received the disappointing news from Harrisburg that the dormitory project had been deferred indefinitely. The adverse bond market and lingering concerns over expansion of housing facilities at the state colleges were given as reasons for the decision.[818]

Certainly one of the most festive and dramatic events on any college campus is the inauguration of a new president, and so it was to be at Slippery Rock when, on May 3, 1980, Dr. Reinhard was formally installed as the College's next president.[819] The entire day was filled with receptions, musicals, luncheons, dining and dancing. The inaugural convocation was attended by representatives of eighty institutions of higher education and learned societies from at home and abroad.[820] Greetings were brought from Governor Thornburgh, the Board of State Colleges and University Directors and the College's faculty, staff, students and alumni.[821] In his inaugural address, President Reinhard voiced his strong commitments to American higher education and to Slippery Rock's promising future. He called upon American colleges to strive for excellence and thus prevent the deterioration of integrity.[822]

To enable Slippery Rock to achieve its academic potential, President Reinhard believed that it was important for the internal structure of the College to be reorganized. His plan called for restructuring the administration of the College's divisions of Academic Affairs, Administrative and Fiscal Affairs and Student Affairs. The greatest changes occurred in Academic Affairs, where the five schools were organized into two faculties each headed by a dean and associate dean. Whereas, the Faculty of Professional Studies now includes the School of Health, Physical Education and Recreation and the School of Education; the Faculty of Arts and Sciences includes the School of Humanities and Fine Arts, the School of Natural Sciences and Mathematics, and the School of Social and Behavioral Sciences. In addition, the areas of graduate programs, summer programs, continuing education, admissions and academic advisement were highlighted and organized under the direct supervision of a dean and assistant dean.

Howard Headland, alumnus and oldest faculty member with
W.O. Magee, Golden Grad President, 1980

the college for well-earned congratulations.[825] In addition, Mrs. Nancy Reinhard graciously received all graduating students, their parents, relatives and friends at a continental breakfast held at the President's Home on the day of commencement.

The summer of 1980 was an exceptionally active one at Slippery Rock with a large number of classes, workshops, camp and parent-student orientations being held. The college also provided an intensive two-day orientation program for the members of the Board of Trustees.[826] Secretary Robert Scanlon and other officials from the State Department of Education visited the campus in August and expressed their satisfaction with the way the college was functioning under its new president. Before they left, President Reinhard once again brought to their attention Slippery Rock's great need for additional dormitory facilities.[827] In the fall, 1980, the College brought a number of representatives of the business and industrial community to participate in its first Business and Industry Day. The College's Student Ambassadors, a new student group on campus, assisted in attending to the many guests who were on campus that day.[828]

December, 1980, was a particularly festive one at Slippery Rock. Medieval-styled Madrigal Christmas Dinners with music provided by the College's Chamber Singers, were held on the fifth and sixth of the month. These dinners which were planned to raise money for the academic scholarship fund, were an immediate success with capacity crowds in attendance both evenings. The Madrigal programs would later be presented at the Seven Springs Resort in the Laurel Highlands.[829] A winter commencement, the first in several years, was also held in December. President Reinhard, with the cooperation of the Alumni Association, hosted all graduates and their parents and friends at a reception at the President's Home.[830]

Throughout this entire period, Slippery Rock was busy preparing for the visit of an evaluation team from the Middle States Association of Colleges and Secondary Schools during the 1980-81 academic year. When Dr. Reinhard arrived on campus, he found that Slippery Rock was to be evaluated by the Middle States Association of Colleges and Secondary Schools sometime during the

A Department of Public Administration was established for those students who were interested in planning for careers in local, state and federal government. The Department quickly established a cooperative program in public administration with the nearby Butler County Community College.[823] Slippery Rock also entered into other kinds of academic cooperative arrangements with Grove City College, the Mercer Correctional Institution, Saint Francis Hospital in New Castle and the Franklin Chamber of Commerce.[824]

At the first College Commencement (1980) over which the new president presided, Dr. Reinhard revived the ancient practice of announcing the name of each graduate and presenting the graduate to the officials of

1980-81 academic year. The College's Middle States Evaluation Steering Committee, under the direction of Dr. N. L. Gamberoni, chairperson, had completed an initial draft of a comprehensive self-study of the school and distributed it to all members of the college community in the fall of 1980.[831] During the fall and winter, the faculty and staff spent an enormous amount of time analyzing, discussing and refining the self-study report. On April 12, 1981, the Evaluation Team, headed by President Nathan Weiss of Kean College, arrived on campus. In the next four days the team conducted an extensive examination of every major facet of the College. They were obviously pleased with what they saw, for their final report to the Middle States Association was a very positive one. President Weiss, in concluding remarks in his report, described Slippery Rock to be "a strong institution with a good promise for an exciting future."[832]

Slippery Rock was delighted to learn that Harrisburg had increased the College's budget for its 1981-82 fiscal year. This was made possible since educational officials in the state capital had not only considered student enrollments in determining the size of the budgets for the state colleges and university, but also these schools' experience in maintaining balanced budgets and other administrative factors.[833]

In 1981, two phonathons were held by the Slippery Rock Foundation, Inc., in cooperation with the Alumni Association to raise money for scholarships and other college programs.[834] President Reinhard joined Dr. Fred Williams, Director of Alumni Affairs and Development, and other campaign workers, in phoning a selected group of alumni and inviting them to support their alma mater.[835] These initial efforts to solicit support by talking to alumni over the telephone of the needs of Slippery Rock State College brought in over twenty-seven thousand dollars.

The faculty approved a collective bargaining agreement in the spring which assured the College of the continuance of effective academic relationships on the campus.[836]

The year 1981 saw Slippery Rock presenting a variety of activities for its students and community. A Miss Slippery Rock State College Student Scholarship Pageant was held in March in Miller Auditorium. Dawn Wilson, a graduate student, won top honors and went on to participate in the Miss Pennsylvania Pageant in June.[837]

A Summer Celebration held on two successive weekends in July brought an estimated twenty thousand people to the campus.[838] A Civil War Battle Reenactment, hot air balloon races, an art exhibition, a military equipment presentation, light aircraft demonstrations and concerts by the Pittsburgh Symphony Orchestra, Peter Nero and Hank Williams, Jr. were among the events which made up this grand celebration.[839] The presence of the Pittsburgh Symphony was, of course, the high point of the festivities. Indeed, the College and community received the orchestra so enthusiastically that

Balloons rising at the Summer Celebration

**President Reinhard and son
enjoying summer celebration, 1981**

Cast of Madrigal Christmas Dinner

some discussions were held to explore the possibility of having the Symphony make its permanent summer home in Slippery Rock.

The second annual Madrigal Christmas Dinners were given for three nights this year and four sold-out performances were staged at the Hotel Hershey, Hershey, Pennsylvania. In early November this popular on-campus event was fully subscribed.

To serve better the various needs of these students, Slippery Rock instituted in September, 1981, a new resident life program administered by a director and several coordinators of resident education/student activities advisors.[841] In each campus dormitory a professional staff supervisor was now available to help students with their academic and social concerns.[842] In addition, in an effort to increase Greek involvement on campus, a Pan Hellenic House was dedicated on September 8, 1981, possibly the first of its kind in the nation.[843] The house can serve as a meeting place for individual sororities, the Pan Hellenic Council, the site of special activities such as rush parties and ceremonies as well as providing overnight accommodations for national

sorority representatives.[844] An experienced food service company assumed operation of the College's cafeteria in August. In addition to offering "quality" meals to students at reasonable prices, it performed these services at considerable savings to the school.[845] While making this important change, the College, at the same time, guaranteed continued employment at the school to its cafeteria personnel.

During these early years of the Reinhard administration, Slippery Rock's athletic teams continued to bring honor to the College in a wide variety of sports. The following teams placed *first* in championship play sponsored by various regional, state, and national athletic associations: Men's Track Team, Pennsylvania Conference, 1979, 1980, 1981, and NCAA Division III National Championships, 1979; Women's Track Team, Pennsylvania Conference, 1979, 1980; Women's Cross Country Team, Pennsylvania Conference and EAIAW Division III, 1979, 1981; Wresting Team, NCAA Division I, Eastern Region, 1979, 1980; Women's Judo Team, Eastern Collegiate Judo Association, 1979, 1980; Women's Gymnastics Team, Pennsylvania Conference,

1980, and EAIAW Division II, 1981; Men's Soccer Team, ECAC College Division, Southern Regional Tournament, 1978; Women's Tennis Team, Pennsylvania Conference, 1980, 1981; Women's Softball Team, EAIAW Division II, 1980, Pennsylvania Conference, 1981; Men's Baseball Team, tied first, Western Division Pennsylvania Conference, 1981.[846] In 1980 and 81, the football team participated in the special Band Day Games at the famous University of Michigan Stadium in Ann Arbor. Well over 100,000 fans watched the two games and enjoyed the over 20,000 band members perform at the half-time ceremonies.

Pennsylvania Conference Tennis Champions, 1980

*Pennsylvania Conference Gymnastics Champions with
Coach Cheryl Levick and President Reinhard, 1980*

189

Marching Band at University of Michigan, 1981

When the Fall Semester began in 1981, President Reinhard, anxious to acquaint the public with the many facets of academic life at Slippery Rock State College, planned a series of events for parents, legislators, community leaders, business and industry representatives and prospective donors, alumni and prospective donors. Ms. Pam Shingler, who was in charge of special programming, arranged many visitations which gave the College "great visibility, improved public relations and the potential for greater outside support. On many occasions, President Reinhard met with campus guests at his home.[847]

During Homecoming of that year, a long-awaited parents' organization was initiated. Mr. Robert Bartsch, father of Brian Bartsch, the current Student Government President, was elected president. Dr. Reinhard underscored the importance of the new parents' organization:

The Quad, late 1970's

"this can be a good organization and will help a number of parents to feel more a part of the institution".[848]

Campus communication among faculty and staff continued to be a focus for Dr. Reinhard. Nearly every week during the academic year, the President hosted coffee sessions with various constituent groups to discuss important issues.[849]

For President Reinhard, increasing student enrollment was a top priority. He appointed Mr. Eliott Baker to be the Director of Admissions. He launched rather quickly a vigorous plan that was designed to attract students who live beyond the waters of Slippery Rock Creek. His extensive campus visitation program provided prospective students and their families with vital information about the many opportunities available to all who attend the College. So successful were his efforts that the freshman class of 1981 was one of the largest in the College's history.[850]

New curricular offerings also made the College more attractive. Students could now earn bachelors degrees in Applied Science and Administration of Occupational Health and Safety Management and a master's degree in Counseling Psychology. [851] The Applied Science degree program was described as a reversal of roles, since accredited community colleges and technical schools provided the student with an associate degree in a technical major while Slippery Rock provided general education and core courses. This was one of the College's first degree programs which attracted the non-traditional students.

A very successful Middle States Association of Colleges and Secondary Schools accreditation visit occurred in 1981. The College's review process and self-study was rated outstanding and used by Middle States in their annual workshop as a case study. At the same time, another very important accreditation review

Rocky

Mrs. Jones, creator of the first Rocky costume, and son, Bob Jones, Rocky mascot, greeted by President Reinhard at his home, Parent's Day, 1981

Bruce Russell, Media Services Center with new equipment, late 1970's

*Presidential Ballerina at the Talent Show,
March, 1982*

was taking place on campus. The National Council for the Accreditation of Teacher Education was evaluating the College's programs in teacher education. Excellent marks were awarded Slippery Rock State College, resulting with continued accreditation.[852]

Increased fund raising efforts began to pay dividends in the spring of 1982. A gift of ten thousand dollars, the largest single gift, was received from Armco's Butler Works in honor of the late Gail Rose. The Slippery Rock State College Foundation was delighted to announce that a total of more than $110,000 had been raised for the campaign period.[853]

Faculty and staff volunteered in March 1982 to participate in a special talent show to raise money for the new Dollars for Student Scholars Program. Various talents at varying levels of ability were demonstrated that evening, including a special surprise visit by a presidential ballerina. Funds sufficient to award ten high school senior scholarships were raised in this effort.

Also that spring, more than $16,000 was raised to support student scholarships during the annual alumni phonathon. Alumni were increasing their efforts to support their alma mater and enjoyed the relationship with President Reinhard. At their annual "Changing of the Guard" banquet, alumni gathered to install Mr. John A. Watson, class of 1940, as its new president.[854]

192

Not all news for students during the spring 1982 was positive. In an effort to develop self-supporting or auxiliary operations in Housing, Food Services and Health Services, the College announced a plan for major fee increases. Lengthy trustee discussions also led to the passage of a 14% increase in the Housing fee, a 12% increase in the Food Services fee, a 40% increase in the Health Services fee and a 22% increase in the General Service Fee.[855]

The summer of 1982 was also a very busy time for the College. In addition to the students enrolled in summer classes, it is estimated that over 25,000 visitors participated in conferences, workshops and the College's summer camps. The attractiveness of Slippery Rock State College continued into the fall with another increase in the freshman class and a record number of more than 400 transfer students. President Reinhard attributed his schools continued expansion in student enrollment to a growing "recognition of the quality of our academic programs, attractiveness of the campus, friendliness and interest in students – expressed and shown".[856]

No sooner after this expanding and revitalized Slippery Rock State College began its fall semester in 1982, a wonderful metamorphosis occurred. It was transformed into a University.

It had been twenty-two years since the State Teachers Colleges in Pennsylvania had been expanded into State Colleges. Now, in Harrisburg, considerable attention was being given to the possibility of a move to university status. Legislative discussions led to the passage of Senate Bill 506 on June 7, 1982, by an overwhelming majority of 41 to 1. Concurrently, the companion House Bill 1949 was in the Education Committee and expected to be voted upon by the House in early Fall.[857]

At a pivotal meeting in Harrisburg on September 15, 1982, the governing board of the State Colleges, the 14 Presidents and the Chairpersons of each of the Boards of Trustees crafted a document of support for the House Bill.[858] Just one week later, September 22, 1982, the House approved the bill by a vote of 181 to 3.[859] At a most celebrated event, with more than 500 citizens in attendance, Governor Dick Thornburg signed into law Act 188 of 1982, granting university status to all 14 state-owned institutions of higher education, effective July 1, 1983. The Act created the State System of Higher Education, Commonwealth of Pennsylvania.[860]

Govenor Dick Thornburgh with Secretary of Education, Robert Scanlon and the
14 State Colleges and University Presidents at the signing of Act 188

Students and Staff at the University Celebration, July 1, 1983

Dr. and Mrs. Reinhard and guests at the University Celebration, July 1, 1983

STATE NORMAL SCHOOL
SLIPPERY ROCK, BUTLER CO., PA.

Fifty-two Dollars, $52
FOR FALL TERM OF SIXTEEN WEEKS FOR
TUITION, BOARD, FURNISHED ROOM, HEAT,
LIGHT, AND USE OF TEXT BOOKS.

We furnish text-books free

Students may board and room in town. During the past year the school has had an attendance of 934 students. Classes in the new required studies, Algebra and Civil Government, are formed each term.

Fall term begins Sept. 5, '05
WINTER TERM BEGINS JAN. 2, '06

Show this circular to your friends and send for a catalogue

ALBERT E. MALTBY, Principal

TUITION FREE
to TEACHERS

The cost of Board and Tuition per year is $200. The State appropriation makes UITION FREE TO TEACHERS, and expenses to such persons reduce to $137 per year. Fall term of Sixteen weeks, to a person receiving State aid, $52; Winter term of Twelve weeks, under same conditions, $39; Spring term of Fourteen weeks, under same conditions, $46; The new Course of Study for Pennsylvania State Normal Schools is now in effect. It adds a full year of required work, and prepares students for higher positions as teachers, or for admission to college. A registration fee of two dollars each term is required.

Original advertisement for Slippery Rock Normal School circa 1905

SLIPPERY ROCK NORMAL SCHOOL
MARCH 1889
SLIPPERY ROCK STATE TEACHERS COLLEGE
AUGUST 1927
SLIPPERY ROCK STATE COLLEGE
JUNE 1960
NOW WE ARE...
SLIPPERY ROCK UNIVERSITY
JULY 1, 1983

SOUVENIR OF SLIPPERY ROCK UNIVERSITY OF PENNSYLVANIA DEDICATION 12:01 A.M. JULY 1, 1983

*Souvenir of Slippery Rock University of Pennsylvania
Dedication, July 1, 1983*

The previous 94 years had witnessed the founding of the Slippery Rock State Normal School in 1889; the movement to a four-year State Teachers College in 1927; the expansion to a multi-purpose State College in 1960 and now the ascension to university status. A glorious celebration was held on campus at the Keister Road entrance, beginning 11:00 pm on June 30, 1983. At the stroke of midnight, a new entrance sign was unveiled.[861] Fireworks were set off announcing Slippery Rock University of Pennsylvania, the State System of Higher Education. Festivities continued well into the morning of July 1, 1983 and included dancing in the streets to a live band, a 250 pound cake and an abundance of refreshments.[862] Hundreds of people from the expanded community attended and participated in the celebration.

One of the first Council of Trustee actions taken after the creation of the University was the approval of the Employee Basic Tuition Fee Waiver Program.[863] Virtually all university employees were provided a spouse and dependent child waiver of the basic tuition fee and the advance tuition deposit fee. The first baccalaureate degree could be earned provided the student maintained good academic standing. President Reinhard expressed his deep appreciation to the Council of Trustees for approving this program which offered such a wonderful opportunity to the families of faculty and staff to receive higher learning at their university.[864]

Extra curricular opportunities also increased during the Reinhard era. A chapter of Phi Eta Sigma, a national freshman academic honorary fraternity, was chartered in the spring of 1982. Members were inducted, officers were installed and President Reinhard hosted a reception at his home for the students, faculty and staff involved.[865] University Union programming expanded dramatically and complemented student life. In the 1981-82 school year more than 125 programs were provided students with more than 500 programs planned for 1983-84.[866]

Students were instrumental in working with members of the Communication Department to develop a new FM educational radio station, which took to the air on July 1, 1983. An advisory council established through the department was initiated under the chairmanship of Larry Berg of Pittsburgh's famous KDKA radio station. The new station would act in cooperation with WRCK; a student coordinated and funded radio station.[867]

The Freshmen Studies Program, coordinated by Dr. Larry Cobb, received acclaim from the State Department of Education in the early 1980s. A presentation entitled "A Glimpse of Freshmen Studies: Teaching and Learning in New Modes" was provided the Council of Trustees in the spring 1983.[868] The interdisciplinary program included experiences in human inquiry, critical thinking and logical reasoning. New freshmen were team taught by faculty and staff from various backgrounds and disciplines.

After a special presentation to the Council of Trustees in the fall, 1983, the ALTER Project, spearheaded by Dr. Robert Macoskey, gained momentum for implementation.[869] The project was designed to create a regional center for experimentation, development and demonstration of practical alternatives in agriculture and energy production at an intermediate scale on the campus. In order to become a reality, the project would need outside financial support. In the spring, 1984, the Council of Trustees adopted a resolution endorsing "a two-fold intensive exploration of both the practical as well as the academic aspects of the ALTER, a project which could serve to stimulate additional agricultural and energy potential of the nation by creating practical alternatives in food and energy production". [870]

Tailgate party with Rocky, Cheerleaders, Rocklettes and Band members, Three Rivers Stadium, 1982

Campus technology took on new form in 1984. The plan called for the acquisition and installation of approximately 30 microcomputers and related equipment in various academic departments for the direct use by faculty, staff and students. Prior to this time, a large mainframe computer, housed in Maltby Hall, provided the technology power to several cathode ray tubes in various administrative offices and academic departments. The CRTs permitted the viewing and processing of information such as registration of classes, student and university accounting, admissions, financial aid and general record keeping. With the purchase of a new central processor and improved academic software in 1984, the computing facilities and capabilities were comparable to those at major universities.[871]

The new Master of Science in Administration program was offered for the first time in fall, 1983, to 23 students. The program was described as "a broad management degree enabling a person to develop administrative and management skills applicable to public, not-for-profit and profit organizations".[872]

While enrollment of new freshmen increased 3% during the fall of 1982, more than 400 new transfer students, which was another record, joined them.[873] The growth continued the next year with nearly 1500 new freshmen, reportedly the most qualified class in nearly 15 years, and again more than 400 transfer students. The total enrollment for the fall semester 1983 stood at approximately 6,200 students.[874]

The athletic program continued to gain prominence during the Reinhard era. The fall of 1982, kicked off the first Butler County Football Classic which was co-sponsored by Slippery Rock State College and the Butler County Chamber of Commerce. Included in the first Classic were a parade and a pep rally in downtown Butler and an elaborate pre-game show at the game site, Butler Area High School Football Field. Slippery Rock, led by its new coach, Don Ault, defeated West Liberty State College by a score of 21-8.[875] The mystique of the college with the unusual name continued throughout the fall with ABC-TV coming to campus to film the Homecoming Football game.[876]

Both the Women's Gymnastic team and the Wrestling team distinguished themselves throughout the winter of 1982. The women won the state conference championships and went on to regional competition. The

College hosted the NCAA Eastern Regional Wrestling Championships. Four SRSC wrestlers won honors, earning trips to the revered national tournament at Iowa State University. Coach Fred Powell received honors from the Board of Trustees for his team's success.[877]

Wishing to recognize the importance of former athletes, the College established the Athletic Hall of Fame. Mr. Bob Prince, a well-known Pittsburgh sports broadcaster, emceed the first ceremony, held in 1983. Seven featured athletes were inducted into the Hall of Fame: N. Kerr Thompson, posthumously, represented by his widow, Margaret, Stan Dziedzic, Shirley Comstock, Elmer "Tuggles" Gross, John Kaufman, Connie Palumbo and Vivian Stringer.[878]

With the development of the new State System of Higher Education, a new athletic conference was formed in the fall 1983, the Pennsylvania State Athletic Conference. Mr. Donald Kelly was hired as Commissioner with an office in Hershey to lead the new NCAA Division II conference.[879]

Given Slippery Rock University's long and distinguished athletic reputation, it was no surprise when, in the spring 1984, Dr. Reinhard was named as one of forty-four college and university presidents to serve on the new President's Commission of the National Collegiate Athletic Association. The new commission was formed to review the relationship of academics and athletics at the NCAA.[880]

Throughout President Reinhard's tenure, there was a persistent effort to promote the College through special programs and activities. These became annual events: Parent's Day, Business and Industry Day, Legislative Day, Community Day and the Madrigal Christmas Dinner. It was planned that the invited guests would not only enjoy the program, but would also learn a good deal about their public institution of higher education at Slippery Rock. Often times, the organized activities included a reception at the President's residence.

Other special programs were planned not as annual events, but nevertheless were conducted with a similar

Computer Center Driector, Gary Goepfert with new IBM 370, Model 148 computer, early 1980's

Special Olympics, 1979

purpose of promoting the College. One such example was in March 24-26, 1983. The College co-hosted with Slippery Rock Area High School, the Region I Band Festival of the Pennsylvania Music Educators Association. One hundred eighty musicians, from 100 high schools participated in this event. For President Reinhard, "having the Festival on our campus was a tremendous privilege for the College and our Department of Music. Of course, while these high school students were participating in the Festival; they were also enjoying Slippery Rock's lifestyle.[881]

International student programs began to flourish during the early 1980s under the direction of Mr. Stan Kendziorski. Due to increased relations with the community, the Town-Gown organization assisted with the welcoming of international students by sponsoring the annual International Student Reception. At the request of the University of Salzburg, President Reinhard visited the University in October of 1981 signing a cooperative agreement enabling Slippery Rock students to participate in summer language programs.[882] The College continued to increase the number of its international students as well as the foreign countries represented. The number of countries represented expanded from 28 in 1981 to 32 in 1983. Peru, Cameroon and Sweden were the countries most represented.[883]

As its influence continued to expand far beyond its local surroundings, Slippery Rock State College decided

Fred McFeely Rogers, first honorary doctorate recipient, December, 1982

President Reinhard with Chief Tom Davis,
S.R. Volunteer Fire Department

to recognize those who were enriching the lives of others by awarding them an honorary doctoral degree. The first to be so honored was Fred McFeely Rogers, well-known Pittsburgh television personality whose morning program enriched the lives of countless children over the past two decades. It was at the College's Commencement on December 18, 1982, that President Reinhard awarded Mr. Rogers the honorary Doctor of Humane Letters degree for his work over the past nineteen years in helping children "grow intellectually and emotionally through his very popular television program."[884] At a reception at President Reinhard's house, children - young and old - welcomed Dr. Rogers to the Slippery Rock neighborhood.

As more students came to college uncertain of an academic major, Slippery Rock allowed, even encouraged students to enroll without identifying a specific academic major. The Undeclared Student Program was immediately attractive to new freshmen, and by the fall of 1983, more than 700 students were registered as undeclared. These students received academic advisors who had been trained to assist them in identifying personal interests, abilities and values in order to make informed major choices.

The topic of desegregation was dominating conversations in higher education in early 1983. Comprehensive desegregation plans of Pennsylvania public colleges and universities were ordered by federal court Judge Pratt to be submitted to the Office of Civil Rights in Washington D.C. by June 20, 1983.[885] On March 28, 1983 Dr. Reinhard and other Slippery Rock officials met with representatives of the other 13 state-owned institutions in Harrisburg to discuss the Pennsylvania Department of Education's Desegregation Plan.[886]

A well known historical landmark, The Old Stone House, located 5 miles south of campus, was the topic of conversation during the fall of 1982. The College proposed a plan to the Commonwealth's Historical and Museum Commission to assume operational responsibility of the property.[887] The plan was approved by the Commission, effective January 1, 1983. A renewable, annual lease agreement recognized Slippery Rock State College as the administrator of the facility and properties as an "Educational and Historical Center", allowing considerable freedom within that context.[888]

As part of the Butler County Chamber of Commerce's Butler County Awareness Week, the first open house and reception was held at the Old Stone House on January 27, 1983. A much larger public program, Old Stone House Day, took place on April 16, 1983. Period craft demonstrations, tours, lectures, a reenactment of a civil war encampment, a bluegrass concert and a one act play by the Theatre Department students comprised the day's festivities.[889]

Early in 1982, members of the newly established Office of Alumni Affairs and Development engaged in discussions with the owners of the Riviera Dormitory. Interest was generated to donate the facility as a major gift to the College. The dormitory had been built by private developers on Main Street across from Morrow Way and opened to 350 freshmen men in the fall, 1966.[890] On December 14, 1982 the Slippery Rock State College Foundation, Incorporated officially received the dormitory from Stanley B. and Marilyn Kraus, Lynn H. and Elaine J. Luxenburg and Arch and Phyllis Lhormer. The dormitory, valued at 4.5 million dollars was by far the largest gift ever received by the College. The renamed Kraus Hall was dedicated October 23, 1983.[891]

Old Stone House, stagecoach post house, five miles south of Slippery Rock, Route 8

Old Stone House in ruins

Old Stone House, reconstructed; managed by Slippery Rock University

At a time when Kraus Hall was undergoing major renovations, other campus facilities were being made handicap accessible. Exterior ramps, special exterior doors and first floor restrooms were constructed in Old Main, Bailey Library, Morrow Field House, Spotts World Cultures Building and the Eisenberg Classroom Building. In late 1983, the University was maintaining more than 4.1 miles of roadways and approximately 12 miles of concrete sidewalks on the more than 600 acre campus. The initial phase of cutting curbs, new sidewalks and barrier elimination in the accessibility plan came with a price tag of more than $660,000.[892]

Through increased promotional efforts, more constituencies better understood Slippery Rock University and its outstanding characteristics. It was a period of awakening for the region and renaissance for this new University. In spite of the political entanglements and resulting difficulties of the 1970s, the Reinhard administration had set the course for a new direction – one of recognition, promotion and advancement as a new regional university.

Rumblings of Dr. Reinhard's candidacy for another presidency began to be heard on campus throughout the spring of 1984. Then, in a special meeting of the Council of Trustees on May 12, the rumors ended after a public announcement that Dr. Herb. F. Reinhard had accepted the presidency at Morehead State University in Kentucky. The Trustees recommended to Chancellor James

McCormick that Dr. Robert N. Aebersold, Vice President for Academic Affairs at Slippery Rock University, serve as the Interim President. Dr. Aebersold would serve effective July 1, 1984 until a permanent president could be identified through a national search.[893]

The regular Council of Trustees meeting June 8, 1984 presented a rather typical agenda. However, other than action to name the University's Art Gallery for Mrs. Martha Gault - longtime teacher and chairperson of the Art Department who retired in January of 1969 - the majority of discussion focused on the departing president. Chairperson Jack Arthurs, along with other members of the Council, gave testimony to Dr. and Mrs. Reinhard's leadership and good work.[894] Dr. Reinhard expressed his deep appreciation to the Trustees for their unfailing support which enabled Slippery Rock University to experience one of the "most dramatic turnarounds that any college or university had ever experienced within what most would view as a relatively short period of time." He assured the Trustees that the University was "a very sound, stable and proud institution with a very good reputation academically …"[895]

And so, the tumultuous times of the 1970s with four leaders at the helm from 1976 to 1979 had ended. Now, Dr. Herb. F. Reinhard, the president, who brought a sense of reconciliation and redirection to the new University was leaving Slippery Rock. The campus was poised, awaiting new and hopefully stable leadership.

Saxigena photo of East/West Gym in the snow, early 1983

Professor Akiko Kotani
teaches student in weaving class, about 1980

Women's basketball, early 1980's

Mary Alice Paul's famous playgroup in the Lab School (McKay Ed. Building)
where parents had to enroll child at birth to get on the waiting list, 1982

Robert McMullen, right, presents to John Watson, left, and Robert Watson,
awards for Rock Athletics Phonathon, early 1980's

President Reinhard, right, Athletic Director Bob Oliver, left and John Watson
show off the new SRSC hat, early 1980's

William Sonntag, president of First National Bank of Slippery Rock,
presents an award to President Reinhard, early 1980's

Professor Robert Macoskey presents President Reinhard with an inaugural gift, May 1980

Dean William Meise prepares to lead administrators into the inaugural arena, May 1980

President Reinhard with the Homecoming Queen, Darci Munn,
and Homecoming King, Scott Pennewill, Fall, 1982

CHAPTER IX

A Century of Success

At his first meeting with the Council of Trustees on September 10, 1984, Interim President Robert Aebersold made it very clear that it was not his intent to play the role of temporary caretaker while occupying the President's chair. As proof, he set forth these very aggressive seven goals for the 1984-85 academic year:

1. Improve the academic programs
2. Establish a student recruitment and retention plan
3. Improve the University's living and learning environment
4. Implement an effective planning process
5. Establish a more effective management process
6. Promote public relations for the University and the State System of Higher Education
7. Establish compliance with the Office of Civil Rights desegregation plan[896]

He also offered the Trustees a status report as the University began its fall term. For example, the fall 1984 freshman class was the best prepared in twelve years and new transfer students had increased about twelve percent over the previous year. The amount of money appropriated to the University from the state had increased ten percent from the previous year.[897] He was pleased to report that a new Honors Program was in place and a degree program in Music Education was also brought to their attention.[898] And, with understandable pride, he reported how the Army ROTC cadets from Slippery Rock University who attended the Advanced Camp at Fort Bragg, North Carolina, during the summer received first honors among the twenty-one units from Pennsylvania and placed fifth among the 111 units from the Eastern Seaboard.[899] He also announced that the new Martha Gault Art Gallery, located in the Eisenberg Classroom Building, was opening with a reception

on September 16,1984.[900] In closing, Dr. Aebersold informed the Trustees that the offering of an accredited five-year master's degree program in Physical Therapy was under consideration.[901]

In late November 1984, Dr. James McCormick, the recently appointed Chancellor of the new State System of Higher Education, visited the campus to review the University's Institutional Goals.[902] Dr. McCormick was no stranger to Pennsylvania. A graduate of Indiana University of Pennsylvania, Dr. McCormick had taught at Shippensburg State College prior to his serving as President of Bloomsburg State College. Through a national search, he was selected to serve as the first Chancellor of the new System.

The Presidential Search Committee at Slippery Rock University was busy reviewing the 117 applications it had received with hopes to reduce the pool to the nine candidates who would be invited to campus the latter part of January, 1985.[903] The Committee would then send their recommendation to the Council of Trustees, which would select three candidates to forward on to the Chancellor in Harrisburg. The governing board of the relatively new State System of Higher Education, the Board of Governors, would then appoint the new president at their March, 1985 meeting.[904]

Meanwhile, the very active day-to-day life of the University continued. Increased development efforts began to pay dividends. The University changed the name of the "Dollars for Student Scholars" program to the "University Academic Scholarship Program" and boasted an increase of $14,000 raised over the previous year.[905] Faculty and staff continued to lead the list of contributors of this successful program.

In order for the University to assume responsibility for its accounting system by July 1, 1985, a structural change took place and the position of Comptroller was created. This adjustment was one of several changes resulting from Act 188, creating the State System of Higher Education, passed by the Pennsylvania Legislature which gave the University more fiscal flexibility. [906]

Upgrades in computer technology prompted Dr. Aebersold to make the following announcement in December 1984: "Slippery Rock began its movement into the modern era of mainframe computing with the installation of an IBM 4361 computer. The eight megabyte 4361 brought with it a four-fold increase in processor memory and three times the processing power of the IBM model 148 which it replaced. More important than the 4361 was the complete systems software conversion to IBM's Virtual Machine (VM) operating system. This system and its vastly enhanced functionality provide computing capabilities, primarily for our students, which are equivalent to those available at large universities such as Penn State. To deliver these capabilities to our students and faculty, approximately thirty-eight new terminals will have been installed by year-end. Fourteen additional terminals have also been provided for administrative offices. The microcomputer lab with nine IBM personal computers has been in operation for most of the year and has been proven to be a welcomed addition to the university's academic computing facilities. Microcomputers have also been integrated into instructional programs in Geography, Physics, Chemistry, Special Education, Psychology and Curriculum and Instruction (Elementary Education and Secondary Education)."[907]

A personal fitness requirement for all undergraduate students was implemented in the fall of 1984. The requirement could be fulfilled by successfully completing the Personal Physical Fitness course in swimming, aerobics or jogging.[908]

The men's tennis team led other spring sport teams with a record of sixteen wins and only five losses in 1984. One of Coach Jim McFarland's player's earned All-America status. The Golf team also enjoyed an outstanding season, earning eleventh place honors in the NCAA Division II Championship with two golfers earning All-America recognition.[909]

Dr. Charles Zuzak, Acting Vice President for Academic Affairs, reported that a total of 50 students from 32 countries had enrolled for the fall, 1984.[910] In addition, more American students

and faculty were traveling abroad. The University had established opportunities for its students majoring in Education to student teach in one of three Department of Defense Dependent schools, Stuttgart or Munich, Germany or Vicenza, Italy. Five students had taken advantage of the opportunity in 1981-82, eleven students in 1982-83 and nineteen students in 1983-84.[911] Thirty-six students studied abroad in 1983-84, an increase from ten students the previous year. Eleven faculty were involved in university-sponsored international experiences.[912]

Presidential level drama unfolded on February 11, 1985, when a special meeting of the Council of Trustees was called. Mr. H. Donald Moss, Chairperson of the

Volunteer fire chief, Tom Davis, receives donation of $10,000 from Dr. Aebersold, 1985

Presidential Search Committee, announced that eight candidates had been interviewed by various constituencies on campus in late January.[913] Mr. Moss went on to say that while "all candidates were extremely well qualified and impressive"; only five candidates would be recommended to the Council of Trustees for their review and action.[914] The Council went into executive session for several hours and at 5:15 p.m. reconvened. The Chairperson of the Council of Trustees, Mr. Jack R. Arthurs, announced to the campus community that the following three names were being forwarded to Chancellor McCormick for his review: Dr. Robert N Aebersold, Dr. Laurence Aianni and Dr. William C. Merwin.[915]

Considerable speculation took place on campus over the next month with various theories being offered for why a particular candidate should get the job. Since the University had not witnessed an interim president appointed since Dr. Norman Weisenfluh nearly thirty years earlier in 1956, there were those who thought it was unlikely that Dr. Aebersold would be selected.

Finally, Chancellor James McCormick in Harrisburg broke the silence on March 19, 1985, with the news that the University's next president would be Dr. Robert N. Aebersold, effective July 1, 1985.[916] Dr. McCormick explained: "We are indeed fortunate to have an educator of Dr. Aebersold's credentials in this System. His seventeen years of experience at Slippery Rock University have been an excellent preparation for his presidency. He enjoys the confidence and support of the entire university community. I am personally pleased that Dr. Aebersold has agreed to serve as the thirteenth president of Slippery Rock University."[917]

A native of Ohio, born in Granville, Dr. Aebersold earned his bachelor's degree in Physical Education and Science from Ohio Wesleyan University in 1957, his master's degree from Ohio University in 1959, and his Ph.D. from the University of Maryland in 1969. He taught in the public schools of Oberlin, Ohio, Hanover College, Indiana, and the University of Maryland. He came to Slippery Rock State College in 1968 as an assistant professor in the Physical Education Department, was promoted to associate professor in 1969, and professor in 1972. Dr. Aebersold served as chairperson of the department from 1972 until 1978; interim vice president for Academic Affairs in 1979; and vice president of Academic Affairs in 1980.[918]

After being selected to be the 13th president of Slippery Rock University, Dr. Aebersold understood so

well that if he were to be successful in achieving his goals for the school, he would have to have the support from the community it served. Increasingly, state universities across the country were coming to realize what private

Robert N. Aebersold, President, 1984-1997

universities always knew that financial support from alumni and other benefactors in the community they served was essential if they were to have the resources necessary to maintain high standards of academic excellence, research and public services. As President Aebersold explained: "There is no question that we will be expected to raise more money than we have in the past, and we need guidance for the right structure".[919] Unfortunately, the steel industry, which was the backbone of the economy of the region surrounding Slippery Rock University was virtually gone by 1985. This, however, did not deter President Aebersold who went out and sought guidance in managing the University's fund-raising campaign from well-known development consultants Ketchum, Inc.[920]

Dr. Russell M. Wright, Class of 1923, (left),
with President Aebersold, September, 1985

It was with pride that Dr. Aebersold recommended to the Council of Trustees, at their April, 1985 meeting, the naming of the physical fitness center being developed in the East Gymnasium, the Russell M. Wright Fitness Center.[921] Dr. Wright, a 1923 graduate of Slippery Rock State Normal School, had realized a distinguished career in osteopathic medicine, focusing on sports medicine. His strong professional network included employment

with the United States Olympic Weightlifting Team, the Detroit Tigers and the Detroit Pistons. Also an author, Dr. Wright published a textbook, *The Making of an Olympic Champion.* Through a generous donation and sale of stock, more than $45,000 was realized for the development of the new fitness center. Formal dedication of the center occurred on September 14, 1985.[922]

Strongly interested in expanding the University's international opportunities, Dr. Aebersold accepted nomination as a representative to the United States Advisory Council traveling to Cairo, Egypt, during the summer of 1985. The Council met with numerous Egyptian university leaders to develop linkages for students and faculty.[923]

Committed to his goal of compliance with the Office of Civil Rights desegregation plan, President Aebersold assembled a representation of faculty and staff for active participation in the Symposium on Desegregation in Harrisburg in June, 1985. He reminded the university community that "the University is committed to improving the admission and retention of minority students, faculty and staff".[924]

In the late 1970s and 1980s, as the steel industry continued its decline in Western Pennsylvania, many residents in the Butler County area lost their jobs. As

Russell M. Wright Fitness Center, East Gym, 1985

an active member of the Community Development Corporation of Butler County, President Aebersold was able to assist in the securing of a $1 million grant from the Commonwealth of Pennsylvania for the development of the former Pullman Standard site.[925] President Aebersold, aware that over the past three decades his university had cooperated informally with the community college in Butler, founded in 1964, decided it was time for these two academic institutions to enter into more formal agreements. In addition to identifying more clearly the general responsibilities of both institutions, the special services which Slippery Rock University would provide the associate degree graduates of Butler County Community College were carefully articulated.[926] It should be remembered that Butler County is one of two counties in the Commonwealth of Pennsylvania which offers to all of its citizens both undergraduate and graduate levels of higher learning in its public community college and a state-owned university.

The fall of 1985 was busy with the traditional Homecoming, Parent's Day and Saturday Visitation activities, along with different workshops and conferences by on-campus and off-campus organizations. Appropriately, the University hosted the Special Olympics competition on campus. For the second consecutive year, the Army ROTC cadets earned the Governor's Trophy for Excellence for the top performing program in Eastern United States.[927] For the first time, a Slippery Rock University cadet, Brad Mifsud, distinguished himself and the University by earning the honor of the outstanding cadet in Eastern United States.[928]

In his search to find ways for Slippery Rock University "to be more efficient in its operation", President Aebersold, at the beginning of the 1985 fall term, formed a committee to review the University's structure.[929]

Improvement of academic programs was also an important goal that President Aebersold addressed

Major Lee Kitchen,(left), officer in charge of Army ROTC at SRU, shares the Governor's Trophy for Excellence, for best ROTC Unit in Pennsylvania with president Aebersold, 1985

President Aebersold (right), presents a plaque to Mrs. N. Kerr Thompson in recognition of her husband's significant contribution to the University, April 1986.

immediately. New degree programs and academic accomplishments were realized during the new president's first year, a Bachelor of Arts degree in Dance and a Bachelor of Science degree in Computer Science – Information System track.[930] The Dance program was the first program submitted for approval since Act 188 created a new program approval process.

On July 1, 1985 Bailey Library acquired its half-millionth volume and celebrated the event by applying this number to a volume entitled *The American Citizen* by former president Dr. Albert Maltby.[931] The second major accomplishment was the listing of the Department of Academic Support Services in the National Directory of Exemplary Developmental Programs.[932]

Chancellor James McCormick (left) and
President Aebersold in discussion with
SRU representatives, April 1986

American poet, Dr. Samuel Hazo, was the guest speaker at the University's seventh annual Academic Honors Convocation.[933] Developed and organized by Mr. Louis Razzano, Assistant Vice President for Academic Affairs, the convocation had grown to be the featured academic honors activity of the year. Although nationally and internationally recognized speakers provided keynote addresses, the convocation always focused on the students receiving honors for their academic achievement.

Good relationships with the borough lead to the development of a gerontology program, supported by grants, in the local United Methodist Church.[934] Senior citizens in the area enjoyed the attention, programs and good lunches they received from students, faculty and staff in charge of the center.

The borough and university police forces benefited from a special ten-week human relations training program developed by Dr. William Shiner, chairperson of the Parks, Recreation and Environmental Education Department.[935] The outcome was the groups "better understand one another, which will result in better service to the community and university."[936]

To demonstrate some of the support often given students, Mr. Dale L. Ekas, Director of Financial Aid, reported growth of financial aid to the Council of Trustees. In 1966-67, students received $871,242 in aid. In 1975-76, the total aid grew to $4,800,953. The financial aid that students received in 1985-86 totaled $12,641,118.[937] This good news was reported on the eve of the Gramm/Rudman/Hollings legislation, which reduced Pell grant awards to 618 students, with 311 students losing their awards completely.[938]

The athletic program enjoyed success in 1985-86 in almost every sport with many capturing titles. The men's cross country team was undefeated going into the conference championship meet.[939] The women's volleyball team was ranked number one in eastern United States and sixteenth nationally with a record of 22-3.[940] The PSAC-West title was captured by the men's soccer team.[941] For the first time in history, the women's basketball team progressed to the NCAA regional finals.[942] Several women swimmers advanced to the national meet in Florida while two wrestlers competed in the National Division I tournament in Iowa City.[943] Finally, the cheerleading squad took top honors at the National NCAA Division II Cheerleading Championships in San Diego, California.[944]

By the end of the spring, the committee on structure had presented its recommendation to the president. On June 16, 1986, Dr. Aebersold announced the structure he felt would best move the University forward under his leadership.[945] The academic side of the house would be divided into five units, managed by deans; Arts and Sciences; Professional Studies; Information Science and Business Administration; Graduate Studies; and Academic Services and Retention.[946] This structure acknowledged for the first time a college of business. With a focus on both, friend raising and fund raising, a

Louis Razzano, (fifth from right in first row), faculty and students of the
Summer Academy for Accelerated High School Students, mid 1980's

new division of University Advancement was announced, the president stating "the primary charge to the division is to coordinate the University's advancement and fund raising programs as the University moves toward its centennial celebration in 1989."[947]

The State System of Higher Education was also engaged in advancement. To honor the members of the

Pennsylvania General Assembly who were System graduates, the Pennsylvania Council of Alumni Associations sponsored the first Legislative Recognition Dinner. Dr. Aebersold attended the activity held in Harrisburg which assisted in establishing a good working relationship between several members of the General Assembly and the new State System.[948]

Paul R. Onuska, (right), Distinguished Alumnus for 1986, meets with
old friends, John A. Watson, center, and Robert J. Watson,
Alumni Association past presidents, 1986

As the University moved quickly into the 1986-87 academic year, nine goals provided direction: "to provide quality academic programming that meets the needs of a changing society; to promote effective programs of student admission and retention; to enhance the environment for academic achievement and personal development; to continue institutional planning; to continue to provide effective leadership and management; to insure equal access to educational opportunities through affirmative action; to insure the recruitment, retention, and promotion of minority faculty and staff; to continue to improve the University's external relations; and to continue to improve the University's internal relations. Special emphasis for this year will be on student retention and enhancements of the liberal studies curriculum in our general education area."[949] These goals were reviewed and approved at the System level.

Enrollment in several monitored areas increased. New freshmen and transfer students admitted for the fall had increased by 169 students over the previous year.[950] African American student enrollment increased to 185 or approximately five percent of the total enrollment, largely due to 89 new freshmen, a thirty-nine percent increase over the previous year.[951] Summer school, 1986 enrollment also climbed 200 students to a total of 2436.[952] The previous year, Mr. Eliott G. Baker had been named Director of Recruitment and Retention.[953] The importance of student enrollment was being realized, identified in university goals and an increasing factor in determining the University's vitality and structure.

Ivan McKeever (left), with President Aebersold at the McKeever Environmental Center, August 1987

Biology professor, Murray A. Shellgren (center), receives recognition from Rep. Joseph A. Steighner (right), and President Aebersold for his years of research of the Muddy Creek Watershed, March 1987

Management of the McKeever Environmental Learning Center, a state owned facility for students of all ages to study the environment, was transferred to the University on August 1, 1986.[954] Formerly under the administration of Clarion University, the State System of Higher Education had requested Slippery Rock University to take over the Center. Located approximately 22 miles north of campus, between Sandy Lake and Stoneboro, the center was situated on a tract of beautiful land donated to the State several years earlier by Mr. Ivan McKeever. A separate $250,000 budget allocated by the State to the

Robert A. Lowry (right), Distinguished Alumnus, 1985, President Aebersold (center) and John A. Watson, Alumni past-president, June 1985

214

University supported the Center.[955]Later that academic year, the Alumni Association Office relocated to the first floor of Old Main. The Association was searching for a facility that would permit it to increase its support to the University. Existing houses, and vacant property close to campus, were under review.

The facility vacated by the Alumni Association, situated adjacent to the President's home on Maltby Avenue, was renovated to house several campus operations including Academic Services, Graduate Studies and Off Campus Programs. Once completed, the facility was named the Robert A. Lowry Center in honor of Dr. Lowry who had been employed at the University from 1956 until his retirement in 1981.[956] Dr. Lowry was the University's first Director of Admissions and served Slippery Rock in several administrative roles including Acting President in 1968. The Lowry Center was dedicated on June 7, 1988.[957]

Academic focus continued with The Middle States Accrediting Association reaffirming the University's accreditation after a 1986 mid-point review.[958] The review recognized continued progress since the 1981 self-study and campus visit, citing the next visit in 1991.[959] Another outstanding Academic Honors Convocation was held on October 22, 1986 with the president stating "this event has grown in stature and is extremely important to the University".[960]

President Aebersold (left), and Shanghai International University President, Dr. Hu Meng Hao sign a faculty and student exchange agreement, April 1987

In 1987, The State System of Higher Education created the Pennsylvania Academy for the Profession of Teaching. President Aebersold was asked to serve as a member of this important academy which was "designed to put school and university leaders in partnership to strengthen teacher preparation programs and the development of teachers at all levels".[961]

That year academic partnerships were being forged not only within the Commonwealth but around the globe as well. An agreement with Shanghai International University, Republic of China provided a new faculty exchange program for the two universities.[962] At an on-campus reception on April 11, 1987, President Hu Meng Hao and President Aebersold signed the agreement.[963]

Off campus, credit-generating programs were on the increase in the mid 1980s. The University offered courses in learning sites such as St. Francis and Jameson Memorial Hospitals in New Castle as well as the Mercer Correctional Facility.[964] However, the location where enrollment was growing dramatically was Cranberry Township in southern Butler County, one of the fastest growing areas in the state. In the fall of 1986, sixty-seven students attended three classes offered by Slippery Rock University. In the 1987 spring semester more than one hundred students registered for five classes.[965] After meeting with the Cranberry Township Chamber of Commerce, President Aebersold was pleased to report "They were extremely interested in the kinds of programs Slippery Rock University has to offer."[966]

Realizing more of a responsibility to assist in development of communities in its region, the University created a Center for Economic and Community Development, effective July 1, 1987.[967] The former Executive Director of the Community Development Corporation of Butler County, Ms. Marthann Rettig, was selected director of the new center.[968]

Greek life for students proved a rewarding experience at this time. In March, 1987, SRU held the Seventh Annual Greek Symposium with more than 500 students and consultants in attendance.[969] Slippery Rock's Interfraternity Council received the Lunsford Award for Excellence while the Pan Hellenic Council was recognized with the Leadership and Officer Training Award, in their regions.[970]

Town-Gown relationships were strong and regular communication took place between

President Aebersold (center) and other representatives from SRU meet with representatives from the Western Pennsylvania Advanced Technology Center to discuss possibilities for economic growth, late 1980's

the University and the town promoting discussion of issues before they became problems. In March, 1987 a Town-Gown open forum was held involving nearly sixty faculty, students, staff and townspeople in discussions about issues that typically confront college communities.[971] The members of Slippery Rock's Volunteer Fire Company were, understandably, very appreciative of the $107,500 the University had donated to them over the last decade.[972]

As the first year of Dr. Aebersold's presidency was drawing to a close, the Council of Trustees carried out its responsibility of formally evaluating his leadership at Slippery Rock University. All of the Trustees were so pleased with everything he had done in the past twelve months that they recommended to the Chancellor of the State System of Higher Education in Pennsylvania that the term of Dr. Aebersold be extended "for the maximum permitted".[973]

A new mission statement was developed for the University, fall 1987. "The fundamental mission of Slippery Rock University is to provide high quality academic instruction. Complementary missions are to conduct scholarly research, promote professional performance, and address the educationally-related economic, social, cultural, and recreational needs of our region."[974]

Affirmative action practices were utilized in employing faculty and professional staff for the fall, 1987. Of the thirty-seven positions advertised, women filled twenty-five positions and minorities filled four positions. President Aebersold announced "we can be proud of the efforts made in the recruitment of qualified females and minorities in an attempt to replenish professional positions now and in the future."[975]

The University's enrollment continued to grow so that by the fall of 1987, a total of 6,871 students were enrolled, a four percent increase over the previous year.[976] However, one area was not growing. In the Operational Audit of the Auditor General, Mr. Don Bailey wrote to Governor Robert P. Casey stating: "declining non-resident enrollment should be addressed," noting that the University's enrollment was growing, while the percentage of non-resident students had decreased from twenty-two percent in 1982 to sixteen percent.[977] The Auditor General went on to recommend that the State System of Higher Education create a committee to propose strategies for stabilization and attainment of non-resident enrollment goals.[978] SRU management responded by sending a written request to the State System asking that non-resident tuition be frozen until the committee could provide a thorough understanding of the importance of non-resident student enrollment.[979] The request was denied.

To provide leadership for the newly created College of Information Science and Business Administration, a national search was conducted. Dr. Frank V. Mastrianna, former Dean and Acting President of Xavier University, Cincinnati, Ohio was selected.[980] The College, primarily housed in the Eisenberg Classroom Building, was composed of five academic departments, accounting, economics and finance, communication, computer science, and marketing and management.[981]

All colleges within the University participated in the Academic Honors Convocation on October 21, 1987. The main speaker was Attorney Patricia Russell-McCloud, Atlanta, Georgia, recognized by President Aebersold "as one of the most dynamic and eloquent orators in America."[982] Honored for outstanding contributions in their fields, were; Mrs. Nien Cheng, author of the *New York Times* best seller, *Life and Death in Shanghai*; Dr. Oswald Ndang, 1972 alumnus and Zimbabwe Ambassador to Moscow; Mr. John C. Jordan, President of Capital Investors, Inc. and Fairlane Development Corporation; and Mr. Lanny Frattore, voice of the Pittsburgh Pirates.[983]

Evening classes were offered in the North Allegheny area.[984] Off-campus enrollment had grown to over 600 students with classes taught in Mercer, Cranberry Township, New Castle, Franklin, Washington, Dubois, Beaver and North Allegheny.[985]

The face of Slippery Rock University students was changing as the University became better known across the United States and around the world. By fall 1987, students from thirty states and forty-five foreign countries were enrolled at the University.[986] New cultures were being introduced and new traditions were being formed. Generally, the international students earned slightly higher grades than their American counterparts.[987] The recruitment and retention of international students was largely the responsibility of Mr. Stan Kendziorski, Director, and Mrs. Pam Frigot, Assistant Director of International Studies. Several faculty and staff also assisted the office. By 1987, the University had established strong relationships with several international schools across the world and the Department of Defense

President Aebersold (left), Mr. Stan Kenoziorski (center) and Mr. Phil Kennedy at The Great Wall of China, April 1988

Dependent Schools where American military dependents received their K-12 education.

More Slippery Rock University students were also getting an opportunity to travel abroad. During the 1986-87 year, 120 students studied overseas in credit generating programs while 196 students participated in non-credit experiences.[988] It was clear that the University had set in motion a well supported initiative providing an international perspective to its students by encouraging both the opportunity to learn by traveling overseas and from international students studying on campus. Educational programs were available to Slippery Rock University students in Austria, Japan, Ireland, Germany, England, Italy, Hungary, Scandinavia, Soviet Union, Canada, Belgium and other areas.[989] Students could even student teach overseas. Faculty and professional staff were also enjoying international experiences. In 1986-87, twenty-two faculty and staff participated in international opportunities.[990]

President Aebersold (second from left) being welcomed by officials of Kangweon National University, Korea, April 1988

Kenneth Wilcox, President of the Senior Class (right), and President Aebersold inspect one of the new signs, on Rt 173 south of the boro, purchased by the Senior Class, May 1988

The internationally recognized Elderhostel program, in conjunction with the University's Gerontology program, offered seniors citizens the opportunity of travel and education. Hungary was a popular travel site in the mid 1980s.[991]

During the spring, 1988, President Aebersold, Mr. Kendziorski and Mr. Philip Kennedy of the Department of Accounting, traveled to Kangweon University in Korea, Shanghai International Studies University in China and Kansai Gaidai University in Japan to develop and expand student and faculty exchange agreements.[992] As President Aebersold explained: "Our students will have the opportunity to take part in programs there that might change the direction of their careers and their lives in the future. It will bring students here who will have a great impact on our students who are unable to go there, and those programs will also provide the opportunity for learning on the part of the faculty."[993]

The use of technology on campus was expanding and a greater demand was forthcoming from all constituents. In his report to the Council of Trustees at the end of 1987, Dr. Aebersold explained: "The main area of growth has been in the implementation of microcomputers for both administrative and academic computing. Among the more significant activities for the 1986-87 year were:

1. Upgraded the University's mainframe computer to an IBM 4381 processor having sixteen megabytes of memory. This upgrade provided the increased processing speed and memory required to support the planned increase in the number of on-line applications and terminal users, and to provide capacity for future requirements.
2. Installed a Xerox laser printer to prepare computer printed reports on 8 ½" x 11" cut sheet paper.
3. Installed the University's second microcomputer lab. This lab in Eisenberg and the other in Spotts provided approximately fifty IBM microcomputers for general use by all students, faculty and staff.
4. Assisted with the planning and installation of two Apple microcomputer labs. One lab

Aerial view of campus, 1988

in Spotts has fifteen microcomputers and the lab in McKay has twenty-four computers.

5. Implemented the mainframe based Wizard Mail electronic mail system, which allows users of the terminal network to send and receive messages via computer terminals."[994]

At Slippery Rock University, student access and success programs had been developed, targeting prospective students residing in urban populations. However, in March 1988, 300 of the 501 school districts in Pennsylvania classified as rural and small, met to discuss common problems relating to curriculum, staffing and opportunities for their students.[995] Many of the issues the districts were dealing with were as a result of the small size of the district and minimal legislative impact. President Aebersold served as a member of the Board of Directors of the Center for Rural Pennsylvania.[996]

After years of development, the University's physical therapy program advanced to the master's degree level.[997] At a special meeting of the Council of Trustees on December 19, 1987, the program was unanimously approved and forwarded on to the Board of Governors of the State System of Higher Education for action.[998]

On January 19, 1988, the Board of Governors approved the program awarding the degree Master of Physical Therapy.[999] The first class of forty students endured a highly competitive admission process. Temporary facilities were constructed to house the program.

With a $1.4 million capital appropriation from the Department of Environmental Resources, water production for the University and the borough of Slippery Rock improved. The project expanded the Slippery Rock Municipal Authority permitting the University to purchase all of its water from the municipal authority instead of producing its own water.[1000]

As one facility was being expanded another facility was being destroyed. Tragically, fire struck the Discovery Building at the McKeever Environmental Learning Center on October 15, 1987, causing more than $20,000 in damages.[1001]

In 1988, Dr. Aebersold established the President's Commission on Race Relations to help set the University's agenda related to the areas of cultural diversity, racism and sexism.[1002] The Commission became an active advisory group from the beginning. It was not a coincidence that Slippery Rock University hosted the Pennsylvania

Women's Consortium annual conference in October 1990.[1003]

Throughout his presidency, Dr. Aebersold expressed a strong interest in developing effective relationships within the local university community. Dr. Aebersold served as president of the Butler County United Way.[1004] Supporting the county's efforts, the University delivered 117 percent of its pledge.[1005] He chose to continue the financial support provided by the University to the local volunteer fire department with another $10,000 gift in December, 1987.[1006] At the same time, an agreement was formed with The Butler County Fire Chiefs Association to use a piece of university property east of Harmony Road to develop and operate a fire school training site.[1007]

SRU staff prepare the donated toys for the community Toys for Tots program, late 1980's

As a former high school teacher, guidance counselor, college professor and coach, Dr. Aebersold put students first in his presidency. From the beginning, he held regular meetings with student leadership, but also enjoyed serendipitous meetings as he managed by walking around campus.[1008] It was no surprise to see the president at student functions especially one as important as Light Up Night. The Association of Residence Hall Students, university personnel and local businesses sponsored the evening of events marking this beginning of the holiday season when they raised money for the Pittsburgh Children's Hospital. In its second year in 1987, the event drew nearly 3,000 people.[1009]

Once students graduated, President Aebersold continued his contact with them as alumni. Nearly 400 alumni and family members attended the Alumni Weekend held in June, 1988. Mrs. Sally Lennox, Alumni Association Director and Mrs. Dorothy Thompson, coordinated this program for Slippery Rock University's many graduates.[1010]

An annual financial audit became the responsibility of the institution with the creation of the State System. "The Slippery Rock University Financial Report, 1986-87 constitutes the first such effort of the University to assess the financial health of the institution in support of the academic program and administrative support services."[1011] The report detailed the solid financial condition of the University.

During the summer 1988, Dr. Charlotte Shapiro, chairperson of the Council of Trustees, announced that the president's contract had been extended to June 30, 1991.[1012] Dr. Aebersold

Dale Liken, class of 1938, surrounded by beautiful women on Alumni Day, from left, Adalin, his wife, Irene Watson and Joy Liken, sister-in-law, June 1988

was honored not only with the good news regarding his contract, but also with the news that he had been selected to receive the Ohio University Alumni Medal of Merit for Achievement in Education Administration.[1013]

Marie Stohrer, flanked by John A. Watson (right) and Robert J. Watson on Alumni Day, after receiving their Distinguished Alumni Awards, June 1988

William Cubbison receives diploma from President Aebersold at graduation, mid 1980's

New degrees, new majors and new partnerships continued to be developed through the late 1980s. During the summer 1988, Pittsburgh Public School students came to SRU to advance their art skills. The Manchester Craftsmen's Guild and university art faculty, coordinated by Mr. Richard Wukich, formed a partnership to support the opportunity. A special Introduction to Studio Arts class was developed for the students.[1014]

The new Bachelor of Science in Cytotechnology degree program was available to students fall 1988. The program offered by the Biology department combined classroom instruction and practical experiences in approved hospitals.[1015]

During the same semester, Dr. Charles Tichy, Chairperson of the Modern Languages and Cultures Department, led a Glasnost Conference on Slippery Rock's campus. Members of the Soviet Embassy and U.S. Department of State participated in the conference with the keynote addresses delivered by an internationally renowned scholar of Soviet Law.[1016]

A campus icon disappeared during the fall 1988. The forty feet tall, steel, water storage tower, located just up the hill from the president's residence and behind Rhoads Hall, was razed. For years, the tower was a prime target of colleges opposing Slippery Rock University in athletic contests. Often times, Slippery Rock students would have to sleep at the tower to discourage invading rivals from attempting to paint opposing slogans on the tower. Now in the late 1980s, it was made obsolete as a result of a new campus fire protection system.[1017]

Slippery Rock University's national notoriety continued to grow. The Marching Band was selected as one of only thirteen bands across America to perform in the famed Macy's Thanksgiving Day Parade, 1988.[1018]

As the University's centennial approached, plans were being developed to launch the first capital campaign, the largest fund raising effort in the history of the University. Mr. C. Bruce Rossiter, Vice President for University Advancement, presented the capital campaign concept and its major gift program, to the Council of Trustees during the summer of 1988.[1019]

Later that year, an All-University Campaign was initiated to raise money from university employees. Begun in mid fall, the campaign touted a goal of $30,000 and would run until mid January. But, by the middle of December, the University family had surpassed its goal with over $35,000 collected with sixty-seven percent of the managers, fifty-five percent of the faculty, fifteen percent of the state university administrators, and nearly eleven percent of the hourly employees contributing to this first of its kind fund raising effort.[1020]

Centennial Gala Banquet, in multipurpose room, University Union, March 29, 1989

On the eve of the University's celebration of its first one hundred years, the Centennial Steering Committee was busy planning a series of dynamic activities, including speaker programs, concerts and special events, throughout the centennial year, beginning in March 1989 and ending March 1990. The Centennial Steering Committee was comprised of Martha J. Haverstick, Chairperson, Timothy L. Walters, Co-Vice Chairperson, John A. Watson, Co-Vice Chairperson, Nancy Aebersold, Robert Allison, Robert Dawson, Donald Kelly, Sandra McKnight and Robert J. Watson, representing the University and the surrounding community.[1021]

The Centennial Convocation was the opening event of the centennial celebration, held on March 29, 1989 in the Morrow Field House. Mr. Terrel Bell, former United States Secretary of Education during the administration of President Ronald W. Reagan, delivered the address. More than 1,500 members of the university family participated in this significant historical event. The convocation was followed by a formal banquet, attended by

nearly 300 friends of the University. President Aebersold reported that this event "kicked the celebration off in a first class manner."[1022]

Throughout this year of celebrating the founding of the University, hundreds of its regular activities incorporated the spirit of centennial. This historic milestone became a sense of great pride for those in the University community especially the descendents of the original families which founded the University one hundred years earlier.

At its annual Changing of the Guard Banquet where new officers are installed, the Slippery Rock University Alumni Association, held a 100th birthday party for the campus on April 15, 1989. Its newly installed president, Dr. Robert J. Watson, member of the class of 1970, commented on the remarkable progress made by the University and its alumni association.

Local history played a role that year in the selection of recipients of the annual Mabel Blyth Town-Gown Awards. Local town historian, Mrs. Shirley Evans Cubbison received the town person award. University historian, Dr. Robert J. Watson received the university faculty/staff award. Student, Deborah A. White of Gibsonia, received the student award.[1023]

During the centennial year, the State Employee Combined Appeal campaign, again exceeded its goals. More than $25,000 was raised with more than 240 employees contributing to local agencies.[1024]

Naturally, the University's Commencement on May 13, 1989, held outdoors in N. Kerr Thompson Stadium, highlighted the centennial celebration. A

Professor Steve Hawk (center), leads the trumpet trio at May Commencement, early 1990's

222

special Processional, "SRU Centennial March" was written and played by University Organist, George W. Bentel. Dr. J. Stanley Marshall, a member of the class of 1947 and former president of Florida State University, presented the address, "Books or Bumper Stickers", to 778 graduates receiving degrees. Dr. Russell M. Wright, a member of the class of 1923, received an honorary doctoral degree from his alma mater. Four university employees received the 1989 President's Award for Outstanding Service, an award established in 1981 by Mr. Robert and Mrs. Donna McMullen. The recipients were Dr. Joanne McKeag, Mrs. Pearl Shaffer, Mr. Roy Martin and Mr. Stan Kendziorski.[1025]

One of the two Centennial bronze plagues mounted on the original stone pillars at the entrance to Morrow Way, 1989

Slippery Rock Postmaster, Everett Bleakney, shows President Aebersold the new SRU Centennial cancellation, May 1989

On August 4, 1989, the Honorable Joe Kolter of Pennsylvania acknowledged Slippery Rock University in the United States House of Representatives. Representative Kolter read a congratulatory statement describing the University's century of excellence, thus making it a part of the Congressional Record.[1026]

An audience of nearly 1700 crowded into the James L. Morrow Field House in October 1989 for the Centennial Academic Honors Convocation. Honor and Dean's List students were recognized for their academic accomplishments. Achievement awards were presented to Dr. M. Richard Rose, a member of the class of 1955 and president of Rochester Institute of Technology; Astronaut Guion Bluford; and actress Edie Adams.[1027]

Just before Christmas 1989, family-owned Cameron Coca-Cola Bottling Co. Inc., also founded in 1889, distributed 80,000 two-liter bottles of Sprite in the Pittsburgh area with labels illustrating both SRU's and Cameron's 100th anniversary logos. SRU's green and white logo depicted the steeple of Old Main outlined by the slogan, "a Century of Excellence".[1028]

One year after the beginning of the centennial, more than 250 faculty, staff, students, alumni and friends of the University gathered on March 23, 1990, in the University Union to begin to bring closure to this historic event. President Aebersold expressed his deep appreciation for their unwavering assistance throughout the year of observance of their university's century of service. "You have all played a part in this yearlong celebration...and it is my special privilege today as president to rededicate

Slippery Rock University and its mission as we move into a second century – through the 'Door of Opportunity' that is education."[1029] He then led the participants through the "Door of Opportunity" and into "SRU's Second Century of Excellence", concluding the ceremony. Later that night, a free concert entitled "SRU Faculty Centennial Sounds" was performed in Miller Auditorium.[1030] The next evening heralded the final event of the centennial, the "Gala Ball." President Aebersold again thanked the Centennial Committee for planning.[1031]

The strong support of the citizens in Slippery Rock given to the University throughout its centennial celebration was reminiscent of those early days back in the 1880s when the townsfolk had a dream. Townsfolk, whose young people had to leave the community for advanced study, labored relentlessly to have their own local institution of higher education. They dared to look forward to the day when their young people would no longer have to travel afar for their advanced studies, thus making higher learning available for all. Governor Beaver of Pennsylvania understood so well that all of this happened because of "the supreme faith of the people that they were doing something worthy of acceptance".[1032] One hundred years later, as town and gown joined in the celebration of Slippery Rock University's one hundredth birthday, there was no evidence that this faith had diminished.

Concerned about the relationship between new students and the University in the centennial year, President Aebersold emphasized the importance of the presence and communication of institutional values. "One of our biggest challenges will be to get people to understand and accept the value system that treats individuals for their personal dignity regardless of race or sex. We will begin to expand further upon the programs which are presently in existence to help educate people for the future of our society and culture."[1033]

During the centennial year, students from forty states and sixty countries of the world were enrolled, with eighty percent of the student body Pennsylvania residents. The University was offering admission to only 59% of its applicants, an effort to provide the best quality of education to those who would profit the most from

it.[1034] The enrollment of well prepared students would continue to be an emphasis into the decade of the 1990s.

As alcohol consumption increased on college campuses across the country, Slippery Rock University took an educational approach to this national issue. A new alcohol policy was passed in March 1988, that took effect in the fall of 1989. President Aebersold announced to the University community "We will continue to monitor behavior which is related to alcohol on or off campus. It is important to understand that we have a concern about behavior, and we are addressing those issues in a way that is intended to be very fair and up front. Our intent is to educate people as to the laws, and their responsibility to the laws in regard to the use of alcohol."[1035]

President Aebersold (center), tying the Mothers Against Drunk Driving red ribbon to his automobile in support of MADD, 1987

Students continued to distinguish themselves through their planning and conducting of numerous community centered events. Throughout the late 1980s, the annual Light Up Night drew record crowds of approximately 4,000 people. The popular Evening Magazine program of Pittsburgh television station KDKA televised the event sponsored by the Association of Residence Hall Students.[1036] In addition, students were actively involved in collecting food for the local food cupboard, performing leadership roles in Special Olympics activities and participating in programs established by the active Mothers Against Drunk Drivers local chapter.[1037] The Pennsylvania Intercollegiate Band Festival came to campus in March 1989. A total of 138 musicians, representing twenty-seven colleges and universities from across the Commonwealth, came together to create the honors band.[1038]

A joint licensing effort of the Council of Trustees and the Student Government Association brought FM radio to campus in spring 1989. Mr. Elliott Wood was selected to serve as manager of the new radio station, WRCK.[1039]

Student athletes performed well throughout the centennial year. For the first time ever, the baseball team, led by Coach Jeff Messer, earned the right to compete at the Division II National World Series and finished third place in the nation. The women's track team, led by Coach John Papa, won the Pennsylvania State Athletic Conference while the men's team finished second. The golf team finished second in the Conference and was ranked eleventh nationally. Water polo, a club sport team trying to advance to varsity status on campus, led by Coach Richard Hunkler, was the only non-California team in the national tournament and finished fourth. Eight student athletes, four in track, three in baseball and one in golf earned all-America status.[1040] The continued attraction of the name, Slippery Rock University, and the quality of its athletic programs led to the men's and women's basketball teams being invited to compete in a Florida tourney. The men's team went on to win the Western Conference title.[1041]

President Aebersold (left), Nancy Peterson, Bob Allison and Connie Emmitt pack food for delivery to the Northern Butler County Food Cupboard, 1992

The International Studies Program continued to grow with the signing of an exchange program in October 1988, with Kangweon National University-Korea. The first faculty exchange through this program took place spring 1989.[1042] After stating his satisfaction for the existing programs, President Aebersold laid out part of the plan for future international programs during the summer 1989. "We are trying to be very careful not to have too many programs, but to have diverse programs. The institution is at a point where we will be getting more selective in the expansion of our international programs."[1043] However, international programming was not without tense moments and anxiety. The University was relieved during the summer 1989, to hear that Professor Jerome O'Malley, teaching at Shanghai International Studies University and student, Karen Curtis, studying at Shanghai were safe in their premature departure of protest torn China.[1044]

SRU staff prepare hotdogs for students after graduation practice, mid 1990's

The president from Kangweon National University in Korea (left) and President Aebersold sign the exchange program, October 1988

As additional exchange programs were developed, more international students attended Slippery Rock University. The Town-Gown Association initiated special activities and programs for these students welcoming them into the Slippery Rock community.[1045]

Regular curricular review often resulted with changes to the curriculum. After many years, the Library Science program was phased out in 1989.[1046] During the same year, a Master of Science degree in Sustainable Systems, a new interdisciplinary program, was approved.[1047] The new Sustainable Systems degree came on the heels of a $55,000 grant from the Pennsylvania Department of Energy to help renovate the existing Patterson house on Harmony Road as a demonstration site for non-chemical farming, local food production and environmentally safe energy.[1048] Mr. Ronald Gargasz, alumnus and International President of the Organic Crop Improvement

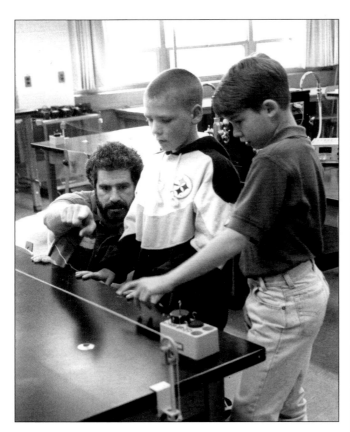

Professor Ben Shaevitz, explains wave forms to Steve Lubinski of Laurel and Andrew Larimore of Karns City at the 1992 Kids Day at College Program

Mrs. Ruth Houk, widow of former president Dale Houk, 1946-1956, stands with President Aebersold at the memorial tree planting ceremony for Dr. Houk, August 1989

Association led course development for the new master's degree. President Aebersold commented, "We are the only site in the U.S. who is doing something in the area of permaculture at the collegiate level".[1049]

The quality of the faculty continued to advance with a higher percentage hired with terminal degrees in their fields and teaching experience from major universities. Faculty members continued to be active in scholarly activities and public service.[1050]

University facilities kept pace with the changes during the late 1980s. As the result of a gift from Joe and Sarah McCandless of Evans City and Dr. G. C. McCandless of Franklin, the McCandless Schoolhouse (formerly the Hickory Corner Schoolhouse in Muddy Creek Township) was donated and moved to the University in the spring 1989.[1051] The McCandless family wished to preserve the schoolhouse in its original form and condition and Dr. G. C. McCandless envisioned the schoolhouse as a memorial to his late wife, Dr. Pauline McCandless. The schoolhouse was dedicated on May 11,1989.[1052]

Two athletic facilities were named at this time. Recognizing Coach Wally Rose for twenty-nine years of service to Slippery Rock University, 1956-1985, the baseball field was named Wally A. Rose Baseball Park. Coach Rose was considered dean of district baseball coaches and served as president of the Tri-State Baseball Coaches Association for four years. His teams posted 410 wins and 309 losses and won several state titles and competed in the NCAA Regional Championships.[1053] The park was dedicated April 22, 1989.[1054] The University's Soccer Field was named the James W. Egli Soccer Field and dedicated on May 6, 1989.[1055] Known as "the Father of NAIA Soccer", Coach Egli was inducted into the NAIA Soccer Hall of Fame in 1965. During his 31 years at SRU, 1955-1986, Coach Egli's teams won 250 matches, losing 141 and tying thirty-eight matches. He coached 19 All-America Athletes and was Coach of the Year in district, regional and national balloting. In addition to soccer, Coach Egli also coached swimming for fifteen years.[1056]

Two new construction projects began during the fall 1989. Groundbreaking for the new racquetball courts in the Morrow Field House took place Homecoming 1989. A major expansion of the Student Government

Dr. Jack C. Dinger (center) and his wife Geri receive a painting of the new Jack C. Dinger Special Education building from President Aebersold, fall, 1989

Association Bookstore in the University Union was also anounced.[1057]

On July 29,1989, Dr. Dale Houk, president of the Slippery Rock State Teacher's College, 1946-1956, was remembered through the dedication of a memorial tree planting on campus.[1058] Dr. Houk was the only University president to have been born in Butler County, Pennsylvania.

The Special Education facility in the Morrow Field House was named for Dr. Jack C. Dinger, former chairperson of the Special Education Department during the fall 1989.[1059] Dr. Dinger founded the Special Education Department in 1963 and served as its chairperson during many of his twenty-four years of service. While chairperson, the department had 750 undergraduate majors, 250 graduate majors and thirteen faculty members and was home to the largest chapter of the Council of Exceptional Children in the world.[1060]

Dr. Muriel Berman, member of the Board of Governors of the State System and her husband, Mr. Philip I. Berman donated a large aluminum sculpture entitled "Benchform 89-5" by Thomas Sternal. In

Members of the Academic Support Services Department are photographed with "Benchform 89-5" donated to the University by Dr. Muriel Berman and her husband Mr. Philip I. Berman, early 1990's

September 1989 the piece was placed between the Eisenberg Classroom Building and the Library and was the first of several pieces to be donated to SRU by the family.[1061] The Bermans donated several pieces to the State System, which were placed on each of the fourteen campuses.

Dr. Roy Stewart, Dean of Graduate Studies, reported to the President in the fall 1989, that after a three-year study, his committee found the University's telephone system inadequate to meet the present and future demands. A recommendation to install a $2.1 million Bell Atlanticom Telecommunications System was approved. The President explained "A new telecommunications system will enhance academic progress and other administrative service, through voice, data transmission, and video services".[1062]

One of the final actions of the Council of Trustees in 1989, was to purchase the Fowler Building at a cost of $165,000 which the University had been renting since fall 1986, for $24,000 per year.[1063] The building, located off Elm Street, housed the University's television and media production studios, coordinated by Mr. Bruce Russell in the communication department.

Dr. Aebersold continued to be active with the NCAA throughout his presidency. Through this relationship, he provided leadership to Slippery Rock University's home conference, the Pennsylvania State Athletic Conference, and other athletic conferences.[1064]

During February 1989, President Aebersold participated in six alumni chapter meetings in Arizona and California.[1065] In April, Dr. Aebersold attended the American Alliance for Health, Physical Education, Recreation and Dance, in Boston, where more than 100 alumni gathered. Three faculty members, Dr. Joanne McKeag, Mr. Gene Boyer and Dr. Susie Knerim, received awards at the meeting. The National Association for Sport and Physical Education named Ms. Marlene Hall, a student, the Outstanding Physical Education Major of the Year.[1066]

The Alumni Association held its annual weekend event, June 9 and 10 during the centennial year. A record number of alumni, more than 450, returned to visit their Alma mater.[1067]

It was truly a good time in the history of the University. Even the budget appropriation from Harrisburg was positive. Governor Robert Casey's budget for the state owned universities represented a seven percent increase over the previous year.[1068] And, to manage that appropriation and be responsible for the Division of Finance and Administration, the President appointed Dr. Charles Curry as Vice President, effective September 25,1989.[1069] Dr. Curry had been serving in an interim capacity the previous year. The appointment of Dr. Curry represented a milestone for the University as he was the first African American to serve in a vice presidential position.

At this time, the University's budget was generally comprised of two entities, the tax dollars allocated to the University from the state legislature and the dollars collected through student tuition and other fees. This

Teeside Polytechnique University President, England (left), signs exchange program with President Aebersold, early 1990s

ratio had been changing over the last few decades with the University receiving proportionally less support from the legislature, thus requiring more from the students. Consequently, the University's enrollment was becoming a greater issue to the health and welfare of the University. Up to this period in the Aebersold administration, enrollment had been growing and appeared to show no signs of leveling much less decreasing. The challenge had been the management of growth. Over the next few years, the issue would change and intensify. The financial well being of Slippery Rock University and other State System Universities would be challenged, resulting with significant competition among the universities of the State System.

As with many public colleges and universities, Slippery Rock was realizing the need for increased fund raising. In June 1990, President Aebersold, in his general Advancement statement, was happy to report: "Four years ago the assets of the Slippery Rock Foundation, Inc. stood at $65,500. Today the asset base has reached $1.3 million."[1070] Dr. Aebersold went on to congratulate the people in the university community who have worked very hard in this effort under the general leadership of Mr. C. Bruce Rossiter. With increased efforts and commensurate results, more support was provided to the division of University Advancement. By the end of 1992, the total assets of the Foundation had surpassed the $2 million mark for the first time in its history.[1071]

The University's international programs continued to develop and prosper through the 1990s. Slippery Rock boasted the first American studying in the International

Queen Margaret College President, Scotland (right) and President Aebersold discuss the existing exchange program, early 1990s

Hungarian University President (center) and President Aebersold (right) with SRU philosophy professor and scholar, Dr. Bernard D. Freydberg on SRU's campus, early 1990s

English professor, Dr. Alden Hart, teaches students in the Eisenberg classroom building in the early 1990's

Coaching Program at the Hungarian University of Physical Education. This occurred while faculty and graduate students from the Hungarian University recip-rocated in their study at Slippery Rock.[1072] During the summer of 1990, the first program of its kind took place in the Soviet Union, with fifteen Slippery Rock University students enrolled. This intensive Russian language program, located in Donesk, was modeled after the very popular and long-standing German language program taught in Salzburg, Austria.[1073] In 1992, the University had signed an agreement for an exchange program with the University of Czecho-slovakia in Bratislava. Slippery Rock was one of the first American universities to sign such an agreement.[1074]

In September 1990, the Alumni Association published the Rock Magazine, the first publication with a multi-colored cover. Mrs. Sally Lennox, Director Alumni Affairs, the staff of the University Relations office and others were commended for this excellent effort.[1075]

Demand for Slippery Rock University graduates continued to grow. In a report compiled by Mrs. Carla Hart, Director of the Career Services Office, ninety-one percent of the 1990 baccalaureate degree graduates were employed a few months after graduation.[1076] Employers of the new graduates expressed their very positive attitude about the graduates in a formal survey.[1077]

The fall term of 1990 was a very busy time for the University since a number of accrediting agencies, including the all-important Middle States Association of Colleges and Schools, visited the campus.[1078] After "Middle States" completed its always careful evaluation of all aspects of academic life on campus, it reaffirmed the University's accreditation. The Association did request that the administration provide a progress report on its intent to develop "a cohesive and structured planning process" for the University and to strengthen its graduate programs by October, 1993.[1079] The teacher education programs were also re-accredited by the National Council for Accreditation of Teacher Education. It should be noted that this came at a time when three out of four universities were being denied this coveted accreditation.[1080] After a very thorough review, the University's new Master's degree program in physical therapy was awarded accreditation by the American

230

Physical Therapy Association.[1081] Before these evaluations were finished, this fall term was dubbed by those on campus as "the accreditation semester".

In 1990, the Pennsylvania Academy for the Profession of Teaching gave "Salute to Teaching" awards to Dr. Larry Cobb, Professor in the Department of Public Administration, and Dr. Robert Arnhold, Associate Professor in the Department of Physical Education, for their outstanding contributions to the State System of Higher Education.[1082]

In Harrisburg, the Board of Governors approved a document defining baccalaureate degrees in its state universities in 1990. Effective fall 1994, all baccalaureate degrees were to require 40% of coursework in liberal arts and sciences, 40% of academic study at the junior or senior level and at least 25% of the student's total program in the major field of study.[1083] President Aebersold responded, "It will be necessary for work to be done to bring that into compliance".[1084]

Before this busy semester ended, the Liberal Studies Committee, chaired by Dean Charles Zuzak, suggested to President Aebersold that major changes be made in the required undergraduate General Education core curriculum. Their proposed core curriculum, Liberal Studies, would require all undergraduates to select courses from each of the following eight areas of study:

1. Basic Skills, 0-11 semester hours of English writing, Mathematics, Public Speaking and Physical Education (dependent upon placement screening)
2. The Arts, 9 semester hours
3. Cultural Diversity, 9 semester hours
4. Global Perspectives, 6 semester hours
5. Human Institutions and Interpersonal Relationships, 6 semester hours
6. Natural Sciences and Mathematics, 12 semester hours
7. Our National Experience, 3 semester hours
8. Challenges of the Modern Age, 3 semester hours[1085]

Regis Scheibel, from the class of 1957, presents Dean Catherine Morsink and President Aebersold with a $10,000 check to initiate the Scholarship for Promising Educators, June 1992

Myron Brown

After considerable debate across the campus, this new Liberal Studies program was accepted. It was scheduled to begin in the fall of 1994.[1086]

The pace of student life seemed to quicken. The campus was alive with activities throughout the week and on the weekends. Athletic events, dramatic productions, musical programs and other activities were strongly supported and attended by students and other members of the University community. When the men's basketball team played at home, in the early 1990s, students had to arrive more than an hour before the game to get a seat to watch the game. Slippery Rock, for many decades, had enjoyed competitive athletic teams and the 1990-91 men's basketball team featuring Myron Brown was no exception. In his last home game, a post-season NCAA Division II East Regional Contest, the Rock won 119 to 101 over its rival Shippensburg. Following the game, The Pittsburgh-Post-Gazette headline read "Flyin' Myron leaves 'em cryin' at Slippery Rock."[1087] Myron Brown went on to play with the Minnesota Timberwolves in the NBA and will be remembered as one of the greatest basketball players at the Rock.

As part of a national exchange program, during the summer, 1991, the Slippery Rock University Jazz Band presented several concerts in the Soviet Union.[1088] In return, the University community was treated in

September to a performance of "The Matroshka", a popular Soviet folk ensemble.

In the fall of 1991, the University strengthened their relationship with WQED, the Pittsburgh based public television channel. The Slippery Rock Foundation had supported WQED in the past by assisting in the underwriting of programs. With "Columbus in the Age of Discovery", October 1991, the University and WQED went beyond the standard series programming. Under the direction of Dr. Catherine Morsink, dean of the College of Education, several members of the faculty and public school teachers collaboratively prepared materials that were shared with more than 100 local schools to be used in conjunction with the Columbus series.[1089] The effort was extremely successful and led to a similar partnership in 1992 with the series, "Today's Changing World " focusing on the breaking up of the USSR and the creation of the Commonwealth of Independent States. This time, joining Dr. Morsink, was Dr. Charles Zuzak and Dr. Jay Harper, dean and assistant dean of the College of Arts and Sciences.[1090] SRU also assisted in the underwriting of the series, "Black Horizons", one of the longest running African American public affairs programs in the country. In 1994, the University engaged in another public school partnership, this time producing teaching materials to coincide with the PBS series, "Baseball", including regional history, economics and cultural development.[1091]

As Slippery Rock University entered the final decade of the Twentieth Century, hopes were high that it would continue its upward spiral of growth. Unfortunately, at the very time Slippery Rock University was forging great plans for the future, the American economy was beginning to slip quickly into a recession. Any prolonged weakening of a country's economy almost certainly means that fewer tax dollars will be available to support state institutions of higher education like Slippery Rock. With reduced Commonwealth revenue, the legislature required the State System to give back nearly five percent of its budget in January 1991.[1092] Since this reduction of state funding came in the middle of the 1990-91 budget year, it was difficult for the state universities to comply with this demand. The Governor's budget increased tuition $350 for state residents and $580 for non-resident students.[1093]

President Aebersold had serious concerns about this legislative action. "It is important that the legislature understands the critical nature of the budget situation. In the state of Pennsylvania where the economic situation is in difficult straits, one of the factors, which insure the future, is the education of the workforce. If we do not fund education appropriately, we are damaging that future in terms of economic status of the Commonwealth."[1094]

Since the state expected its universities to reduce their enrollments during this economic recession, President Aebersold was prepared to admit a smaller freshman class. Of course, this would enable the University to be more selective as it recruited its freshman class.[1095]

Dr. Aebersold explained to the university community in September 1990, "In order to attempt to level off our enrollment, we have admitted approximately 100 fewer students this year as compared to last year. During this period of time, we are pleased to see the quality of students increase."[1096] This cut in freshmen marked the first such action in years and was seen as a measure to attempt to curb the dramatically increasing enrollment. In spite of the 100 freshmen reduction, the president went on to explain "We are off slightly in obtaining our goal between zero and two percent increase, for at the present time, there is an increase of approximately two and one half percent credit hour as a result of more returning students." The total enrollment of the University had surged to another high of 7,800 students. Minority student enrollment was also at the highest level to date.[1097]

Even with the reduction of new freshmen and increase in tuition, the University's 1991 enrollment increased 1.3% to another all-time high, 7928.[1098] However, actions soon to be taken by the Board of Governors would create a different environment.

After the first year of budget austerity, President Aebersold reported in December of 1991 to the Council of Trustees on the status of enrollment at the University. "There have been enrollment bands placed on each of the State System Universities through the State System of Higher Education. We will be looking toward being within that band and in fact, probably decreasing our enrollment for the fall by approximately 250 students. We also have a new target of ten percent out-of-state enrollment. Our enrollment is approximately fourteen percent out-of-state, and we will be reducing out-of-state enrollment to meet that requirement."[1099]

Then in the spring 1992, Governor Robert Casey sent more bad news to all fourteen state universities. "Downsizing education" became the clarion call heard throughout the Commonwealth, the State System of Higher Education and on the Slippery Rock University campus. Instead of the universities getting their request for a ten percent increase in funding to accommodate recent enrollment increases, they learned that the Governor was reducing their budgets by three and one-half percent.[1100] He explained that the declining fiscal health of the Commonwealth offered no other choice. Mr. Michael Hershock, Secretary of Budget for the State, shared his fear that "The recovery will be long and slow, and it is not a very healthy picture".[1101] The operating budget of Slippery Rock University was reduced by $3,750,000 as a result of the Governor's actions.[1102]

President Aebersold, however, believed his University could weather this new fiscal storm by "capping enrollment, implementing hiring freezes, delaying deferred maintenance projects, suspending instructional equipment purchases and library acquisitions, and cutting student wages".[1103] He felt his proposal to have 250 fewer students on campus "was in line with the enrollment cap scenario with the State System Enrollment Management and seems to fit the comments made by Governor Casey for the need to downsize education in Pennsylvania".[1104]

During this time of budgetary crisis, the University Planning Council, in 1992, composed a new mission statement defining the purposes of the University which were consistent with those the Board of Governors of the State System of Higher Education outlined in its *Priorities for Pennsylvania's State System of Higher Education During the 1990s*.[1105] It reads: "The fundamental mission of Slippery Rock University is to provide high quality undergraduate and graduate academic instruction. Complementary missions are to conduct scholarly research, to promote professional performance, and to address the educationally-related economic, environmental, social, cultural, and recreational needs of the region served by the university."[1106]

The Board of Governors also recommended that the principle of Continuous Improvement be used as a format for planning and assessment in the State System. Slippery Rock University adopted the principle and appointed Dr. Susan Hannam and Dr. James Laux as Directors of Continuous Improvement.[1107] The new directors worked with several hundred members of the University community to identify the areas of campus life which would benefit most from the application of the principle of Continuous Improvement.[1108] Six Areas of Emphasis were identified as aspects of University life where the process of Continuous Improvement should be applied in planning their future.

1. The Teaching-Learning Process will focus upon the success of the student in the classroom.
2. The Living-Learning Environment will examine the various aspects of the classroom and non-classroom environments that impact upon the success of students in their education.
3. Financial Equilibrium. The financial condition of the University is critical in providing resources necessary to bring about successful learning.
4. Enrollment Management is crucial to the ability to plan and provide resources to support the learning process.
5. Increasing External Service and Support.
6. In order to improve the function of the University, assessment will play a critical role.[1109]

After considerable review, the University's College of Education and Human Service Professions underwent a major restructuring in 1991.[1110] A new College of Education was formed and included the following areas of study:
- Counseling and Educational Psychology
- Educational Studies
- Elementary Education/Early Childhood
- Supervision and Student Teaching
- Developmental Programs
- Special Education
- McKeever Environmental Learning Center[1111]

Concurrently, a new College of Allied Health, Physical Education, Recreation and Dance was formed and included the following areas of study:
- Allied Health
- Physical Education
- Recreation
- Dance
- Nursing
- Environmental Education
- Military Science
- Athletics
- Russell Wright Fitness Center
- Physical Therapy.[1112]

In January 1992, Mr. William H. Gray III, President and Chief Executive Officer of the United Negro College Fund and former Majority Whip of the U.S. House of Representatives, spoke to the University community as part of the Martin Luther King Day observance. Mr.

*Salt-n-Pepa rap artists, Salt (Cheryl James, left), Spinderella
(DeeDee Roper, center), and Pepa (Sandy Denton)*

Gray, the first African American to hold a post in the House leadership, spoke with students, faculty and staff as part of planned activities.[1113]

Female rap stars, Salt-n-Pepa performed on-campus during Spring Week in 1992. These internationally known recording artists brought their smash hit songs and popular concert tour to the Morrow Field House.[1114]

Fall 1992 enrollment declined 138 students, less than the target of 250, nevertheless it marked the beginning of several years of declining enrollments for the University.[1115] Chancellor James McCormick addressed the Council of Trustees in September 1992 stating "This is the first time in the history of the public university system that the System has received a cut in funding, and provides further evidence that Pennsylvania and its neighboring states are struggling with the national economic recession".[1116] President Aebersold added that based on national and state college going rates, "college age populations in this country are continuing to drop until the year 2000, high school graduation numbers are down and low income students are less likely to go to college in greater numbers." Dramatic rises in

tuition rates, especially for non-residents, enrollment caps, state funding cuts, reduced high school graduation rates and mandated enrollment decreases all spelled trouble for SRU.[1117]

Just as SRU was developing a plan to dramatically reduce its non-resident enrollment to the ten percent maximum desired by the state legislature, significant tuition increases were implemented in the fall of 1992. The state legislature had decided it would not subsidize State System students from states outside Pennsylvania. The result was a tuition increase of $1200 for non-residents and only a $100 increase for Pennsylvania residents.[1118] This sent a message rippling through the non-resident community and precipitated the exodus of hundreds of non-resident students and a rapid decline in non-resident applications.

This action pleased those Pennsylvanians who never understood why their tax dollars were being used to educate students from other states. Others, including state legislators, obviously forgot that as recently as the late 1980's, Pennsylvania's Auditor General, noting with deep concern the decline of non-resident student enrollment, called for immediate action to reverse the

*Artist, John Seitz (right), class of 1972, presents President Aebersold with a
handcrafted glass sculpture as a "thank you" to SRU for his education, 1992*

*Madam Nien Cheng presents her scholarship to a
student as Louis Razzano looks on, 1992*

trend. Because of the higher tuition costs for non-resident students, there were 276 fewer who applied for admission in 1993.[1119] The non-resident student enrollment dropped more than one thousand students during the 1990s, from over 1,250 to less than 250.

The student enrollment at Slippery Rock University declined in the 1993 fall term to 7,625.[1120] To offset this steady decline in the size of the student body, the University began to explore ways of attracting transfer students to its campus. After contacting community colleges in the area, President Aebersold, in 1994, informed the Council of Trustees: "We have an articulation program with community colleges that deals with our new curriculum attempting to improve the transferring from community colleges".[1121] The articulation agreements soon spread from community colleges to technical schools and branch campuses of four-year colleges and universities. Those students who transferred to the University served to enhance Slippery Rock's image as being a friendly university.

By 1993, the University's off-campus educational programs were enrolling hundreds of students to credit and non-credit courses. The programs were located in Cranberry Township, southwestern Butler County, and at the St. Francis Hospital and the Jameson Hospital in New Castle.[1122]

Old Main, the oldest building on campus, had not seen an interior renovation for a very long time. With the

help of personnel from the Facilities division, this work was completed in 1993. An "open house" celebration was arranged so that the University community could see the restoration of this beautiful historic structure.[1123]

During the spring of 1993, the Student Government Association received approval to expand its Bookstore in the Student Union.[1124] This two-story, 10,000 square foot addition, which would cost $1.42 million, was totally funded by the Student Government Association.[1125] When the addition was opened the following year, students immediately noticed the increase in display space for books, educational materials and Slippery Rock University T-shirts and sweatshirts worn throughout the world.[1126]

In the fall of 1993, the Association of Collegiate Business Schools and Programs arrived on campus to evaluate the College of Information and Business Administration. Obviously impressed, it fully accredited all of the College's programs.[1127] President Aebersold was extremely pleased and praised Dean Frank Mastrianna for his outstanding leadership and his faculty for their hard work.[1128]

When Dr. Douglas Covington became President of Cheyney University in 1992, Edward Hess, Comptroller at Slippery Rock University, volunteered to assist him as he assembled his executive team. This practice of loaning academic personnel among Pennsylvania's State universities when there is a need is a rather remarkable example of academic philanthropy. During his six-month stay at Cheyney University, Mr. Hess served as President Covington's Vice President of Business Affairs. In March, 1993, Chancellor McCormick was quick to praise Mr. Hess for the valuable assistance he gave to one of his fellow state universities.[1129]

In 1993, the University's International Program was at an all-time high. Students from 68 foreign countries were studying at Slippery Rock. One hundred and sixty-two American students and more than sixty faculty members took advantage of diverse overseas opportunities.[1130] In an effort to keep in touch with the over 700 former international students who studied at Slippery Rock, the University was sending a bi-annual newsletter.[1131]

As the United States was down-sizing its military presence in Germany, fewer student teaching

Elderhostel group on campus, 1994

opportunities existed for Slippery Rock's students. A new opportunity, however, in an English-speaking school in Mexico City was created through the assistance of an alumnus.[1132]

One of the University's outstanding students, Mr. Eric Holmes, former student member of the Council of Trustees, was selected to serve in the prestigious White House internship program in 1993.[1133] Gabriel Tate, a very talented photography student, finished third in a National Photo Journalist competition in Houston, Texas. Most of the photo journalists, including those placing first and second in the competition, were professionals working with national news publications.[1134]

On August 2, 1993, the University took a major step by announcing its first capital campaign, "Invest in Opportunity." The campaign, with a five-year goal of $4.5 million, was kicked off on September 12, 1993. Centerville Day, a series of local and regional activities, were held on the historic part of the University's campus.[1135] Hundreds of members of the University community participated in the activities, coordinated by Mrs. Shirley Jones, focusing on the roots of the University and the town.

By the end of 1993, the capital campaign had reached 72% of its $4.5 million goal with approximately $3.2 million committed.[1136] The campaign was managed by Mr. William Sonntag, Campaign Chairman, 1970 alumnus and President and Chief Executive

A sampling of brochures representing the many international opportunities available to students, 1993

William Elliott (left) receives congratulations
from President Aebersold, early 1990's

Executive Chef Aebersold serves an omelet to faculty
and staff at the kick-off breakfast for the
All University Fund Raising Campaign, early 1990's

Guy McUmber (second from left) Pennsylvania Department of Environmental Resources
presents a $152,000 check to establish a leaf composting facility on campus.
Slippery Rock Mayor, Howard Meyer (left), Ron Steele, Boro Council president
(second from right) and President Aebersold receive the check jointly, 1994

Athletic Director, Bill Lennox, (far right, standing) and his coaches, 1980's

Officer of the First National Bank of Slippery Rock; Mr. C. Bruce Rossiter, Vice President of University Advancement; Mr. Ed Bucha, Executive Director for University Advancement; Mr. Walter Williams, Director of Annual Giving; and Mr. William Kirker, Director of Prospect Research.[1137] The $4.5 million goal was comprised of five sub-goal areas, including Student Scholarships ($1.5 million), Academic and Instructional Support ($700,000), East/West Gymnasium Complex ($500,000), West Hall ($1.5 million), and Internationalism ($300,000).[1138]

Concurrently, a university-wide capital campaign was announced involving faculty, staff, townspeople and retirees. A goal of $300,000 was established for the University community as part of the capital campaign.[1139] Working with the Advancement division and coordinating the University-wide effort, Dr. Robert J. Watson announced that the University community had exceeded its goal with $330,853 pledged.[1140] Slippery Rock University employees had demonstrated that they

were the most supportive of any employee group among the fourteen State System universities.

The Homecoming celebration in the fall of 1993, coordinated by Ms. Tese Calderelli, was a huge success, in spite of high winds and heavy rains. Alumni will never forget this Homecoming since it was the one when the large alumni tent blew away.[1141] Family Day, coordinated by Ms. Lynn Swisher, was enjoyed by a large number of families who had come to campus to spend the day with their students.[1142]

The University named two major athletic facilities in September, 1994. The new track in N. Kerr Thompson Stadium was named the William C. Lennox Track, in honor of the University's cross country and track and field coach and director of athletics. President Aebersold had these words of high praise for his colleague: "Bill Lennox exemplifies the great professional who has reached the pinnacle of his profession and has attained recognition at the state and national levels for his exceptional work ethic. He dedicated the past 25 years to insuring that Slippery Rock University maintained its long traditions of excellence in academics and athletics."[1143]

The playing field for the women's field hockey team was named in honor of Dr. Patricia Zimmerman. Before coming to Slippery Rock, she was a member of the United States field hockey team. During her thirty years in the Department of Physical Education, she served as director of equal opportunity in sport, assistant department chairperson, graduate coordinator, associate athletic director and, for twenty-two years the women's field hockey coach. President Aebersold admired the fact that "Her special focus has always been on improving opportunities for women in sport."[1144] Dr. Zimmerman was a member of the United States field hockey team, early in her career.[1145]

Always interested in property contiguous to the campus, the University, in 1994, was pleased to have the opportunity to acquire the home of Dr. Frederick W. and Mabel Vincent. This property, located at the corner of Main and Cooper Streets, would be quickly developed to accommodate faculty in the Department of Educational Psychology and Counseling.[1146] The Vincent name was synonymous with the pioneers in the community. Dr. and Mrs. Vincent's son, Fred served for a time as Director of the Budget for the University and met and married his wife, Kathleen at Slippery Rock.

Unfortunately, tragedy struck off campus in the early morning hours of October 15, 1994, when a group of apartments in the Keister Road Apartment Complex was destroyed by fire.[1147] Thankfully, no students were injured but four firefighters received minor injuries. The fire left seventy Slippery Rock University students homeless.[45] In traditional Slippery Rock fashion, the University community responded with food, clothing and alternative housing for the displaced students. President Aebersold, deeply moved by this outpouring of support, explained: "While it is impossible to thank everyone who has lent a hand or contributed in some way to this incident, I want everyone to know that their help is truly appreciated by the University, the students affected by the fire, and the rest of the community which has pulled together so well and so quickly during this event. I am proud to live in Slippery Rock."[1148]

The University's Academic Advisement Center was honored in 1994 when the National Academic Advising Association granted it the Outstanding Institutional Advising Program Award. The Association was very impressed with the book, entitled "Transitions: Changes, Choices, Values and You" which prospective students and their parents use during the two-day orientation program. Written by faculty and administrators and compiled by Dr. Amanda Yale, Director of the Academic Advisement Center, this book introduces the student to the various aspects of academic and social life at Slippery Rock University and to the helpful role the Advisement Center can play.[1149]

Since the Board of Governors of Pennsylvania's state university system was interested in knowing what its students thought about their higher education experience, they selected two to serve on their Board. In September of 1994, Slippery Rock University was honored to have the President of its Student Government Association – Jennifer Alexander - chosen to be a member of this prestigious group of educational leaders.[1150]

A long time leader in student recreation and sport, Slippery Rock University decided to conduct a feasibility study for a recreation complex in early fall, 1993. Interested students, faculty and staff discussed the recreational needs of the campus with architects throughout the fall and winter of 1993-94.[1151] In the spring of 1994, architectural drawings, developed after listening to the University community, were offered to the students for consideration.[1152] An election was held and the majority of students voted in favor of constructing the new recreation facility.[1153] The Council of Trustees approved the proposed design of the complex. This facility would include a swimming pool, running track, basketball and volleyball courts, exercise areas, weight lifting facilities and locker rooms.[1154]

Since, as President Aebersold reminded everyone involved in this project that Pennsylvania law prohibited the use of tax dollars to build such a center, it was agreed that student fees would fund this $12 million enterprise.[1155] Mr. Peter Oesterling, Chairperson of the Student Affairs Committee for the Council of Trustees, "commended the students for taking the responsibility for a project of this magnitude and he looked forward to being a part of it."[1156]

Students majoring in Elementary Education and wishing to student teach in a bi-lingual environment were immediately attracted to the new minor in Spanish, created in 1994.[1157] Student teaching opportunities were available in Mexico City for these students through the international studies program.

A new program leading to the Master of Public Administration degree was approved by the Council of Trustees at their summer meeting in 1994.[1158] As

NKT Golf Outing, 1994 with President Aebersold (left), and
Bill Lennox (right) present the Green Jacket to Mike Bazzone, winner,
for the second consecutive year, with a score of three under par, 69

In December of 1994, President Aebersold proposed to advance the physical therapy program from a master's level to a doctoral degree program. This bold move would make Slippery Rock University only the second university in the nation to award a doctorate in physical therapy.[1162] The proposal included a phasing in of the doctoral curriculum one year at a time beginning in the fall of 1995. The Board of Governors approved the Council of Trustees' action in January, 1995. By March, 1995, more than 750 students had applied for the fifty vacancies in the new program.[1163]

The University jumped into the technological world of distance learning by developing a master of science degree program in nursing to be offered beginning with fall of 1995. The program, offered jointly, with Clarion University, would prepare nurse practitioners for rural service. Dr. Roy T. Stewart, Dean of Graduate Studies and Research, Dr. Anne M. Griffiths, Dean of the College of Health and Human Services, Dr. Leona Parascenzo, Assistant to the Dean and Dr. Catherine Rosenlieb, Chairperson of the Nursing Department were commended for their efforts in developing the University's first distance learning degree program.[1164]

required, the program was then forwarded to the Board of Governors in Harrisburg for their approval.

As a center for higher learning in a rural setting, Slippery Rock University understood well the challenges facing rural youth. In 1994, grants totaling nearly $160,000 were awarded to the University for the "Project to Strengthen Rural Participation in Higher Education," and for teachers in rural Pennsylvania to teach students with special needs.[1159]

The year 1994 marked the twentieth anniversary of the University's participation in the Act 101 grant program that enabled disadvantaged young people to attend college. Directed by Dr. Harry Budd for fourteen years, and, since then by Rev. Wil Hadden, this program has provided life-changing opportunities to hundreds of Pennsylvanians.[1160]

In the summer of 1994, the University renamed the outdoor adventure program as the Helen "Susie" Knierim Leadership Institute-Reach Program.[1161] Dr. Knierim, a member of the physical education faculty, was instrumental in developing the Reach Program, which included a ropes challenge course and other outdoor adventure activities.

Dr. David James (center), President of the International Mentoring
Association chats with student, Casie Hampton (left) and
Dwight Greer (right), Director of Minority Affairs, October 1995

During the evening of March 8, 1995, tragedy struck the McKeever Environmental Learning Center. The Roy Wilt auditorium was destroyed by accidental fire. Ten volunteer fire companies responded promptly to the emergency, but could not save the building and approximately one half million dollars of damages resulted. President Aebersold reported: "Arrangements are being made to relocate existing programs public schools were involved in related to the auditorium's use."[1165]

The Art Building underwent major renovation in 1994-95, enabling improvement and consolidation of some of the art instruction.[1166] The building, utilized for several decades as a student union, had been called "The Hut" and housed a small restaurant/grille, dance floor, student lounge with fireplace, and bowling alleys. Renovation was completed in early summer, 1995, with its dedication on May 4, 1996.[1167]

Outstanding progress was made by the University regarding residence hall technology by the spring 1995.

The University had purchased the necessary equipment to bring all of the residence halls and academic buildings technologically online, an accomplishment very few colleges and universities in the country had achieved.[1168] Every academic building and residence hall accommodated students with a well equipped computer laboratory.

The newly constructed and developing Harmony Homestead, located on Harmony Road, on the east edge of campus, was named the Robert A. Macoskey Center for Sustainable Systems Education and Research in honor of Dr. Macoskey. The late philosophy professor was the founder and supporter of the program housed at the campus Harmony Homestead Complex.[1169]

During the fall of 1995, for the second time in three years, Slippery Rock University's Army Reserve Officers Training Corps received the General Douglas McArthur Award as the best small-sized ROTC detachment in the nation. The award is presented each year

Art building under major renovation, 1995

Game day, President Aebersold cheers on Slippery Rock football team, mid 1990's

to ROTC units with cadets who exceed all established evaluation standards and the unit, which exceeds yearly commissioning goals.[1170]

Off campus courses were offered in a new facility in Cranberry Township in the fall of 1995. The site located on Executive Drive, owned by Butler County Community College, was leased to the University through a partnership. This new venture was testimony to the continued, strong relationship that existed between the two public institutions in the county, forged nearly twenty-five years earlier. Classes offered by the University prior to the fall, 1995, were offered at a facility leased through the Cranberry Professional Park.[1171]

Scholar student athletes are few and far between on some college campuses, but not the case at Slippery Rock. In 1995 and 1996, Slippery Rock University had the largest number of scholar athletes within the Pennsylvania State Athletic Conference. In order to qualify for the honor, a student athlete had to earn a minimum 3.25 grade point average. In 1995, Mr. Mark

Metzka, a member of the men's basketball team, was the top male scholar athlete in the State System and, in 1996, Ms. Lori Robinson, a member of the women's basketball team, was the top female scholar athlete.[1172]

Caring for others has been a characteristic of the Slippery Rock University community since it's founding. In the mid 1990s, the organization "Kids that Care", coordinated by Dr. Alice Kaiser-Drobney, completed several volunteer projects in Butler and Allegheny Counties. At the same time, "Kids that Care" traveled to Illinois and Albany, Georgia to aid victims of the massive floods.[1173] "The spring 1995 "Care Break" involved several Slippery Rock University students and faculty working with Native Americans through the National Youth Leadership Council in Albuquerque, New Mexico and the Navajo Nation Americorps Program.[1174] While in New Mexico, Slippery Rock alumni, Paul Onuska and Bob McGuire, assisted in facilitating the "Care Break" efforts.

Greek life, during the mid-90s, involved 319 brothers in twelve fraternities, and 401 sisters in ten sororities. The annual Greek Week fund raising events provided more than $1,100 for local charities.[1175]

The Pittsburgh Symphony returned to Slippery Rock's campus for a holiday concert on December 12, 1995. The concert marked the first performance of the symphony on the University's campus since the Summer Celebration in 1980.[1176]

Initiated by the class of 1954 alumni and personal friends, a memorial honoring Michael J. Estocian was dedicated during alumni weekend in June of 1995. The Navy pilot, killed in the Vietnam War, was a recipient of the Congressional Medal of Honor, the US Navy's highest honor, and the Distinguished Flying Cross and Air Medal.[1177] The memorial, located on the main floor of the University Union, invites the university community to pause and reflect.

By the mid 1990s, housemothers in Slippery Rock's residence halls were a thing of the past. However, one, Mrs. Lillian Yartz, former North Hall housemother for more than twenty-seven years, would not be forgotten. The fireplace lounge, located north of the main entrance, was named for Mrs. Yartz in recognition of her outstanding service. "During this period of time, she viewed North Hall as if it were her own home and the students who lived there as her own children," commented Dr. Aebersold. She has touched the lives of thousand of women and men and was the last house mother at Slippery Rock University.[1178]

The students of Dodds Residence Hall nominated their custodian, Mr. Lenny Szybka for the Building Service Contractors Association Custodian of the Year Award. Mr. Szybka, an employee of the cleaning contractor, Systems Management, Inc., was selected to receive the national honor. Affected by Down Syndrome, Mr. Szybka, accompanied by his parents, received his honor at the national conference in Chicago.[1179]

By September 1995, the capital campaign was closed, surpassing its $4.5 million goal with approximately $6 million in funds and commitments received. The Student Scholarship and Academic and Instructional Support areas received funds nearly double their goals. While the bricks and mortar portion of the campaign saw giving more in line with the original goal, the Internationalism goal was not met. On September 30, 1995 the University celebrated its extremely successful "Invest in Opportunity" capital campaign, which had exceeded its goal six months ahead of schedule.[1180] This first and critical capital campaign elevated Slippery Rock University to a new level of fund raising. Largely assisted by the campaign, the Foundation, by March 1996, reported assets of $5.4 million.[1181]

After the conclusion of the first and successful capital campaign, a national search was conducted to replace the retiring head of University Advancement. In August, 1996, President Aebersold introduced the new Vice President, Mr. Robert J. Mollenhauer, to the university community. Mr. Mollenhauer brought more than 15 years of fund raising experience while at the University of Pittsburgh.[1182]

At the very next meeting of the Council of Trustees, Mr. Mollenhauer announced the development of the Robert N. Aebersold Scholarship. Its purpose was to reward excellence, both inside and outside the classroom, and to attract and retain talented students.[1183] This scholarship was the first four-year, renewable scholarship rewarding excellence at Slippery Rock University. In just six months, more than 400 alumni and university friends contributed to the scholarship, resulting with $270,000 in the endowed fund.[1184]

Heritage Days, sponsored by the Slippery Rock Borough, in celebration of its history, combined efforts with the University's Community Day to create a joint

Senator Tim Shaffer (left) presents President Aebersold with Boy Scouts of America, Moraine Trials Council, Distinguished Citizens Award, April 1995

celebration on September 21, 1996, on the University's campus.[1185] This action was further testimony to the excellent relationship between the Borough and the University.

In spring 1996, the Pennsylvania Department of Education and the National Council for the Accreditation of Teacher Education visited the University as part of their review of the College of Education for re-accreditation. Since both professional agencies found that the College met their standards, its accreditation continued. Dr. Aebersold reported, "We will remain among the elite college and university programs". The NCATE team chairperson indicated that "two exemplary ratings have been bestowed and how unusual that feat is to accomplish as there is usually only one exemplary rating granted".[1186] Dr. Catherine Morsink, Dean of the College of Education and Dr. John Hicks, Assistant to the Dean were commended for their outstanding work.

In the fall of 1996, the Chronicle of Higher Education reported that among master's degree institutions, Slippery Rock University ranked fifth in the Nation by sending 298 students abroad. Among all American colleges and universities, only fourteen sent a higher percentage of their students abroad.[1187] SRU had succeeded in developing a nationally ranked international program.

In 1994, the State System negotiated a contract with Pepsi-Cola Corporation that resulted with Pepsi products being sold exclusively on the State System's fourteen university campuses. The contract provided Slippery Rock University $50,000 each year for ten years.[1188]

The Division of Advancement played important roles for the University other than strictly fund raising. The Advancement Division often supported activities and programs which promoted the name of Slippery Rock University. The University's Camps and Conferences Program was becoming very popular to high school students by the 1990s. Boasting nearly 100 camps and conferences during the summer of 1996, the program was up nearly fifteen percent from the previous year. More than 12,500 participants and 27,500 visitors were involved with the program. Notable camps included a football camp, featuring several Pittsburgh Steelers, including Coach Bill Cowher and players Greg Lloyd, Carnell Lake, Rod Woodson, and retired player Merrill Hoge.[1189]

The Sigma Pi social fraternity was disbanded in 1996. Its house and land located at 223 Harmony Road was purchased later by the Council of Trustees.[1190]

After several years of operation in university quarters, the Slippery Rock University Alumni Association announced receipt of a $50,000 gift and their intention of pursuing the possibility of purchasing or building an alumni house.[1191] In August, 1996, the Alumni Association, working with the University, announced plans for the construction of a new Alumni Center on the historic part of campus just north of the East/West Gymnasium Complex at an approximate anticipated cost of $500,000.[1192] The total cost of the project would come from the operating budget of the Alumni Association and gifts from alumni. Groundbreaking for the new Russell Wright Alumni Center took place June 21, 1997 during alumni weekend. Dr. Wright, a member of the class of 1923 and long-time friend of Slippery Rock University attended the groundbreaking with his wife, Rose, and other family members.[1193] President Aebersold paused to comment that the University and the Alumni Association have worked in harmony for more than eighty years. The University providing office space and staff for the Alumni Association in exchange for services and programs provided.[1194] Dr. Aebersold

commended the Board of Directors of the Slippery Rock University Alumni Association, Mr. Franklin Carr, its President at the time of the ground breaking, and Mrs. Sally Lennox, Director of the Association. More than $550,000 in cash and pledges had been received for the new Alumni Center.[1195]

To accommodate the housing shortage on campus, President Aebersold asked the Council of Trustees to accept the lowest bid, from the firm Burt Hill Kosar Rittelmann Associates, to conduct a feasibility study for an apartment-style residence complex at a cost of $44,968.07.[1196] After an extensive study by students, faculty, administration and staff to determine student housing needs and options, Dr. Aebersold presented to the Council a proposal for a $5.4 million apartment-style residence complex to be built east of Founders Hall.[1197] Initially, the sixty-unit complex would include forty, two-person apartments and twenty, four-person apartments. Twenty-year bonds retired by student paid residence hall fees would provide funding for the new facility.[1198] By fall 1995, the architect had been selected and contracts prepared.[1199] Bids for construction were released during the spring of 1996 and site preparation and construction began during the summer.[1200] Students fully occupied the new Rock Apartments fall 1997.[1201]

In December 1996, President Aebersold announced that the men's basketball program had violated NCAA regulations and, as a result, was issued sanctions. Most of the violations however, had been discovered and corrected before the university was sanctioned.[1202] This occurred at a time when nearly fifty percent of all Slippery Rock University students were involved in sport at some level; intramural, club or varsity.

The Rock Apartments, 1997

For more than twenty years, the University had been developing integrated programs focusing on the environment. Midway through the 1996-1997 academic year President Aebersold announced this further development: "On February 24, 1997 Governor Tom Ridge and the Commonwealth of Pennsylvania officially launched the newly created Pennsylvania Center for Environmental Education with Slippery Rock University as the designated home office. The Center will facilitate quality environmental education and help create partnerships that facilitate cooperation between state agencies, business industry, and grass root programs dealing with various segments of the Commonwealth's environmental health."[1203] Dr. Paulette Johnson, Associate Professor of Parks, Recreation and Environmental Education, directed the Center that would assist Pennsylvania with the design of environmental education programs for the Twenty-First Century. Only the second center of its kind in the nation, it would also assist in securing funding for environmental education programs throughout the state.[1204]

Rev. Bernice King autographs her books for SRU faculty and staff
Rev King was the keynote speaker at SRU's
Dr. Martin Luther King, Jr. Day Observance, January 1997

The report, "Crime at College: The Student Guide to Personal Safety", listed Slippery Rock University as the second safest college area among the more than 200 areas in Pennsylvania and the ninth safest of the more than 3,000 college areas in the nation. President Aebersold commended the campus police, led by Mr. Eric Thomas and all the staff, who helped to make the University community safe. The President also recognized the excellent work of the Slippery Rock Borough Police and other supportive officials.[1205]

A movement throughout the United States was requiring certified public accounting candidates to complete 150 clock hours of education after the baccalaureate degree as a requirement for certification. This prompted the Accounting faculty to develop a Master of Science degree in Accounting. Students began in the program January, 1997.[1206]

By the mid 1990s, the McKeever Environmental Center, was having a significant impact on public school, elementary and secondary students. During the 1996-97 academic year, approximately 5,200 students and 500 teachers from more than seventy schools representing thirty counties within the Commonwealth had been served at McKeever.[1207] The McKeever Environmental Center was recognized by many as a model program for environmental education.

In March 1997, Dr. Aebersold formally recognized the First Year Studies program as an integral unit within the University. The effort that had been underway informally for more than a decade, facilitating various first year, student success programs and activities. An intrusive academic advisement system, an individual student tracking program, personalized tutoring and other activities were designed to increase student retention at the university. Dr. Aebersold observed: "We must marshal the services of Academic Affairs, Student Affairs, and other parts of the university in helping students not only through the orientation process, but also to track these students more intensively for the first year and one half trying to assist their transition to college."[1208]

What was formerly just a track within the physical education program, sport management was promoted to degree program status in June, 1997. Programs at the bachelor's and master's levels were approved and immediately garnered student interest.[1209]

245

*Dr. and Mrs. Stanley Kraus (right) with President Aebersold
prior to December, 1996 commencement*

While several improvements had been made over the previous decades to the East/West Gymnasium complex, President Aebersold announced a plan for a major renovation of the facility. The renovation would be made possible through a shared capital facilities project negotiated with the Governor's Budget Secretary.[1210] Slippery Rock University would be responsible for a percentage of the cost of renovation. By the summer, 1995, the project had moved into design stage awaiting construction.[1211]

In December 1996, the Council of Trustees approved a proposal presented by student member, Ms. Charity Blakely to name the new center, the Robert N. Aebersold Student Recreation Center.[1212] Ms. Blakely stated, "It is an honor for me as a student to take part in this, and I don't think there is a more appropriate or deserving person."[1213] In accepting the honor, President Aebersold said, "I am humbled. I appreciate the hard work of the

*President Aebersold (left) hosts Mr. F. Eugene Dixon (center), Chair Person of the State System's
Board of Governors and Chancellor James McCormick, mid 1990's*

President and Mrs. Aebersold at
December 1996, commencement

a special meeting of the Council of Trustees called for December 21, 1996.[1218] At that meeting, three candidates were approved by the Council of Trustees and forwarded for further consideration to Chancellor James McCormick. The candidates were Dr. Manuel L. Ibanez, President, Texas A&M at Kingsville; Dr. Kay Schallenkamp, Provost and Vice Chancellor for Academic Affairs, University of Wisconsin at White Water; and Dr. G. Warren Smith, served ten years as President, Southeastern Louisiana University.[1219]

At the March 3, 1997, Council of Trustees meeting, Chancellor James McCormick joined many others in commending Dr. Robert Aebersold for his leadership, "Bob, it is with great thanks and respect that I publicly acknowledge your tremendous service to the University, to the System, and to the people of the Commonwealth. I know you will close your chapter as the President of Slippery Rock University with great success and recognition. Congratulations to you."[1220]

Student Government Association and our students to make this facility possible. I am particularly honored because the plan for naming the building has come from students, and I thank them all."[1214]

Nearly thirteen years after his selection as President, Dr. Aebersold announced his intention to retire on July 1, 1997.[1215] Mr. Edward P. Kelley, Vice Chancellor for Employee and Labor Relations of the State System for Higher Education, discussed the procedure for replacing Dr. Aebersold with the Council of Trustees during their June, 1996, meeting.[1216] It was anticipated that the search would run from summer, 1996, through the early part of 1997, with the new President assuming the position on July 1, 1997.

The presidential search committee held its organizational meeting on August 19, 1996.[1217] Committee work continued throughout the fall and early winter with

President Aebersold was bestowed with the title, President Emeritus, in a unanimous act by the Council of Trustees, each thanking him for his service.[1221] The President responded: "I am overwhelmed by your generosity. I simply want to thank all of you for your comments. I will cherish them."[1222]

By the conclusion of President Aebersold's tenure, the Slippery Rock Foundation assets totaled more than $7.2 million. At the same time, the Slippery Rock Alumni Association net worth approximated $1.2 million, both all time high figures to date.[1223]

Nearly three months had passed since the announcement of the names of the three presidential candidates. The campus was anxious to learn of the decision. And then, on March 3, 1997 the Chancellor informed the university community "on the tenth of April, the formal offer of appointment will be extended to Dr. G. Warren Smith".[1224]

Student Sam Thangiah, now professor, Computer
Science, works on early PC, mid 1980's

"The Rock" relocated to N. Kerr Thompson Stadium, 1988

1989 Regional Baseball Champions

1997 Regional Baseball Champions

Rock apartment building

Vacation College group, 1987

CHAPTER X

Advancing to the Millennium

Born and raised in State College, Pennsylvania G. Warren Smith, with a quest for a higher education, traveled to Grinnel, Iowa where he earned a Bachelor of Arts degree from Grinnel College. He returned to the East to earn a Doctor of Philosophy degree from Cornell University in New York.

Dr. Smith served as associate professor, professor and head of the department of Chemistry at the University of Alaska in Fairbanks and American Council of Education Fellow and visiting professor of Chemistry and Chemical Engineering at Cornell University.

From 1979 to 1984, Dr. Smith served as Dean of the School of Science and Technologies at the University of Houston, Clear Lake. From the deanship in Texas, he rose to the academic affairs vice presidency at Southeastern Louisiana University in Hammond, Louisiana. Just two years later in 1986, Dr. Smith was chosen president of SLU, a position he held for nine years. Before being selected as the fourteenth president of Slippery Rock University beginning July 1, 1997 Dr. Smith served as honors professor of Arts and Sciences at SLU.

President Smith understood the importance of developing good faculty relationships, and made it a priority to meet with every academic department during his first semester on campus. At the conclusion of the departmental meetings, "He was impressed by the commitment to excellence and the dedication to students shared by every group."[1225]

Beginning President Smith's initial days at the helm, he saw the need for an increased planning effort for Slippery Rock University. The Future Watch task force was created to facilitate Slippery Rock University's preparation for the future. According to President Smith, "Future Watch was designed as an initiative for university self-renewal at a time when we are adjusting to new leadership and state wide systemic change. Its purpose

Dr. G. Warren Smith, President, 1997-2002

was to identify issues, collect and review information and make recommendations to the Cabinet that will culminate in the development of a new vision statement for SRU."[1226]

A few months after President Smith assumed office, the University received a $100,000 grant from the State System of Higher Education to create a technology-based career laboratory.[1227] Housed in the Maltby Center, the Career Lab became a major service utilized by students at all levels of their education.

President and Dr. Constance Smith at Welcome Reception, July 1997

In his first year, Dr. Smith established a President's Advisory Council comprised of a small group of alumni and friends of the University, who had distinguished themselves nationally and internationally as successful leaders. "The mission of the President's Advisory Council will be to provide the opportunity for the University's leadership to benefit from their insight and experience regarding issues and concerns of the University."[1228] President Smith relied on the members of his Advisory Council for advice, especially as he moved through the transition of his first few years of leadership.

It was evident to the new president that alternative revenue sources would be necessary if Slippery Rock University was to enjoy increased fiscal flexibility. Fundraising efforts would need to increase significantly. As a result, President Smith charged the division of University Advancement with this critical responsibility. During the fall of 1997, the Slippery Rock University Foundation reported total assets of $10 million. This was an increase of 37% when compared with the previous year and an increase of 207% over the previous five years.[1229]

During his first semester of leadership, President Smith was informed by the State System of Higher Education in Harrisburg that Slippery Rock University would need to create a five-year master plan of campus development. DRS / The Saratoga Associates was selected

by the University to conduct this important planning process. Concurrently, the campus was undergoing a comprehensive facilities study to review the location of underground service lines, pedestrian and vehicular traffic patterns and the current conditions of all and buildings and general infrastructure.[1230]

That fall 1997, the football team was enjoying its best season in the University's 108-year history. After winning the Pennsylvania State Athletic Conference championship, the Rock hosted and won the first round NCAA Division II playoff game with Ashland University before losing the regional playoff game at the Yale Bowl in New Haven, Connecticut.[1231]

Before the students left campus for the end of the fall semester, a major student-focused initiative took place. December 11, 1997 marked the ground breaking for the long awaited, new Robert Aebersold Student Recreation Center. President Smith commented, "Our Student Government Association is to be congratulated for its many efforts to see this project to its completion."[1232]

As President Smith learned of the University's various academic programs and services, he showed particular interest in the activities that were developed with first-year students in mind. He was familiar with the concept of front-loading services for traditional freshmen and wanted to see the support services expanded at Slippery Rock University. Subsequently, the First

President Smith greets a family in his home during Family Weekend, September 1997

Year Studies Program (FYRST) was formally adopted in 1998 with one primary goal, "to facilitate the student transition from high school or work to the University."[1233]

On the cutting edge of library services, in 1998, the Pennsylvania State System of Higher Education developed the Keystone Library Network, a virtual library network for all students at the fourteen state owned universities. The State System of Higher Education was the only System in the nation enabling its students to read electronic text of approximately 1,350 journals and to review summaries of articles printed in approximately 1,400 additional journals online.[1234]

Together with the University's Public Relations Office, the Alumni Association launched a new Rock Magazine concept in early 1998, creating a forty-eight page multi-color publication to replace the former Alumni publication. Now, instead of being sent to only its dues paying members, the new publication would be sent to all alumni, nearly 40,000, informing them of their Alma Mater's major events, programs and news.[1235]

Concurrently, the Rock Net Alumni program was created. As a mentoring program, connecting students with alumni and friends of the University, it was developed to assist students with career goals.[1236] Within three months, alumni from nineteen states and nine foreign countries were involved with Rock Net. And within a

University police on bike patrol, about 1997

year, alumni from twenty-seven states were engaged in the new program.[1237]

At the September 3, 1998 academic assembly President Smith reported, for the first time, to the University community, and beyond via television broadcast. The focus of his report was the progress and success of Future Watch. Over the previous ten months more than 300 campus, community, and regional leaders comprised the six study teams, which sought intensely the University's internal strengths and weaknesses and external threats and opportunities. The information was comprehensively reviewed and competitive advantages and driving forces considered. One of the results was the vision statement, "Slippery Rock University will excel as a caring community of lifelong learners connecting with the world."[1238]

After the formation of a continuous improvement model, President Smith commented "we are now at a critical crossroads in the overall process. Through this process SRU will become more efficient and more quality-oriented—all to the benefit of our students and their families. The continuous improvement coordinating council has been charged to launch strategic action plans conducive to

Faculty and staff at the Academic Assembly, September 3, 1998

each of the ten university goals and the Trustees will be kept apprise as the plan unfolds."[1239]

In September 1998, Dr. Anne Griffiths, long time faculty and administrator, was appointed Interim Provost and Vice President for Academic Affairs. Dr. Griffiths immediately took charge of the development of the self-study in preparation for the Middle States Association of Colleges and Schools upcoming visit

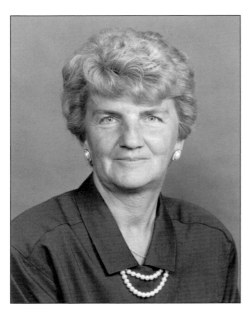

Dr. Anne Griffiths, Interim Provost
and Vice President for
Academic Affairs, 1998

2000-2001.[1240] She announced a new student enrollment of 1,300 freshmen and 509 transfers, an increase from the previous year. However, the University's total enrollment again decreased primarily due to the continued loss of non-resident and part time students.[1241]

With enrollment in mind, two new academic programs were developed in 1998. A bachelor's degree program in Exercise Science and a major in Human Resource Management were added to Slippery Rock's academic offerings.[1242]

Two new facilities were dedicated during the fall 1998. On October 3, the Russell Wright Alumni House was opened to the University's alumni, students, faculty and staff. Just a week later on October 10, the Jerry Bejbl Athletic Training Facility, attached to the N. Kerr Thompson football stadium, was dedicated.[4] The facility was made available by Mr. Jerry Bejbl, class of 1963, contributing the single largest gift in the University's history.[1243] Also that fall, former head football coach Bob DiSpirito was honored with the naming of the football field inside N. Kerr Thompson stadium, the Bob DiSpirito Field.[1244] Coach DiSpirito and his very successful teams established a dynasty in area collegiate football beginning the early 1970s.

Serving the community had been a common practice for Slippery Rock University students since the founding of the University. In the late 1990s Slippery Rock University's Community Service Learning Institute (CSLI) again gained national recognition through its extensive volunteer programs. "The Community Service Learning Institute operates a system for leveraging knowledge to develop socially responsible, civic minded youth. The Institute prepares young people, in partnership with their communities, to use personal strengths, academic preparation, and community resources to address pressing needs." A variety of programs are provided including the "Kids that Care" program which sponsors "Care Breaks" assisting flood victims in various states, providing hurricane relief with Native Americans, promoting urban redevelopment and creating affordable housing through Habitat for Humanity. The activities normally take place during spring breaks. The Connector Core is a cadre of SRU student leaders who collaborate with Allegheny, Butler, Lawrence and Mercer County communities to address needs in the areas of

Wright Alumni House construction, April 1998

President Smith (left), Senator Rick Santorum (center) and Dr. Griffiths meet on campus, 1999

community development, education and literacy, youth leadership development and the environment.[1245]

A record eighty-two varsity athletes were recognized for their academic accomplishments by the Pennsylvania State Athletic Conference (PSAC) as scholar athletes during the President's first year on campus. In addition to this honor the University also ranked number one in the PSAC for the number of athletes gaining National Academic All-America status.[1246]

Slippery Rock University continued to develop national recognition when, during the fall 1998, "the play" was featured on ESPN as the play of the week. Occurring in the last second of the football game, a Rock receiver caught a pass to defeat long-time rival Indiana University of Pennsylvania (IUP).[1247] The *New York Times* featured Slippery Rock University in an extensive article on western Pennsylvania football and enhanced its national notoriety.[1248] The Rock football team enjoyed another great regular season, resulting with its second consecutive PSAC championship. It went on to win two regional playoff games permitting them to advance to the final four Division II competition where it lost to Carson-Newman College of Jefferson City, Tennessee. For its outstanding efforts the football team was selected the Division II Team of the Year 1998 with the Lambert Meadowlands Award. Established in 1936, the award is among the oldest and most prestigious awards in collegiate athletics. At the same time head coach Dr. George Mihalik was selected one of the five regional

winners of the American Football Coaches Association's 1998 GTE Coach of the Year.[1249]

Awards were also earned in other areas of the University. The State System for Higher Education established the Eberly Awards for philanthropy and volunteerism in 1998 to recognize 30 individuals, two from each of the fourteen universities and the System office. The awards were created "to honor those who have advanced the cause of public higher education through their acts of philanthropy and volunteerism."[1250] Slippery Rock University's recipients, Dr. Jerry Bejbl for philanthropy and Mr. Kenneth Blair for volunteerism, were recognized in October at a special ceremony in Harrisburg.[1251]

At the end of the fall semester 1998, President Smith announced the formation of the Teaching and Learning Technology Roundtable (TLTR). Primarily a group of volunteer faculty who meet to discuss concerns and issues of technology and how technology can improve learning, the TLTR quickly became an active organization.[1252]

The Rocket, the weekly student newspaper, earned the National Pacemaker award for its overall journalistic excellence in 1999. Other universities vying for the coveted title were Penn State University, University of Pennsylvania and Carnegie Mellon University.[1253]

Slippery Rock University was recognized as a leader in transfer articulation with the community colleges since the early 1970s. In 1999 the University

Grand Marshall Wilma Cavill passes the University Mace to the newly inaugurated president, December 1998

F. Eugene Dixon (left), Chairperson of State System Board of Governors, President Smith (center) and Chancellor James McCormick at President Smith's inauguration, December 1998

expanded its articulation efforts leading to the Bachelor of Science degree in Applied Science to twenty-three proprietary schools, all tied to workforce development in Pennsylvania.[1254] The University went on to sign an articulation agreement with the Pennsylvania Association of Private School Administrators to encourage more graduates of accredited proprietary schools to consider SRU.[1256] By the summer of 2001 more than sixty articulation transfer agreements had been developed and signed with the community colleges and proprietary schools.[1257]

The University's facilities master plan was completed during the summer 1999. The plan called for the improvement of many facets of the University's physical plant, resulting with a more effective use of classroom space; reallocation of space; reorganization of departments; redesign of pedestrian and vehicular traffic patterns; and renovation and new construction projects.[1258] While the University was reviewing its existing facilities, its inventory increased. The Old Stone House, situated five miles south of Slippery Rock at the intersection of Routes 8 and 173, had been managed by the University since 1982 and was now being transferred to the University. Through a memo of understanding with the Pennsylvania Historical and Museum Commission, the University assumed ownership of the Old Stone House, seventy-two acres of land, two modern residences and several service buildings.[1259]

In June 1999, after an extensive national search, President Warren Smith announced the appointment of Dr. Robert M. Smith, Provost and Vice President for Academic Affairs. Dr. Smith had been serving the University of Tennessee at Martin as Dean of the School of Arts and Sciences.[1260] President Smith said of the new Provost, "Dr. Smith will take this University very far on the next level where we need to be."[1261]

Almost immediately, Provost Robert Smith began working on reversing the declining enrollment trend. Much of the decade of the 1990s had witnessed a persistent enrollment decline resulting with a loss of more than 800 students. An expert in the enrollment management area, Dr. Robert Smith quickly implemented a three-year enrollment management plan identifying immediate needs and initiatives.[1262]

Aerial view of campus from west, 1999

Aerial view of campus from east, 1999

*Artist sculptor, James Myford (left), music faculty,
Kate Brennan and Maribeth Knaub (center, left and right),
with President Smith at sculpture dedication, late 1990's*

During the summer 1999, the new Provost created three priorities for the fall. Enrollment was at the top of the list. Professional development of faculty, especially in the use of technology, to promote learning and increase faculty student research was second. A performance-based funding program for the division, which would reward academic departments and units successful in achieving important goals completed the list.[1263]

The fall semester, 1999 began with serious concern. The faculty, represented by the Association of Pennsylvania State College and University Faculties, had been working without a contract since June 30, 1999. A strike authorization vote was scheduled for the end of September. President Smith commented, "we want to insure that our faculty continue to be well compensated for the excellent job they do, but we recognize the limitations imposed by appropriations and how much one can ask students for increases in tuition. It is the State System's intent to keep the universities open for our students, and to continue good faith bargaining until an agreement is reached."[1264] Negotiations between APSCUF and the State System

took place in Harrisburg. Before the end of the fall semester, a new contract was approved retroactive to July 1.[1265]

In September 1999, The State System announced that all fourteen universities would be assessed in three broad performance areas—student success, institutional efficiency, and diversity. The President commented, "More and more the State System is using assessment indicators to determine how well the universities are doing."[1266] "Slippery Rock University is poised for a very exciting future. Improvements to the curriculum and university infrastructure will continue in the upcoming year. Enrollment issues remain a paramount concern. The enrollment management committee is looking ahead five to ten years, a twenty-year Facilities master plan is underway and we are preparing for our Middle States Association reaccredidation, which is slated for 2000-2001."[1267]

Slippery Rock University opened a new off-campus center halfway between the campus and Pittsburgh, at the Waterfront property in Wexford (Cranberry Township). The new center provided part time students, many of whom were employed full time, the opportunity to continue their undergraduate and graduate education closer to their workplaces.[1268] Initially, three classrooms,

Marching Rockets, Homecoming, late 1990's

Very large spruce near old main blows down, late 1990's

President Smith (right) entertains guests in his home, 1999

Football team's 1999 PSAC Championship trophy hoisted

a computer lab, a TV lab for distance learning, an office and reception area were provided.[1269]

The United States Government turned over control of the Panama Canal to the Panamanian Government in late 1999. Former U.S. Ambassador to Panama, Mr. Ambler H. Moss, and a major influence in the development of the new treaty visited campus and spoke to a capacity audience in the University's Swope Music Hall auditorium .[1270]

Graduates of Slippery Rock University were increasingly sought by prospective employers. During the fall 1999, more than sixty-five recruiters representing more than thirty states attended the fall education consortium and teacher job fair hoping to recruit Slippery Rock graduates. The program was presented by the office of Career Services and the College of Education.[1271]

The Slippery Rock University football team continued its domination over the other state owned universities by earning its third consecutive PSAC championship, fall 1999 and Coach Mihalik earned his third consecutive PSAC Western Division Coach of the Year honor.[1272] A total of thirteen players were named to the All-Conference team, more than any other university in the State System. For the second consecutive year Coach Mihalik earned the GTE Regional Coach of the Year honors by the American Football Coaches Association. A $10,000 academic scholarship was awarded by GTE to SRU in Coach Mihalik's honor. The team ended its season ranked second in the nation.[1273]

Three more degree programs were added to Slippery Rock's academic offerings in 1999, two at the undergraduate level and one at the graduate level. Bachelor degree programs in Information Science and Communication (Journalism, Public Relations and Emerging Technology Multi-Media) were instantly popular with undergraduate students. Building upon the very successful bachelor degree program in Exercise Science first offered the year before, a master's degree program in Exercise Science was added to the graduate offerings.[1274]

The McKeever Environmental Center celebrated its twenty-fifth anniversary during the fall of 1999. Established in 1974, McKeever provided environmental education programs to schools, undergraduate students, teachers and the public. SRU administered the center on behalf of the Commonwealth. The State System's Board of Governors recognized the center and its importance during the fall and Mrs. Opal McKeever,

widow of Dr. Ivan McKeever, was present to receive congratulations.[1275]

Major renovations to the East/West Instructional Complex (East and West Gymnasia) were completed during the fall of 1999. These renovations supported the University's instructional process.[1276]

The long anticipated new Physical Therapy building was finally designed and construction began during the fall 1999.[1277] And Old Main, the University's oldest facility, was being fitted for an elevator to service all four floors in order to comply with the Americans with Disabilities Act.[1278] Rocky's Grille, a popular area for student dining, last renovated in 1986, received a major face lift in late 1999.[1279]

The construction project the student body was focused on concluded its first phase before the students ended the fall semester 1999. After two years of construction, phase 1 of the new Robert Aebersold Student Recreation Center was opened the first week of December, featuring a new Russell Wright Fitness Center. Initially, more than 700 students per day utilized the 7,714 square foot workout center

East view of Art building, 1999

New International students with office staff at Myford sculpture, 2000

260

featuring a 44-foot high climbing wall.[1280] The other areas of the center, including the pool and aquatic area, the indoor track and two large general gymnasium areas, were opened to the students January of the new millennium.[1281]

On the eve of the millennium, an aggressive advertising campaign was planned for the University. Included for the first year in this diverse plan were the development of new brochures, billboards, Pittsburgh bus ads and a new *Rock Magazine*.[1282] In the second year, beginning September, the University introduced a three-month advertising campaign to reinforce the institutional image and attract further interest of prospective new students. The plan incorporated the theme of "Rock Solid Education" and called for strategic placement of print, radio, television and transit advertisements.[1283] Mr. Ross Feltz, Director of University Public Relations, was instrumental in the design, development and initiation of this successful campaign.

Dr. Kerchis, Director, International Programs (left) with President Smith on Asia tour, December 1999

President Smith (left) receives Bangladesh Official, 2000

In December 1999 President Smith was honored at the North South University Convocation in Bangladesh as Chief Guest and Convocation Speaker. At that time, Slippery Rock was enjoying the enrollment of eleven students from Bangladesh, five from North South University.[1284]

As part of the regular 1999 and 2000 presidential evaluations, members of the Council of Trustees met with constituents of the University community regarding the leadership of President G. Warren Smith. The following motion was unanimously approved in 1999, "It is the Council of Trustees' recommendation to you, Chancellor McCormick, and to the Board of Governors, to continue Dr. Smith's contract of service to the maximum permitted as Dr. G. Warren Smith fulfills adequately his position as President of Slippery Rock University."[1285] In 2000 a letter was sent requesting a one-year extension of President Smith's contract.[1286]

In January 2000, the Board of Governors, in order to monitor and assess the periodic progress of each of its universities, required the development and submission of a Performance and Outcomes Plan.[1287] President Smith presented the University's plan in June 2000, including targeted performance goals for thirty-six categories and a strategic plan covering 161 initiatives.[1288] Clearly, this was the beginning of increased accountability linking State System directions to specific university goals. By the spring 2001, President Smith had received feedback on the University's Performance and Outcomes Plan, "while the Board of Governors believes that the University's performance overall is generally good; they also believe that there are opportunities for improvement and increased efficiency which should and must be pursued in light of its legislative purpose, plans and goals. The POP report calls for monitoring assessment and periodically reporting to the Board of Governors on a quarterly basis our progress in a host of different areas. Further, there is a strong indication that performance plans and outcomes will be directly linked to all future management reviews and compensation adjustments."[1289]

President Smith announced a $1.2 million initiative to improve the University's technology during the spring

Azaleas blooming in front of Maltby, Spring 2000

Former President Aebersold (left) is congratulated by President Smith (center) and Chancellor McCormick at the dedication of the Robert Aebersold Student Recreation Center, March 10, 2000

semester 2000. "This will afford greater opportunities in research and scholarship" and "we must be progressive in providing our students with sophisticated equipment and functional labs to build skills for critical thinking, effective problem solving and decision making."[1290]

Workforce development and creation of jobs, especially through the use of technology became a statewide initiative of Governor Tom Ridge. In response to the Governor's request of Pennsylvania colleges and universities for technology proposals, Slippery Rock submitted three significant proposals:

1. To construct a new Science and Technology building replacing Vincent Science Hall.
2. Renovation of Vincent Science Hall to become a learning-centered hub focusing on student services.
3. The North Hills Educational Alliance will serve as a model for future educational cooperatives and a national showcase for how the State System can serve workforce development, community education and lifelong learning needs.[1291]

The University received $126,000 in spring 2000 through a Heinz endowment fund grant to connect rural and urban schools that work with pre-service teachers. Three school districts, the Pittsburgh Public Schools, the Moniteau School District and the Sharon School District would receive benefits coordinated by the University. The grant will provide resources to create an important training ground for the University's pre-service teachers, a research setting for our faculty, in-service training resources for public school teachers, and a cooperative learning environment for students.[1292]

During the spring 2000, the Board of Governors mandated the installation of automatic fire suppression systems in all state owned university residence halls. Slippery Rock University had already installed sprinkler systems in Dodds, Bard, Harner and Founders Halls leaving North, Kraus, Patterson and Rhoads Halls and the Rock Apartments to be completed.[1293]

On March 10, 2000, the new student recreation center named in honor of President Emeritus Robert N. Aebersold was dedicated. Dr. Aebersold and Chancellor of the State System of Higher Education, Dr. James McCormick were on hand to assist in the dedication of the immensely popular student-funded facility containing more than 80,000 square feet of recreation area.[1294]

Within a year after it's opening, campus recreation director, Mr. Greg Sferra announced that the Aebersold Student Recreation Center had received a major accolade—the Athletic Business Magazine recognized the center as one of ten National winners of their "Facility of Merit" award. The average student use per day had reached 1,000 students, affirming the need for such a facility.[1295]

Students enjoyed diverse programs in the millennia year. The modern day version of the Broadway musical "Jesus Christ Superstar" was performed in Miller Auditorium. The forty-member cast and thirty-member crew performed five times and presented the largest production in more than a decade. The daughter of Malcolm X, Ilyasah Shabazz, spoke about the life of her father to students, faculty and staff in a lecture sponsored by the University's Black Action Society and University Programming Board.[1296]

The "ARC", May 2001

The University signed another formal, international agreement in mid-June 2000, this time with the University of Costa Rica. The agreement was the eighteenth international exchange agreement for SRU.[1297]

After a somewhat abrupt departure of the Vice President of Student Affairs in June 2000, President Warren Smith announced Dr. Robert J. Watson, Dean of Academic Services, had been appointed to the position, Interim Vice President for Student Affairs. "President Smith expressed that he is confident in Dr. Watson's abilities to lead the division during this time of transition and is delighted that he is willing to accept this important assignment."[1298] After a national search had been conducted, Dr. Watson, in his 30th year at Slippery Rock University, was appointed to the permanent position, June 2001.[1299]

The millennia alumni weekend, June 2000, was coordinated by the new Alumni Director, Mr. Michael Saraka, class of 1989. More than 250 alumni returned to enjoy a comprehensive schedule of activities and celebrate the golden graduate class of 1950.[1300] The class of 1970 presented the Alumni Association with more than $5,000 to provide landscaping around the new Russell Wright Alumni Center.[1301]

At the fall 2000, Council of Trustees meeting Mr. Brad Kovaleski, Student Government's Vice President for Student Affairs, and Student Trustee, Susan Davis, introduced the "Rock Pride" campaign coordinated through the Division of Student Affairs. Utilizing the term "Rock Pride" which originated in the athletic program years before, the campus wide program promoted the re-establishment of strong school spirit at the Rock. Students encouraged faculty, staff and trustees to attend

Coach George Mihalik (center) with his 2000 football captains, Randy McKavish (right) and Mike Waszczuk holding the four consecutive PSAC Championship trophies from 1997, 1998, 1999 and 2000

Rock Pride photo with President Smith holding right edge of sign, 2001

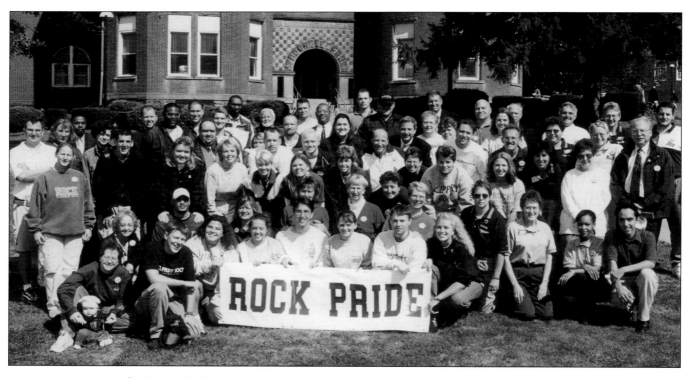

Student Life division in front of Old Main with President Smith (far right), 2000

an all-university, fall photograph in front of North Hall, revisiting what Dr. Maltby had initiated nearly a hundred years earlier. President Smith stated, "You know, our students are the pride of The Rock." The same week the new mascot, "the lion" leading the pride of Slippery Rock, was unveiled in the quad to hundreds of students in attendance.[1302]

At a time when assessment inside the classroom was critical to measuring the outcomes of learning, the Student Affairs division developed a day-long workshop for university faculty and staff entitled, Student Learning and Development Outcomes: Assessment Strategies. Dr. Virginia Wagner, Dean of Students at Alverno College, conducted the collaborative Assessment Strategies workshop.[1303]

The Association of Residence Hall Students, with university support, initiated a student readership program delivering to students in every residence hall and the University Union, the local daily newspaper, *The Butler Eagle*; the regional daily newspaper, *The Pittsburgh Press*; and the national daily newspaper, *USA Today*. In addition to students being able to read for enjoyment the daily newspapers, faculty incorporated the newspapers into their classroom assignments.[1304]

As a state-owned university, Slippery Rock clearly recognized its mission to the community. In 2000, as an effort to improve communication with landlords within the community, a group was formed for the purpose of sharing information.[1305] The group proved effective benefiting the University and the off-campus landlords, however the real benefits of the collaborative efforts were realized by the students.

The magnitude of the University's renovation and construction of its physical plant was represented in

late fall 2000 with President Smith's statement, "We have completed more than $30 million worth of new construction and renovation in the past five years." The President went on to say, "this campus' infrastructure has been essentially rebuilt from power plant improvements to our telephone system, utility lines to computer cabling and networking systems." [1306]

In November 2000, the traditional community light-up night was held in the memory of Slippery Rock Mayor and University Alumnus, Mr. Pat Madden, who had recently passed away. President Smith commented, "Pat Madden was our Mayor, our alumnus and most of all, our friend."[1307]

Pat Madden, Mayor of Slippery Rock and alumnus

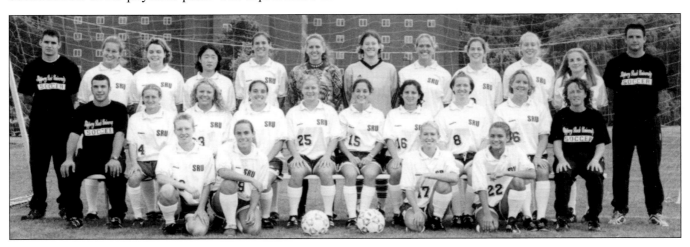

2001 Women's Soccer Team with Coach Noreen Herlihy, seated, far right

A new graduate degree program was added to Slippery Rock University's list of offerings in 2000. In cooperation with Clarion University, the Master of Science in Nursing degree would now be offered graduate students through coursework required at both universities.[1308]

The Physical Therapy doctoral program received excellent news at the close of the fall term 2000 . The Commission on Accreditation on Physical Therapy Education granted, effective November 2000, an eight-year certificate of accreditation, the maximum allowable, to the University.[1309] The Nursing program also received a maximum period of accreditation, five years, from the National League for Nursing Accrediting Commission. The department of Dance received accreditation from the National Association of Schools of Dance, effective October 10, 2000, becoming the first accredited dance program in the state.[1310]

Dr. James H. McCormick, Chancellor of the State System of Higher Education announced December 2000, his resignation to assume the Chancellorship of the Minnesota State College and University System. Dr. McCormick, a State System alumnus, had served as a faculty member, an administrator and president at State System universities before being selected the first Chancellor in 1983.[1311] Within a year, a new Chancellor, Dr. Judy G. Hample, was selected and toured the Slippery Rock University campus speaking with students, faculty and staff.[1312]

State conference championships were earned during the spring semester 2001, by the women's track team and the men's baseball team. After winning the PSAC championship, the baseball team went on to the North Atlantic Regional tournament where it lost in the final championship round.[1313]

In June 2001, a month before the next regularly scheduled presidential review, President Smith submitted a progress report to the Council of Trustees. "In 1997, I inaugurated *Future Watch*, a strategic planning process involving more than fifty university and 300 community leaders, to define the University's core values, driving forces, comparative advantages and key measures of success. We emerged from the process with the University's

Student Leadership Tour, University of Edinburgh, Scotland, March 2001

2001 Women's Track/Field Team, PSAC champions

first vision statement upon which so much has been built to date: Slippery Rock University will excel as a caring community of lifelong learners connecting with the world."[1314] The President went on to identify a number of accomplishments:

1. "We have undergone a significant and systematic transformation in response to goals and guidelines established by the State System of Higher Education."
2. "We have established programmatic areas of distinction recognized by the State System."
3. "The Board of Governors has approved our three-year business plan (the Performance Outcomes Plan) through 2003."

4. "Last January I announced a major reorganization of all academic departments across the University. This restructuring evolved from *Future Watch*."

5. "Through these efforts, we've created a Rock Solid foundation, which presents a clear, bright and ambitious picture of what Slippery Rock University should be like in the twenty-first century."[1315]

By September of 2001, the Council of Trustees had completed their review of the President. By a vote of five to one, the Council forwarded a recommendation to the Chancellor and to the Board of Governors to extend President Smith's contract the maximum three years.[1316]

Constructed at the same time as North Hall, the 1938 President's residence was approved by the Board of Governors for a major renovation in early 2001. The project was to begin summer 2002, with the funds appropriated from a state system reserve account established for that purpose. The function of the house had changed considerably over its sixty-five-year history from a single family home to a multi-purpose residence used for public relations and development activities.[1317]

Then in the fall 2001, Ms. Deb Pincek, Director of University Dining Services, introduced to the student body a substantial expansion of Rocky's Grille, which doubled the seating and added an attractive outdoor deck.[1318] The name, Rocky's Grille was a partial carry-over from "The Grille" located in the former student facility, The Hut, on the upper part of campus. The Hut was converted into the Art Building in the early 1970s,

President's house under a blanket of snow, 2001

after the University Union was opened in 1970. Now, the renovations to Rocky's Grille were well received and it was very much the place to be between classes and in the evenings and on weekends.

President Smith ushered in the second year of the millennium with the bold announcement that Slippery Rock University was launching the most ambitious capital fund campaign in its history. The goal of this five-year effort called the "Rock Solid Investment" was $11 million. These funds were to be earmarked as follows:

Scholarships	$4,000,000
Campus Environment	$2,500,000
Honors Program	$2,500,000
North Hills Regional Development	$1,000,000
Service Learning	$500,000
Internationalism	$500,000[1319]

The campaign got off to a blazing start with a pledge from Mrs. Ethel Carruth of $2.5 million – the largest single gift in the history of Slippery Rock University. This was her way of honoring her daughter, Dr. Carolyn Carruth-Rizza and her son-in-law, Dr. Paul Rizza, who, collectively gave over half a century of service to the University.[1320] Mrs. Carruth desired to stimulate a "culture of giving" at Slippery Rock University and her gift enabled the renovation and restoration of West Hall, particularly as a site for International Initiatives and Modern Languages.[1321]

The First National Bank of Slippery Rock continued its strong support of the University's scholarship program with a major gift of $1,000,000.[1322]

Mr. and Mrs. Stanley Kraus, who were long-time friends of the University, were also quick to present a gift of $700,000.[1323]

Jack Critchfield, class of 1955, quickly stepped up to the plate with a gift of $500,000 – the largest ever given by an alumnus.[1324] Retired as CEO and Chairman of the Board of Florida Progress, he and Mary, his wife, were determined to help his alma mater build the finest collegiate baseball park in Pennsylvania.[1325]

Lockheed Martin Corporation, based in Bethesda, Maryland, contributed $120,000 for Science and Technology. President and Chief Operating Officer, Robert Stevens, a 1976 alumnus, was instrumental in facilitating the gift.[1326]

The Mine Safety Appliance Corporation in western Pennsylvania, deeded a twenty-acre parcel of land valued at $2.09 million to the University so that it would be able to develop an educational alliance in the North Hills of Allegheny County. This was the single largest charitable gift given by the Mine Safety Appliance Corporation.[1327]

With such early and generous support from these donors in this "Rock Solid Investment;" Slippery Rock University reached over half of its $11 million goal in the opening months of this campaign.

Though not a gift to the capital fund drive, the $13 million grant which Pennsylvania's Lieutenant Governor Mark Schweiker presented to the University in May of 2001, for the construction of a new Science and Technology facility was also greatly appreiciated.[1328]

At the same time the University was beginning its capital fund campaign, Slippery Rock Development Inc. was busy seeking $1.5 million from local sources to attract matching funds from the state of Pennsylvania for the revitalization of Slippery Rock's Main Street. Recognizing that the University's image is enhanced by a prosperous looking local business community, the Slippery Rock University Foundation pledged $400,000.[1329]

Early in March of 2001, a team from the Middle States Accrediting Association of Colleges and Schools arrived for their cyclical, ten-year visit. As usual, Slippery Rock's Middle States Self-Study Committee, comprised of faculty, students, administrators and alumni, had prepared an extensive self-evaluation for this visitation. The examiners were particularly impressed with the University's plans in the areas of enrollment and human resources, information technology, student retention and town-gown relationships. The commitment of the faculty to improve the retention rate of first-year students was something else they admired.[1330] The progress in the town-gown revitalization of Slippery Rock's business district gave ample evidence that the relationship between the University and the local community was a healthy one.

At their closing meeting with President Smith and his Committee, the Middle States team in their oral summary shared such commendations as: "Good things are happening

at Slippery Rock University;" "Your fiscal position is of extreme noteworthiness;" "People are our greatest resource," and "Slippery Rock University proves itself way too modest."[1331]

When the Accrediting Association for Ambulatory Healthcare approved the program at Slippery Rock's Health Center in the spring of 2001; the University became the first State System University to receive this coveted accreditation.[1332]

President Smith, Dr. Paul Rizza, Dr. Carolyn Rizza,
Dr. Constance Smith (from left to right)
in the president's home, 2001

Jack and Mary Critchfield with President Smith (right), 2002

The Therapeutic Recreation program was also accredited by the National Recreation and Parks Association in the fall.[1333]

Following the recommendations of the Future Watch strategic planning team to create a higher level of synergy among the University's related disciplines, the following four new Colleges were created.

- College of Business, Information and Behavioral Sciences
- College of Health, Environment and Science (including the School of Physical Therapy)
- College of Humanities, Fine and Performing Arts
- College of Education[1334]

Four academic "areas of distinction" were requested by the State System of Higher Education. The University submitted the following:

- Communication and Information Technology
- Environmental Sciences and Studies
- Health, Wellness and Recreation
- The World as Community

Concurrently, the Board of Governors also approved the University's three-year business plan.[1335]

Pennsylvania Act 48 mandating all public school teachers to earn a minimum of six college credits or its equivalency in continuing education units every five years sparked a review of related course work and workshops providing new opportunities for teachers. Several new courses were offered at the Waterfront campus near Wexford.[1336]

With the founding of the Frederick Douglas Institute for the purpose of identifying, promoting, and assessing the practices and experiences influencing minority students' growth; Slippery Rock, with grant money from the state, enrolled their students in an 18-month program.[1337]

As a result of more aggressive marketing for potential students and an expansion of the number of new academic programs; the enrollment in the fall of 2000, rose to 6,952. This was also the fourth highest percentage gain in enrollment among the fourteen universities in Pennsylvania's Higher Educational System.[1338] After nine years of eroding enrollments, Slippery Rock University's student population began, once again, to increase. This critical reaction was largely due to the very well developed and successfully executed enrollment management plan involving the entire university community.

The University added a post master's degree program to its curriculum in 2001. Focused at those in the public schools wishing to advance to the principal's level, a program was created leading to Principal's Certification.[1339]

All of the students who majored in health and physical education and biology programs scored 100% in the Praxis I examination required by the Pennsylvania Department of Education. Ninety-six percent of the majors in the College of Education passed that examination.[1340]

The Institute for Learning in Retirement - an alumni related organization affiliated with the Elderhostel Institute network – was formed in 2001, for mature adults who loved learning. Nearly 100 alumni, community members, and retired faculty and staff paid the $60 membership fee that enabled them to attend one or more of ten classes offered at Slippery Rock University.[1341]

By the summer of 2001, the construction of the Physical Therapy Building, and renovation of the Morrow Field House were completed.[15] Other renovations of the Stoner Instructional Complex, the Hickory Corner Schoolhouse, and the McLachan Health Center were also finished.[1342]

Considered to be one of the most beautiful buildings on campus, North Hall was selected to be the site of the University's new Welcome Center. By relocating the Office of Admissions, Enrollment Management, Graduate Studies, Lifelong Learning and Academic Records in a renovated North Hall, services to all of the students at Slippery Rock University would be greatly improved.[1343]

At the beginning of the fall term of 2001, Provost Robert Smith offers this ardently enthusiastic view of Slippery Rock University's present and future.

"The new Slippery Rock University dispels old stereotypes and replaces them with a newfound awareness of a vibrant campus culture, the promise of new opportunities, and a growing commitment to excellence. We will be called upon more frequently to deliver more and different services to more and different people. I believe that we are well prepared, out in front, paving the way. Addressing higher education challenges and providing forward-thinking solutions to positioning this University for the future will continue to be our priorities."[1344]

Slippery Rock's success in enrolling 7,195 students – a 3.5% increase over last year – was certainly evidence that the University indeed was the place to be.[1345] Compared with the other thirteen universities

North Hall in winter, late 1990's

in Pennsylvania's system, Slippery Rock ranked fifth in percentage increase in enrollment for the 2001 fall term. The University was also pleased that there was a 43% increase in the number of African Americans in attendance in the fall term.[1346] A survey of this Freshman Class revealed that the chief reason students selected Slippery Rock University was the quality of its academic programs.[1347]

Through a major curricular change, the University revised the minimum number of credits required for graduation from 128 to 120 beginning the 2001-2002 academic year.[1348] The Board of Governors adopted the new graduation requirement for the majority of Slippery Rock's degree programs and also made the change for a number of the other State System universities. In addition, the State System began to require of all universities that forty percent of baccalaureate degree programs cover a broad range of coursework in Humanities, Fine Arts, Sciences Mathematics and Communications. A minimum of twenty-five percent of coursework was

required in a specific academic discipline with the remainder of the curriculum consisting of coursework related to the major field of study, advanced coursework in liberal arts or sciences, or electives.[1349]

A Week of Welcome, WOW, was initiated in the fall of 2001, as part of the University's continuous improvement effort. The comprehensive program began with assisting all freshmen and transfer students moving into residence halls. Several subsequent social and academic activities were provided through the leadership of the Student Affairs division. More than 500 students, faculty, staff, alumni and townspeople volunteered to make this community effort a huge success. The response by new student families was overwhelmingly enthusiastic.[1350] The new University Health Center, moved from North Hall to Rhoads Hall, was opened August, 2001, just in time for WOW.[1351]

Slippery Rock's football team traveled to Miami, Florida for its opening game with Florida Atlantic University, on September 5, 2001. The game was

President Smith (center), with Coach Mihalik (left) and Coach Schnellenberger, September 2001

President Smith with Jerry Bejbl at ProPlayer Stadium

played in Pro Player Stadium, home to the NFL Miami Dolphins. It was FAU's inaugural year for football and the University had hired former NFL coach Howard Schnellenberger to jump start the program. An extensively publicized game attended by many SRU alumni and broadcasted through the Sunshine Cable T. V. network to about six million homes in Southern Florida, the Rock defeated the Owls by a score of 40-7.[1352]

No sooner did the freshmen, along with the upper classmen begin their studies than the world was shaken on September 11 with the frightful news that terrorists had launched attacks on the United States. The American flags in front of Old Main and at the main entrance to the University were quickly placed at half-staff.

Slippery Rock, explains President Smith, "joins the nation in morning the loss of life in the disaster of this week. Our sincere thoughts are with those whose lives have been irreversibly changed through the course of these events."[1353] He also reminds us "the University is truly an environment for learning. This is equally true in times of joy and times of grief. Therefore, the campus community has continued with a regular class schedule as we seek understanding and comfort together. ....We know that everyone has been touched and saddened

Coach Foster talks with the defense during the game, 2001

271

Flight #93 Memorial on campus

by these tragic events, and we must all come together at this moment to provide comfort and support in the entire campus community."[1354]

Communication centers were set-up immediately in all the residence halls and dining halls, the University Union and the Aebersold Recreation Center so that students could keep in touch with family members. Faculty were encouraged to allot time in their classes for discussion about this national tragedy. Special faculty panels discussed with students such issues as "The Attack on America in Historical, Political and Moral Perspective," media interpretation; "Response to Rhetoric of Terrorism and Implications for Individual Freedoms of Speech, Movement and Privacy," and "Death and Dying." A meditation room was set up in the University Union. A candlelight vigil was held on September 12 with more than 1000 students in attendance. Students were also invited to prayer services which were held in local churches. The Student Government Association assisted with a blood drive with the local Red Cross Chapter. Amazingly, no family member of the more than 7,000 students was injured in the tragedy.[1355]

Three days after the terrorists' attack, at the request of Mr. Kenneth Blair, Chairman of the University's Council of Trustees; Slippery Rock University's Choir sang the National Anthem at the opening of their meeting. A moment of silence followed.[1356]

Mr. Tim Rowe, an admission counselor and a soldier in the Army Reserve who joined the University in August, was the first member of the Slippery Rock University family to be called up for active military service.[1357] Other staff, faculty and students who were Army Reservists also returned to active duty.

The increased use of technology in academia drove the need for improved technology. Beginning the fall semester 2001, sixty internet connected classrooms and two "smart classrooms" with computers at each student station were available for instruction.[1358] President Smith summarized the substantial technical work completed on campus fall 2001: which cost the University over $8.5 million. "There are 53 buildings on the campus network, 83 wiring closets, 10,653 connections on campus for data and voice, 2 data jacks per residence hall room, 83 triple rooms with 3 data jacks, lounge areas in residence halls are wired for laptop use by students, 1.6 million feet of new cable inside the buildings, and 64,235 feet of fiber optic outside cable."[1359]

The Physical Therapy Building, located on the lower quadrangle between Vincent Science Hall and Spotts World Culture Building, opened in the fall of 2001. It was for President Smith, a "magnificent new facility" which "matches the quality of the School of Physical Therapy program".[1360]

With a $180,000 curriculum initiative grant from the Pennsylvania State System, Slippery Rock was able to equip a classroom in Vincent Science Hall with the twenty new computers necessary for using a new method of teaching an introductory course in physics.[1361]

Slippery Rock's expanded Nurse Practitioner Program offered jointly with Clarion and Edinboro Universities was enormously strengthened when the United States Department of Health and Human Services gave it a federal grant of $553,668 in 2001.[1362]

During the Christmas season, the University's Chamber Choir, directed by Paul LaPrade of the Music Department, traveled to Washington D. C. where, on December 12, performed at the White House for President Bush's Cabinet and members of Congress. Other concerts were held in the Capitol and the Supreme Court Building. Their last performance was for Slippery Rock alumni in a church in Virginia.[1363]

A snapshot of all students who registered for classes at the University in January 2002, was provided by the Office of Institutional Research. The top five states Slippery Rock attracted students from were (in rank order) Pennsylvania, Ohio, New York, New Jersey

Old Main staff during the holidays, 2001

A holiday production with President Smith standing, 2001

President Smith at winter commencement, 2001

President Smith in his vintage Land Rover

A presidential violinist

and Maryland. As to those residing in Pennsylvania, it is no surprise that more students came from Butler County since it is the home of Slippery Rock University. Allegheny County, where Pittsburgh is located, ranked second; followed by Mercer, Lawrence and Beaver Counties. Surprisingly, on the global scene, more students came (in rank order) from Nepal, Sri Lanka, India, Japan and Kenya. Ninety percent of the students were undergraduates and ten percent were graduate students. As to the areas of study of these undergraduates, seven percent were in the College of Humanities, Fine and Performing Arts; twenty percent in the College of Health, Environment and Science; twenty-three percent in the College of Business, Information and Social Sciences; and thirty percent in the College of Education. Ten percent of the students were listed as "exploratory". Fifty-nine percent of the student body were women and forty-one percent were men.[1365]

Compliance with Title IX became more prominent as the millennium unfolded. Athletic Director, Mr. Paul Lueken, regularly monitored the University's progress in this important area and contracted with Dr. Betsy Alden, a nationally recognized athletics consultant, to conduct a thorough examination of Slippery Rock University's program. All varsity teams were involved in the comprehensive process.[1366]

In celebration of "Black History" month in February of 2002, students entered the Martin Luther King Speech Competition, Sonia Sanchez was the keynote speaker, the professional ensemble produced "Ain't Misbehaving" and the Black Action Society concluded the celebration with a Soul Food Dinner.[1367]

To meet the ever-expanding technological needs of students and faculty, the University contracted with the Collegis Corporation for consulting and delivery services. Collegis quickly helped in developing the University's three-year Information Technology Plan.[1368]

An on-site Director of Instructional Technologies helped faculty design and implement web-based courses, and vendor support training programs. The Director also helped the Center for Teaching Excellence in its search for ever-better practices in e-learning.[1369]

President Smith saw that this investment of $8.5 million in technology and technological-related infrastructure is giving Slippery Rock students" a foundation for successful learning".[1370]

During the 2001-02 academic year, the staff of The Rocket received a number of outstanding awards from various state and national journalistic associations. The Pennsylvania Newspaper Press Association gave them three Keystone Awards; the Society of Collegiate Journalists, two first place honors and twelve individual awards; and the Columbia Scholarship Press Association, two Gold Medals and five individual awards. The Society of Professional Journalists was so impressed with the quality of The Rocket that it ranked it "the best all around student newspaper".[1371]

During the spring semester of 2002, the Association of Residence Hall Students asked President Smith to eliminate smoking in all of the University's residence halls.[18]

The students also recommended to the president that a twenty-four hour residence hall visitation program be adopted if eighty percent of the hall residents approved. Dr. Smith supported both proposals. In the fall of 2002, one residence hall adopted the new visitation program.[1372]

Slippery Rock University's five-year $11 million capital campaign, which was launched in 2000, was so highly successful that it reached its goal in just eighteen months. Subsequently, it was decided to roll the campaign into a $33 million ten year effort. Forty-one percent ($4,500,000) of its gifts came from the friends of the University; 33% ($3,600,000) from corporations; 21% ($2,300,000) from alumni and 5% ($500,000) from foundations and other organizations.[1373]

In April 2002, the Board of Governors adopted a new process to reward universities for outstanding performance in the key areas of student advancement, fiscal management and diversity. Set aside through contributions from each of the fourteen university budgets, $9 million would be awarded as performance funding during 2002-2003. Three measurement tools would be used in determining the amount of money to be distributed: 1) an accountability matrix (quantitative), 2) a narrative assessment (qualitative) and 3) the University's performance plan.[1374]

Both divisions, Academic Affairs and Student Affairs, were increasing their efforts in support of the enrollment management plan. On April 11, 2002, Dr. John Gardner, senior fellow of the National Resource Center for the First-Year Experience and Students in Transition, presented a campus symposium sponsored by the two divisions, entitled, "Successful Student Learning and Transition."[1375] Dr. Gardner was no stranger to SRU, having visited the campus for the first time in February 1990.

The dedication of the new Jack Critchfield Stadium on April 20, 2002, was an enormous success. Legislators, trustees, alumni, students, sports celebrities and citizens of Slippery Rock all joined in the grand opening of one of the finest collegiate parks in the region. An effort to encourage student attendance was coordinated by the athletic department and the "Pack the Park" was successful resulting with a new NCAA Division II attendance record. The Rock baseball team played their rival Edinboro and won both games of the doubleheader in the new stadium dubbed "The Jack".[1376]

The Jack, 2002

275

During spring 2002, former professor and football coach Mr. C. Douglas Clinger was honored posthumously by the naming of the exercise science laboratory in the Pearl Stoner Instructional Complex (East Gymnasium). "Dad" Clinger was described by his students, colleagues and friends as an outstanding educator, professional leader and coach, role model and mentor.[1377]

Later in the year, former marching band director and faculty member, Mr. Blase S. Scarnati, was honored through the naming of the marching band field. Many former students, colleagues and friends were on hand to recognize "Mr. S" and his thirty-two years of dedicated service to Slippery Rock University.[1378]

The University's Therapeutic Recreation program received the 2002 award for excellence in education from the American Therapeutic Recreation Association. The national award recognized Slippery Rock's program as one of the best in the country.[1379]

In April 2002, twenty-five hundred attended the annual Spring Academic Honors Convocation where the University honored its top twenty sophomores, juniors and seniors as Presidential Scholars. Students on the Dean's list and others earning scholarships for their academic efforts were also saluted.[1380]

Over 10,000 guests gathered in the N. Kerr Thompson Stadium on May 11, 2002, to witness the graduation of one of the largest classes at Slippery Rock University in the past decade. President Emeritus Herb. F. Reinhard, Jr., who retired in 1984 after serving five years as President, was granted an honorary doctorate in recognition of his service to Slippery Rock University.[1381]

Renovation of a university building located off Main Street in the town center began in May 2002. It originally housed the TV studio, which had been relocated to the Vincent Science Hall. The vacated building was earmarked for activities and programs dedicated to business and industry training, short-term workshops, conferences, the Institute for Learning in Retirement and community enrichment programs. When renovated it would provide a thirty-seat distance learning room, a fifteen-station computer lab and a forty-seat community learning room.[1382]

Processional at spring commencement, 2000

The Evolution of Slippery Rock cheerleaders, 1920's-1990's

During the summer 2002, the collaborative effort of Slippery Rock, Clarion and Edinboro Universities to offer an expanded Family Nurse Practitioner degree program became a reality when the Department of Health and Human Services of the United States granted $553,668 in support of this very important and timely endeavor.[1383]

Capitalizing on their quality and the University's international reputation, the jazz ensemble toured Paris and four cities in Italy during the summer 2002. The "big band" sound of the jazz ensemble was presented to Euro Disney as part of a fourteen-day European tour under the direction of Mr. Steve Hawk, Associate Professor of Music.[1384]

Beginning July 1, 2002, the non-teaching faculty coaches were represented by the Association of Pennsylvania State, College and University Faculties in negotiating a rolling two-year contract. More than 350 coaches were employed at the 14 State System

Universities. This action marked the first collective bargaining agreement for non-teaching coaches in Pennsylvania.[1385]

Governor Mark Schweiker, who was a strong supporter of the Main Street Development Project, came to Slippery Rock in July of 2002, to deliver, in person, a grant of $2 million granted by the Commonwealth of Pennsylvania for this important community and University undertaking. When President Smith accepted the check, he underscored the critical importance of this three and one-half block project in the center of town to both the community and Slippery Rock University of this joint effort.[1386]

The summer of 2002, marked the 5th anniversary of Dr. Smith's tenure as Slippery Rock University's president. His leadership accomplished much that prepared it for the Twenty-first Century.

His successful fundraising strategies enabled the University to reach its $11 million goal in just one and one- half years.[1387]

Aware that the North Hills in Western Pennsylvania was increasingly becoming a center of businesses and industries, President Smith promoted the creation of an alliance to meet the educational and training needs of this region. To his great delight, the Mine Safety Appliance Company granted in 2002 a 20 acre parcel of land in the North Hills valued at $2.1 million. This enabled him to put in motion plans to design, build and manage a multi-functional center of education.[1388]

In July 2001, Governor Mark Schweiker of Pennsylvania presented $2 million in capital budget redevelopment assistance to the town/gown revitalization project which President Smith initiated. He described it as "an exceptionally cooperative venture between the community and the University" and an "outstanding example of people working together."[1389]

Anxious to enhance excellence by providing quality technological tools for students and faculty, President Smith launched in 2001, an $8.5 million project that would completely revamp and expand the University's existing network. This undertaking was the largest of its kind among Pennsylvania's fourteen state universities.[1390]

His success in reversing the University's nine-year enrollment erosion was remarkable. In the fall of 2001, the enrollment of 7,195 students – which was an increase of 3.5% over the previous year – was the fifth largest

percentage increase among Pennsylvania's State System universities. Equally impressive was the diversity of this student body that came from 55 countries, 31 states and all of the counties in Pennsylvania.[1391]

The enrollment management program continued on its successful path for the fall 2002, semester. Applications for admission continued to increase in number and in quality. Slippery Rock University enrolled 7,542 students.[1392]

The University unveiled on September 30, 2002, its new web site. President Smith proudly stated, "This new site will enable people to own and better manage their information on the web. It also will enable visitors to navigate quickly to the information they want."[1393]

The University's marketing plan and aggressive promotion and advertising materials gained national recognition, winning awards in seven categories in the 2002 Admissions Advertising Awards. Conducted by the *Admissions Marketing Report,* the national newspaper of Admissions Marketing, the honors were awarded nationally to colleges and universities distinguishing themselves in this area.[1394]

By the close of the fall semester 2002, the College of Education had been granted continuing national accreditation at the initial teacher preparation and advanced preparation levels by the National Council for Accreditation of Teacher Education. "NCATE Board of Examiners specifically remarked upon the high quality of SRU's professional education unit as well as the quality of professional education offerings available to its students."[1395]

The University's Exercise Science degree program became the first exercise physiology undergraduate program in the nation to be accredited by the American Society of Exercise Physiologists.[1396]

At the same time, the University's Therapeutic Recreation program received the 2002 award for excellence in education from the American Therapeutic Recreation Association. The national award recognized Slippery Rock's program as one of the best in the country.[1397]

As President Smith was preparing for a new fiscal year, he acknowledged that the commitment of those affiliated with Slippery Rock University over the past year "has truly been remarkable." And he added: "We have created a special kind of momentum within this university."[1398]

Not surprisingly, President Smith had every reason to believe that the fall term of his sixth year at Slippery Rock University would be another "wonderful semester."[1399]

On October 8, he received the shocking news from the Board of Governors of the State System of Higher Education that his contract was not going to be renewed upon its expiration on June 30, 2004.[1400]

As this tragic news spread on the campus and town; the University's Council of Trustees, faculty and students, along with the local citizens quickly rallied to his support. The appeals that were sent to Harrisburg, however, were interpreted by the members of the Board of Governors as President Smith's "divisive campaign" to force them to reverse their October decision.[1401]

During this time of unrest, President Smith was elected to the rank of Fellow in the American Association for the Advancement of Science for his distinguished efforts on behalf of the advancement of science and its applications. He is honored for his contributions to the field of chemistry; service to professional, scientific and higher education associations; and for academic leadership, particularly as a university president.[1402]

SLIPPERY ROCK UNIVERSITY PRESIDENT OUSTED BY STATE BOARD

This headline of the Pittsburgh Post Gazette tells the story of what transpired at a special meeting on December 9, of the Board of Governors of the Pennsylvania State System of Higher Education in Harrisburg.[1403]

It was a hastily arranged Saturday morning meeting on December 9, that the Board of governors quickly voted to remove Dr. Smith as the president of Slippery Rock University, effective immediately. Chairman Charles Gomulka explained the Board's action: Dr. Smith was removed for one reason only: unsatisfactory performance. That is not to say that he did not do some things well. He did. But doing some things well is not the standard for a State System university president."[1404] He also was certain that Dr. Smith did indeed participate in a divisive campaign "to get the Board to cancel their earlier decision.[1405]

Dr. Robert Smith, Provost at Slippery Rock University, was asked by the Board of Governors to serve as Acting President.[1406]

Paul LaPrade with choir in Washington D.C., 2001

Missy McKavish drives to the hoop

International Student Dinner

In control

Shot on goal

280

2000 Regional Baseball Champions

Randy McKavish rolls out

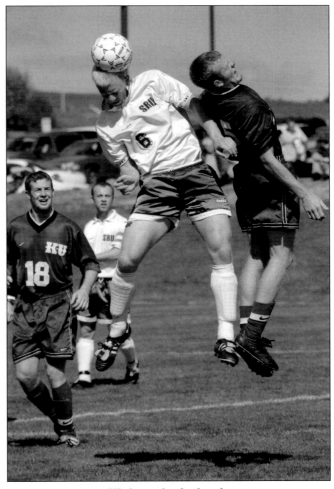

High to win the header

281

CHAPTER XI

Becoming a Premier Residential Public University

It is certain that when Dr. Robert Smith accepted the Provost and Vice President for Academic Affairs position in 1999, he did not anticipate his appointment as Interim President in December 2002. The environment in which he began working was initially difficult because of the timing and manner in which President G. Warren Smith was removed from office. However, armed with a professional commitment to succeed, excellent organization and communication skills, a solid understanding of the University and a personable nature, by the time President Smith presented his first report to the Council of Trustees in March 2003, he had adjusted to the environment and the position. Dr. Smith commented, "I am grateful to the Trustees for their support over the past three months and their commitment to Slippery Rock University. I appreciate their service and loyalty to the University during this transition." President Smith welcomed the newest member of the University's Council of Trustees, Mr. John Thornburgh, son of Richard Thornburgh, the Commonwealth's former Governor and an instrumental partner in the development of Act 188, which created the Pennsylvania State System of Higher Education.[1407] Mr. Thornburgh was also serving as a member of the Board of Governors.

Four issues were addressed by the Interim President in his first trustees meeting, issues that would remain as focal points during his interim presidency:

1. Enrollment, Retention and Academic Quality—Strategic Enrollment Management was one of Dr. Smith's strengths. It was under his leadership as Provost that the University began to reverse the nine-year enrollment decline.

2. Diversity—"The University took significant steps in the past three months to raise awareness about the importance of diversity to our campus. In January 2003, I appointed a new President's Commission on Racial and Ethnic Diversity."[1408]

3. Communication—"We promised we would improve the Chancellor's awareness of our work. Chancellor Hample visited campus February 2003 to meet with Student Government Association officers. Both the Chancellor and the students reported positively on the experience."[1409]

4. Moving Forward—"The last line in my speech to the University community was: We are going to move forward. Slippery Rock University is going to be okay. Now, let's make it happen."[1410]

With an agenda inclusive of enrollment management through facilities improvements, the new Interim

President Smith with students

President embarked on his challenging task with a quickened pace.

Anticipating a four percent growth in the number of new freshmen fall 2003, additional finances were made available to employ new faculty to accommodate the student increase. "I've authorized an expenditure of $1 million for additional faculty over the next two years to adjust to enrollment increases. We are also working to maximize the quality of the learning experience by managing class size. We believe that the best learning experience comes from close student and faculty contact within appropriate teacher-student ratios."[1411]

Regarding the academic quality of the students, the Interim President commented, "We are raising the academic bar. Although we require fewer hours for completing a degree, we are requiring more stringent standards for the degree through an increase in residency requirements for the new degree program and the major, a new standard for hours required in upper division work and stronger standards for completing the major and minor programs."[1412]

Beginning with the Eisenberg Classroom Auditorium, the University planned to completely

Dr. William Williams

remodel and bring to a state-of-the-technological-art the four major instructional auditoriums. More than $600,000 was set aside to redesign the Eisenberg Auditorium in 2003. "We are remodeling facilities to enhance the learning environment for those spaces traditionally serving freshmen and lower division students."[1413]

One of the first human resource decisions made by Dr. Robert Smith as interim president was to appoint Professor William Williams, Chairperson of the Department of English, and president of the faculty union, APSCUF, as Interim Provost. In his two decades at the University, Dr. Williams had earned considerable respect within the faculty and administration.[1414] Dr. Smith understood the value of shared governance and collaboration in higher education and chose Dr. Williams to assist in developing and fostering that environment. Beginning with student quality, the teaching/learning experience, class size, technology needs and teaching facilities, Dr. Williams tackled the daunting task of understanding the issues from all sides and continuing to move forward the core mission of the University.

As the interim president began his duties, the University was hosting in Old Main, the oldest building on campus, one of its relatively new traditions, The Celebration of Giving. The event invited the University's more benevolent donors to celebrate fund raising accomplishments and enjoy the festive seasons. That year, it was the venue for the official announcement of the University's extension of their capital campaign. The campaign goal was extended to $33 million within a ten year time period. Pledges and gifts to date totaled $12.3 million or thirty-seven percent of the goal.[1415]

Jammin at the field house

*President Smith provides a tour of
RLA construction to US Rep. Melissa Hart*

Early on, Dr. Robert Smith developed a general theme for Slippery Rock University - building an engaged intellectual community. Dr. Smith identified to University constituents, five major components of the engaged intellectual community he was committed to building.

- An engaged intellectual community creates and maintains enriched learning experiences for its students.
- An engaged intellectual community determines its own destiny.
- An engaged intellectual community gathers diverse people.
- An engaged intellectual community creates accepting space.
- An engaged intellectual community promotes hope.[1416]

The project formerly known as The North Hills Educational Alliance was changed to the Regional Learning Alliance and a separate 501(C)(3) was established. The President along with Dean Jim Kushner met with the Chancellor and her senior staff in February 2003, to review the plans for the project and discuss strategies for acquiring funding. "The primary purpose of the educational alliance is to efficiently and effectively meet the training and educational needs of the businesses and industries within the Western Pennsylvania and Eastern Ohio region."[1417] The Renaissance 3 firm with Zimmer, Gunsul and Frasca from Washington D. C. were selected to be the architects of the project and in early 2003, were developing the plans for the facility. A $200,000 grant,

in part through the efforts of U. S. Representative Phil English, was announced in March 2003, by the offices of U.S. Representative Melissa Hart and U.S. Senator Arlen Specter to assist in the development of the project.[1418] In December 2003, President Smith reported " The Regional Learning Alliance (RLA), is under construction in the Cranberry Woods Corporate Park. Staying on an aggressive schedule, the facility is expected to open in August 2004. Leases are being negotiated with the other academic partners and a loan is being completed with Pen Trust and the ERECT fund to assure financing of the project while we wait the outcome of the Governor's budget."[1419]

Work began on the renovation of the Eisenberg Classroom Building Auditorium in early 2003. At a cost of $600,000 the facility would be converted from a 200 seat, large lecture hall to a 100 seat, state-of-the-art, high-tech instructional classroom, accommodating wireless technology. The two remaining lecture halls in The Spotts World Culture Building and the Strain Behavioral Science Building were scheduled to be renovated in 2004.[1420]

SRU students on tour of Trinity College, Dublin, 2003

In the spring 2003, the Vice President for Student Affairs and two staff members led a group of 43 student leaders to Ireland to meet with student leaders from Trinity College, University College Dublin and Dublin City College. President Smith commented, "The program gives both groups the opportunity to share ideas and offer solutions to common problems of campus life".[1421] Over the next four years, more than 125 student leaders would discuss student issues with their counterparts in Ireland, Czech Republic, Spain, Scotland, England and France.

Care packages were assembled by students several times during the spring 2003, for students, faculty and staff who were serving their nation in the Iraqi Freedom/War on Terror effort. At one time more than 30 students and several faculty and staff had enlisted or were called up to serve in the military during the war.[1422]

The student newspaper, *The Rocket* captured more than 30 national journalistic awards in the spring 2003, including first-place honors from the Society of Professional Journalists, the American Scholastic Press Association, the Columbia Scholastic Press Association, Society for Collegiate Journalists and the Pennsylvania News Press Association. *The Rocket* was the only State System University to receive recognition from the Pennsylvania News Press Association.[1423]

The Athletics program, under the direction of Mr. Paul Lueken experienced another successful year in 2002/03 finishing third overall in the fourteen State System Universities, All-Sports, Dixon Trophy competition. Eight athletes were named to All-America status and three athletes were named to Academic All-America status.[1424] The Baseball team finished the regular season with their best ever record of 48-13. Through regional play, the team coached by Mr. Jeff Messer qualified for the Division II National World Series in Montgomery, Alabama.[1425]

Slippery Rock University received two national awards at the end of the spring semester 2003, the Noel-Levitz National Award for Excellence in Student Retention presented for

SRU students with Irish students on their campus radio, 2003

Packing care packages for the troops, 2003

2003 Women's Tennis PSAC Champions

2003 Regional Baseball Champions

the "Learning Community Cluster and FYRST Seminar" and The Association of Higher Education Facilities Officers National Award for Effective and Innovate Practices, presented for Streamlining and Creating a Stockless Custodial Supply Chain.[1426]

The Nursing program was re-accredited in the spring 2003, marking more than 60% of the University's academic programs now accredited. Concurrently, the Liberal Studies program including basic skills, arts and sciences was reduced from 52 credit hours to 48 to comply with the Board of Governors' policy requiring programs to include 40% liberal studies coursework.[1427]

The Division of Student Affairs made a major change in the Dining Services contractor on June 1, 2003. After fifteen years with one contractor, the University hired AVI Food Systems, Inc., the nation's largest independent family-owned food service company. The co-presidents, Anthony Payiavlas and his sister, Patrice were responsible for more than 6,000 national employees. The five year, student focused contract could be extended for two additional years. The President commented, "We are confident this will be a positive partnership."[1428]

Technology was becoming more a part of the daily life on college campuses and even with the creation of a $100 per semester student technology fee more of the University's budget was required to maintain the high-tech campus that students expected. More than $2.9 million was spent during 2002, on new and upgraded technology. "Black Board" became an important classroom management tool for faculty with 408 course shells in place to better serve students. More than 7,000 university web pages were created in 2002. A program entitled My Rock-1 Stop permitted students the opportunity to personalize

Stadium gets new turf, summer, 2003

N. Kerr Thompson Stadium, Robert DiSpirito Field and William Lennox Track, mid 2000's

their own web page which would include specific SRU news and information updated daily.[1429]

Over the summer 2003, the technology staff, headed by Mr. Dean Lindey, replaced the hardware in 18 computer labs, installed 726 new campus work stations and completed 1,203 faculty and staff work orders. The week students moved into the residence halls, the Blaster worm struck the campus, the same virus that closed down computer systems all over the world. Working 24 hours a day, the technology team disinfected 4,389 faculty, staff and student computers across campus in less than a week.[1430]

A greater emphasis was placed on student research and faculty fostered the concept. During 2002-2003, more than 200 students, guided by faculty, presented their research at state, regional, national or international academic conferences.[1431]

The new Carruth-Rizza Hall, formerly West Hall, and earlier, the Model School and the town's school building was dedicated on August 22, 2003. "The massive renovation including reopening a long closed, two-story, sky-lit atrium, restoring the building's original woodwork, and installation of state-of-the-art fiber optics systems as part of a modern language laboratory, was funded by a $2.5 million gift to the University from Mrs. Ethel Carruth. The Houston, Texas, philanthropist donated the funds in honor of the teaching dedication of her son-in-law and daughter, Drs. Paul and Carolyn Carruth Rizza. Both are professor emeritus at SRU with 52 years of combined service."[1432] The new facility would serve as home to the Office of International Studies and the department of Modern Languages and Cultures.

In June 2003, the fall athletic rosters indicated, 49.1% women athletes and 50.9% men athletes. And, for

288

the first time in the University's history 50% of all scholarship dollars would be issued to women and 50% would be issued to men.[1433]

As part of the University's strategic enrollment management effort, the Student Affairs division, took the lead in designing the Week of Welcome (WOW) program as an extended orientation program for all new students. In August 2003, more than 700 students, faculty, staff, alumni and townspeople volunteered to help the more than 1400 first year students move into the residence halls and begin their first week on SRU's campus in an up-beat environment. ROTC cadets directed traffic, volunteers helped carry luggage and other items into the residence halls, The SGA Bookstore delivered students' books to their residence hall rooms, musical groups strolled through

Chancellor Hample (second from right), and President Smith with Drs. Paul and Carolyn Rizza at the Carruth-Rizza Hall dedication, 2003

the campus, the cheerleaders and Rocky, the mascot, greeted the families, the mayor handed out cookies, AVI Food Services set up "picnic sites" across campus for hot dogs and cold drinks and President Smith placed welcome mints on the pillows of hundreds of new students as they moved into the halls, talking with the new students and families. The President described the WOW activities, "It was truly remarkable. I said to those new students, you are at a very special place. You are at a place that's more than just 4 walls in a classroom. We

reinstated traditions and expectations of being part of the Slippery Rock Community into the Week of Welcome, too. Students taught (as a group) the Alma Mater, the Fight Song, supported by the Rock Pride Marching Band and the nation's largest student based fan club, the Rock Rowdies."[1434]

WOW included the University's first night-time, home football game, September 13, 2003, in the newly renovated stadium with artificial turf and lights. In preparation for WOW, more than 1,000 members of the Rock Rowdies had purchased and assisted in putting up on street light poles on campus, a series of three different Rock Pride banners. The Student Government Association was recognized before the game for their support in funding the majority of the cost of the stadium lights to permit such an event.[1435] The football team was just one of several teams that would compete on the new turf field. Other teams included Women's Field Hockey, Women's and Men's Soccer and Women's and Men's Track and Field.

Fall 2003, enrollment was up for the eighth consecutive semester, to 7,791 students, an increase of 14% over 1999. Students of color had also increased. Not only did more students want to come to SRU, but a greater percentage of those enrolled wanted to remain at the Rock. The focus on quality was expressed in the

First night football game, 2003

freshmen class, which had earned a cumulative high school grade point average of 3.18 on a 4 point scale. Nearly all of the new freshmen were enrolled in the FYRST seminar program, created to assist students in the transition to college life. More than 70% participated in structured, small, learning communities. These efforts were made to further increase every student's opportunity for success.[1436]

All of the international student programs in American colleges and universities were impacted by the effects of 9-11 and SRU was no exception. In 2003, the University's international student enrollment dipped to 135 students from 50 countries of the world.[1437]

In an effort to provide more professional development opportunities to women students, faculty and staff, the president announced the creation of the Women in Leadership Series fall 2003. Sponsored by Sprint Telecommunications, the program brought women leaders to campus to speak formally and also engage with different campus organizations.[1438]

In 2003, the Commonwealth's Guaranteed Free Training Program reimbursed qualified companies for much of their training expenses. That year the University administered training contracts for 33 Western Pa companies. Under the leadership of Dr. Jim Kushner, SRU was an active participant in Workforce and Development Network of Pa.[1439]

When President Robert Smith was Provost and Vice President for Academic Affairs, he and Dr. Robert Watson, Vice President for Student Affairs developed a strong working relationship between their divisions. The two leaders realized if the University was going to continue to become stronger through its growth in enrollment, programs and opportunities, the two divisions must recognize common goals and work collaboratively toward their accomplishment. The faculty and staff of the two divisions began to create new opportunities for student success with positive results for the University and its students. When Dr. Smith became the interim president and Dr. William Williams assumed the interim provost's position, the collaborative efforts of the two divisions continued to develop. The result was noticeable. In September 2003, the *Princeton Review*, one of the college and university national rating services listed Slippery Rock University among the Best 98 Colleges and Universities in the Mid-Atlantic Region. The *Princeton Review* cited "Students praise the small class size and the excellent tutoring as well as the writing center and resident hall study groups. Our sources make

claims such as "my professors (at least in my major) all know me by name, and are very approachable, and help in any way they can so that you will succeed".[1440]

The following general goals of the Student Affairs division were tied to university goals:

- Actively engaging in all aspects of strategic enrollment management
- Developing collaborative efforts with the other divisions of the University
- Fostering responsible decision making by all students
- Increasing the understanding of the importance of diversity
- Enhancement of a division-wide model for assessment and quality improvement
- Developing a sense of "Rock Pride" within campus constituents

During the fall 2003, the Vice President for Student Affairs, restructured the division. Collaboration between departments within and outside the division was emphasized in the restructuring creating a name change to the Division of Student Life.[1441]

The executive officers and Senate of the Student Government Association, Inc. also became more collaborative with campus leadership. In 2003, when the University announced a major renovation program for the NKT Stadium, The SGA Senate under the leadership of president Jeff Milliner funded the majority of

Army ROTC Leadership, 2003

the construction costs for stadium lights so that night activities could be scheduled for students.[1442] SGA actions were noticed by Council of Trustee member and chairperson of the Student Affairs Subcommittee, Mr. Howard Meyer and he publicly commented, "This is a wonderful group of diverse individuals who are working cooperatively with the administration to meet goals and initiatives for the betterment of SRU".[1443]

As success with fund raising began to increase, so did the dramatic need for the funds. At the beginning of the fall 2003, the Slippery Rock University Foundation, Inc. announced for the first time it had awarded in excess of $1 million in student scholarships. The Foundation maintained more than 400 named student scholarships.[1444]

Four additional national or regional honors were received by the University fall 2003. The National Award for Marketing and Advertising for University Public Relations; the Macarthur Award for the Number One ROTC Program in the Eastern United States Region; the Outside Magazine National Award for the Best Park Ranger Graduate Program; and the American Marketing Association Higher Education Marketing Symposium Award for University Marketing and Branding recognized through the National Strategic Enrollment Management Conference were awarded.[1445]

On October 25, 2003, Slippery Rock University volunteers collaborated with Lowes Home Center employees and refurbished a Victorian house in New Castle. The empty house, which was in part donated to and purchased by SRU, was transformed into a neighborhood community center to provide tutoring to low income children, lunches for senior citizens, and dozens of other community revitalization programs. The I-Care House engaged nearly 50 university students who tutored

Twelfth Night play in the tent, 2003

Veterans memorial, 2004

approximately 100 children in grades one through twelve, served lunches to 25 senior citizens and organized dozens of other activities for children and adults.[1446]

A new Leadership Reaction Course, located on the north end of campus, was made possible in large part to a federal grant arranged by the Army ROTC department. Finished in November 2003, the first group to use the facility was Leadership Butler County.[1447]

Fittingly, the dedication of the new Alumni Memorial took place on Veterans Day, November 11, 2003. The classes of 1951, 1952 and 1953 raised funds for the construction of the memorial recognizing all alumni who had served in the military. The Memorial was located just outside the front entrance of the Russell Wright Alumni Center.[1448]

After the Women's Soccer Team won the 2003 PSAC championship and advanced for the first time to NCAA Div. II regional competition, the team was awarded the National Soccer Coaches Association of America "Team Ethics Award for Merit" and the "Team Academic Award" for academic performance. Coach Noreen Herlihy was named "Regional Coach

Midnight Madness, opening of basketball season, 2003

Old Main, winter, 2003

of the Year". Athletes Sarah Arsenault and Meghan McGrath were awarded first team All America honors. Student athletes representing other teams and receiving honors were Jennifer Zuzak, the first individual PSAC swimming champion since 1989 and Brad Cieleski for winning his second, in as many years, PSAC wrestling championship.[1449]

Shortly after the new millennium, the State System of Higher Education, on behalf of its 14 universities, signed a 100 million dollar contract with the German-based SAP Corporation to develop a shared administrative system. Each of the universities would be assessed a portion of the contract. By December 2003,

Old Main holiday party, 2003

2003 women's soccer PSAC champions

Student Leaders Tour, London and Paris, 2004

Unity Week, 2004

Gospel choir, 2004

Slippery Rock University was able to interface with the SAP software to bring online the first phase, purchasing and human resources, including the important payroll process.[1450] Additional phases of the system would be brought online to eventually connect the Universities and the System in ways not previously connected.

In February 2004, more than 1,300 people thoroughly enjoyed the world premier of Mr. Luke Mayernick's "Requiem for Mr. Rogers", performed by the SRU Chorus and Orchestra. The work, featured on National Public Radio's "All Things Considered" included original cast members "Neighbor Aber" (SRU alumnus Chuck Aber), "Mayor Maggie" and "Handyman Negri".[1451]

The First Year Advocate Award was presented in March 2004, by The National Center on the First

The ARC, 2004

Year Experience and Students in Transition to Dr. Amanda Yale, assistant vice president for academic affairs, recognizing her outstanding work with first-year students.[26] Concurrently, the University received another national award, The Top Fifty Colleges and Universities for Women recognized by Cosmo Girl Magazine.[1452]

Springtime on a university campus is always alive with student activity and 2004 was no exception for Slippery Rock University. "A very successful and energized Unity Week brought hundreds of students, faculty and staff together for a week full of different programs, attractions and events that not only engaged the campus but also embraced the larger community in attracting hundreds of visitors." Unity Week was developed and coordinated for the campus by the Office of Intercultural Programs. Attending many of the Unity Week events, president Smith commented "The campus continues to experience constant and consistent messages of inclusion, tolerance and opportunity."[1453]

The Aebersold Student Recreation Center was the venue selected for the March 4-6, 2004 National Women's Wheelchair Basketball Tournament. More than 250 volunteers, mostly students, lead by Mrs. Karen Perry, Assistant Director of the Center, hosted the 11 national teams competing and trying out for the Athens, Greece, 2004 Paralympics. The national committee was so pleased with the organization and venue that it announced that the tournament would return to SRU for 2005.[1454]

Relay for Life, coordinated largely by student leaders and staff members registered

858 walkers raising $31,000. Much of the money donated went to cancer research with a portion staying within the local area to assist cancer survivors. Many of the student organizations responded to the appeal for involvement.[1455]

The Rocket, once again earned journalistic awards and honors in national level competition. New to the competition, *The Online Rocket* earned top honors from the Pennsylvania Newspaper Press Association. More than 25 awards were earned.[1456]

New academic programs, created by articulation agreements, were announced in the spring 2004. Slippery Rock University and its Ohio neighbor, Youngstown State University had worked to create a five year engineering degree program. Students majored in physics at SRU for three years and completed the final two years at YSU. A second partnership with the Lake Erie College of Osteopathic Medicine provided students the opportunity to complete a three year program in the natural sciences at Slippery Rock University and then a three year program at LECOM to earn a doctorate in Pharmacy.[1457]

Relay for Life, 2004

Three students received state or national recognition through their major fields of study. Matt McCusker was named Pennsylvania State Association of Health, Physical Education, Recreation and Dance "Outstanding Major of the Year". Chris Hoaks received the NASPE "Major of the Year" award. Francie Lloyd, majoring in Dance, won the New England Regional Dance Festival and went on to compete in the National American College Dance Festival in the Kennedy Center in the nation's capital.[1458]

Mr. Timothy Wilson, class of 1962 received the Distinguished Alumni Award at the Academic Honors Convocation April 4, 2004. Mr. Wilson was

Francie Lloyd, Lady of the Lake,
national performance at the Kennedy Center, 2004

Francie Lloyd and professor Nora Ambrosia, 2004

Vice President and Camp Director of Seeds of Peace International Camp in Otisfield, Maine. The world renowned camp seeks to foster understanding, friendship and tolerance in the Middle East by nurturing mutual respect between Arab and Israeli teenagers.[1459]

At the conclusion of the spring semester, the University finished fifth in the Dixon Trophy competition. A total of 110 student athletes won 2003-2004 PSAC Scholar Athlete awards, requiring a minimum 3.25 grade point average. Jesse Bungo, Women's Tennis and Karen McCready, Women's Track and Field were also named PSAC Spring Top Ten Scholar Athletes. The Women's Outdoor Track and Field Team earned top honors with

Advocacy Day with Chancellor Hample (center), May 2004

Advocacy Day with Representative Stevenson (center), May 2004

another PSAC Championship and sent four women to compete in the NCAA Div. II National Championships. Karen McCready, a three time All America athlete, won the national competition in javelin and went on to compete in the Olympic Team Trials. Coach John Papa was named USTCA Eastern Region "Women's Track and Field Coach of the Year". Two women tennis players, Jessica Bungo and Ashley Michaux were awarded NCAA Div. II All America honors by the Intercollegiate Tennis Asssociation.[1460]

The University's Facilities staff worked with the Athletics Department to put in place prefabricated modules on a site east of Harmony Road, during the spring 2004.[1461] This was the first time such a construction process was used on Slippery Rock University's campus. The units were constructed in an environmentally controlled indoor facility, transported to the university and placed on site with a large crane. The result was a new women's soccer and softball complex on the property of the former Sigma Pi fraternity. Complete with locker rooms, storage areas, coaches' offices and reception areas, the facility was dedicated in March 2005.[1462]

Collaboration became a common practice for so many entities of the University under President Smith's leadership. The creation of the campus water falls was a good example of such collaborative efforts. The Student Government Association wanted to create a campus focal point where students would gather, near the quadrangle, but did not have all the money to make it happen. The Advancement Division approached Maggie and Bud Headland, longtime friends of the University. Maggie graduated Slippery Rock State Teachers College in 1940 and Bud's father was a long-time professor both at Slippery Rock State Normal School and Slippery Rock State Teachers College. They had been benevolent in previous projects and on this occasion wanted to do something significant with the students. The final piece fell into place when two other alumni, Bob and Karen Watson donated more than 190 tons of large field rocks from their nearby farm, needed in the construction of the new focal point. Bob, class of 1970 and Karen, class of 1973 had been active in support of their alma mater since graduating. The result was a beautiful, new campus focal point dedicated May 6, 2004, for students, faculty, staff

Waterfalls construction, 2004

Bud and Maggie Headland, donors

SGA leadership at the waterfalls

and alumni to enjoy - a prime spot for photographs after graduation and other significant campus events. The back to back waterfalls, designed and constructed by local contractor, Mr. Jay Hill, circulated 36,000 gallons of water per hour. One of the adjacent rocks bears a bronze plaque citing the first few lines of the University's Alma Mater, "Where the Slippery Rock Creek wanders, with her sparkling falls, there in stately grace and beauty stands old SR halls…".[1463]

More college bound students were expressing a desire to attend SRU resulting with the closing of admissions for the fall in May 2004. The increase in the number of new students was matched by an increase in quality. To ensure a positive academic experience for the new students, President Smith allocated another one million dollars for new faculty hires, commenting

Wright Aumni Center, 2004

May, 2004, Commencement

Senator White (left), Governor Rendell with trustees

President Smith speaks with graduates

Academic Leadership

The President awards a diploma

The Governor addresses grads

Col. Bialozar administers oath to ROTC graduates

"quality students expect a quality academic institution focused on their education".[1464]

The speaker for the May 2004, outdoor commencement was Governor Ed Rendell. More than 900 graduates received his personal congratulations as well as their long awaited diplomas.[1465]

Throughout the winter and spring of 2004, the Presidential Search Committee, responsible for reviewing all applications and recommending a short list of candidates to the Council of Trustees, met regularly. After interviewing nine applicants in Pittsburgh, the Committee invited the top six to campus for two-day interviews in mid April. At the conclusion of the campus-wide scrutiny, the Committee selected the following three candidates for Council of Trustee review and approval.

* Dr. Don Betz, provost and vice president for academic affairs, University of Central Oklahoma

* Dr. Norman Bregman, provost and vice president for academic affairs and professor of psychology, Longwood University

* Dr. Robert Smith, interim president, Slippery Rock University [1466]

The Trustees approved the three candidates and forwarded the names to the Chancellor. All were interviewed in Harrisburg and introduced to the Board of Governors before the Chancellor, Dr. Judy Hample, made her selection. On May 20, 2004, after nearly a year long, nationwide search, Dr. Robert M. Smith was selected the fifteenth president of Slippery Rock University.[1467] The announcement was less than a surprise and one hoped for by the overwhelming majority of the university community. Many were to say, he was the right choice at the right time. The new president commented "I said to the State System Board of Governors that I accept their appointment not for myself personally but as affirmation that the faculty, administration, staff, students and community constituents have come together as one united team moving the institution forward in a positive direction and that their decision was that we continue together to build a great university".[1468]

Robert M. Smith was born in Kansas and raised in Wichita, where he attended Wichita State University earning a Bachelor of Arts degree in 1967, with a major of speech communication and minors in mathematics and education. A year later he earned a Master of Arts degree at Ohio University in interpersonal communication. After serving as debate coach at Princeton University, he returned to his undergraduate alma mater as a faculty member and chairperson of his major department while

engaged in doctoral study at Temple University. Upon completion of a Ph.D. in communication theory and research methodology in 1977, he was named associate dean, College of Liberal Arts and Sciences at Wichita. His professional career prior to his appointment in 1999 as provost and vice president for academic affairs at Slippery Rock University included dean of the School of Arts and Sciences at the University of Tennessee at Martin, director of the Tennessee Governor's School for the Humanities and director of the West Star Leadership Development Program.

Robert M. Smith, President, 2002-2012

President Smith wasted no time between his appointment and the announcement of a new strategic plan for Slippery Rock University. The plan, shared through 17 interviews with all university stakeholders, introducing three major themes, was presented to the University's Council of Trustees in June 2004.

* "We must continue to raise the academic value of the SRU degree."

* "We need to assert our presence as a premier, regional, public, residential university."

* "It is imperative that we intensify our efforts to generate alternative revenue sources to ensure our ability as a public institution to control our destiny."[1469]

All five components in the University's engaged intellectual community plan and all three major themes in the University's strategic plan were important to the overall success of the University. However, the desire for determining its own destiny was critical in the first decade of the 21st century. The University needed to develop a stronger financial foundation of private fundraising and university advancement to create the margin of excellence for Slippery Rock.

The importance of the University's Foundation was paramount. The need for the non-profit, tax exempt, corporate partnership became increasingly important in 2004, as competition and controls increased. Regardless of the need, student scholarships, capital construction or increased opportunities, the Foundation would be called upon for increasing support.

The charitable giving to Slippery Rock University in 2003-2004, set a new record of $3.6 million, surpassing the previous $2.97 million record. The capital campaign approached fifty percent of its goal with more than $16 million in gifts and contributions collected. The combined endowment of the Slippery Rock University Foundation, Inc. and the Slippery Rock University Alumni Association, as of June 30, 2004, was approximately $14.3 million.[1470]

Wonderful news came in June 2004, from Phi Kappa Phi, the nation's oldest, largest and most selective honor society. The organization visited to campus during the late winter as part of a formal review for membership. Phi Kappa Phi approved a Slippery Rock Chapter with

The Regional Learning Alliance, 2004

RLA Entrance

RLA Technology

RLA Lobby

President Smith provides a tour of the RLA

Main Street construction, summer, 2004

the first official installation scheduled in November in conjunction with the presidential inauguration. Only the top 10% of seniors and top 7.5% of juniors were eligible for membership.[1471]

An aggressive construction schedule permitted the Regional Learning Alliance, in the center of the bustling Cranberry Township area, to open August 2004. "The 76,000 square feet, state-of-the-art facility will prove to be a national model for delivery of post-secondary education. The unique collaboration of eleven education institutions along with a number of other education services devoted to workforce development will be a positive contributor to economic recovery in Southwest Pennsylvania."[1472]

Students returning to Slippery Rock University for the fall semester, 2004 realized a number of campus improvements. Millions of dollars had been spent on construction and renovation projects over the summer including: a new pedestrian corridor from North Hall to the Morrow Field House, air conditioning in Miller

Advanced Technology and Science Center construction, 2004-2005

301

President's residence renovation, summer, 2004

Auditorium and the Vincent Science Hall, more than 400 new parking spaces, several athletic facilities, the painting of the campus water tower including the "Varsity S", and a new water distribution system.[1473]

Several of the faculty and staff hired in the 1960s and 1970s were now retiring resulting with more than 70 national searches. On the eve of the University's celebration of the 50th anniversary of Brown vs. Board of Education, Mrs. Lynne Motyl, director of the Human Resources Office announced the hiring of 18 tenure track faculty positions. Twelve of the new hires were women including five individuals of color.[1474] Slippery Rock University was continuing to become more diverse, resembling the Commonwealth's society.

Fall 2004, opened with Week of Welcome with more than 800 volunteers helping first year students move into residence halls and begin the transition to the University. The desired campus environment had been created focusing on new and continuing students.

SGA Executive Committee, 2004

SGA Senate, 2004

Week of Welcome, 2004

As anticipated, fall 2004, saw the second largest enrollment in the university's history, 7,918, just seven students shy of the record, 7,925. International student enrollment continued to slide an additional 20%, now standing at less than half of the September 11, 2001, number. With the initiation of a new non-resident tuition policy, rewarding students with 3.0 or better averages, non-resident enrollment was up 19%. Actively recruited

Pedestrian walkway construction, 2004

Emma Guffey Miller tales in North Hall, 2004

students of color increased in numbers too, African American students increasing by 13% and Hispanic students by 27%.[1475]

On September 18, The Athletic Department and the Alumni Association celebrated 70 years of Soccer at the University. Long-time coach Jim Egli, after whom the varsity field is named, was on hand to welcome back dozens of alumni soccer players from all over America.[1476]

Continuing in their persistent effort to increase the quality of the students' academic experience, Provost Williams and President Smith discussed their plan for increased program accreditation with the University community fall 2004. The goal was to have every program accredited by its affiliated professional organization. The University had met the rigorous standards for full,

national accreditation through the Middle States Accrediting Association of Colleges and Secondary Schools for nearly half a century and now it was taking professional external review to a programmatic level.[1477]

As a culminating statement, the president offered the following: "In 2001-2002, the University was publicly criticized for being at the bottom of the State System Universities in performance. In 2002-2003, we began to show the results of our concerted work to improve and we moved to eighth place among the universities. The 2003-2004, results show us in third place behind Bloomsburg and Shippensburg".[1478] "If we are to become a great regional public university as I described in my last report, we have to increase the value of the SRU degree for our students and in the minds of our constituents. I believe there are four ways we can do that:

1. We must increase the academic rigor of our programs.
2. We must integrate the classroom with experiential learning.
3. We must engage our students with individualized learning experiences.
4. We must produce competent, civil and caring citizens willing to make their communities better places for all people to live and work.".[1479]

A new organization for men, MAN2MAN, was formed fall 2004. The organization, promoted relationships between men and women based upon respect and

Don McPherson (left) and vice presidents Williams,
Curry and Watson join MAN2MAN

Don McPherson speaks to a
packed crowd about violence against women

Homecoming, 2004

equality, encouraged positive expressions of masculinity and promoted men to become allies for women. On October 11, 2004, MAN2MAN and the grant funded, women-focused Bridge Project co-sponsored a campus-wide program "advocating men's involvement in the prevention of violence against women". A standing room only crowd of more than 500, mostly male students, filled the Swope Music Building Auditorium to listen to former NFL quarterback, Don McPherson speak frankly about the role of men on college campuses.[1480] Recognizing the importance of their efforts, State Senator Mary Jo White presented a $10,000 check to Dr. John Bonando, assistant vice president for student life, representing the MAN2MAN organization.[1481]

Amidst a very busy semester, on a cool, crisp fall day—November 5, 2004—Slippery Rock University's campus community officially welcomed its fifteenth president with the inauguration of Dr. Robert M. Smith.[1482] A committee of more than two dozen faculty, staff, alumni and townspeople planned the extensive celebration, rich in traditional pomp and circumstance. Included in the day-long event was a processional across campus involving nearly 400 participants clad in colorful academic regalia, witnessed by hundreds of students, faculty and staff flanking the processional route; the formal presidential installation performed by the Chancellor and members of the Board of Governors and Council of Trustees; and elaborate receptions and meals. President Smith offered the following creed during his inaugural address:

> "May our lives in this community be motivated
> By goals that have deep meaning
> By dreams that need completion
> By truths that demand expression, and
> By a willingness to learn that remains
>   unquenched".[1483]

Delegates from more than 150 colleges, universities and learned societies attended, offering their greetings and congratulations to the new president. Many of

Phi Kappa Phi first class

Phi Kappa Phi Charter

the visiting delegates were surprised to find marching in the processional approximately 125 SRU students representing academic departments, academic honoraries and organizations. This was no surprise to the campus community knowing the strong relationship the president had forged with students. Mr. Robert Taylor, 1973 alumnus and member of the Council of Trustees commented in their December meeting "I thank Dr. Bob Watson, chair and the entire Inaugural Committee – this was an exciting and well-executed event and SRU never looked better".[1484]

308

Inauguration of Robert M. Smith, Fifteenth President, November 2004

Inauguration of Robert M. Smith, Fifteenth President, November 2004

After months of discussion, the possibility of a campus equestrian center became a reality in December 2004. The Council of Trustees unanimously approved the proposal for the Storm Harbor Equestrian Center with Trustee Suzanne Vessella stating "this is going to be a rather revolutionary program in therapeutic riding and it will center everything right here on campus".[1485] The center included several indoor facilities; stalls, tack rooms, reception area, offices, small classrooms/conference rooms and a large riding arena and outdoor facilities; riding areas, training areas, pastures and parking lots. It was constructed on top of the hill east of Harmony Road and just north of the Women's Soccer and Softball facility with a commanding view of campus. When it was dedicated on October 16, 2005, the president stated "This facility adds to the national reputation the university is building for helping people with disabilities. Made possible by the generous contributions of Carolyn and Paul Rizza, the center provides a place for therapeutic horseback riding opportunities and practical experience for students in the adapted physical activity minor. The facility is named after one of Carolyn Rizza's prized horses. The Center is under the guidance of a board of directors including Trustee Suzanne Vessella."[1486]

Go Greek, 2005

Like so many other colleges and universities across the nation, SRU grew in the 1960s and 1970s. As a result, dormitory facilities were constructed and now were in need of major renovation. For Slippery Rock, the list included Patterson, Harner, Bard, Dodds and Founders Halls. Various options were considered. The dilemma was the University would be required to invest millions of dollars into facilities, difficult to redesign, that would upon completion, resemble institutional dormitories. The new millennial student was most discriminating in the college search process. It was feared that the dormitories with little privacy, gang showers and bathrooms would not help the university in the highly competitive process. The State System was no longer funding student residence facilities, knowing private corporations were interested in this endeavor. A window of opportunity was created for state system universities allowing them to utilize a private, third party to serve in the capacity of private developer, thus expediting the entire construction process. It was decided not to renovate the aging dormitories and to move ahead with construction of new, larger, private, suite-style residence units. The Slippery Rock University Foundation, Incorporated, existing to support the University, stepped up to take charge of the largest construction project in the history of the University. The Council of Trustees unanimously approved the proposed plan at their December 2004, meeting.[1487]

The State System decided that student unions, like student housing, should be constructed, maintained and operated with student dollars, not state funding. The

Going to class, winter, 2005

University's student union, constructed in 1970 for 3,000 students, also needed major renovation. In December 2004, the Council of Trustees approved the undertaking of a feasibility study.[1488] Subsequently, WTW Architects, Pittsburgh was selected.[1489]

At the end of the semester, the President took time to talk with the Council of Trustees about the quality of Slippery Rock University students. He cited Valerie Williams, Karen Buono, Laura Lubinski, Melanie Sugar and Michael McNamara for receiving awards in their major areas of study. He went on to describe the caring nature of students, citing dozens of examples where organizations or individual students accomplished significant community or humanitarian efforts.[1490]

Packed house, Mr. Belding, Saved by the Bell

Mr. Belding, Saved by the Bell

A packed house at Pittsburgh's Heinz Hall enjoyed a heart-warming production by the Pittsburgh Symphony and the All-Star College Chorus under the direction of the masterful and award winning, Principal Pops Conductor, Marvin Hamlisch in January 2005. Slippery Rock University celebrated the largest representation of any college or university with 15 students performing in the All-Star Chorus. At the conclusion of the production, all of the students, their families and dozens of alumni and friends joined President Smith at a reception where Mr. Hamlisch was honored.[1491]

The Regional Learning Alliance continued to gain notoriety. In January 2005, about six months after its opening, the president reported "This week, Governor Edward Rendell toured the building and announced funding of $2 million for the construction of the building. In the last two months, Senator Arlen Spector announced a third $200,000 grant to support development of the RLA. We are working with Senator Spector to secure a major demonstration grant to showcase our unique approach to workforce development."[1492]

A Student Union Task Force, composed primarily of students, was assembled by the vice president for student life in January 2005. Initially, the task force looked at the need for a performing arts center and dining facilities as well as a student union and traveled to several colleges and universities to review distinguishing features of student unions.[1493]

The Vincent Science Hall was aging and in need of major renovations. For years the University had been working through the State System to obtain funding to construct a new facility for some science and technology departments. Finally, a funding partnership was forged with the State System allowing construction to begin in 2005. It was understood that upon completion of the new building, major renovation would begin on the Vincent Science Hall.[1494]

In order for the student housing construction project to progress smoothly and effectively, all divisions of the University would need to collaborate on the massive project lead by the Foundation's Board of Directors. In March 2005, Trustee John Thornburg reported to the rest of the Council "All SRU divisions are working together toward the construction phase of the project".[1495] WTW Architects from Pittsburgh was selected along with the general contractor, Mistick Construction Corporation and the work pace quicken throughout the spring. President Smith noted "Arguably the largest single construction project in Butler County history, this project will forever

Student residence construction, 2005

313

change the way the campus looks and the way it develops our students as leaders. The housing project fully complements how Student Life helps develop the social and leadership skills of our students in harmony with our academic development."[1496]

The need for President Smith to move the University to a position where it could have more financial control of its destiny became more evident in early 2005. In March, the President reported "One of our goals has been to create our own options and insulate us from the financial vagaries of the political process".[1497] Referring to the State System budget process, he went on to say, in early 2005, Chancellor Hample told the Pennsylvania House and Senate Appropriations Committees, "In Fiscal Year 2005-2006, we are facing significant obligations in the area of personnel compensation, due to mandated increases in salary and health care benefits". The projected increase for health care for the State System was in excess of $20 million.[1498] The President continued, "SRU began its own transformation in 2003. We can be well protected if we are able to hold to our plan. Our work depends on the continued success of two initiatives: the Regional Learning Alliance as an alternative income stream and the Foundation as the building block for financial security and enhancement

Off campus landlords

of our aspirations."[1499] "Over the next year, we will give considerable attention to alternative funding methods and you should expect similar transformations such as those we have experienced in enrollment management. We must be aggressive and we must establish bold audacious goals if we are to be successful in the face of declining legislative appropriations."[1500]

At the Academic Honors Convocation, April 3, 2005, the University recognized one of its long-time leaders, also an alumnus from the class of 1961. Dr.

Coach Messer on the mound, 2005

Coach Johnson and women's softball team, 2005

314

Robert Marcus, Chairperson of the Council of Trustees received the distinguished Alumnus Award and served as keynote speaker at the prestigious event.[1501]

That spring, two faculty received national awards. Mr. Steve Hawk, Music department, played trumpet on Ms. Nancy Wilson's "R.S.V.P." album which was

Joanne Rogers recital, 2005

Joanne Rogers (right) signs book with Chuck Aber, alumnus (Neighbor Aber) for local teacher, Karen Watson, alumna, 2005

Professor Richard Martin advises SGA, 2005

Swearing in of new SGA officers, 2005

Swearing in of SGA Senate, 2005

SGA Orientation, 2005

Dance Recital, 2005

Dance Recital, 2005

One Act Play, 2005

awarded the Best Jazz Vocal Album of the year. Mr. Hawk had been featured previously on the Oprah Winfrey Show. Ms. Susan Kushner, Physical Therapy department, was recognized for her more than 16 years of involvement with the National Multiple Sclerosis Society as "Volunteer of the Year". The award was presented at the national leadership conference in Denver, Colorado.[1502]

Student life on campus flourished under President Smith's tenure. In just four brief years, the number of recognized student organizations increased 50% from 85 to more than 130.

For the second time in as many years the University hosted a high ranking state government leader as commencement speaker. Dr. Francis V. Barnes, Secretary of Education and a graduate of the class of 1971, presented remarks to the more than 1,000 graduates and their families and friends at the May 7, 2005, commencement.[1503]

On June 9, 2005, a groundbreaking ceremony was held to mark the beginning of the formal construction of the student residence complex. President Smith reported the following day, "On June 9, the university and the Slippery rock University Foundation closed on the financial package for $79 million of bonds to begin the construction of Phase I of the new student housing

Military Ball, 2005

Trace Adkins, 2005

Rising Star

Rising Star

Office of Intercultural Programs

ACT101

Gospel Choir

Student Awards Programs, spring, 2005

Drinking the lucky green juice before finals

Midnight at the Fluh, free food, 2005

Equestrian Center construction, 2005

Equestrian Center interior construction, 2005

May Commencement, 2005

A wet Commencement

President Smith with speaker, Dr. Barnes, alumnus

complex. This construction project represents the largest single housing project to date in the Pennsylvania State System for Higher Education and, we are told, when coupled with phase II, is the largest of its kind in the nation. When finished in 2009, we will have replaced 2,200 of our 2,800 residential beds.

It is hard to adequately describe the significance of this project to the transformation of the university. Located in the center of the campus, this project compellingly proves that students are the focus of the campus and that the total emersion within a living-learning environment is the core of becoming a truly educated person at Slippery Rock University."[1504] It was reported that the project was the largest LEED Certified student residence construction project, at that time, in the nation.[1505]

In June, President Smith announced to the campus community his appointment of Dr. William Williams as Provost and Vice President for Academic Affairs. "Following more than two years as interim provost, Dr. Williams has proven himself an able leader of our academic mission and a visionary guide for academic excellence."[1506] Dr. William's continued his work relative to the accreditation of academic programs, announcing the accreditation of programs in Theatre, Computer Science, the graduate School Counseling program, and the re-accreditation of four other departments.[1507]

By the next Trustees meeting in June, the President's fiscal concerns had only increased. "In a departure from previous quarterly reports, I am devoting almost the entirety on the fiscal events facing Slippery Rock University in the coming months and through the next two years. My hope is to inform the Council members of the circumstances of our budget and the challenges we are facing for the next 18 months."[1508]

319

"We essentially receive revenues from three sources: Tuition and fees from students; a state appropriation received form the Pennsylvania State System of Higher Education as our allocation from the approved appropriation from the State Legislature; and other incidental revenues such as interest on investments and auxiliary services. About ten years ago, the state allocation was approximately 60% of the total revenues. Now it is closer to 38%."[1509] The president went on to explain that the allocation from the legislature for the current year was 5% less than the previous year, in spite of a 12% growth in enrollment. "The single greatest factor in play for 2005-2006, is the Governor's desire that no tuition increase be approved."[1510] The net result was more than a $4 million deficit. "Contractually obligated salaries and benefits will increase next year by $3,533,449 or 86% of the projected shortfall. Of those salaries and benefits, health care costs are the fastest growing component, comprising $1,575,000 of the increase or 45% of the total compensation increase. The increases for 2006-2007, are even more severe. Based on no tuition increase, the total shortfall next year could be $8,943,770."[1511]

By the beginning of school, August 2005, the Board of Governors had approved the smallest tuition increase in several years ($96) but the appropriation to SRU was more than originally predicted due to improved performance and greater attention to the funding attributes. Having dodged a major fiscal bullet, the president commented, "Our budget issues may only be symptomatic of the challenges we face in the future. The larger issue is the erosion of the underlying social contract that charters us as a public university in Pennsylvania."[1512]

The freshman class that fall, again increased in quality, and established another enrollment record, nearly 8,100 students.[1513] In order to appropriately accommodate the increase, twenty-one faculty were hired; twelve females, and ten minorities.[1514] The emphasis on diversity of new employees continued the next year with women comprising 80% of the management hires and 60% of the faculty hires and 26% of the faculty hires were persons of color.[1515]

Students sign in for Town Gown International Student Reception, 2005

Town Gown says welcome to Slippery Rock, 2005

The campus responded compassionately to the national disaster, Hurricane Katrina, the costliest and one of the deadliest hurricanes in the nation's history. Occurring in late August 2005, millions of Americans in southeastern United States were affected by Katrina. Student organizations along with faculty and staff immediately went into fundraising operations for the victims. President Smith commented to the campus community at the beginning of the semester, "By the end of the first week of classes, nineteen students have been called into duty by the National Guard and deployed to the flood sites".[1516]

With a greater interest in campus traditions, the Student Government Association Senate led by Mr. Jude

Week of Welcome, August 2005

Week of Welcome, August 2005

2005 Women's Soccer PSAC Champions

Butch, president, decided it wanted to foster the return of a long-time tradition. After nearly ten years without a campus yearbook, the Senate voted in late November to bring back the Saxigenia. The fall semester had past when a student editor and staff, and a faculty advisor were chosen, but they immediately went to work. After seven months of focused effort, the new edition of the Saxigenia was released in the Fall 2005.

During the fall 2005, the campus was treated to outstanding soccer as both the men's and women's teams earned PSAC Championships. Coaches Matt Thompson and Noreen Herlihy were awarded their teams' PSAC honors.[1517]

The impact the student housing project had on the campus community was positive and expansive. That fall, applications for admission were up nearly 40%, with non-resident applications up over 100%.[1518] Considerable economic impact was realized in the area with more than $13 million spent with Butler County contractors which employed nearly 500 workers. The payroll had generated almost $4,000 in local income taxes and nearly $300,000 in federal and state income taxes.[1519]

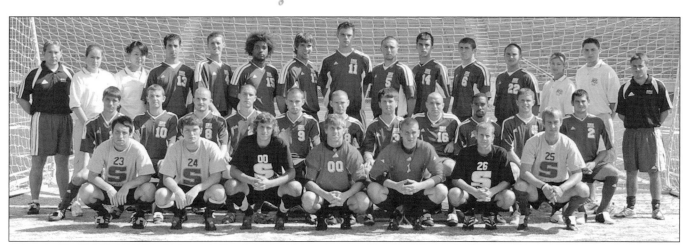

2005 Men's Soccer PSAC Champions

Homecoming, 2005

Under snow, 2005

Trustee Robert Taylor reported in December 2005, that 100% of the Council of Trustees had made financial contribution to the University. A committee of trustees had established a $1000 annual goal for each Trustee, however, it was understood that Trustees would contribute according to their individual means.[1520]

Since the student union construction project would be funded by the students, a referendum was necessary to determine whether the students wanted to renovate the existing facility or construct a new union. The student union task force coordinated the activity with all students and the architectural firm, WTW.[1521] In December 2005, the students voted to construct a new facility.[1522] It was a time for major construction like non other in the University's history.

While the student housing construction project was running smoothly and ahead of schedule, the advanced technology and science building construction project seemed wrought with issues. Before construction started, the design of the building was changed due to reduced funding. In a critical location, sited at the south end of the quadrangle, the new building would be the first building visitors would see when turning into campus from the main Kiester Road entrance. President Smith reported in December 2005, "we had hoped to present to you at this meeting our new science building, scheduled to be completed mid-November. A state-supervised project, the building is more than 140 days behind completion with limited workers on site in any given day

and a backlog of architectural and construction problems that may take months if not a full year to resolve after the building is turned over to the university."[1523] In March 2006, the President reported "Next month we will move into the new Applied Technology and Science Hall. This new home to the departments of chemistry; computer science; geography, geology and environmental sciences will provide our faculty and students expanded space a d new laboratories for research and teaching. The Advanced Technology and Science Hall will be first used for the Pennsylvania Association of Councils of Trustees meeting in April."[1524]

For several years the University Athletic Council, comprised of representatives of the faculty, staff, students and coaches and led by the University's Faculty Athletic Representative, Dr. Brian Crow, had been reviewing the athletic program. With 23 varsity sports, Slippery Rock University was one of the largest NCAA Division II programs in the country, well above the average of 14 teams. Costs were increasing dramatically for everything including, transportation, equipment, officiating, coaching and facilities, and the University's athletic budget was nearing the national average for a Division I program. As the University's fiscal concerns increased, recommendations were made by the UAC and an experienced outside consultant to reduce the number of varsity sports.[34] After discussions with the UAC, student athletes, coaches and their union representatives, and a significant review of related

Winter, 2005

326

factors, a decision was reached. President Smith reported the decision, "We announced on January 30, 2006, that we will end competition in golf, all of our water sports (swimming and water polo), field hockey, men's tennis and wrestling.[1525] "Our decision to eliminate these programs was driven by the necessity to effectively manage the institutions fiscal resources in a time of significant budgetary constraints without eroding our commitment to academic quality".[1526]

"Following the announcement, our first priority was to serve as well as we could the needs of the 122 students directly involved in these sports. We will continue the scholarships for up to four years for each scholarship student for those students impacted by this decision and who wish to stay at SRU. For those seeking a transfer to another institution to continue their competition, we have taken steps to help them with that process and removed whatever barriers might stand in their way to a smooth transfer."[1527]

On March 27, 2006, President Smith convened the head coaches of those teams that were retained to discuss the importance of achieving compliance with Title IX requirements. With a new direction for the athletic program, he believed this was the opportunity to overcome a long-standing question of Slippery Rock University's conformity with the federal law. He challenged them to work together to reach compliance by the start of the 2006-07, sport seasons. This meant adjusting their recruitment strategies and team composition such that opportunities for women were in proportion to the population of women in the undergraduate class, a common test for Title IX conformity. The coaches were to develop their plan and present to the president before the end of the school term.

The coaches presented a plan on May 1, 2006, that included reinstatement of field hockey and adding women's lacrosse. By adjusting the roster counts for each team, the coaches felt that everyone could be competitive but the additional women's sports were necessary to reach proportionality. They argued that adding lacrosse would result in needing only one coach who would be responsible for both sports, one in the fall and one in the spring. The president endorsed the plan on May 4, 2006.

On June 14, 2006, twelve women student-athletes representing the sports that had been cut sought the

SGA holiday party, 2005

SGA holiday party, 2005

help of the Women's Law Project, a nonprofit women's legal aid organization, to successfully get a preliminary injunction in Federal Court, Western Pennsylvania District, from eliminating women's swimming and water polo until the court could decide the legality of the university's decisions to cut sports. The plaintiffs argued that the university could not cut women's sports while knowingly out of compliance with Title IX without first becoming in compliance with Title IX.

U.S. Chief District Justice Donetta Ambrose ruled July 24, 2006, that the University had discriminated against its female student-athletes by eliminating their sports when they were already under-represented by the

Student leadership picnic, 2006

expectations of Title IX law.[1528] The Court then ordered mediation between the university and the Women's Law Project, who was now representing all female student-athletes, to finalize how the University would be able to meet one of its own goals, compliance with federal law.

By April 2007, the Court ruled that the University had successfully settled gender equity in the athletic programs and had a plan in place to assure continued compliance. By the end of the process, the University had 17 varsity teams, the same number and same sports as in May 2006, but much more expanded facilities, coaching opportunities, equipment, and scholarships for women student-athletes. Water polo star and lead plaintiff Beth Choike said, "This lawsuit was definitely worthwhile. We've already seen some definite improvements, and the progress just keeps on going."[1529]

Disaster struck the Slippery Rock University community March 2006, when an early morning off-campus, house fire left three students and one non-student homeless, losing all material possessions. By noon the campus community had rallied providing, meal passes in the dining halls, apartment accommodations, new clothing, new text books and supplies and cash for the students and their friend.[1530] The local media heralded the response as "the Slippery Rock University way".

Normally, two shifts worked seven days a week on the student housing project and it was well ahead of schedule. By the end of March 2006, it was reported that buildings A and B would be ready for the fall and building C, including the administrative center would

be ready before January 2007. So much progress had been realized in phase I construction of four buildings, 1400 beds, that the Foundation prepared to begin phase II, 800 beds, in February, 2007.[1531]

In March 2006, the University still had more than a million dollars of budget deficit to trim to balance the 2006–07 budget. The President was examining a few academic programs for possible elimination as well as hopeful cost-savings from various operational processes such as travel, vehicle fleet costs, campus energy usage and assignment of overtime within the facilities operations. The University's plans would produce a balanced budget, providing the legislature increase the appropriation by one-half of one percent over the Governor's recommendation, and the Board of Governors increase tuition modestly at their July meeting.[1532]

The Trustees acted to name two facilities during their March 2006, meeting. A resolution to rename conference room 108 in Old Main, the "Dr. Robert Marcus Executive Conference Room" was unanimously approved. Trustee Kenneth Blair noted "Dr. Marcus is a wonderful example of someone who truly supports his alma mater as a caring and generous alumnus through his dedication to provide financial support for students from non-majority backgrounds as well as for an absolute passion for the students of Slippery Rock University and giving of his time and talents as a trustee".[1533]

The Trustees unanimously approved a resolution to name building C of the new student housing complex "Dr. Robert J. Watson Hall". Watson Hall was the central

Julie Hepner, SGA president makes presentation to retiring vice president Watson, 2006

328

Watson Hall

building in the new housing complex and housed the Residence Life offices, the Honors Program and many of the Education students. Dr. Watson, Vice President for Student Life at SRU was attending his final trustee meeting as he was retiring at the end of March. Trustee Blair commented "Dr. Watson has served the University through tremendous service for many, many years and has shown great compassion for the students of this University – he will be very much missed and we thank him for his service. This is such a fitting way to honor his dedication and selfless leadership."[1534] Mr. Kyle Kekic, representing the 2800 student members of the Association of Residence Hall Students, presented Dr. Watson with a framed design of "Robert J. Watson Hall".[1535]

At that same meeting, President Smith announced that Dr. Constance L. Foley would be joining the University on July 1, 2006, as the next Vice President for Student Life. Dr. Foley was serving as Assistant Vice President for Student Affairs at Florida Atlantic University.[1536]

During the spring semester 2006, the College of Education received good news with the award of a $1.3 million grant for construct of a model for recruiting and retaining teachers of diverse backgrounds.[1537]

At the Academic Honors Convocation, spring, 2006, Mr. Marvin Hamlisch, Principal Pops Conductor with the Pittsburgh Symphony Orchestra and the National Symphony Orchestra received the honorary Doctor of Humane Letters degree.[1538]

Led by Coach John Papa, the Women's Track and Field Team, again captured the coveted PSAC championship that spring 2006.[1539]

At their June 2006, meeting, six months after the students voted to fund the construction of the new student union, the Council of Trustees approved the proposed construction project. "The proposed student union will serve as gateway between the academic quad and the residential community. It will provide our students greater space and service for their needs. The university union is projected to be a 122,500 gross square foot facility to house the bookstore, retail shops, a food court, a new Rocky's dining room, a movie theater, ballroom for special events, greatly expanded student club and

Fran Hensler, Computer Center pioneer, receives forty years award from President Smith

Dr. Marvin Hamlisch (center) awarded a personalized seat at the Jack by President Smith, with Deb and Eliott Baker, 2006

organization meeting rooms, five different student lounges as well as student offices and staff offices for some Student Life employees. The projected cost is broadly estimated at $3.7 million."[1540]

The Council of Trustees also approved the proposed Alumni House expansion construction project. "The Alumni Association Board of Directors has generously offered to pay for a major expansion of the facility. The Board's goal is to provide the University an inviting, warm, first-class place to host events, meetings and socials that serve the University's goals."[1541]

In a little more than three years, more than 20 major projects involving new construction or renovation were either started, under construction or completed. Without question, Slippery Rock University was creating a new campus image. As the largest State System university in terms of physical size, with a campus of more than 650 acres, the University was making substantive changes to move from its appearance as a "state built" institution of higher education to a premier residential public university.

As Slippery Rock University prepared for the opening of the fall semester, it was reaping the benefits of strong leadership and an excellent faculty and staff. The University had enrolled 8,234 students, not only the largest number of students in its history, but also one of the best prepared student bodies. The first two buildings of its comprehensive student residence project were ready for occupancy. Due to an aggressive construction schedule, the third building, Watson Hall, originally scheduled for opening in January 2007, was ready for its students October 14, 2006, several months early. The new Advanced Technology and Science building was ready for student and faculty occupancy. Plans for the new student union were quickly moving forward. Many of the academic departments had earned professional, national accreditation. The State System's Performance Indicators Program evaluated Slippery Rock University second among the 14 universities.[1542]

According to President Smith, "The beginning of the 2006-07, year could not have been more spectacular: record-breaking enrollment on the first day of classes, opening a new academic building for three of our departments, and the move-in of 714 students in the first completed phase of our $110 million residential housing complex.

What an extraordinary start for the year. We have expectations of even more pivotal events to come."[1543]

Indeed, enrollment was up nearly 200 students over the previous year with 8,234 students attending classes. The quality of all freshmen also increased as measured by the SAT scores and the percentage of students graduating from the top quarter of their high school class. The number of African American students rose from 96 in 2005 to 133 in 2006.[1544]

Setting forth the University's short term enrollment plan, President Smith stated, "We do not intend to increase enrollment beyond an average of one percent per year. We are entering the period of time when the pool of available college-aged students will decline sharply and remain down for eight years. We believe we has positioned the reputation of the university to hold our own through our careful management of our reputation and continuing to increase the proportion we take from the market. In addition, we will continue to seek out-of-state students from places not facing declining numbers of college-age students and international students. We have in place the necessary policies and strategies to achieve our goal."[1545]

The new Advanced Technology and Science Hall, home to the Chemistry, Computer Science and Geography, Geology, and Environmental Studies departments completed the footprint for the academic quadrangle on the lower part of campus. The 76,000 square-foot building has two fronts, one facing the southern entrance to campus off Kiester Road and the other facing the interior of the quad. The new building includes twenty science

Quad side of Advanced Technology and Science Center, 2006

teaching and research laboratories, a 120 unit computer science laboratory, study lounges and faculty offices. It is equipped for multimedia display as well as wired for the internet and other "smart classroom" technologies. A gift from the Snyder Charitable Foundation provided the lobby outside the main auditorium.[1546]

At the beginning of the 2006-07 school year, President Smith took the opportunity to report on the University's three strategic goals.

"Goal One: To raise the value of the SRU degree

We are pursuing a number of strategies that will continue to enhance the quality of the Slippery Rock University degree. Primary among our strategies is to enhance the reputation of our academic majors by:

1. Assuring that we know and can articulate what learning takes place and at what level of accomplishment.

2. Tracking the success of our graduates.

3. Certifying through successful accreditation that we meet the highest standards set by our national professional organizations.

4. Assuring the highest qualifications of our faculty as demonstrated by the percent that hold the highest degree within their profession.

5. We want our students to have an enriched education through a range of experiences beyond simply acquiring 120 credit hours. We believe that these add considerable value to our students' education. Among the key experiences we provide are service-learning, internships, international experiences, joint student-faculty research, leadership development, and respect for diversity.

Goal Two: To be a premier residential public university

Strategies for achieving this goal include the ways we integrate academic life with student life to create enhanced intellectual experiences, to provide for leadership development that fosters civic responsibility and skills in civil discourse, and to create respect for diversity.

Also among our strategies is to continue to transform the entire campus to be an intentional learning laboratory with areas that teach people about our environment, provide opportunities for meditation and reflection, remind us of our heritage and culture, and, through art, provoke observations and contemplation.

As part of the continuing development of our campus, we will aggressively pursue completion of

phase II of the residential housing project, the dining services renovation plan, development of the recreational athletic complex, and construction of the student union and performing arts center. These projects are vital to the living-learning environment we are building for our students.

Goal Three: To control our own financial destiny

We are concentrating on three strategies to achieve our goal: careful and prudent management of our existing resources, establishment of independent revenue streams to the campus, and attraction of private gifts and bequests."[1547]

Over the summer 2006, several students enjoyed enriched experiences. Ms. Laura Smiley and seven of her theater students performed to "five-star" reviews at the 60th Edinburgh Fringe Festival in Scotland, the largest international arts festival in the world. Their play, "Dark North", was written by Slippery Rock University Theater faculty member, Dr. David Skeele.[1548]

The Slippery Rock University Jazz Ambassadors, under the direction of Dr. Steve Hawk, performed at the Montreux Jazz Festival in Switzerland as well as the North Sea Jazz Festival in Rotterdam, Holland. The Montreux Festival is the oldest and most respected in the world and Slippery Rock's jazz group was the first college band from Pennsylvania to have been chosen to perform.[1549]

At the two year anniversary of the Regional Learning Alliance, it was reported that more than 75,000 people had received training and educational development amounting more than 420,000 hours, not including the General Motors training programs and those credit courses offered by the fourteen partner institutions of higher education. More than 270 different companies had used the facility for their training.[1550]

President Smith introduced to the Trustees at their December meeting, Ms. Rita Abent, recently hired as the University's Executive Director of Public Relations. Ms Abent had more than 30 years experience as a higher education marketing and communication administrator and former newspaper editor.[1551]

Four years had passed since President Smith had been appointed interim president. He reflected: "The changes we have seen in those four years have been remarkable. Most noticeably, our enrollment is up 9.3% and we have broken previous records every single year while simultaneously reducing or holding steady the size of the freshman class for the last three years. All measures of the quality of the entering freshman class

(SAT, grades, percent from the top tiers of their high school class) are at record levels. Admission of students of color is up (31% for African Americans and 138% for Hispanics and Latinos). Retention and graduation rates are up for all measures. We have had a successful four years in overcoming our greatest challenge at that point of time."[1552]

Every program evaluated within the past four years had received accreditation or re-accreditation. The Exercise Science Program was one of only six programs in the nation to receive the maximum five-year accreditation by the Commission on Accreditation of Allied Health Education Programs. In addition, the Pennsylvania Department of Education re-accredited all of the College of Education's teaching certification programs.[1553]

During the fall 2006, the Department of Counseling and Development, for the second time, was awarded the "Outstanding Counselor Education Program" by the Pennsylvania Counseling Association.[1554]

Individual faculty and staff members also received state, regional and national awards. Dr. James Strickland, English, received the Conference on English Leadership Exemplary Leadership Award for 2006. The award was presented at the annual National Council of Teachers national conference. Dr. Thomas Flynn, Communications, received the Neil Postman Mentor's Award from the New York State Communication Association at its annual conference. Dr. Stephen Barr, Music, was chosen as an ASCAPLUS Award recipient by the American Society of Composers, Authors and Publishers in the Concert Music category.[1555]

Also during the fall 2006, Dr. Charles Curry, vice president for finance and administrative affairs, was honored as one of the top 25 chief financial officers in the region. The awards were sponsored by the Pittsburgh Business Times. Dean of the College of Education, Dr. Jay Hertzog was presented the Pennsylvania State University College of Education Alumni Society Excellence in Education Award.[1556]

President Smith felt strongly that faculty and staff of this caliber increased the quality of the Slippery Rock University degree. Students also agreed as measured by the 2006 National Survey of Student Engagement results. The results showed that Slippery Rock University students consistently rated their experiences at SRU higher than do students attending peer institutions.[1557]

Standing for many decades, the record of most football victories, was held by the legendary coach, N. Kerr Thompson. The record was finally broken by the

Coach Mihalik with family after 127th win, 2006

Rock's football coach, Dr. George Mihalik in his 19th season. The record 127th win came at Indiana University of Pennsylvania during a nationally televised game, when the Rock defeated IUP, 21 to 17.[1558]

The Center on Disability and Health received two new grants totaling $216,000 to continue providing horseback riding, exercise programs and health education through 2008 to area residents with disabilities. In addition, the University also received a $116,000 grant from the FISA Foundation, a Pittsburgh charitable foundation working to improve quality of life for girls, women and people of both genders with disabilities, and $100,000 from DSF Charitable Foundation in Pittsburgh which supports health and human-services programs.[1559]

Three students earned regional or national honors for their research, during the fall 2006. Jennifer Basich, an exercise science major, received a regional award from the Mid-Atlantic Region of the American College of Sports Medicine. Chemistry major, Amanda Henry, earned first place honors and Biochemistry major, Kimberly Negrin received a second place award at the Annual Undergraduate Research Symposium in the Chemical and Biological Sciences.[1560]

The University continued to take steps toward its goal of becoming the region's premier residential public university. A ribbon-cutting ceremony on September 15, 2006, marked the official opening of the Slippery Rock University Foundation, Inc., suite-style residence hall complex. Participating in the opening ceremony of the $110 million project were: members of the Foundation's Board of Directors, Mr. Regis Schiebel, Mr. William Thomas, Mr. William Sonntag and Mr. Barry Welsch; students, Amy Homa, president of the Student Government Association and William cooper, president of the Association of Residence Hall Students; and President Smith.[1561] Building A was occupied by 366 students, Building B with 346 students and Watson Hall, had 326 students and administrative offices. Building D, the last building in phase I construction, was nearing completion, five months ahead of schedule. Buildings E and F, housing 446 students, would mark the beginning of phase II construction scheduled to begin March 2007. When completed, the University will have replaced approximately 86% of its student residential inventory.[1562]

Homecoming weekend, 2006 was a perfect time for the Alumni Association to conduct a ground breaking ceremony for its new $600,000 addition to the Russell Wright Alumni House. The 2,600 square-foot project would provide a state-of-the-art conference center and much needed meeting space. The new facility would be ready during the fall 2007.[1563]

Significant strides were made toward the University's goal of financial stability when it received the largest amount of money in the four years of the performance funding program. The University added $4,341,344 to its 2006-07, operating budget based on outstanding results from the previous year's performance indicators. The performance funding program, developed by the State System, encouraged the fourteen universities to improve both student achievement and success in all of their daily management operations, and to reward them when they do.[1564]

In December 2006, the Frontier League of professional baseball announced that Slippery Rock University would be the host location for an expansion team beginning May, 2006. The team, later named as the Slippery Rock Sliders, would play 32 home games in the

SGA sign and Advanced Technology and Science Center, 2007

Jack Critchfield Stadium on campus beginning May 29, 2007. Not only would this opportunity provide a modest revenue stream to the University, the team provided many students, especially sports management majors, a chance to gain first hand experience in the operation of a professional franchise.[1565]

Ms. Amy Homa, SGA President informed campus in March 2007, that the senior gift project was nearing completion. The project, a new sign at the main entrance to the lower part of campus off Kiester Road was a culmination of several months work of solicitation and construction.[1566]

Martin Luther King Day of Service had developed into a major event for the University, led by the Office of Intercultural Programs. One of its major activities

Alumni Expansion, 2006

Martin Luther King Day On, Not Off

Homecoming, 2006

was "a day on not off" resulting with more than 300 student volunteers serving the community in various capacities.[1567]

As a unionized campus, Slippery Rock University operated through several collective bargaining agreements. Nearly all personnel groups, such as the faculty, nurses, police, coaches, some levels of administration and others were unionized. Staff members working in maintenance and the trades were represented by the American Federation of State County and Municipal Employees (AFSCME), Slippery Rock's largest union. The Association of Pennsylvania State College and University Faculties (APSCUF), represented the teaching faculty. In January 2007, both unions had not yet settled their agreements, resulting in considerable difficulty in attempting to project the budget to begin July 1, 2007.[1568]

On the revenue side of the budget, the Governor had recommended an increase of 3.5% in the state-owned universities' budget, yet to be voted on by the legislature. A tuition increase would be decided by the Board of Governors of the State System to complete the majority of the income to the University. This was an annual process, normally completed in advance of the beginning of the fiscal year, July 1.[1569]

During the spring of 2007, Slippery Rock University was in the midst of a campus-wide energy audit led by BCS, a specialty engineering company. At the completion of the audit, BCS submitted an extensive list of capital projects that were guaranteed to save energy equal to or exceeding the cost of the implementation. As an effort to achieve energy savings over the next 15 to 20 years and as a part of the Governor's initiative to save energy consumption and to reduce costs, the University prepared to propose an extensive portfolio of projects based on the audit.[1570]

In addition, the University was in the process of establishing a host of demonstration projects that would showcase energy savings and methods of alternative energy. One such example was the award of Silver LEED certification for the Regional Learning Alliance building. The RLA was the only building in Marshall Township to be certified as an environmentally "Green" building at this level of performance. The University had set LEED certification as a goal for all of its campus construction projects.[1571]

Macoskey Center

During the spring of 2007, the University installed a solar and wind turbine system to generate electricity for the Robert A. Macoskey Center for Sustainable Systems Education and Research. The University monitored and managed the use of both to efficiently utilize alternatives to electricity to power the facility. A geothermal well was soon to be drilled, adding a third dimension of alternative energy sources. The plan was to establish, if feasible, additional geothermal wells for buildings that were beyond the central heating system serving the main campus buildings.[1572]

The University Energy Conservation Committee was created to guide the development of several creative savings projects. One of the first projects adopted was to mandate the automation of the sleep mode in the Energy Star computer monitors across campus. The result was an annual savings of $27,000 in electricity costs on 2,000 faculty and staff computer monitors. President Smith commented "The intent of these efforts is not only to realize financial savings but to establish the university as a leader in environmental work and energy research."[1573]

Michael Zieg, assistant professor of geography, geology and the environment, had just returned from a two-week research expedition in Antarctica. He collected 150 rocks for his students, majoring in geology, to analyze to discover more about the separation of the continents. Professor Zieg was one of nine geologists for the National Science Foundation Office of Polar Programs Project.[1574]

Students as well as faculty demonstrated significant interest in the environment. Two seniors, David Fuji and Matthew Batina developed an abstract on their findings on air pollution research and were invited to present their findings at the American Geophysical Union's National Conference before 14,000 scientists from around the world. Conferees were so impressed that NASA scientists approached them about working together.[1575]

Also during the spring 2007, the plan submitted by the School of Business for accreditation was accepted by the national association, setting in motion the final stages for acquiring that important accreditation. The most recent graduates of the athletic training program scored significantly higher than the national average on the National Athletic Trainers' Association Board of Certification Exam. Students must pass all three sections of the exam to work as athletic trainers and Slippery Rock graduates earned above average marks in all three sections of the national exam.[1576]

The Slippery Rock University Jazz Ensemble I, directed by Stephen Hawk, associate professor of music, performed at the oldest jazz festival in the United States, the annual University of Notre Dame Collegiate Jazz Festival. Dr. Hawk's personal work as a performer in the jazz ensemble for artist, Nancy Wilson, was also recognized for his work. Ms Wilson's CD, "Turned to Blue" was honored with a Grammy Award in the "Best Vocal Jazz Ensemble" category.[1577]

Kaleidoscope, the annual spring arts festival provided a wonderful opportunity for the University to showcase its outstanding fine and performing arts programs. Usually lasting for about a week, special presentations from around the nation established a festive atmosphere on campus.[1578]

Events occurring on Virginia Tech's campus on April 16, 2007, would change practices and procedures on college campuses across the United States. A troubled student killed 32 other students and wounded 25 more students before taking his own life. It became the deadliest shooting in history involving a single gunman. Procedures throughout the Student Life division at Slippery Rock University were immediately reviewed bringing together operations such as campus police, counseling center, health services, residence life, judicial

Deans Russell, McKinney, Hannam and Hertzog

affairs and others. Emergency operational and communication procedures and practices were scrutinized at the local and state levels.[1579]

The Student Life and Academic Affairs divisions continued their collaborative efforts with a joint conference brought to campus, spring 2007, focusing on student learning outcomes both inside and outside the classroom. These developments created practices that became part of the University's strategic plan.[1580]

Only ten campus health centers in Pennsylvania had met the standards set by the Accreditation Association for Ambulatory Health Care. The University Student Health Services proudly announced, June 2007, their continuing accreditation.[1581]

The new Professional Studies department within the College of Business, Information and Social Sciences began operation on July 1. 2007. The department was created at the request of Dean Bruce Russell to restructure the Applied Science major into a high quality degree that met the needs of students wishing to customize their degree program. The major was chosen primarily by students transferring into Slippery Rock University from technical institutions. The creation of the new department also met concerns of the Association to Advance Collegiate Schools of Business (AACSB) for accrediting Slippery Rock University's School of Business.[1582]

In June 2007, President Smith introduced Ms. Barbara Ender, the new Vice President for Advancement to the Council of Trustees. Formerly Vice President for Development and CEO of the Moorehead State University Foundation, Ms. Ender brought with her more than twenty years of experience in the field.[1583]

Recognized as one of the best processes in the State System, the Board of Governors asked President Smith to present Slippery Rock University's strategic planning and budgeting computerized process at its spring meeting, 2007. The Board had a concern regarding how State System universities would manage through the predicted downturn in the number of high school graduates over the next eight to ten years. Board members witnessed how the University was maximizing its fiscal resources through micro-targeted recruitment

Women's Field Hockey and Lacrosse Locker Room, 2007

and retention programs and how carefully the University managed its marketing and recruitment plan. After the presentation, President Smith explained to the campus community, "This allowed us to showcase our utilization of financial reserves to enhance the living/learning environment and our development of alternative funding sources such as the Regional Learning Alliance and our SRU Foundation housing project to buffer unpredictable changes in our base budget."[1584]

The presentation to the Board led to an invitation to a national forum for budgeting and planning processes. In May, President Smith was invited to present the University's methodology through a national web cast. The program featured George Mason University and Slippery Rock University with more than 400 colleges and universities tuning in to see and hear how the University was strategically driving its vision.[1585]

A huge feather was placed in Slippery Rock's cap in June 2007, when the *Consumer's Digest* ranked the University as one of the "Top 5 Best Values among Public Colleges and Universities." The magazine analyzed approximately 3,800 institutions of higher education and ranked the very best.[1586]

That summer, the art department earned associate status in the National Association of Schools of Art and Design. This was the first step toward full accreditation for the department. Once completed, all performing art programs at Slippery Rock University will have earned accreditation.[1587]

Considerable attention was paid the University's facilities over the summer 2007. A $1.4 million upgrade to the chemistry labs in the new Advanced Technology

and Science Hall, a complete renovation of the McKay auditorium, a new women's athletics locker room at the stadium, an expansion of the alumni center and the demolition and rehabilitation of the abandoned residence halls took place over the summer 2007. An additional paving project was completed just to assist traffic around the large amount of campus construction.[1588]

Also that summer, the New Castle Thunder of the North American Football League, a minor league football organization, signed an agreement with Mr. Paul Lueken, Director of Athletics, to use Bob DiSpirito Field at the N. Kerr Thompson Stadium as its home.[1589] The Thunder joined the Slippery Rock Sliders baseball team as the second professional sports franchise to use Slippery Rock University facilities as their home.

Nineteen new tenure track faculty members were hired in preparation for the fall semester, 2007. Eleven were women, five minorities and sixteen hold terminal degrees in their fields.[1590]

Fall semester 2007, was an affirmation that Slippery Rock University was continuing to attract more and better prepared students to its campus. A total of 8,325 students, an increase of nearly 100, enrolled at the Rock. The profile of these students showed better preparation as measured by standardized test scores, high school grades and class rank.[1591] Black student enrollment was up 5.6 percent compared to a year ago while Hispanic enrollment was up 16.7 percent.[1592]

The University reported the registration of 2,767 resident students during the Week of Welcome, a 100% occupancy of their facilities. It marked the first full use of the 2,190 beds in the four new buildings of phase

I construction. Phase II construction, including two buildings and 746 beds would begin in April 2008.[1593]

In addition to the Consumer's Report accolade received in June, the Princeton Review again cited Slippery Rock University as one of the top 225 public and private universities in the Northeast United States. The student evaluations conducted by the Princeton Review placed the University among the elite in the Northeast.[1594]

The University's two strategic planning initiatives continued to be top priorities during the fall – The Foundation of Excellence project and the University Strategic Planning Committee. The Foundation of Excellence project involving 104 faculty, staff and administrators compiled a set of 101 recommendations for action. A council was appointed to review and give priority to the listing during the fall. The University Strategic Planning Committee spent the previous year compiling all planning activities throughout the University into a single document. Now, the task at hand required the group to set priorities and strategies for sustaining the University' drive of excellence.[1595]

President Smith defined the work of the University, fall 2007, within three broad categories. The first were the efforts to increase the value of the Slippery Rock University degree. The second was to celebrate the careers of the distinguished faculty who retired. The third was to begin developing viable commercial projects in anticipation of the opening of the business incubator facility on the former Vincent property owned by the Slippery Rock University Foundation.[1596]

President Smith, 2007

It was clear to the University community that the strategic direction established a few years earlier by President Smith was still very much his dream; the building of a premier residential public university. An integral part of that community was a new student union for the University. The council of Trustees had approved the plan to build the new union and the process was now at the level of the Board of Governors of the State System. The president believed, "The union brings people together. It broadens the academic experience by offering a diversity of programs and activities that enrich the quality of campus life".[1597]

Dr. Connie Foley, vice president of the Division of Student Life, put in place the fall 2007, an innovative program to engage students in leadership development. Under the theme of "learning reconsidered" student life

SGA Gazebo, ATS in background

338

was integrating with academic life to form a seamless relationship. The new "Compass" program, led by Mr. Brad Kovaleski, Director of the Center for Student Involvement and Leadership, was a integral part of the new initiative. A series of cascading certification challenges for students to demonstrate their leadership competencies comprised the exciting "Compass" program.[1598]

The new Rock ID card and a separate contact less token designed to be used with the student's mobile phone created an international technological attraction at Slippery Rock University. The system was made possible by the partnership with Heartland Payment Systems. The chip in the student's mobile phone was read by scanners in dining halls, for residence hall admittance, laundry services, vending machines, copying machines and library services. Over fifty national and international articles were written about the innovative technology on the Slippery Rock University campus.[1599]

The Student Government Association began construction fall 2007, of a large pavilion in the middle of the quad as a gift to the University. It was intended to create another outdoor meeting place for students between classes.[1600]

On October 12, 2007, the Advancement Division hosted a very successful fundraiser, the Storm Harbor Equestrian Center's Sunset Serenade. More than $40,000 was raised for the Equestrian Center helping children with disabilities.[1601]

In November, the Office of Intercultural Programs, in conjunction with the Western Pennsylvania Diversity Consortium, hosted the fourth annual Harambee Summit Diversity Conference. The Slippery Rock based summit had grown to more than 130 in attendance.[1602]

The University launched an accountability website during the fall 2007, in response to the U. S. Department of Education Secretary, Margaret Spelling's challenge to colleges and universities to provide potential student students, parents, general public and policy makers with accessible, transparent information about the University. Considerable information was place on the website, "SRU Institutional Profile: Accountability 2008."[1603]

In keeping with the desire to celebrate each faculty retiree, a seminar concept in honor of the retiree was developed. The seminar, featuring a presentation by the retiree was sponsored by the president's office as a fitting remembrance of the individual's service to the University. Dr. Francene Haymond, a 33-year employee,

Harambee Summit, 2007

Professor Ramona Nelson with President Smith, 2007

339

*Maureen McGovern (right) with President
and Mrs. Smith, 2007*

was the inaugural speaker for the President's Capstone Lecture Series.[1604]

Several Slippery Rock University faculty and administrators were recognized by professional organizations for contributions to their respective fields. Some were: Ramona Nelson was named a fellow in the Academy of Nursing Education by the National League for Nursing; Randy Nichols was named Physical Education Teacher of the Year by the Pennsylvania State Association of Health, Physical Education, Recreation and Dance; and dean Jay Hertzog was named Pennsylvania Teacher Educator for 2007 by the Pennsylvania Association of Colleges and Teacher Educators.[1605]

Student accolades were given to Christie D. Willison, a secondary education and English major, who won the "Meritorious Student Paper Award" at the 2007 Information Systems Education Conference for her paper "Teaching Students How to Evaluate Sources in Online Research" and freshman Justin Brown who received several awards for "The Real Enslavement," a web site he co-created that examines the legacy and enduring problem of human slavery.[1606]

Understanding the significant expenses required in emergency response situations, the University increased its donation December 2007, to the Slippery Rock Volunteer Fire Department to $20,000. In addition, a $2,000 donation was made to be split between the Sandy Lake and the Stoneboro Volunteer Fire Departments.[1607]

Begun in 2001, the Student Leadership International Program taken annually during spring break had

developed into a competitive opportunity for students. During the spring 2008, vice president Foley led the group of sixteen student leaders to Italy where they met with student leaders from Italian universities.[1608]

Recognized nationally for his work in adapted physical education, Dr. Robert Arnhold was the creator of the adaptive physical education program at Slippery Rock University. On April 10, 2008, the program was recognized as the Adapted Physical Education Program of the year at the national convention of the American Alliance for Health, Physical Education, Recreation and Dance.[1609]

Throughout 2007-2008, President Smith met with twenty-seven academic departments as well as faculty and student leadership groups to discuss Slippery Rock University's strategic plan. In addition, the President's Cabinet met for a two day retreat to discuss the important topic. As a result, the plan was updated and placed on the University's web site with hyperlinks to subordinate plans and assessment results of various divisions and offices. "The Strategic Plan sets sights on the long-term and presents a continuing exciting future for our students, faculty, staff, alums, and constituents. Among the key elements is continuing measured growth in enrollment, including students of increasingly higher quality despite a forecasted drop in the state's number of high school graduates, most especially in the western region."[1610]

Even though the western region of the state was projecting a decline in the number of high school graduates, more students wanted to attend Slippery Rock

*Professors Arnhold and Leeds presented
25 year medallions by President Smith*

University. In February, the University closed freshmen admissions for the 2008 fall semester, the earliest in recent decades.[1611]

The University's marketing efforts played a major role in building the image of the University and its enrollment success. Competing against more than 1,000 colleges and universities from all fifty states, the Office of University Public Relations won five national awards in the 23rd Annual Admissions Advertising Awards competition during the spring 2008.[1612]

In concert with the University' Strategic Plan, President Smith saw the need to development a very sophisticated, comprehensive, university-wide assessment program, one that would incorporate and coordinate all aspects of assessment occurring at the University. "A yearly cycle of assessment activities has been established that includes interactions among faculty members, department chairpersons, and deans, curricular changes resulting from assessment, and a yearly report of assessment progress submitted by each department to their dean. A Degree Coherence Matrix has been developed that links university-wide learning outcomes with degree program and liberal studies (the University's general education program) goals, program curriculum, "out of class" experiences, and assessment data sources and results. The DCM now serves as each department's annual report of assessment progress, and the college deans use these reports, along with specific

budgetary requests related to strategic planning goals, when drawing up their annual budgets."[1613] The president went on to explain to the Council of Trustees, "As of February 2008, 36 of the 42 academic departments and student life offices have developed and implemented comprehensive plans for assessing student learning. Each of these plans articulates expectations for student learning at various levels, the methods used to assess whether the expectations are being met, and descriptions of how the assessment results are influencing teaching approaches and curricula. The remaining six academic departments have developed student learning goals and instruments for assessing the learning that is taking place, and are expected to demonstrate how the assessments are applied to curriculum, student activities, or teaching by June 2008."[1614]

Two administrators earned awards during the spring 2008, Mr. Gordon Ovenshine, senior writer in University Public Relations, was awarded a Gold Cuppie award from The College and University Public Relations Association of Pennsylvania and Dr, Connie Foley, vice president for student life, was named an American College Personnel Association Diamond Honoree Award recipient and.[1615]

The previous year in athletics was significant for Slippery Rock University. The women's and men's track teams both won Pennsylvania State Athletic Conference team championships. For the women, it was their second championship in as many years. Coach John Papa, a Slippery Rock University alumnus and standout track athlete under coach Bill Lennox was coaching both teams. Danielle Cooper, a forward on the women's soccer team, was the only PSAC soccer athlete to be named to the National Soccer Coaches Association of America/Adidas Scholar All-America third-team College Division. In addition, Jen Blasko and Mike Butterworth were named as recipients of the PSAC "Fall Top Ten Award" for their distinction in the classroom and in athletics.[1616]

Slippery Rock University was very proud of its Army ROTC program. Cadet Zachary Foster earned the Air Assault Badge from the U.S. Army's Sabalauski Air Assault School at Fort Campbell, KY. At the fifteen day training program, cadet Foster placed first, earning him the distinction "Honor Graduate", among the nearly 200 soldiers and cadets who began the training.[1617]

On April 4, 2008, the University enjoyed something very few colleges and universities have the opportunity to enjoy. Slippery Rock University recognized one of its faculty members, Ms. Wilma J. Cavill, an alumna of the

Grand Marshall Wilma Cavill

Wilma Cavill, fifty years of service

University, for fifty years of service. The Wilma J. Cavill award for service was created to honor and recognize her for her outstanding contributions to her alma mater. In addition, one of the many honors and gifts bestowed to professor Cavill was a highly coveted, assigned parking space.[1618]

President Smith and his wife, Ramona, in addition to hosting many events in their home, also hosted numerous events on and off campus. Often, the events benefited and recognized students. On April 5, 2008, they hosted their annual Celebration of Scholarship luncheon in the University Club, with more than 100 scholarship donors and student recipients in attendance. The next month, in Cranberry Township, they hosted the President's Scholarship Gala, "Swing Time at the Rock", and a major fundraiser for student scholarships. More than 225 guests attended the formal event which raised more than $105,000 for scholarships.[1619]

Also during the spring 2008, the Division of student life in partnership with AVI Food Services, held the annual Rising Star Awards Program, honoring outstanding students. The awards program was initiated by AVI when it received the food services contract at the University.[1620]

In June 2008, the president reported to the Council of Trustees several actions taken by the Board of Governors at its most recent meeting in April. First, it had approved a new master's degree program for Slippery Rock University in Adapted Physical Activity. Second, the Board approved a Guaranteed Energy Savings Agreement project to begin immediately, estimated at $4.6 million with a

simple payback of fifteen years. Third was the approval to construct a 4,500 square-foot art studio. Although all actions were important, the University had been waiting for more than eight years for the last one, approval to build a new student union. The Board permitted the construction of a new 76,500 net-square-foot building using State System bond funds of approximately $37 million. Construction would begin as soon as possible.[1621]

At the same meeting, a number of student accolades were reported but one was especially well received. Mr. Paul Lueken, athletic director, introduced to the Council of Trustees, the Dixon Cup, awarded to the university within the Pennsylvania State Athletic Conference with the top athletic program. This was Slippery Rock University's first award of the Cup. Each individual team has the ability to earn points based upon their overall standing in the PSAC. The university with the most points at the end of the year, wins the coveted Cup. Universities vying for the Cup must be competitive in just about all its athletic teams.

Some of the athletic honors earned by Slippery Rock University during the 2007-2008 year were as follows:

- Women's softball team earned a first-ever berth to the NCAA regional tournament,
- Women's tennis team earned PSAC runner-up and a berth in the NCAA round of sixteen for the second time in university history,
- Women's tennis team coach Matt Meredith was selected Intercollegiate Tennis Association's East Regional "Coach of the Year",
- Women's track and field team won its third consecutive PSAC championship,

Women's Tennis team with Coach Meredith, 2008

342

- Men's track and field team won its first PSAC championship since 2000,
- Women's and men's track and field coach, John Papa, was selected as the winner of both the U.S. Track and Field and Cross Country Coaches Association men's and women's track and field "Coach of the Year" awards as well as the PSAC Outstanding Coach award,
- Women's track and field assistant coach, Dave Labor, was selected the U.S. Track and Field and Cross Country Coaches Association's East Regional women's track and field "Assistant Coach of the Year",
- Nicole Blaesser, Jennifer Hansen, Jen Harpp, Whitney Hendershot, Allison Smith, Nate Hardic, Brad Mueller, Pat Reagan and Jeff Weiss each earned individual berths to the NCAA Division II outdoor track and field national championships,
- Seventeen spring sport student-athletes earned all-Pennsylvania State Athletic Conference-Western Division status, and
- 181 Slippery Rock University student-athletes earned PSAC Scholar-Athlete status, a university record and conference best total. This represented 45% of the University's total student-athletes.[1622]

The NCAA recognized Slippery Rock University with two Diversity in Athletics Awards, "Overall Excellence in Diversity" and "African American Graduation: Male Student-Athletes and Gender Diversity." In addition, the University was awarded the Division II Community Engagement Award of Excellence for creativity in advancing relationships within the community.[1623]

Head Coach, Track and Field, and Cross Country, John Papa

2008 Women's and Men's Indoor and Outdoor Track and Field PSAC Champions

Upon receipt of the Dixon Trophy at the PSAC luncheon in Harrisburg, President Smith said, "Two and one-half years ago we set out to do the right thing for our women athletes and to be in compliance with the law. Receiving this trophy means to our campus that you can do the right thing and remain competitive."[1624]

The University was recognized by professional organizations as well that spring. First, for its "Promising Practices in Student Affairs and Academic Affairs Collaboration" by the National Association for Student Affairs in Higher Education during the spring 2008. Its Student Government Association Preschool was asked by the Pennsylvania Department of Education to allow publication of its Preschool Curriculum and Daily Schedule as a model for others. And, the Bartramian Audubon Society honored the University with four awards for establishing Audubon wildlife sanctuaries.[1625]

Over the summer 2008, the dance program was honored as one of the top 200 programs in the country by "Creative Colleges: A Guide for Student Actors, Artists, Dancers, Musicians and Writers." In addition, a $160,000 grant from the Edith L. Trees Charitable Trust was awarded to the University's Center on Disability and Health to fund student-faculty research on a program for youth and adults with intellectual disabilities.[1626]

One of the University's alumni, Ms. C. Vivian Stringer, was the third woman, the second coach, and the first African American woman to have a building named after her on the Nike World headquarters campus. The 35,000-square-foot Child Development Center houses twenty-six classrooms serving approximately 300 children. One of the four wings of the building, all named for universities which have touched the 800-win coach is The Rock.[1627]

Slippery Rock University had entered a stage in its life when more students were being denied admission than were being offered admission. For the fall 2008, the 1,552 new freshmen were selected from a total of 5,792 applications for admission. The total enrollment for the University had topped 8,500 students.[1628]

The construction of student residence buildings, E and F was completed in August 2008, just in time for the beginning of the fall semester. Both new and returning students flocked to the new suite style facilities with private or semi-private bedrooms and bathrooms, a common living area and a mini-kitchen. The upgrade from the old dormitories with gang showers was well received and subsequently, all six new suite style buildings were fully occupied. In order to completely modernize the two remaining dormitory buildings, North Hall and Rhoads Hall were renovated. Patterson Hall was converted from a traditional dormitory to an exciting academic building permanently housing the Department of Exercise and Rehabilitative Sciences and several administrative offices, and temporary housing for departments during the renovation of Vincent Science Hall.[1629]

While dormitory renovations were occurring, the University also renovated Boozel Dining Hall. Located on the lower campus, Boozel provided students with another option to dining, in addition to Weisenfluh Dining Hall on the upper part of campus and Rocky's in the university union. Boozel renovations began May 2008, and would re-open for students, faculty and staff in 2009.[1630]

For many reasons, Slippery Rock University continued to capture national light in higher education. Nearly all of its academic programs were professionally accredited, approximately ninety percent of its faculty with earned terminal degrees in their fields, its first rate facilities and its unparalleled name. It was no surprise when the Princeton Review again, found them one of the best public and private colleges and universities in the eleven states of the Northeast U.S.. Sometimes quality is not easily recognized closer to home but that was not the case when the *Pittsburgh Magazine* featured Slippery Rock University in their August 2008, edition as one of only ten institutions in a three state area and the only State System university.[1631]

Early in the fall 2008, the Student Government Association, courtesy of a Pittsburgh 250 Green and Growing grant, purchased benches, picnic tables, and a message board for the SGA Pavilion in the center of the campus quad. Later, the SGA held a Green and Growing grant ceremony inviting special guests as well as faculty, staff and students. A dedication concluded

Vivian Stringer, alumna

Five Guys Named Moe plus one president, 2008

Rock University. Senior Jaime Wright placed 20th in the individual competition leading the team to an 11th place finish. The men's cross country team also sent two runners to the national championship. Senior Jeff Weiss and junior Pat Reagan both earned U.S. Track and Field and Cross Country Coaches Association All-America honors. The women's and men's soccer teams, as a result of their play in the PSAC championships both earned the right to go on to compete in the NCAA soccer championships. For the women it was their third straight trip and fifth trip since 2001. The women's volleyball team also competed well in the PSAC championships and went on to the NCAA volleyball championships. Senior Jen Blasko received ESPN The Magazine Academic All-America first-team honors. As expected, several other student-athletes from the fall sports also received post-season honors.[1633]

the ceremony with the planting of two memorial trees for faculty members who had passed away the previous year, Dr. Claudia Balach and Dr. David Dixon. Pittsburgh 250 officials were so impressed with the way in which students utilized the grant that they decided to showcase Slippery Rock University in a future publication.[1632]

Rock athletics earned post season opportunities as a result of outstanding regular season performances. The women's cross country team finished second in the NCAA Atlantic Regional competition and was awarded a berth to the national championships, hosted by Slippery

Dr. Stephen Barr, assistant professor of music, was chosen by the American Society of Composers, Authors and Publishers to receive its 2008-09 ASCAPLUS Award in the concert music division. Vice president for finance and administration, Dr. Charles Curry, was recognized by Minority Opinion Magazine with a Minority Achievement Award.[1634]

The Center for Student Involvement and Leadership reported over 700 students actively involved in the Compass Leadership Program. In addition to this exciting

2008 Cross Country Nationals, hosted by Slippery Rock University

345

Members of the Cross Country Team not competing at Nationals, supporting the Rock

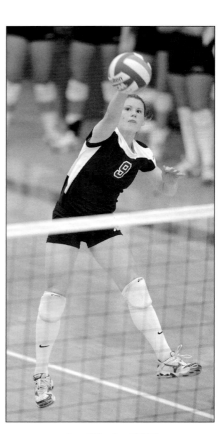

Pat Reagan, 2008

Jeff Weiss, 2008

Jen Blasko, 2008

program, the Center officially launched an online co-curricular transcript program for students to document their experiences while enjoying their years at the Rock.[1635]

Student Life staff members invested a great deal of time developing a showcase event that would incorporate the learning outcomes of global citizenship, personal development and lifelong learning. The result was "Up till 2am", a major fundraising event benefiting St. Jude Children's Research Hospital. More than 300 students participated in 2007, the first year of the event, raising more than $21,000. During the fall 2008, the number of students participating increased and so did the event's financial outcome.[1636]

Up Till 2am organizers

To begin the Council of Trustees meeting in December 2008, President Smith referred to the economical problems of the nation and the commonwealth. "The governor had asked all state-owned universities to return 4.25% of the state's appropriation as a result of the shortfall in tax collections. For Slippery Rock University, it meant a total $1,700,879. In addition, the governor had asked the University to identify another three percent, or $1,200,621 in the event that the situation should worsen. A total give back could mean $2,901,500. The President stated, "I want to assure you that Slippery Rock University has well-prepared itself to weather these times and to remain this region's premier residential public university."[1637]

"We are looking ahead to 2009-2010 budget planning. No prognosticator suggests that all will be well on July 1, 2009. Therefore, we are taking steps to examine our state appropriation funds and prepare early decisions on how we would respond to a request this spring to make further cuts. It is in times like these that I am particularly happy with the budgeting methods we use at Slippery Rock University. We fund on performance and project initiatives. Consequently, we build in flexibility. We also have generated one of the nation's best enrollment management systems. Consequently, our applications are up and our commitments from admitted student's are up. We are in full control of our enrollment for 2009, and can manage that as a resource for contending with budget needs."[1638]

Dr. Amanda Yale, associate provost for enrollment services, reported to the University community regarding the results of the National Survey of Student Engagement. "With first-year students, our students scored significantly higher that our Carnegie Classification peers, our state system peers and all institutions in NSSE on three of those benchmarks: academic learning, student-faculty interaction and enriching educational experience. This shows that students, overall, are engaged with the campus and are involved with activities in and out of the classroom.

Seniors gave SRU higher ratings than their peers did at other Pennsylvania State System of Higher Education schools, Carnegie peers, and all NSSE institutions in the categories of collaborative learning, student-faculty interaction, enriching educational experiences and supporting campus experiences."[1639]

In another survey, Slippery Rock University students responded regarding some of their daily habits. Ninety percent of them brought computers, mostly laptops, to campus; fifty percent of them spend at least one hour per day on social networks and sixty-eight percent of them spend up to an hour per day texting and instant messaging.[1640]

Slippery Rock University received additional national recognition when the National Council for Accreditation of Teacher Education re-accredited its teacher education programs in late 2008. This marked the fifty-third consecutive year of the programs' accreditation. One of the very first programs in the nation to receive NCATE accreditation in 1955, the University was now one of only 20 of the 95 teacher preparation institutions in the state to bear the NCATE symbol of approval.[1641]

The University earned another accreditation distinction when its Storm Harbor Equestrian Center became the

President Smith and Dr. Carolyn Rizza, Sunset Serenade

only university-based equestrian center in Pennsylvania to receive a premier center accreditation from the North American Riding for the Handicapped Association. The Center made possible by the benevolence of Drs. Carolyn and Paul Rizza had advanced quickly in its first few years of operation. During the fall 2008 the Center raised over $50,000 through its Sunset Serenade Celebration fundraiser to expand its successful services.[1642]

In a related area, Slippery Rock University's "I Can Do It, You Can Do It" mentoring program was selected to be the national role model for launching nine new I Can Do It programs across the country. In addition, the University received a three-year, $850,000 contract from the U.S. Department of Health and Human Services Office on Disability to become the charter institution for a national expansion of the program.[1643]

In October 2008, the University broke ground on a $1.3 million development of 12 acres on the north side of campus for an intramural sports complex. The project, funded by campus recreation, included four multi-purpose recreation sports fields and two softball fields. A walk/jog path along the east side of the fields was paid for by a state grant.[1644] A significant contribution to the University's athletic and recreation facilities, the project was concluded in December 2008, and later named "The Mac" in honor and memory of Dr. James P. McFarland, a beloved faculty member and coach.[1645]

Early in 2009, The Slippery Rock University Foundation Board of Directors announced a ground lease with Butler Health Systems for the construction of

a medical services facility on the Foundation's property just off route 108 at the eastern edge of the village. The former Vincent Farm, now being developed by the Foundation as the Slippery Rock Technology Park also included the location of the new entrance to the University's campus.[1646]

The Council of Accreditation of Counseling and Related Programs re-accredited the University's Community Counseling Program and School Counseling Program at the beginning of 2009. The Council also accredited for the first time the Student Affairs in Higher Education program.[1647]

Wireless internet became a reality in the Quad during the spring 2009, and students appreciated the convenience of the new service. This upgrade in service matched what had been done in most of the buildings on campus.[1648] In a related matter, through a $20,000 grant from the new campus green fund, matched by Student Government Association, a GPS tracking system was installed on both of the Happy Buses during the spring 2009. This enabled students to track the buses on their computers or smart phones and also assisted in monitoring the on-campus and off-campus routes.[1649]

The Rock 's women's track and field team continued to collect honors over the winter 2009, as the women's indoor team won the PSAC championship. Whitney Hendershot was named the Outstanding Field Athlete of the championship, while Jenn Harpp and Whitney earned All-America Honors. Coach John Papa was named Atlantic Region Indoor Women's Coach of the Year. In men's basketball, Denell Stephens was named PSAC Player of the Year and the relatively new coach Kevin Reynolds was named PSAC West Men's Basketball Coach of the Year.[1650]

A new program leading to a Master of Arts degree in Criminal Justice was approved by the Board of Governors at their spring meeting 2009. The innovative program was designed to be offered on-line.[1651]

The University was awarded two new accolades during the spring 2009. First, the Institute of International Education named Slippery Rock University as one of the top 40 Universities in the nation for travel abroad opportunities. Next, the University was featured as one of only four nationally outstanding programs in *Beyond the Books, A Guide to Service Learning Colleges and Universities*.[1652]

At the April 17, 2009, Council of Trustees meeting considerable time was spent on the state of western Pennsylvania, the Commonwealth and the nation. The

Students abroad with Professor Bruce Orvis

All-America 4x4 team, Tedesco (left), Seigworth, Smith, Cochran, 2009

economic problems had worsened over the year, creating other issues with which the University had to contend. Nation-wide, giving to higher education had flattened or declined. Costs to attend a college or university were escalating. States across the nation were cutting dramatically their support of higher education. Students were concerned that they would be admitted but may not be able to afford college. The number of high school graduates in Pennsylvania was declining. To relieve college costs to students and their families, the University initiated the Slippery Rock University Tuition Assistance Program.[1653]

The State System and subsequently all of its fourteen universities were also facing major financial issues. A $56.8 million unfunded gap existed for 2009-10. For Slippery Rock University it meant more than a $6.2 million deficit.[1654] Over the next several months, the Commonwealth's budget process would decide the issue.

The outdoor women's track and field team continued its domination in the PSAC by winning the championship again, in 2009. Eight student-athletes from the team went on to compete at the NCAA National Championships. The women's tennis team went on to compete at the NCAA East Regional and the women's softball team qualified for the first time for the PSAC playoffs.[1655]

2009 Women's Outdoor Track and Field PSAC Champions

Allison Smith (left) and Amanda Seigworth, 2009

The University decided that the traditional May commencement held outdoors would be split into two ceremonies, both to be held indoors. However, in May 2009, just prior to conducting the two ceremonies for the first time, twenty-two students returned from their student teaching experience in Mexico City, ready to participate in their commencement. Concurrently, Mexico had been deemed to be the epicenter of an H1N1 flu outbreak. The media became involved and within hours, the University had received hundreds of phone calls from students and family members fearful of being exposed at the commencement ceremonies. However, the students returning from Mexico felt they were safe and did not want to be denied their ceremony. The controversy was fed by considerable media attention. A separate and special graduation ceremony was held for the returning students and their families between the two regularly scheduled ceremonies. A great number of staff spent inordinate hours to create a positive situation for all involved. The event generated a great deal of positive attention for the University, thanks to all the good work of the University Office of Public Relations.[1656]

The spring semester ended and the summer began without a budget for the Commonwealth. The University developed a series of estimates in order to prepare for the fall semester, focusing on a $4 million shortfall.[1657]

The implementation of a new Student Information System Project demanded considerable staff time over the summer 2009. In addition, a complete transformation of the University's web presence was taking place, expected to be in place by November.[1658]

Boozel Dining Hall was being well received by the students and also honored by the *American School and University Magazine's Educational Interiors Showcase.* The magazine awarded the University with an Outstanding Design Award in the Cafeteria/ Food Service Areas category during the summer 2009.[1659]

New faculty hires over the summer were fewer than desired given the unresolved budget issue. Nevertheless, twenty-six outstanding tenure-track teachers were hired, seventeen women and five minorities. Twenty-two faculty had already earned their terminal degrees with the additional four defending their dissertations during the fall.[1660]

A record 8,648 students enrolled for classes at Slippery Rock University fall 2009. The new students were treated to the Week of Welcome traditional activities, including the President's lecture on the summer reading book, The Ultimate Gift.[1661]

The October Council of Trustees meeting opened with a presentation to Dr. Robert Arnhold, honoring the

May Commencement

Old Boozel Cafeteria

New Boozel Dining Hall, 2009

Boozel Lobby

Boozel Inside

exceptional achievements of the University's Adapted Physical Activity program. A resolution was awarded designating November 11, 2009 as Adapted Physical Education Day at Slippery Rock University.[1662]

President Smith began his report to the Council in October 2009, "For more than a decade we have embraced one compelling vision that Slippery Rock University will excel as a caring community of lifelong learners connecting to the world. We believe fulfillment of this single vision is to be the premier residential public university for this region. Seven years ago, we acknowledged what we do best is serve students who are part of a residential experience within the intellectual community made possible by capable, committed faculty and staff members."[1663]

He proceeded to add to the list of awards the University had received, supporting the premier status of Slippery Rock University:

- Eight consecutive years of being listed in The Princeton Review as one of the Best Northeastern Colleges and Universities.
- One of only 150 colleges selected as s "Great College to Work For".
- One of the select "military friendly" universities. Only 15 % of the colleges and universities in the U.S. are on the list.

Presidential foursome at the Women's Golf Outing, 2009

- Ranked as the 14th safest college and university in the nation by current issues Web site, *The Daily Beast*.
- Included as one of the nation's top service learning colleges and universities in the 2009, edition of *Beyond the Books, Guide to Service Learning at Colleges and Universities*.[1664]

However after identifying all the premier characteristics of the University, President Smith reported: "As of this meeting, Pennsylvania remains the only state without a budget and no clear prospect for resolving the political squabbling necessary to pass a budget. Each month that passes, cost the University $3.2 million in the state revenues used to pay our obligations.

As of this meeting, we are one quarter of the way through the fiscal year and just short of $100 million due from the state. We are meeting our obligation to our employees, students, and vendors by using cash for tuition and fees paid by our students. To say the least, this is an untenable situation for much longer.

In addition, The SRU Foundation has suffered a significant loss in their assets and a sharp falloff in contributions such that the Finance Committee has recommended a reduction in their scholarship allocation for 2010-11, in the amount of $335,000. If this decision prevails, it will devastate our work to attract the highly qualified and most competitive students to next year's freshman class.

We have begun a review of our budget at all levels with the expectation that we will need to reduce a gap of $8.9 million either through enhanced revenue or reduction of expenses."[1665]

The President went on to affirm the guiding principles of the University embedded in the Strategic Plan:
- "Students come first. Educating students is always the highest priority.
- Consultation with faculty, students and administration on matters of the strategic plan and budget decisions are an inherent integral part of the shared governance of the University.
- Cuts and/or increases are not made "across-the-board". Doing so violate the purpose of the strategic plan and is a formula for mediocrity.
- The University cannot be all things to all people. The budget reinforces the strategic priorities of the University to preserve the overall quality of the institution.
- Specifically, we have added that we will:
- Invest in quality,
- Commit to a faculty that is full-time and professionally credentialed,
- Commit to enhancing academic programs to assure accreditation and national recognitions,
- Commit to upgrading our teaching/learning environment, campus safety and security, and
- Commit to recruiting, educating and graduating high quality engaged students."[1666]

Less than one month later, the state passed a budget. The reduction to the State System's base budget was nearly $33 million. The result for Slippery Rock University was a reduction of nearly $3.56 million or approximately 9.8% Federal stimulus monies were used to offset the decrease but it was cautioned that this money would be "one-time" money. Fortunately, the University again, faired well in the performance funding allocation so that the final result was not as devastating.[1667]

The Honor's Program had enrolled nearly three hundred students by the fall 2009. Housed in Watson Hall, the program was providing qualified students with experiences to learn and grow through honor classes, student-faculty research and conference participation.[1668]

On November 12, 2009, President Smith signed the American College and University Presidents Climate

2009 men's soccer PSAC Champions

Commitment stating that Slippery Rock University would help lead the region in reducing global emissions of greenhouse gases, starting with our own campus. Begun in 2007, more than 660 institutions had signed the Commitment representing all 50 states and the District of Columbia.[1669]

Fall 2009, marked the fifth anniversary of the Regional Learning Alliance which had been created to help provide Pennsylvania businesses with workforce training facilities. It had grown to the largest such cooperative program in the nation with more than 500 different companies including the primary facility for Westinghouse Electric Corp., H.J. Heinz Co., MSA, McKesson Automation Corp., Verizon Wireless, PPG Industries, MEDRAD Inc. and Siemens Water Technologies. In addition, twelve partnering colleges and universities were using the facility to teach their courses. Since its opening, more than 150,000 students had used the campus and more than one million people hours of workforce training had been completed.[1670]

Complementing the tradition of excellence within the faculty, Mrs. Pam Arnhold, of exercise and rehabilitative sciences, was named the Adapted Physical Activity Professional of the year fall 2009. In addition, Dr. Joanne Leight, of physical education, was been named "Teacher of the Year" for the college/university division of the Pennsylvania State Association of Health, Physical Education, Recreation and Dance. Ms. Jessamine Jovelina Mozo Montera, special assistant to the president and senior officer for diversity and inclusion, was recognized with a Minority Achievement Award by *Talk/Minority Opinion Magazine*.[1671]

In terms of construction on campus, the ESCO project was on schedule, the new sculpture studio was completed, the Vincent Science project was underway and ahead of schedule, the Harmony Homestead (Macoskey Center) was completed, and the McFarland Recreation Complex was nearing completion.[1672]

During the fall 2009 the Women's Center was awarded more than a quarter of a million dollars in federal grant money to address violence against women on campus. The grant also included a scholarship to a two-year course for advocacy programs funded by the Office of Violence Against Women.[1673]

For many years, the Rocket, the student newspaper received awards for outstanding journalism. In March 2010, its editor-in-chief, Mr. Josh Rizzo, was named the Arthur Barlow National Student Journalist of the Year by the Society of Collegiate Journalists, the National

Care Break, 2010

Stately Grace and Beauty, 2010

New SGA Executive Committee

SGA Executive Committee, with President Smith and Vice President Foley, 2010

Honorary Journalism Society at their national convention in New York City.[1674]

Over spring break 2010, more than three hundred Slippery Rock University students traveled to eleven countries as part of organized programs. Eighteen students and four staff traveled to a St. Lucia Ministry to deliver 3,000 pairs of shoes that were collected by Bishop Canevin High School and packaged by SRU students.[1675]

After several years of providing outstanding dining services to students, faculty, staff, alumni and guests, AVI Food Systems was awarded a second contract. In the review process, AVI stood out with an exceptionally creative and highly personal proposal. [1676]

Co-chaired by Ms. Cindi Dillon and Dr. Neil Cosgrove, the Middle States Accreditation Self Study Committee was busy at work for two years preparing for the review committee to visit campus March 2011. More than 100 participants actively engaged in the extremely

President and Mrs. Smith donate campus clock, April 2010

detailed preparation process. Middle States Accreditation was without question becoming increasingly more difficult to earn.[1677]

Through the University's strategic plan process, a new plan had evolved including five transformational themes. The themes were the centerpiece for how the University would educate its students and how those students would become global leaders over the next twenty-five years.[1678]

Presidential Commissions were reinvigorated in 2010, by Dr. Jessamine Monterro, Senior Officer for Diversity and Inclusion. A campus-wide climate study would be conducted in the fall 2010. To enhance the work, two new presidential Commissions were named in the areas of Disability and Sustainability.[1679]

The third annual Slippery Rock University Campus Family Campaign was successfully conducted in 2010, and was the most successful to date. More than five hundred of the University's employees combined to donate $142,375.[1680]

In April 2010, President Smith reported to the Council of Trustees, "This has been the year of change for our technology,...this is the greatest massive technology change undertaken in any one time period in our University history."

* The Banner Student Information System is being built and installed.

* A change in learning management system from Black Board to Desire2Learn.

* The transformation of tens of thousands of web pages to create a new University web presence by August.

* Installing new equipment and upgrading fiber network to match the need to provide high speed and responsive network access.

* As part of a $100 million federal grant, to provide ultra-high speed broadband networking throughout Pennsylvania, the University was selected to become one of the major off/on ramps to the network. The Core Node Location for the new Pennsylvania Research and Education Network had been proposed to be in the Slippery Rock University Innovation Center.[1681]

In the midst of a continued budgetary crisis in Pennsylvania and the rest of the nation, the State System was expected to again reduce its operating budget. For Slippery Rock University it was a proposed reduction of nearly $9 million. In April 2010, the President was examining the proposed budget reductions of the four divisions. "Soon, we will post on the web all of the

recommended cuts by department and budget office. This is complete transparency of our process and results."[1682]

The President was reminded of the significant enrollment decline in which the University found itself in 2000 when he came to Slippery Rock. "We now have the most robust, responsive enrollment management plans

Jen Hansen, 2010

President Smith with students discussing budget presentation

2010 Women's Track and Field PSAC Champions

in the country...not just Pennsylvania. It would not have become possible without the full commitment of the entire campus. It would not have been possible without the willingness to change. Those changes resulted in avoiding layoff, introducing new programs, attracting highly qualified students to Slippery Rock University. Change was clearly for the better.

Now, in 2010, we are facing our next crisis. The absence for state financial support, and the lack of control over how our revenue sources are determined, has created an even more severe challenge than we faced before.

It is time that we look more seriously at how we can establish economic independence. I believe that we can do that by "Changing the Equation" for how we approach our work.

Here is the bottom line: The challenges we face are real. They are the creation of circumstances we can't control. However, how we choose to attack them is entirely under our control. We could choose to wallow in self-pity (and some will) or in the engage in the blaming of others for our plight (and there will be those who will). Or we can rise up and change the equation to our betterment.

I believe we have consistently proven we can do amazing things when we work together. And, I believe we have the capacity as well as destiny on our side. It is consistent with a statement I made at the beginning

Budget Forum

of the year: A crisis is a terrible thing to waste. Now is our moment."[1683]

As a result of combining cost savings and revenue enhancements, the University was able to balance the 2010-11 budget, closing an $8.9 million deficit. The President expressed his gratitude to the campus community, 300 of whom attended on of his more than 12 forums, and suggesting more than 150 ideas. Many of the ideas were implemented to meet the deficit.[1684]

Over the summer 2010 the University completed its reorganization of the service-learning program. The program was combined with the Center for Student Involvement and Leadership within the Student Life Division.[1685]

Fall 2010, enrollment set new records with 8,852 students registered for classes at Slippery Rock University. Not only did more new students enroll, but a higher percentage of those enrolled the previous year wished to continue their studies at SRU.[1686]

The University earned repeat honors in several areas in 2010, such as the Office of Public Relations received five national awards for marketing from the Higher Education Marketing Group and for the eighth year, the Princeton Review recognized Slippery Rock University as one of the Best Colleges in the Northeast United States. The University was ranked number two in the nation's top rural colleges and Universities and for the first time Slippery Rock University was selected by

President and Mrs. Smith

the U.S. News and World Report as one of the top 100 universities in the north.[1687]

Two individual academic programs also earned accolades. The therapeutic recreation program was named one of the top twelve programs in the nation and sport management was one of the first two programs in the nation to receive accreditation from their national accrediting agency.[1688]

In July 2010, construction was begun on the new 104,000 square foot student union. A ground breaking ceremony was held for this long-awaited project on October 1, 2010. Five major construction projects were identified for the future, including the renovation of the old student union into the new student success center; the renovation of

In the Quad

West Gym; an addition to McKay Education Building; completion of Patterson Hall phase II; and renovation of the Bailey Library.[1689]

Performance funding has always been a critical part of the revenues for the University. In 2010, an announcement was made that the methodology for evaluating institutional performance would change in 2010-11. For the next five years ten new performance indicators would be pursued. The University had begun making careful strategic decisions regarding the pursuit of the indicators.[1690]

In his closing comments to the Council of Trustee in October 2010, President Smith offered these thoughts. "These questions are the challenges we should take up in

the context of our financial decision making. How we deliver our form of education defines us. When we say that our aspiration is to be the region's premier public residential university, then something very special has to happen in this network, beyond the classroom, beyond the exam, beyond the term paper.

We will be left to our own devices in this economy and in this political arena. Some would say that the path ahead is foreboding, threatening. Given our strengths in our creative faculty and our innovative administration and staff, united to one vision, I think left to our own devices is a great opportunity."[1691]

The Institute of International Education ranked Slippery Rock University 10th nationally among

Compass, 2010

Homecoming, 2010

Homecoming concert, 2010

Homecoming, 2010

masters-degree granting institutions for the number of students participating in short-term study abroad programs. More than 400 students participated in study abroad programs the previous year. Not satisfied with the status quo, the Office of International Services worked with academic departments to offer short-term programs in Italy, France, Ireland, The Bahamas, Mexico, Egypt, The Netherlands, England, China, Canada and others during spring break and summer.[1692]

On October 17-19, 2010, Dr. John Ettling, SUNY Plattsburg, chairman of the Middle States Accreditation Review Team, visited campus and met with the co-chairs of the Self Study Committee and others to prepare for the Review Team's visit in March 2012. The campus was fully engaged in this important process.[1693]

Dr. Eva Tsuquiashi-Daddesio, dean of the College of Humanities, Fine and Performing Arts, received the Minority Achievement Award sponsored by the *Minority Opinion/Talk Magazine*. This was the second time the magazine had recognized one of Slippery Rock University's administrators with the award.[1694]

Dr. Steve Hawk, music professor and Jazz Band director had long been recognized on and off campus as a highly talented jazz musician. Invited to perform with several notable professional groups, Dr. Hawk was honored among his peers with two Grammy nominations. The first for Best Jazz Instrumental Album, individual or group and the second in the Jazz Category, Best Large Jazz Ensemble.[1695]

Rock Athletics continued their winning traditions, fall 2010. The women's and men's soccer teams competed in the PSAC Championships. The women's soccer team also advanced to the second round of the NCAA Division II Women's Soccer Championships. The men's soccer team had two players, Patrick Conley and Tom Pool named to first team All-Region honors and two other players, Greg Blum and Toby Bowser named to second team honors.[1696]

The women's and men's cross country teams also competed in the PSAC Championships and in the NCAA Atlantic Regional Cross Country Championships. Ms. Jen Harpp placed third and Crystal Burnick placed eleventh in the regional championships, both earning All-Region honors and a trip to Nationals. The women's team placed third overall and barely missed a team berth to Nationals. In the men's division, Brian Ulrich and Jason Leonard placed 26th and 27th to lead the Rock to a fourth place finish at the NCAA Atlantic Regional Championships.[1697]

President Smith with AKPsi and ghost busters, fall, 2010

Jen Harpp, 2009

*Brandon Fusco, alumnus
and Minnesota Viking*

Most Division II football players end their competitive football days with their last college game. However, Brandon Fusco, offensive center for the Rock, 2007-2010, took his abilities to much higher levels, the

National Football League. After his last game for the Rock, Brandon became the first Slippery Rock University player to be invited to play in the prestigious Senior Bowl. He earned the eighth annual Gene Upshaw Division II Lineman of the Year Award. Also, Brandon, a native of Cranberry Township, Butler County, was named to the first team Football Gazette All-America team. Naturally he had earned countless team and PSAC honors as well.

Brandon became the highest drafted player in school history when he was selected 172nd overall in the fourth round by the Minnesota Vikings.[1698]

Late in 2010, newly elected Pennsylvania governor, Tom Corbett put all on notice of his intentions to slash a number of expenses in the Commonwealth. For the State System, it meant a proposed 50% cut in their state appropriations. After the proposed cut, it left the State System with $2.5 million less than the initial appropriation to the System in its initial year, 1983-84. The amount of the proposed cut equated to the entire budgets of Cheyney, Mansfield and Lock Haven Universities combined. For Slippery Rock University, it meant a cut of $24.3 million. President Smith commented, "Our strategy is a combination of advocacy for restoration of

Winter Commencement

359

the funds and planning for the reduction. With only four months to assemble a budget (and conclude negotiations on five labor contracts), we obviously have much to do before July 1, 2011."[1699]

The University developed an advocacy group, Rock Nation, expecting advocates to share with a variety of involved parties in the budget process the value of Slippery Rock University. Through the web based program, developed and managed by two students, advocates were provided timely updates on University and legislative issues, periodic calls to action, and invitations to legislative strategy briefings. Lou Bouselli designed the format for the *ROCKNation* web site and linked with FaceBook software. Nicole Vandyke managed the database for the *ROCKNation* advocates and made sure the messages got out both on the web site and the FaceBook page.[1700]

Simultaneously, the University worked to prioritize its budget reductions in a similar manner as in the recent past. The basic fundamentals that had been observed for previous budget crisis were utilized in this critical situation.[1701]

President Smith was noticeably concerned about the possible creation of a perfect institutional storm. The development of this significant budget crisis was occurring in late March 2011, just days before the on-campus review of the University by the Middle States Accreditation Review Team. However, the President commented, "Our preparation for the review has been an absolute act of pride for Slippery Rock University. The incredible team approach, the engagement of the University, the countless hours of preparation by hundreds of committed faculty, staff, and students has been nothing short of inspirational."[1702]

The Middle States Review team found just that and after their four days of intensive review, the Team found all that Slippery Rock University had hoped they would find. "Most notably, The University was reaccredited for the full ten years with no stipulations, no requirements, nor recommendations. Not only did the University receive full credit for each of the fourteen standards of excellence, but also earned nine commendations. No other PASSHE institution has received such a positive report in this current re-accreditation round. In fact, few public or private institutions in the entire Middle States region have received a clean report, let alone commendation."[1703] The report noted, "Since its last full Middle States accreditation review a decade ago, Slippery Rock University has made enormous progress toward its goal of becoming a premier residential university."[1704]

Early in 2011, Slippery Rock University and West Virginia University announced a cooperative agreement for students wishing to earn a bachelor's degree in engineering. The program allowed a SRU student majoring in Physics to transfer to WVU after three years and complete a prescribed two-year program. The result was a bachelor's degree in Physics from Slippery Rock University and an engineering degree from West Virginia University.[1705]

When the spring term 2011, opened, The Vincent Science Hall reopened following a three-year, $14 million renovation. The state of the art science facility housed the departments of biology, mathematics, nursing, physics and psychology.[1706]

Concurrently, the University Counseling Center earned accreditation by the International Association of Counseling Services for a five year period. This marked the first accreditation for the Center, which was under the direction of Dr. Carol Holland.[1707]

Dr. Michael Ignelzi, professor and graduate coordinator of counseling and development received a

Stan Savron, FSN sports broadcaster, presents President Smith with a personalized Pittsburgh Penguins jersey after an interview, 2011

Physical Activity for Wellness Spokespeople

Diamond Honoree Award from the American College Personnel Association during the spring 2011. The award, recognizing leadership and scholarship, was given to only seventeen honorees nationwide.[1708]

Akeem Satterfield of Erie, was named to the second team Football Gazette All-America team. Akeem and his teammate, Brandon Fusco were honored by this prestigious organization.[1709]

Rock athletes finished strong in the winter season. Finishing second in the PSAC Championships, the men's basketball team made its first trip to the NCAA tournament since 1991. The women's indoor track and field team finished second in the 2011 PSAC Championships. Nine women earned all-region honors from the U.S. Track and Field and Cross Country Coaches Association. The men's team placed fourth in the PSAC with six student athletes earning all-region honors. Cameron Daugherty earned All-America honors in the pole vault at the NCAA National Track and Field Championships.[1710]

The spring season student athletes performed well and the University hosted post season competition in two sports. The women's tennis team hosted the NCAA Division II Atlantic Regional Championships and finished second in the team competition. The men's baseball team qualified for and hosted the PSAC Championships. The women's lacrosse team tied the

school record for the number of wins in a season with eleven victories.[1711]

However, it was a member of the women's track and field team that left a national impact on the sport. After the team placed second in the PSAC Championships, they sent six student athletes to the national championships to compete while the men's team sent four student athletes. It was senior Whitney Hendershot who capped off her outstanding track and field career at the 2011 NCAA Division II National Championships by winning the high jump. With that win, Whitney became the fifth Slippery Rock University woman track and field student athlete to earn a national championship.[1712]

Women's Indoor Track and Field PSAC Champions

Men's basketball team, 2010-11

Amanda Seigworth,
Outstanding PSAC Track Athlete, 2011

Kevin Jewel, 2011

Lexi Arnold, 2011

Cameron Daugherty, 2011

Brady Wert, 2011

Women's 2011 Track and Field PSAC Champions

363

Whitney Hendershot, 2011

Chris Warning, 2011

Slippery Rock University was named to the 2010 President's Higher Education Community Service Honor Roll by the Corporation for National and Community Service. The Honor Roll recognizes colleges and universities that reflect the values of exemplary community service and achieve meaningful outcomes in their communities.[1713]

Construction was progressing well through the spring on the student union building and was on schedule to open in the spring 2012. The Weisenfluh Dining Hall was vacated as soon as the students left campus for the summer in order that its major renovation project could begin.[1714]

In a related topic, construction of the new Butler Health Systems facility at the Slippery Rock Technology Park had concluded during the spring 2011. A grand opening of the new health services facility occurred on

May 2, 2011.[1715] Soon thereafter, large numbers of local community members were utilizing the new facilities services instead of traveling to facilities outside of Slippery Rock.

On the eve of his forty-fourth year in education, at the spring faculty and staff assembly, President Robert Smith announced his plan to retire in January 2012. The campus was surprised with the announcement as so many felt he would stay on in the position for several years. It was a difficult time for the entire campus community. A search committee would be formed in order for the new

Weisenfluh renovation, 2011

Weisenfluh renovation, 2011

Innovation Drive, the new entrance to campus off route 108 E, 2011

Butler Health System facility in Slippery Rock Technology Park, 2011

President Smith announces his goodbye, April 2011

A standing ovation for President and Mrs. Smith

President and Mrs. Smith return from bidding goodbye

President Smith and his office staff, Tina Moser (right) and Kelli Rensel, 2011

president to be on campus by the January date. President Smith focused upon preparing the University to be an attractive place for the very best qualified candidate for the presidency and worked to that end.[1716]

Mr. Eric Holmes, member of the Council of Trustees and Slippery Rock University alumnus was selected as chair of the search committee. The Committee would follow the Board of Governor's policy identified for the recommending of a president. The first meeting was set for June 10, 2011.[1717]

Much of the president's primary focus over the spring months was to restore the governor's recommended budget cuts. As of the Council of Trustees meeting

President Smith with former SGA presidents during his presidency, September 2011

in June, the House of Representatives had passed their version of the budget that would restore $195 million of the $232.6 million cut by the governor. The percentage of the overall reduction went from 54% to 15% with this action. For Slippery Rock University it would mean finding $6.6 million in savings or cuts. To assist the University, the Trustees passed the implementation of a Student Life Enhancement Fee of $5 per credit hour for all undergraduate students enrolled.[1718]

Amidst the budgetary struggles of the spring 2011, great accomplishments were still being made by the University. Exercise Science faculty and students developed an "Exercise is Medicine" program for entry in the national competition, Exercise is Medicine Active U Challenge. The University's entry was competing with entries from the likes of the University of Michigan, Mississippi State University and others and still it was Slippery Rock University who won the competition.[1719]

Fall 2011, Slippery Rock University earned the "College of Distinction" honor. Only fourteen colleges and universities in Pennsylvania were selected and Slippery Rock was the only public institution selected.[1720] And, for the ninth consecutive year, the *Princeton Review* recognized the University as one of the "Best Colleges in the Northeast".[1721]

Selected for the first time, the University was named to The President's Higher Education Community Service Honor Role. The national registry award is designed to recognize "exemplary commitment to service and volunteering from institutions of higher education."[1722]

The Association for the Advancement for Sustainability in Higher Education designated Slippery Rock University as a STARS Bronze Institution based on the campus accomplishments in sustainability. In a related matter, the Harmony House at Slippery Rock was awarded LEED Silver Certification.[1723]

The U.S. Track and Field and Cross Country Coaches Association awarded the women's and men's teams with All-Academic Team honors after the conclusion of their outstanding 2011, outdoor season. This was the third consecutive award for the women's team which ranked eleventh nationally with a 3.21 grade point average. Ranking eighteenth in the nation, the men's team had earned a 3.12 grade point average.[1724]

The University announced fall 2011, that the Computer Science programs had earned triple accreditation. ABET accreditation utilized a very stringent program review and very few institutions were accredited in the three areas of Information Technology, Information Science and Computer Science.[1725]

The Council of Trustees honored President Robert M. Smith on September 9, 2011, with the naming of the new student building, The Robert M. Smith Student Center.[1726] This tribute was especially meaningful because it was the building that President Smith wanted for the students. It was the building in which he invested so much of his personal time and effort, from beginning to fruition. It was the building that would be the center of the life of each student, the very individual that Dr. Smith kept in the center of his life, every day as president. Students, faculty, staff, alumni, and community members joined the Trustees in recognizing President Smith's outstanding leadership and service to the University.

Fall is a wonderful time to be on a college campus and certainly Homecoming is one of those

Mihalik-Thompson stadium dedication, September 2011

Alumni Tent Homecoming, 2011

Some Golden Grads, 1961, and others at Homecoming, 2011

Golden Grad Class of 1961

Coach Mihalik congratulates his team after a big 2011 Homecoming win

Like father, like son for the Shaws, Homecoming, 2011

Men's Soccer team with old grads, after the big Homecoming game win, 2011

Director, Paul Lueken (right) and men's soccer coach, Mike Bonelli (left) with some of the Ring of Honor recipients at half-time of the Homecoming game, 2011

special activities during the fall. Slippery Rock University's Homecoming was October 15, 2011, and in spite of temperatures being low, the spirit was high. For President and Mrs. Ramona Smith, it was their last Homecoming in their leadership positions at the Rock. The festivities were grand. Nearly fifty members of the "Golden Grad" class of 1961 returned to enjoy the weekend with their former classmates and activities with President and Mrs. Smith.

Almost all of the home athletic contests ended with the Rock winning. Both, the women's and men's soccer teams won their matches. The men's coach, Mike Bonelli and Patrick O'Hare, 1965 alumnus, coordinated the first Ring of Honor ceremony, inducting nine members into the new varsity soccer honor organization on Friday evening, the night before Homecoming.

The Rock's NCAA Division II football team, with the number one ranked defensive team in the nation, proved too much for the nationally ranked California University of PA team, defeating Cal U by a score of 17-3. After the big win, Slippery Rock University's football team was ranked number 18 in the nation, Division II.

Much will be said and written about the presidency of Dr. Robert M. Smith. Descriptors like leadership, quality, advocate, growth, change, passion, student-focus, accreditation, championships, accomplishment, and other terms will be used in describing his era. As a Slippery Rock University alumnus said when Robert Smith was named president in 2004, "he was the right person at the right time."

In the closing of his quarterly report fall 2011, President Smith addressed the Council of Trustees:

"You will embrace our next leaders(s). I am confident you will provide great mentoring and wise counsel. Around these tables in Old Main or the Alumni House, your experience and enthusiasm will inspire. You will need to do more. You need to model advocacy for Slippery Rock University with your colleagues and friends within your communities and across the Commonwealth. Invite our new leader(s) to community events or the Capitol and provide introductions that begin the process of building great relationships. Be present at significant events so all can see that you are an active partner in the leadership of the University. Continue to tell others that something special is happening at Slippery Rock University unlike "those other places." Be audacious in your support. Remind all that this is still a great time to be at Slippery Rock University."[1727]

President Smith with Ed Cottrell (left) and Bruce Adams, two football players from Coach Thompson's 1939, undefeated team, Homecoming, 2011

Campus Scenes, 2011

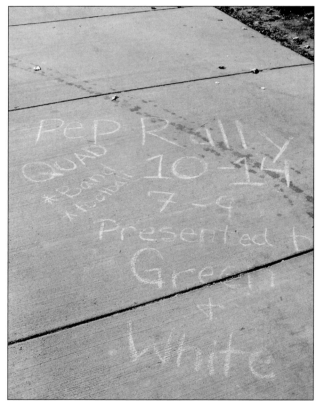

Homecoming, 2011

APPENDIX

2011 PASSHE BOARD OF GOVERNORS

Guido M. Pichini
Marie Conley Lammando
Aaron A. Walton
Leonard B. Altieri, III
Rep. Matthew E. Baker
Jennifer Branstetter (designee for Governor Corbett)
Gov. Tom Corbett
Sarah C. Darling
Rep. Michael K. Hanna
Ronald G. Henry
Kenneth M. Jarin
Bonnie L. Keener
Jonathan B. Mack
Joseph F. McGinn
C.R. "Chuck" Pennoni
Sen. Jeffrey E. Piccola
Harold C. Shields
Robert S. Taylor
Ronald J. Tomalis
Sen. John T. Yudichak

2011 PASSHE EXECUTIVE STAFF

Dr. John C. Cavanaugh
Chancellor

Dr. Peter Garland
Executive Vice Chancellor

Dr. Kathleen Howley
Associate Vice Chancellor for Academic and Student Affairs

James Dillon
Vice Chancellor for Administration and Finance

Karen Ball
Vice Chancellor for External Relations

Gary Dent
Vice Chancellor for Human Resources and Labor Relations

Leonidas Pandeladis
Chief Counsel

Arthur C. Stephens
Vice Chancellor for Strategic Initiatives

PREVIOUS PASSHE CHANCELLORS

Dr. Judy G. Hample
2001 – 2008

Dr. James H. McCormick
1983-2001

2011 SLIPPERY ROCK UNIVERSITY COUNCIL OF TRUSTEES

383

SLIPPERY ROCK UNIVERSITY PRESIDENT'S CABINET 2011

Dr. Robert M. Smith
President

Dr. William F. Williams
Provost and Vice President for Academic Affairs

Dr. Charles T. Curry
Vice President for Finance & Administrative Affairs

Dr. Constance L. Foley
Vice President for Student Life

Ms. Barbara Ender
Vice President for University Advancement

Ms. Rita Abent
Executive Director for University Public Relations

Ms. Tina Moser
Assistant to the President

SLIPPERY ROCK UNIVERSITY ALUMNI ASSOCIATION BOARD OF DIRECTORS

Effective July 1, 2010, Updated October 2011

Executive Committee

Kimberley Hudak Jones '96
President
Grove City, PA

Don Huddart '87
Treasurer
Bridgeville, PA

Bonnie McElhaney Lukasik '63
Immediate Past President
The Villages, FL

Lisa McCullough Holmes '88
Secretary
Grove City, PA

Richard Manning '75
Acting President-Elect
Slippery Rock, PA

Expires 2012

Brian Cashman '72
Hannover, PA

David Haddad '88
Pittsburgh, PA

Lorraine Troiano-Barron '57
Vandergrift, PA

Jason Wagner '93
New Castle, PA

Susan Whelpley Greaves '80
Slippery Rock, PA

Expires 2013

Kenneth Hanby '63
Emlenton, PA

L. Michael Ross '77
Chambersburg, PA

Dominic Williams '88
Middletown, OH

Larry Young '66
Slippery Rock, PA

Expires 2014

Marce Pancio '86
State College, PA

Marcie Popeck '96
Pittsburgh, PA

Bruce Russell '72
Slippery Rock, PA

Keith Warcup '75
Slippery Rock, PA

Linda Williamson '73
Grove City, PA

Other Voting Board Members

Ben Addison '87
Past Presidents' Representative
Columbus, OH

Sam Zyroll '78
Honorary Board Member
Pittsburgh, PA

Ex Officio

Dr. Robert Smith, President
Slippery Rock, PA

PAST PRESIDENTS OF THE SLIPPERY ROCK UNIVERSITY ALUMNI ASSOCIATION

1911-14	Origen K. Bingham '01	1964-65	C. Foster McGarvey '39
1914-15	Frank Campbell '09	1965-67	Shirley Butler Comstock '40
1915-17	Augustus T. Clutton '09	1967-68	Earl Birdy '51
1917-18	William Barron '14	1969-70	Raymond Haynes '37
1918-19	Howard Headland '06	1970-72	Eugene Boyer '50
1919-20	Thomas Duff '02	1972-73	Shirley Butler Comstock '40
1920-21	William Barron '14	1973-74	William Byrnes '61
1922-23	Claire Book '18	1974-75	Douglas Clinger '60
1923-25	Beatty Dimit '11	1975-76	Martha Schaaf '47
1925-26	Jessee C. Uber '11	1976-77	Louis Rossi '50
1926-27	Calvin Hogg '08	1977-78	Duane Conway '56
1927-28	Bruce Denniston '20	1978-79	Paul Stieman '67
1929-30	Arthur Hogg '08	1979-79	Thomas C. Gazda '69
1930-31	Jessee C. Uber '11	1979-81	Robert J. Watson '70
1931-32	Howard Headland '06	1981-82	Elizabeth A. Berkely '70
1932-33	A.P. Vincent '13	1982-83	John A. Watson '40
1933-34	N. Kerr Thompson '08	1983-84	William Sonntag '70
1934-35	John Bingham '09	1984-85	Jerome F. Bejbl '63
1935-36	Norman Doer '14	1985-86	Fred Van Dyke '55
1938-39	F.A. Barkley '97	1986-87	H. Charles Shultz '54
1940-41	Willis Schidemantle '36	1987-88	Fred Van Dyke '55
1945-46	Paul Varnum '33	1988-89	Martha Schaaf '47
1946-48	Earle Stoops '13	1989-90	Robert J. Watson '70
1948-50	Ralph Horsman '25	1990-91	William T. Beatty '56
1950-51	Porter McCandless '18	1991-93	Susan Whelpley Greaves '80
1951-52	Joseph D. McClymonds '34	1993-95	William T. Beatty '56
1952-53	Howard S. Steward '25	1995-97	Frank M. Carr '50
1953-54	John Mixer '26	1997-99	Ben L. Addison '87
1955-56	Bruce Adams '43	1999-01	Sam Zyroll '78
1956-57	Margaretta Eisenberg Hanford '34	2001-03	Phil Wanchick '67
1957-58	Clair Axtell '37	2003-05	Bill Kirker '73
1958-59	Raymond Haynes '37	2005-07	Eric Holmes '93
1959-60	Loyal Liken '34	2007-09	Dick Manning '75
1960-61	Wallace Kerr	2009-11	Bonnie Gangone McElhaney '63
1961-62	Jack Denbow '38	2011-13	Kimberley Hudak Jones '96
1962-63	Orlando Lucidore '42		
1963-64	Thomas Carmody '51		

SLIPPERY ROCK UNIVERSITY ALUMNI ASSOCIATION
DISTINGUISHED ALUMNI AWARDS

1968	Dale Liken*	1938
1969	J. Stanley Marshall	1947
1970	Clarence Kelly*	1904
1971	Jack Critchfield	1955
	Raymond Haynes	1937
	Jean Negley Zucchelli	1961
	Leila Watson Vincent*	1917
1972	Anthony Annarino	1949
	Rose Margaret Barber*	1911
	Joseph Ferderbar*	1953
	Walter Winner*	1916
1973	Esther Silveus*	1921
	Samual Sava*	1953
	M. Richard Rose	1955
	Michael Wargo*	1934
	Russell Wright*	1923
1974	Frankin Brittain*	1909
	Catherine Furbee*	1931
	John Graham*	1927
	Raymond Norris*	1948
	Edward Raney*	1931
1975	John Anderson*	1969
	Beatrice Davis Lowe*	1933
	Marjorie Christy Maquire*	1937
	Robert McMullen*	1951
	Peter DeLonga*	1943
1976	Timothy Wilson	1962
1977	Stan Dziedzic, Jr	1972
1978-79	No Awards Given	
1980	Howard Stewart*	1925
1981	No Awards Given	

SLIPPERY ROCK UNIVERSITY ALUMNI ASSOCIATION
DISTINGUISHED ALUMNI AWARDS (CONTINUED)

1982	Tut Melman*	1932
	Harry Spataro	1951
	Vivian Stoner Stringer	1970
1983	John Watson*	1940
	Robert Watson	1970
1984	Marcia Carlson	1948
1985	Catherine McLaine Fuller*	1925
	Robert Lowry	1948
	Joanne Genova Sujansky*	1972
1986	Paul Onuska	1969
1987	No Awards Given	
1988	Robert Hannan	1961
	Josie Metal-Corbin	1967
1989	Joanna McKeag	1955
1990	Anthony Daniels	1963
1991	Patricia Monteson	1967
1992	Anthony Miklausen*	1942
	Stanley Zagorski	1957
1993	Donald Eichhorn*	1954
1994	No Awards Given	
1995	All Veterans	
1996-98	No Awards Given	
1999	James Dull*	1950
	Carol Matteson	1968
2000	William Sonntag	1970
2001	Charles Sheetz	1974

SLIPPERY ROCK UNIVERSITY ALUMNI ASSOCIATION
DISTINGUISHED ALUMNI AWARDS (CONTINUED)

2002	Jack Critchfield	1955
2003	Kenneth Wilcox	1989
	Robert Stevens	1976
2004	Sheila Drohan	1974
2005	Robert Marcus	1961
2006	Robert Taylor	1978
2007	Thomas Zaucha	1967
2008	Janet Westerwick Sargert	1963
2009	Dorotha Anderson	1937
	Quentin Currie	1962
	Rose Spataro Dillner	1957
	Daniel Gillen	1978
	Gary Lancaster	1971
2010	Patrick Cappatt	1973
	Dr. Richard Hudson	1968
	Dr. Robert Murray	1971
	Dr. F. Dennis Riegelnegg	1972
	Dr. Anne Wuenschel	1976 & 2006
	Tine Hansen-Turton	1982
2011	Kathlene Contres	1977
	Sandra Kalin	1964
	Samuel Kiefer	1979
	Peter Oesterling	1978
	Bruno Raso	1961 & 1966

SLIPPERY ROCK UNIVERSITY FOUNDATION, INC.
BOARD OF DIRECTORS

As of January 28, 2011
Updated September 15, 2011

Mr. Richard L. Allen '83
Term Ends: 2013

Office:
Committee: Resource Development

Ms. Elizabeth A. Berkely '70
Term Ends: 2012

Office:
Committee: Special Events

Mr. Harry Bertrand, CPA '81
Term Ends: 2011

Office:
Committee: Finance; Executive

Mr. John W. Conway
Term Ends: 2011

Office:
Committee: Investment

Ms. Mary Crawford
Term ends: 2011

Office:
Committee: Finance; Executive

Mr. James Culligan '92
Term Ends: 2013

Office:
Committee: Resource Development

Mr. David C. Knopp '98
Term Ends: 2013

Office:
Committee: Resource Development

Mr. Douglas McMullen
Term Ends: 2011

Office:
Committee: Investment; Special Events

Dr. Paul Rizza
Term Ends: 2012

Office:
Committee: Investment

Mr. Regis I. Schiebel '57
Term Ends: 2012

Office: CHAIR
Committee: Investment; Executive; Chair of Nominations

Mr. William C. Sonntag '70
Term Ends: 2012

Office: SECRETARY
Committee: Executive; Chair of Finance

Mr. William K. Thomas
Term Ends: 2012

Office:
Committee: Resource Development

Mr. Barry E. Welsch '73
Term Ends: 2011

Office: VICE CHAIR
Committee: Investment

SLIPPERY ROCK UNIVERSITY HONORARY DOCTORATE RECIPIENTS

Dr. Fred McFeely Rogers, December 1982
Doctor of Humane Letters

Dr. Russell M. Wright, May 1989
Doctor of Science

Mr. Albert R. Puntureri, May 1990
Doctor of Science

Dr. Vincent E. Reed, May 1991
Doctor of Pedagogy

Mr. John C. Jordan, December 1991
Doctor of Laws

Mr. Louis D. Pappan, May 1992
Doctor of Laws

Dr. Samuel Hazo, December 1992
Doctor of Humane Letters

Mr. Robert L. McMullen, May 1993
Doctor of Humane Letters

Dr. Robert E. Eberly, December 1994
Doctor of Humane Letters

Mr. James E. Winner, Jr., December 1995
Doctor of Laws

Mr. Jerome F. Bejbl, May 1996
Doctor of Laws

Mr. Stanley Kraus, December 1996
Doctor of Laws

Dr. Csaba Istvanfi, May 1997
Doctor of Pedagogy

Mr. F. Eugene Dixon, Jr., April 2001
Doctor of Public Service

Mr. William E. Strickland, December 2001
Doctor of Humane Letters

Dr. Herb. F. Reinhard, Jr., May 2002
Doctor of Pedagogy

Mr. Marvin Hamlisch, April 2006
Doctor of Humane Letters

SLIPPERY ROCK UNIVERSITY PRESIDENT'S AWARD FOR OUTSTANDING SERVICE

2011   Ms. Kathy Jack, University Advancement

2010:   Mr. Eliott Baker, Academic Records/SS

2009:   Ms. Sandra Busch, Public Relations

2008:   Ms. Mary Ann King, Academic Affairs

2007:   Dr. Christopher Cole, Student Life

2006:   Ms. Tracy Allison, University Advancement

2005:   Ms. Jean Richardson, Academic Affairs

2004:   Mr. Tom McPherson, SGA Bookstore

2003:   Mr. Dennis Colosimo, Facilities & Planning
            Ms. Patricia Hladio, Financial Aid

2002:   Dr. Patrick Burkhart, Geog, Geol, Environment

2001:   Ms. Beverly Lumley, Student ID Services

2000:   Dr. John Hicks, Asst to the Dean, College of Education

1999:   Dr. Kurt W. Pitluga, Art

1998:   Mr. Michael Vigliotti, Office of Housing
            Dr. Carolyn Steglich, Biology

1997:   Dr. Paulette Johnson, Parks & Rec/EE
            Dr. Daniel Dziubek, Parks & Rec/EE
            Ms. Marcia Miller, Human Resources
            Ms. Mary Ann Nagel, Donor Records
            Ms. Barbara Kristufek, Health Services

1996:   Ms. Pamela Frigot, International Studies
            Ms. Lynne Motyl, Human Resources
            Dr. Clarie Settlemire, History
            Mr. L. Andrew Stoughton, User Services

1995:   Dr. Ferenc Szucs, Geology
            Dr. Catherine Morsink, Dean, College of Education
            Mr. William Martin, Storekeeper, Vincent Science Hall
            Dr. Paula Olivero, Director of Residence Education
            Mr. John Bonando, Assistant Dean of Student Affairs
            Ms. Bonnie Montgomery, Printing Services

1994:   Mr. Allen McClymonds, Business Services
            Dr. Robert Sattler, Special Education
            Mr. Francis Hensler, Computer Center
            Mrs. Sara Jane "Sally" Foust, Printing Services

1993:   Ms. Wilma Cavill, Allied Health
            Mr. Robert "Dick" McFeaters, Facilities & Planning
            Mr. William Kirker, Prospect Research/Donor Records
            Ms. Lynne Swisher, Greek Affairs/Family Foundation
            Ms. Alice Kaiser-Drobney, Gov & Public Affairs

1992:   Mr. John Snyder, Career Services
            Ms. Amanda Yale, Academic Advisement Center
            Ms. Alice Holden, Academic Affairs
            Mr. Edward Leone, Facilities and Planning
            Dr. Richard VonMayrhauser, History

1991:   Ms. Linda Beatty, Health Services
            Mr. William Lennox, Athletics
            Dr. Roy Stewart, Graduate Studies
            Mr. Richard Wukich, Art

1990:   Dr. Anna McLee Austin, Super & Student Teaching
            Mr. David Collins, Admissions
            Ms. Katherine Hogg, Student Affairs
            Ms. Shirley Jones, University Relations
            Dr. Michael Ross, Computer Science
            Mr. Joseph Stahlman, Sr., Maintenance Center

1989:   Mr. Stan Kendziorski, International Studies
            Mr. Roy Martin, Receiving/Stores
            Dr. Joanne McKeag, Physical Education
            Ms. Pearl Shaffer, Athletics

1988:   Mr. Furrie Bonnetti, Residence Life
            Ms. Joan Condravy, Academic Support Services
            Mr. Charles Curry, Finance & Administration
            Mr. Robert DiSpirito, Parks & Recreation
            Ms. Katherine Edes, Computer Center

1987:   Reverend P.A. Harmon, Newman Center
            Dr. Helen Knierim, Physical Education
            Ms. Kathy Moore, Health Services
            Mr. Louis Razzano, Academic Affairs
            Mr. Mark Shiring, Curriculum/Instruction

1986:   Mr. J. Robert Bruya, Art
            Mr. Philip Kennedy, Accounting
            Mr. Robert Konnen, Budget & Fiscal Planning
            Ms. Carol Latronica, Residence Life

1985:   Mr. Douglas Clinger, Physical Education
            Ms. Carla Hart, Career Services
            Dr. Gary Pechar, Physical Education
            Mr. Murray Shellgren, Biology
            Ms. Nancy Szymarek, Counseling Center

1984:   Dr. Anne Griffiths, College of Professional Studies
            Mr. Barry Hammond, Public Administration
            Dr. Stephen Hulbert, Administration & Public Affairs
            Dr. Robert Macoskey, Philosophy
            Dr. Al Matthews, Student Affairs
            Mr. Carl Miller, Computer Center

1983:   Dr. Robert Aebersold, Academic Affairs
            Dr. Robert Hart, Biology
            Dr. Richard Hunkler, Curriculum/Instruction
            Ms. Claire Schmieler, Health Services
            Mr. Alvin Walters, Budget

1982:   Ms. Mildred Barnes, Health Services
            Ms. Leah Brown, Library
            Ms. Minnie Colosimo, Maintenance Center
            Dr. Leona Parascenzo, Nursing
            Mr. Blasé Scarnati, Music

1981:   Mr. Thom Cobb, Physical Education
            Mr. James Leone, Maintenance Center
            Ms. Rhonda Mangieri, Affirmative Action
            Dr. Tim Walters, Communication
            Ms. Lillian Yartz, Residence Life

SLIPPERY ROCK UNIVERSITY STUDENT LEADERSHIP

Student Government Association (SGA)

SGA Senate

Executive Board:
President-Jordan Bailley
Vice President of Financial Affairs-Josh Rodgers
Vice President of Student Affairs-Jim Henry
Vice President of Campus Outreach-Katie Campbell
Vice President of Internal Affairs-Kimberly Sloan
Speaker of the Senate-Carmen Fortunato

SLIPPERY ROCK UNIVERSITY STUDENT LEADERSHIP

University Program Board (UPB)

Left to Right: Johnson, Foreback, Street, George and Wolfe

Executive Board:
President-Audrey Foreback
Vice President-Corey Street
Vice President of Marketing-Marcie Johnson
Vice President of Speakers-Rebekah George
Vice President of Cultural Arts-Terrell Foster
Vice President of Concerts-Dave Wolfe

SLIPPERY ROCK UNIVERSITY STUDENT LEADERSHIP

Association of Residence Hall Students (ARHS)

Left to Right (Back): Wolfe, Holzman and Laniear
Left to Right (Front): Malloy and Sladden

Executive Board:
President–Madison Holzman
Vice President for Education–Oliver Laniear
Vice President for Financial Affairs–Dave Wolfe
Vice President for Administration–Kelly Sladden
National Communications Chair–Hannah Malloy

SLIPPERY ROCK UNIVERSITY STUDENT LEADERSHIP

Student Union for Multicultural Affairs (SUMA)
President-Anissa Rutledge
Vice President-Cicely Jackson
Secretary-Tynasha Barnes
Public Relations-Randell Boyles

Black Action Society (BAS)
President-Mariah Banks
Vice President-Deronda Strothers
Treasurer-Fielding Vaughn
Secretary-Roxy McLaughlin

Student Athlete Advisory Council (SAAC)
President-Skylar Brosse
Vice President-Erin Moran
Secretary-Lauren Rojek
Treasurer-Carter Haponski

2011-2012 SLIPPERY ROCK UNIVERSITY GREEK LIFE

Interfraternity Council

National Pan-Hellenic Council

2011-2012 SLIPPERY ROCK UNIVERSITY GREEK LIFE (CONTINUED)

Interfraternity Council

President
Patrick Scherer

Vice President
John Guerrieri

Administration
Brian Gabriel

Public Relations
James Miller

Student Affairs
Corey DeSantis

Chief Justice
Kyle Scatena

IFC Fraternity Presidents

Alpha Sigma Phi
Michael DiCocco

Theta Xi
Evan Croyle

Kappa Delta Rho
Ian Heilman

Kappa Sigma
Curt Hesidenz

Pi Kappa Alpha
Pat Cole

Pi Kappa Phi
Ryan Phillips

Sigma Tau Gamma
Thomas Weaver

Panhellenic Council

President
Alex Evans

VP of Recruitment
Antonia Arch

VP of Administration
Madeline Stump

VP of Public Relations
Kaylee Kirsch

VP of Education
Megan Scott

VP of Community Service
Amber Whitton

VP of Student Affairs
Kristin Thomas

PHC Sorority Presidents

Alpha Xi Delta
Elle Naughton

Alpha Omicron Pi
Megan Scott

Alpha Sigma Tau
Kasey Hazi

Delta Zeta
Morgan Bonekovic

Sigma Sigma Sigma
Jordan Mojzer-Brown

Phi Sigma Sigma
Tara Robinson

Multicultural Fraternity

Theta Delta Sigma
James Hull

National Pan-Hellenic Council

President
TBD

Public Relations
TBD

Treasurer
TBD

Jr. Panhel Council

President
Brooke Miller

VP of Recruitment
Elle Naughton

VP of Administration
Jessica Mawhinney

VP of Public Relations
Kayla Haid

VP of Education
Sarah Rothrock

VP of Community Service
Kaitlin Hart

VP of Student Affairs
Jessica Smith

NPHC Fraternity/Sorority Presidents

Zeta Phi Beta
Keeyaira Murray

Alpha Kappa Alpha
Tracey McPherson

Phi Beta Sigma
Martin Akers

Omega Psi Phi
Charles Allen

2011-2012 SLIPPERY ROCK UNIVERSITY ROCKET STAFF

Top row: Advisor Dr. Mark Zeltner, Sports editor Tim Durr
Second row: News reporter Will Deshong, Assistant Campus Life editor Jim Meyer
Third row: News editor Brian Brodeur, Campus Life editor Andy Treese
Bottom Row: Assistant photo editor Liana Pittman, Assistant news editor Stephanie Holsinger,
Web editor James Intile, Assistant sports editor Madeline Williams, Editor-in-chief Courtney Nickle,
Photo editor Lexi Kovski, Ad manager Emily Hunter.
Missing from the photo is Copy editor Stephanie Martincsek.

SLIPPERY ROCK UNIVERSITY CHAMPIONSHIPS

NATIONAL CHAMPIONSHIPS
1979 Men's track and field
1995 Women's water polo

REGIONAL CHAMPIONSHIPS
Baseball: 1989, 1997, 2000, 2003
Women's basketball: 1999-2000
Football: 1998
Women's tennis: 2003, 2008, 2010

PSAC CHAMPIONSHIPS
Baseball
1978, 1982, 1991, 2001
Men's basketball
1963
Women's basketball
1986
Men's cross country
1959, 1061, 1962, 1963, 1969, 1991
Women's cross country
1981, 1995
Football
1962, 1972, 1973, 1974, 1976, 1997, 1998, 1999, 2000
Men's golf
1958, 1960, 1961, 1962, 1970, 1972, 1974, 1985, 1987, 1988, 1993, 1994, 1995, 1996
Men's soccer
1952, 1953, 1954, 1974, 2005, 2009
Women's soccer
2003, 2005
Women's softball
1981
Men's swimming
1966
Men's tennis
1962
Women's tennis
1980, 1981, 2003
Men's indoor track and field
2008
Men's outdoor track and field
1960, 1964, 1966, 1968, 1972, 1978, 1980, 1981, 1987, 1994, 2000, 2008
Women's indoor track and field
2007, 2008, 2009
Women's outdoor track and field
1979, 1980, 1982, 1986, 1987, 1989, 1996, 1999, 2001, 2003, 2004, 2006, 2007, 2008, 2009
Women's volleyball
1984, 1993
Wrestling
1975

SLIPPERY ROCK UNIVERSITY ACADEMIC ALL-AMERICA® SELECTIONS

Selected by the College Sports Information Directors of America (CoSIDA) and sponsored over the years by GTE, Verizon, ESPN The Magazine and Capital One

2010-11: Jen Harpp, Women's Track/Cross Country - 1st team
2009-10: Jennifer Hansen, Women's Track/Cross Country – 1st team
2009-10: Shardea Croes, Softball – 3rd team
2009-10: Jeremy Deighton, Men's Soccer – 3rd team
2009-10: Jen Harpp, Women's Track/Cross Country – 3rd team
2008-09: Jen Blasko, Women's Volleyball – 1st team
2008-09: Jennifer Harpp, Women's Track/Cross Country – 2nd team
2007-08: Mike Butterworth, Football -- 1st team
2007-08: Clint Forsha, Football -- 1st team
2007-08: Jennifer Hansen, Women's Track/Cross Country – 1st team
2006-07: Mike Butterworth, Football -- 1st team
2005-06: Jen Zuzack, At-Large (Women's Swimming) -- 1st team
2004-05: Jen Zuzack, At-Large (Women's Swimming) -- 2nd team
2003-04: Karyn McCready, Women's Track/Cross Country – 1st team
2002-03: Karyn McCready, Women's Track/Cross Country – 2nd team
2002-03: Ella Reilly, At-Large (Women's Tennis) -- 2nd team
2001-02: Louis Jamison, Football -- 2nd team
2000-01: Tracy Whitling, Women's basketball --2nd team
1998-99 Tim Kusniez, Football -- 2nd team
1998-99 Mark Dolan, Baseball -- 2nd team
1997-98 Tom Wise, At-Large (Track & Field) -- 1st team
1997-98 Lori Robinson-Nuzzo, Women's basketball -- 1st team
1997-98 Mark Dolan, Baseball -- 2nd team
1996-97 Mike Habalar, At-Large (Soccer) -- 1st team
1996-97 Dave Sabolcik, Football -- 2nd team
1996-97 Tom Wise, At-Large (Track & Field) -- 1st team
1995-96 Mike Habalar, At-Large (Soccer) -- 1st team
1995-96 Joan Mount, At-Large (Women's Track & Field) -- 2nd team
1995-96 Julie Bravin, At-Large (Women's Track & Field) -- 2nd team
1995-96 Lori Robinson, Women's basketball) -- 3rd team
1994-95 Joan Mount, At-Large (Women's Track & Field) -- 3rd team
1994-95 Mike Habalar, At-Large (Soccer) -- 2nd team
1994-95 Mark Metzka, Men's basketball -- 1st team
1993-94 Greg Hopkins, Football -- 2nd team
1993-94 Mark Metzka, Men's basketball -- 2nd team
1984-85 Julie Morrow, At-Large (Women's Gymnastics) -- 2nd team
1984-85 Todd Olsen, At-Large (Men's Soccer) -- 2nd team
1983-84 Julie Morrow, At-Large (Women's Gymnastics) -- 3rd team
1983-84 Harold Lueken, At-Large (Tennis) -- 2nd team
1982-83 Bob Petrini, At-Large (Track & Field) -- 1st team
1982-83 John Samsa, Men's Basketball -- 1st team
1982-83 Darlene Bullock, Softball -- 1st team
1982-83 Jayne Beatty, At-Large (Women's Track & Field) -- 1st team
1982-83 Julie Morrow, At-Large (Women's Gymnastics) -- 3rd team
1982-83 Cristel Smith, At-Large (Women's Swimming) -- 2nd team
1978-79 Mike Hardy, Men's Basketball -- 1st team
19-7576 Sid Manchester, Baseball -- 1st team
1975-76 Nick Forese, Baseball - 2nd team
1974-75 George Spetar, Baseball -- 1st team
1973-74 John Hoffman, Baseball -- 1st team
1970-71 Robert Wiegand, Men's Basketball – 1st team

SLIPPERY ROCK UNIVERSITY PETE NEVINS SCHOLAR-ATHLETES OF THE YEAR

The following Rock student athletes have received the Pennsylvania State Athletic Conference's Pete Nevins Scholar-Athlete of the Year Awards, which are presented to the top student-athletes who have achieved at least a 3.50 cumulative grade point average while competing at an outstanding athletic level. Student-athletes must have been recognized as a conference Fall, Winter or Spring Top Ten Award Winner to be eligible for the honor. The Scholar-Athletes of the Year are chosen by the league's sports information directors and were renamed in 2007 to honor East Stroudsburg's long-time sports information director, Pete Nevins, who passed away in 2007. Nevins held his position at ESU for 33 years and it is estimated that he wrote articles on more than 12,000 ESU events that covered more than 5,000 student-athletes.

2008-09: Jen Blasko, Women's Volleyball
2007-08: Jennifer Hansen, Women's Track and Field
2003-04: Karen McCready, Women's Track and Field
1999-2000: Tim Kusniez, Football
1997-98: Dave Sabolcik, Football
1995-96: Lori Robinson, Women's Basketball
1994-95: Mark Metzka, Men's Basketball

SLIPPERY ROCK UNIVERSITY PSAC TOP-10 AWARD WINNERS

The following Rock student-athletes have earned Pennsylvania State Athletic Conference "Top-10 Awards" as one of the top five male or five female student-athletes in the conference during the fall, winter or spring sports season. In order to be eligible for voting, a student-athlete must maintain above a 3.5 cumulative GPA.

Year: Name, Season, Sport
2010-11: Chris Warning, Spring, Men's Outdoor Track and Field
2010-11: Chris Warning, Winter, Men's Indoor Track and Field
2010-11: Jen Harpp, Fall, Women's Cross Country
2009-10: Jeremy Deighton, Fall Men's Soccer
2009-10: Jen Harpp, Fall Women's Cross Country
2009-10: Jen Hansen, Winter, Women's Indoor Track and Field
2009-10: Jen Hansen, Spring, Women's Outdoor Track and Field
2008-09: Jennifer Blasko, Fall, Volleyball
2008-09: Jen Harpp, Winter, Women's Indoor Track and Field
2007-08: Mike Butterworth, Fall, Football
2007-08: Jennifer Hansen, Winter, Women's Indoor Track and Field
2007-08: Jennifer Hansen, Spring, Women's Outdoor Track and Field
2006-07: Mike Butterworth, Fall, Football
2006-07: Andi Rose, Winter, Women's Indoor Track and Field
2006-07: Jennifer Hansen, Spring, Women's Outdoor Track and Field
2006-07: Jeff Weiss, Spring, Men's Outdoor Track & Field
2005-06: Jason Cardillo, Winter, Wrestling
2005-06: Jen Zuzack, Winter, Swimming
2004-05: Preston Gibbs, Spring, Men's Track and Field
2003-04: Karyn McCready, Spring, Women's Track and Field
2002-03: Ella Reilly, Spring, Women's Tennis
2001-02: Shelbey Wardman, Winter, Women's Basketball
2001-02: Ella Reilly, Spring, Women's Tennis
2000-01: Tracy Whitling, Winter, Women's Basketball
1999-00: Tim Kusniez, Fall, Football
1998-99: Nicole Frey, Spring, Women's Track and Field
1998-99: Heather Kearney, Winter, Women's Basketball
1998-99: Rick Magulick, Fall, Football
1998-99: Tim Kusniez, Fall, Football
1997-98: Mark Dolan, Spring, Baseball
1997-98: Tom Wise, Spring, Men's Track and Field
1997-98: Lori Robinson-Nuzzo, Winter, Women's Basketball
1997-98: Dave Sabolcik, Fall, Football
1997-98: Joan Mount, Fall, Women's Cross Country
1995-96: Lori Robinson, Winter, Women's Basketball
1994-95: Mark Metzka, Winter, Men's Basketball

SLIPPERY ROCK UNIVERSITY HALL OF FAME

CLASS OF 2011
Derek DelPorto 1999
Scott Hendry 1997, 2000, 2002-M
Dr. Richard "Doc" Hunkler............. Coach
Sue Bow Kolczak................1977, 1982-M
Owen Long...1975
Bill Raush...1983
Carol Sprague......................1971, 1974-M
1979 Men's track and field team

CLASS OF 2010
Jack Fullen 1963
Michael Hambrick 1984/1993
Heather Kearney 1999/2003
Randy McKavish 2001
Craig White.......................................1986
John Zack..1978

CLASS OF 2009
Garry Benford 1977/1979
Roger Flynn 1968
Laurel L. Heilman.................... 1986/1988
Duane Kirklin....................................1964
Bob Ogoreuc 1996
William C. Rometo 1946
Chuck Vietmeier 1982

CLASS OF 2008
Walter Esser 1960
Lori Way Gulati 1991
Rita Belavic Harrell 1974
Blair Hildebrand...............................1948
Bridget Sheehan 1977/1990
Jerry Skocik 1976
Wilma Cavill
Dr. Anne Griffiths
Dr. Martha Haverstick
Dr. Marie Wheaton
Carolyn Williams
Dr. Patricia Zimmerman

CLASS OF 2007
Laurie Flynn Cortazzo 1995
Anthony Emanuele.............................1983
Janice Forsty 1975/1989
Chad Vogt..1997
Joseph Walters......................... 1968/1972
Judith Whalen-Geist...........................1991

CLASS OF 2006
Gary Aldrich............................. 1982/1989
Mark Balbach.......................... 1969/1973
Jon C. Boyd......................................1966
Jim Cichra 1979
Deb Feather......................................1984
Dr. Richard Hudson 1968
Dr. Robert J. Watson 1970

CLASS OF 2005
Joan Anderson...................................1995
Stephen Banjak .... Coach
Greg Hopkins....................................1995
William Kelly....................................1965
William Miller...................................1964
Dr. Albert Schmittlein .... Coach
Jay Wagner..1970
1972-74 football coaching staff (Head coach Bob DiSpirito and assistant coaches Paul "Bear" Bruno, Doug "Dad" Clinger, Rod Oberlin and Mike Pariseau)

CLASS OF 2004
William T. Beatty 1956
Joseph R. Daniels..............................1964
Virginia Kelly Grindle 1960
Edward J. Olkowski...........................1953
Kory Fielitz Malkus 1994/1998
Dr. John A. Samsa.............................1983
Mark Seybert.....................................1979

CLASS OF 2003
Charles Armstrong 1969
Robert Byler......................................1965
Edwin B. Cottrell 1943
Linda Derk 1987
Thomas Dolde....................................1960
Jim McFarland .... Coach
Bob Skaneski 1973
Juanita Vetter....................................1984

CLASS OF 2002
Jeanne Arbuckle.................................1979
John Carpenter 1975
Jean Condo..1962
Quentin Currie 1962
John Dahlstrand 1983
Robert Hannan 1961
Herb Lauffer......................................1963
Fay Steving 1973

CLASS OF 2001
Patti Bucklew 1978
Darlene Bullock 1983
Rudy Corona 1956
Jack Denbow 1938
Jeanne Powell Furrie 1945
Robert Siar 1955
George Spetar 1975

CLASS OF 2000
Earl Birdy 1951
Loyal Briggs 1938
Carol DeVenzio 1965
Charles Dunaway 1962
James Geist 1989
Bob Raymond .... Admin.
Richard Sauers 1951
Elizabeth Smiley 1932

CLASS OF 1999
Wade Acker 1985
Harry Brownfield 1950
Marvin Donaldson 1952
Sue Fatcheric Hawes 1986
Bill McGinnis...................................1961
Ruth Podbielski 1949
Judy Zarenko....................................1971

CLASS OF 1998
Bruce Adams..................................... 1943
Dave Barnes 1961
Barb Skrbin Crupie 1966
Jana Sipes Porter 1986
Jeff Siemianowski 1974
Doug Zimmerman.............................1972

CLASS OF 1997
Kamal Houari 1979
George Mihalik 1974
Nancy Olson.....................................1979
Charles Sanders................................1986
Richard Shirey 1986
Tom Stabile 1968
Gordon Vietmeier.............................1989

CLASS OF 1996
Jayne Beatty 1985
Julie Morrow Caito 1985
Dick Dilts...1955
Joe Duffy...1956
Troy Mild 1984
Ray Nedwidek...................................1948
Bob Petrini 1983

CLASS OF 1995
Sal Agostinelli..................................1983
Hank Baierl....................................... Coach
Jim Hagstrom 1987
Elaine Jewart 1966
Mike Kish..1973
Bill Lennox 1959
Sally Ward 1971
John Watson 1940

CLASS OF 1994
Jon Paul Albitz 1960
Jodi Kest...1984
Tim Nunes...1973
John Papa..1979
Wally Rose ....Coach
Bruce Seaman 1979
Bill Shuffstall...................................1975

CLASS OF 1993
Tom Beck 1954
John Daller..1967
Carol DeSalvo Lidfeldt 1968
Terry Factor......................................1974
Ray Haynes 1937
Nancy Kunkel 1981
Ricky Porter 1983

CLASS OF 1992
Corrie Convis....................................1986
George Crunkleton............................1979
Kathy Lisman Wood 1982
Tut Melman.......................................1932
Fred Powell .... Coach
Jack Spates 1975
Fran Webster 1947

CLASS OF 1991
Sally Benedict Baum.........................1977
August J. Catanese 1966
Lynn Comer Kachmarik....................1979
Charles L. Klausing 1948
Beverly Corll Lewis..........................1959
Bruno Raso..1961
John Ross 1970

CLASS OF 1990
Angelo Albanese 1979
Alfred Barnes....................................1938
Patrick Campbell...............................1961
Denny Douds 1963
William J. Logue...............................1955
Dr. Richard McLachlan.... Team physician
Billl Purvis 1965
Dennis Tilko.....................................1974

405

CLASS OF 1989
Tom Campion.....................................1979
Tom Carey..1943
Tom Erdos..1968
Jodi Gault..1979
John Madden.....................................1942
Jim McElhaney 1964
Bill Meise..1947

CLASS OF 1988
Patricia Connolly 1961
Jan Kasnevich 1968
Pat Madden 1962
Chuck Neuschwander 1953
Art Rex..1977
Milan Tatala 1935
Bill Temple.......................................1941

CLASS OF 1987
Chuck Godlasky............................ Coach
Oliver Gordon 1925
Ed Hepe..1954
Darrell Hess 1954
Bob Phillips......................................1950
George Stonis....................................1935
Janet Schwab Wilson 1962

CLASS OF 1986
Jerry Bejbl.......................................1963
Jim Egli .... Coach
Bill Flecher.......................................1975
Jean Heard..1962
Paul Uram 1949
Roy Van Horn...................................1940
Dr. Russell Wright.............................1928

CLASS OF 1985
Edward Boyle....................................1958
Bob Di Spirito................................ Coach
Janet Hollack....................................1967
Edward McFarlane............................1962
"Hooks" Sample................................1941

CLASS OF 1984
Shirley Comstock.............................1940
Stan Dziedzic 1972
"Tuggles" Gross...............................1941
John O. Kaufman 1940
Connie Palumbo................................1957
C. Vivian Stringer 1970
N. Kerr Thompson 1908

Received Special Recognition Award

SRU ATHLETIC HALL OF FAME COMMITTEE
Paul Lueken * ....Chair
Joan Anderson..................................1995
John Carpenter 1975-M
Mike Franko.....................................1976
Ed Gould 1987
John Hicks..1962
Jan Hollack.......................................1967
Jan Kasnevich 1968
George McDowell.........................1982-M
Randy Nichols...................................1990
Bill Richter............................. Ex-Officio
Pearl Shaffer........................ 1991, '93-M
Kathy Wood 1982
* non-voting member

SLIPPERY ROCK UNIVERSITY CONTRIBUTIONS TO THE SLIPPERY ROCK
VOLUNTEER FIRE DEPARTMENT

In Accordance with legislation enacted in 1975, the fourteen constituent institutions within the State System of Higher Education are authorized to make a contribution, at the discretion of the Presidents, to those volunteer fire companies that provide fire protection to the institutions. The action by the President is subject to approval of the Council of Trustees.

Since this legislation was passed, Slippery Rock University has given annual contributions to the Slippery Rock Volunteer Fire Department, which is also shared with the Rescue Squad. The dollar amounts and the corresponding fiscal years for each of those contributions are as follows:

$20,000	**2009 -2010**
$20,000	2008 - 2009
$15,000	2007 – 2008
$15,000	2006 – 2007
$15,000	2005 – 2006
$15,000	2004 – 2005
$15,000	2003 – 2004
$15,000	2002 – 2003
$14,534	2001 – 2002
$14,111	2000 – 2001
$14,111	1999 – 2000
$13,700	1998 – 1999
$13,700	1997 – 1998
$13,300	1996 – 1997
$13,300	1995 – 1996
$12,900	1994 – 1995
$12,500	1993 – 1994
$12,000	1992 – 1993
$12,000	1991 – 1992
$10,000	1990 – 1991
$10,000	1989 – 1990
$12,500	1988 – 1989
$12,500	1987 – 1988
$12,500	1986 – 1987
$10,000	1985 – 1986
$10,000	1984 – 1985
$10,000	1983 – 1984
$10,000	1982 – 1983
$10,000	1981 – 1982
$10,000	1980 – 1981
$10,000	1979 – 1980
$13,500	1978 – 1979
$10,000	1977 – 1978
$14,100	1976 – 1977

SLIPPERY ROCK UNIVERESITY CONTRIBUTION TO THE SANDY LAKE AND STONEBORO VOLUNTEER FIRE DEPARTMENTS

McKeever Environmental Learning Center through Slippery Rock University began giving annual contributions to the Sandy Lake Volunteer Fire Department in 1994–1995. In 1995-1996 McKeever (SRU) began to split the contribution between the Sandy Lake and Stoneboro Volunteer Fire Departments. The amounts and the corresponding fiscal years for each of these contributions are as follows.

Sandy Lake/Stoneboro	**$2,000**	**2009 – 2010**
Sandy Lake/Stoneboro	$2,000	2008 - 2009
Sandy Lake/Stoneboro	$1,000	2007 - 2008
Sandy Lake/Stoneboro	$1,000	2006 – 2007
Sandy Lake/Stoneboro	$1,000	2005 – 2006
Sandy Lake/Stoneboro	$565	2004 – 2005
Sandy Lake/Stoneboro	$565	2003 – 2004
Sandy Lake/Stoneboro	$565	2002 – 2003
Sandy Lake/Stoneboro	$547	2001 – 2002
Sandy Lake/Stoneboro	$531	2000 – 2001
Sandy Lake/Stoneboro	$531	1999 – 2000
Sandy Lake/Stoneboro	$515	1998 – 1999
Sandy Lake/Stoneboro	$500	1997 – 1998
Sandy Lake/Stoneboro	$500	1996 – 1997
Sandy Lake/Stoneboro	$500	1995 – 1996
Sandy Lake	$500	1994 – 1995

SRU Overall Enrollment Headcounts: Spring 1889 to Present

Fall Term	Headcount	Fall Term	Headcount	Fall Term	Headcount	Fall Term	Headcount	Fall Term	Headcount
1889*	168	1913	506	1938	654	1963	2,155	1988	7,360
1889	298	1914	589	1939	625	1964	2,589	1989	7,484
1890	340	1915	604	1940	622	1965	3,164	1990	7,825
1891	434	1916	522	1941	520	1966	3,640	1991	7,925
1892	513	1917	432	1942	376	1967	4,026	1992	7,777
1893	601	1918	433	1943	193	1968	4,411	1993	7,677
1894	634	1919	524	1944	234	1969	4,952	1994	7,563
1895	631	1920	496	1945	317	1970	5,446	1995	7,493
1896	604	1921	245	1946	593	1971	6,020	1996	7,291
1897	626	1922	376	1947	720	1972	5,897	1997	7,038
1898	598	1923	402	1948	821	1973	5,985	1998	6,923
1899	537	1924	514	1949	928	1974	6,299	1999	6,803
1900	490	1925	660	1950	884	1975	6,350	2000	6,952
1901	566	1926	761	1951	762	1976	6,244	2001	7,197
1902	490	1927	830	1952	776	1977	6,059	2002	7,530
1903	605	1928	867	1953	755	1978	5,845	2003	7,789
1904	680	1929	892	1954	829	1979	5,694	2004	7,928
1905	724	1930	925	1955	925	1980	5,690	2005	8,105
1906	670	1931	899	1956	901	1981	5,715	2006	8,230
1907	713	1932	832	1957	1,035	1982	5,782	2007	8,325
1908	782	1933	761	1958	1,192	1983	6,159	2008	8,458
1909	787	1934	729	1959	1,273	1984	6,479	2009	8,648
1910	768	1935	728	1960	1,445	1985	6,496	2010	8,852
1911	777	1936	720	1961	1,606	1986	6,599	2011	8,712
1912	768	1937	617	1962	1,790	1987	6,851		

Headcount is the total number of full- and part-time undergraduate and graduate students

*Spring term when the university opened

SRU History of Degrees Awarded (1925 to Present)

Year	Diploma (2 Yr.)	Bachelor's	Master's	Doctorate	Total Degrees
2010-2011		1548	306	51	1905
2009-2010		1547	248	46	1841
2008-2009		1654	270	49	1973
2007-2008		1506	193	51	1750
2006-2007		1532	222	41	1795
2005-2006		1252	216	48	1516
2004-2005		1268	226	31	1525
2003-2004		1265	188	58	1511
2002-2003		1180	153	43	1376
2001-2002		1156	168	45	1369
2000-2001		1046	135	49	1230
1999-2000		1062	183		1245
1998-1999		1145	197		1342
1997-1998		1095	161		1256
1996-1997		1153	213		1366
1995-1996		1148	212		1360
1994-1995		1198	191		1389
1993-1994		1240	137		1377
1992-1993		1269	168		1437
1991-1992		1168	206		1374
1990-1991		1062	157		1219
1989-1990		1079	135		1214
1988-1989		1068	124		1192
1987-1988		1083	99		1182
1986-1987		1095	115		1210
1985-1986		872	113		985
1984-1985		933	110		1043
1983-1984		862	99		961
1982-1983		862	126		988
1981-1982		931	135		1066
1980-1981		947	108		1055
1979-1980		1025	149		1174
1978-1979		907	136		1043
1977-1978		1019	142		1161
1976-1977		1057	158		1215

SRU History of Degrees Awarded (1925 to Present)

Year	Diploma (2 Yr.)	Bachelor's	Master's	Doctorate	Total Degrees
1975-1976		1079	209		1288
1974-1975		1227	241		1468
1973-1974		1235	190		1425
1972-1973		1106	184		1290
1971-1972		981	183		1164
1970-1971		1012	136		1148
1969-1970		877	124		1001
1968-1969		831	71		902
1967-1968		636	85		721
1966-1967		514	53		567
1965-1966		434	18		452
1964-1965		410	3		413
1963-1964		353	1		354
1962-1963		312			312
1961-1962		332			332
1960-1961		271			271
1959-1960		208			208
1958-1959		219			219
1957-1958		214			214
1956-1957		177			177
1955-1956		172			172
1954-1955		154			154
1953-1954		184			184
1952-1953		187			187
1951-1952		185			185
1950-1951		196			196
1949-1950		222			222
1948-1949		169			169
1947-1948		113			113
1946-1947		86			86
1945-1946		63			63
1944-1945		65			65
1943-1944		102			102
1942-1943		144			144
1941-1942		134			134

SRU History of Degrees Awarded (1925 to Present)

Year	Diploma (2 Yr.)	Bachelor's	Master's	Doctorate	Total Degrees
1940-1941		129			129
1939-1940		71			71
1938-1939		120			120
1937-1938		98			98
1936-1937		114			114
1935-1936		97			97
1934-1935	128	125			253
1933-1934	185	132			317
1932-1933	160	91			251
1931-1932	198	82			280
1930-1931	195	70			265
1929-1930	245	67			312
1928-1929	212	30			242
1927-1928	263	17			280
1926-1927	262	9			271
1925-1926*	167				167

*Data on degrees awarded priort to 1925 currently not available

Note: Degrees awarded data;1981-92 through 1984-85 sources
   Snyder Amendment Report (Feb. 1987 & Feb. 1991 eds.)

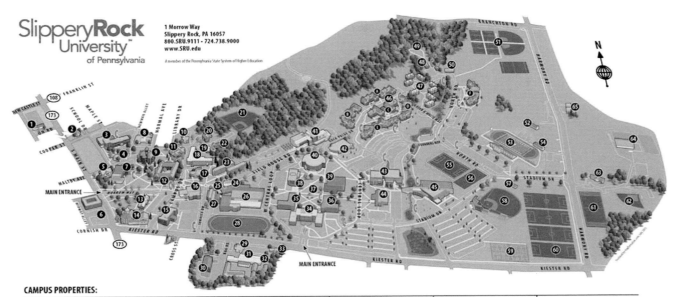

Slippery Rock University of Pennsylvania

1 Morrow Way
Slippery Rock, PA 16057
800.SRU.9111 · 724.738.9000
www.SRU.edu

A member of the Pennsylvania State System of Higher Education

CAMPUS PROPERTIES:

1. Extended Learning Center
2. Counseling and Development Training Facility
3. McKay Education Building
4. Hickory Corner Schoolhouse
5. Drs. Paul and Carolyn Carruth Rizza Hall
6. Kraus Hall Parking
7. Miller Auditorium
8. Rock Catholic Center
9. Old Main
10. Robert A. Lowry Center
11. Maltby Center (Financial Aid, Martha Gault Art Gallery)
12. North Hall Welcome Center (Admissions, Residence Hall*)
13. Russell Wright Alumni House / Conference Center

14. Pearl K. Stoner Instructional Complex (East/West Gym)
15. Strain Behavioral Science Building
16. Weisenfluh Dining Center
17. Art Building
18. Rhoads Hall* (McLachlan Student Health Center and Student Counseling Center)
19. Art Metals Building
20. President's Residence
21. Wally Rose Field
22. Art Sculpture Building
23. Patterson Hall
24. Jack Dinger Special Education Building
25. Special Education Annex
26. Morrow Field House

27. Art Ceramics Building / Heating Plant
28. Old Thompson Field
29. University Police / Parking Office
30. Maintenance Center
31. Printing Services
32. Central Receiving / Stores Building 1
33. Art Fibers Building
34. Advanced Technology and Science Hall
35. Spotts World Culture Building
36. Eisenberg Classroom Building
37. Student Government Association Gazebo
38. School of Physical Therapy Building
39. Bailey Library
40. Vincent Science Center
41. Student Center

42. Boozel Dining Hall
43. University Union (SGA Bookstore)
44. Swope Music Hall
45. Robert N. Aebersold Student Recreation Center
46. Residential Suites*
  A. Building A*
  B. Building B*
  C. Robert J. Watson Hall*
  D. Building D*
  E. Building E*
  F. Building F*
47. R.O.C.K. Apartments
48. Ski Lodge
49. Knierim Leadership Institute, Reach Program

50. Leadership Development Center
51. James P. McFarland Recreational Sports Complex
52. Gail L. Rose Lodge
53. Mihalik-Thompson Stadium Complex
  · DiSpirito Field
  · Lennox Track
  · Jerry Bejbl Weight Training Facility
54. Field Hockey and Lacrosse Center
55. Jim Egli Soccer Field
56. Blaise S. Scarnati Marching Band Field
57. SRU Alumni Pavilion
58. Jack Critchfield Park
59. Tennis Courts
60. Patricia Zimmerman Field Hockey Field

61. Athletic/Intramural Practice Field
62. Softball Field
63. Women's Soccer/Softball Facility
64. Storm Harbor Equestrian Center
65. Robert A. Macoskey Center for Sustainable Systems Education and Research

* Residence Hall

C Emergency Phone

NOTES

[1] Reverend George Bowden, ed., *Souvenir History of Slippery Rock, Pennsylvania*, (Butler, Pennsylvania: Ziegler Printing Company, 1925)

[2] *Ibid.*, The five hundred acre tract of land located near Wolf Creek, purchased by the Coopers, remained in the family until 1920 when it was purchased as a summer home by Mr. Carroll Miller and his wife, Mrs. Emma Guffey Miller. Emma Guffey Miller donated a forty-two acre parcel of the farm, which included the Sugar Maple Grove and the Kuskuski Indian camp on the banks of Wolf Creek, to Slippery Rock State College in 1961.

[3] Pi Gamma Mu Fraternity, *Thru Fifty Years of Normal School and Teachers College*, (Slippery Rock, Pennsylvania, 1939), p. 5

[4] *Ibid.*

[5] *Ibid.*

[6] *Ibid.*

[7] *Ibid.*

[8] C. Hale Sipe, *History of Butler County, Pennsylvania*, Vol. I, (Topeka-Indianapolis: Historical Publishing Company, 1927), p. 644

[9] Robert C. Brown, ed., *History of Butler County, Pennsylvania*, (R.C. Brown & Co., 1895), p. 628

[10] *Ibid.*

[11] *Ibid.*

[12] C. Hale Sipe, *History of Butler County, Pennsylvania*, Vol. I, (Topeka-Indianapolis: Historical Publishing Company, 1927), p. 644

[13] Robert C. Brown, ed., *History of Butler County, Pennsylvania*, (R.C. Brown & Co., 1895), p. 628

[14] *Ibid.*

[15] C. Hale Sipe, *History of Butler County, Pennsylvania*, Vol. I, (Topeka-Indianapolis: Historical Publishing Company, 1927), p. 644

[16] Robert C. Brown, ed., *History of Butler County, Pennsylvania*, (R.C. Brown & Co., 1895), p. 628.

[17] *Ibid.*

[18] *Ibid.*, p. 629

[19] *Ibid.*, p. 629

[20] Pi Gamma Mu Fraternity, *Thru Fifty Years of Normal School and Teachers College*, (Slippery Rock, Pa.: 1939), p. 7.

[21] Robert C. Brown, ed., *History of Butler County, Pennsylvania*, (R.C. Brown & Co., 1895), p. 629.

[22] Rev. George S. Bowden, ed., *Souvenir History of Slippery Rock, Pa.*, (Butler, Pa.: The Ziegler Printing Company, Inc., 1925), p. 33.

[23] *Minutes*, Board of Trustees, Slippery Rock State College, March 9, 1888.

[24] *Ibid.*

[25] *Ibid.*

[26] *Ibid.*, March 16, 1888.

[27] *Ibid.*

[28] *Ibid.*, March 19, 1888.

[29] *Ibid.*

[30] *Ibid.*, March 23, 1888.

[31] *Ibid.*, April 3, 1888.

[32] *Ibid.*, May 7, 1888.

[33] *Ibid.*, May 12, 1888. Shortly after awarding the building contract to Joseph F. Gorely, the Trustees awarded the water well contract to the Watson Company of Butler, Pennsylvania (*Minutes*, May 18, 1888). Some time later, W. H. Tanker of West Sunbury, Pennsylvania, received the carpentry contract while McGinn of Pittsburgh, Pennsylvania received the steam heating contract. (*History of Butler County*, p. 629). Wages for labor outside the contract were established by the Trustees to be $1.25 cash per day. (*Minutes*, May 18, 1888).

[34] Pi Gamma Mu Fraternity, *Thru Fifty Years of Normal School and Teachers College*, (Slippery Rock, Pa.: 1939), p. 8-9.

[35] *Minutes*, Board of Trustees, Slippery Rock State College, May 3, 1888.

[36] Rev. George S. Bowden, ed., *Souvenir History of Slippery Rock, Pa.*, (Butler, Pa.: The Ziegler Printing Company, Inc., 1925), p. 34.

[37] *Minutes*, Board of Trustees, Slippery Rock State College, May 18, 1888.

[38] Rev. George S. Bowden, ed., *Souvenir History of Slippery Rock, Pa.*, (Butler, Pa.: The Ziegler Printing Company, Inc., 1925), p. 34.

[39] *Ibid.*

[40] *Minutes*, Board of Trustees, Slippery Rock State College, November 30, 1888.

[41] Rev. George S. Bowden, ed., *Souvenir History of Slippery Rock, Pa.*, (Butler, Pa.: The Ziegler Printing Company, Inc., 1925), p. 33.

[42] Pi Gamma Mu Fraternity, *Thru Fifty Years of Normal School and Teachers College*, (Slippery Rock, Pa.: 1939), p. 9.

[43] Robert C. Brown, ed., *History of Butler County, Pennsylvania*, (R.C. Brown & Co., 1895), p. 628.

[44] Rev. George S. Bowden, ed., *Souvenir History of Slippery Rock, Pa.*, (Butler, Pa.: The Ziegler Printing Company, Inc., 1925), p. 34.

[45] Rev. George S. Bowden, ed., *Souvenir History of Slippery Rock, Pa.*, (Butler, Pa.: The Ziegler Printing Company, Inc., 1925), p. 34.

[46] *Ibid.*

[47] *Ibid.*, p. 35.

[48] It is interesting to note that W. H. Wilson, the Board's Treasurer and stockholders' thirteenth representative, was not officially listed as one of the twelve Trustees. *History of Butler County, Pennsylvania*, p. 630.

[49] *Ibid.*

[50] Pi Gamma Mu Fraternity, *Thru Fifty Years of Normal School and Teachers College*, (Slippery Rock, Pa.: 1939), pp. 27 and 28. Today, Dr. Morrow is remembered by those who stroll along Morrow Way, a shaded lane with a cul-de-sac adjacent to North Hall.

[51] *Slippery Rock State Normal School Catalog*, 1889 (Slippery Rock, Pennsylvania), no pagination.

[52] *Ibid.*

[53] *Ibid.*

[54] *Ibid.*

[55] *Ibid.*

[56] *Ibid.*

[57] *Ibid.*

[58] *Ibid.*

[59] *Ibid.*

[60] Pi Gamma Mu Fraternity, *Thru Fifty Years of Normal School and Teachers College*, (Slippery Rock, Pa.: 1939), p. 27.

[61] *Slippery Rock State Normal School Catalog*, Vol. I., 1889-93.

[62] *Slippery Rock State College Catalog*, 1889-90, p. 17. Of the 294 students in attendance, 189 were women and 105 were men. Eleven Pennsylvania counties and two other states were represented. One hundred sixty students were from Butler county. *Ibid.*, pp. 9-17.

[63] *Slippery Rock State Normal School Catalog*, 1894-94, p. 27.

[64] *Ibid.*

[65] *Ibid.*

[66] *Ibid.*

[67] *Ibid.*

[68] *Ibid.*

[69] *Ibid.*

[70] Pi Gamma Mu Fraternity, *Thru Fifty Years of Normal School and Teachers College*, (Slippery Rock, Pa.: 1939), p. 14.

[71] *Ibid.*

[72] *Ibid.*

[73] Robert C. Brown, ed., *History of Butler County, Pennsylvania*, (R.C. Brown & Co., 1895), p. 630.

[74] Pi Gamma Mu Fraternity, *Thru Fifty Years of Normal School and Teachers College*, (Slippery Rock, Pa.: 1939), p. 14.

[75] *Ibid.*

[76] *Ibid.*, p. 15.

[77] *Ibid.*

[78] *Ibid.*, p. 10.

[79] *Ibid.*

[80] *Ibid.*

[81] *Slippery Rock State Normal School Catalog*, 1890-91, pp. 34-35.

[82] *Ibid.*, p. 26.

[83] *Ibid.*, p. 24.

[84] *Ibid.*, p. 23-24.

[85] *Ibid.*, p. 23.

[86] *Ibid.*

[87] *Slippery Rock State Normal School Catalog*, 1890-91, p. 32.

[88] *Slippery Rock State Normal School Catalog*, 1890-91, p. 20.

[89] *Slippery Rock State Normal School Catalog, 1890-91*, p. 30.

[90] *Ibid.*

[91] *Ibid.*, p. 48

[92] *Slippery Rock State Normal School Catalog*, 1890-91, p. 29.

[93] *Butler Eagle*, (Butler, Pennsylvania: Eagle Printery), May 16, 1895.

[94] *Ibid.*

[95] *Ibid.*

[96] Pi Gamma Mu Fraternity, *Thru Fifty Years of Normal School and Teachers College*, (Slippery Rock, Pa.: 1939), p. 15.

[97] *Ibid.*

[98] *Butler Eagle*, (Butler, Pa.: Eagle Printery), July 2, 1896.

[99] Pi Gamma Mu Fraternity, *Thru Fifty Years of Normal School and Teachers College*, (Slippery Rock, Pa.: 1939), p. 16.

[100] *Ibid.*

[101] *Ibid.*

[102] Howard Headland, *interview*, February 20 and 21, 1977.

[103] Pi Gamma Mu Fraternity, *Thru Fifty Years of Normal School and Teachers College*, (Slippery Rock, Pa.: 1939), p. 16.

[104] Howard Headland, *interview*, February 20 and 21, 1977.

[105] Pi Gamma Mu Fraternity, *Thru Fifty Years of Normal School and Teachers College*, (Slippery Rock, Pa.: 1939), p. 16.

[106] *Ibid.*, p. 17.

[107] *Slippery Rock State Normal School Catalog*, 1893-94, pp. 11-29.

[108] *Ibid.*

[109] *Ibid.*, pp. 33-34.

[110] *Ibid.*

[111] *Ibid.*

[112] *Ibid.*

[113] *Ibid.*

[114] *Ibid.*, p. 39.

[115] *Ibid.*, pp. 39-40.

[116] *Slippery Rock State Normal School Catalog*, 1895-96, pp. 43-44.

[117] *Slippery Rock State Normal School Catalog*, 1898-99, p. 43.

[118] *Slippery Rock State Normal School Catalog*, 1900-01, p. 33.

[119] *Ibid.*

[120] *Ibid.*, pp. 33-35.

[121] *Ibid.*, p. 38.

[122] *Ibid.*

[123] *Slippery Rock State Normal School Catalog*, 1904-05, pp. 41-58.

[124] *Ibid.*, p. 62. Although the sport of basketball originated at Slippery Rock State Normal School prior to the turn of the century, the records are very sketchy. Football, however, saw its first "intercollegiate" game in 1900. Slippery Rock State Normal School defeated Westminster College, 11-0. (*The Rock*, 1975 Slippery Rock State College Football Brochure, John Carpenter, ed.).

[125] Pi Gamma Mu Fraternity, *Thru Fifty Years of Normal School and Teachers College*, (Slippery Rock, Pa.: 1939), p. 17

[126] *Ibid.*

[127] *Slippery Rock State Normal School Catalog.* 1910-11, p. 69.

[128] *Slippery Rock State Normal School Catalog*, 1903-04, p. 36.

[129] *Slippery Rock State Normal School Catalog*, 1904-05, pp. 67-68.

[130] *The Slippery Rock State Historian*, Vol. I, No. 1, Fall, 1969, (Slippery Rock, Pa.) p. 1.

[131] Class of 1917 of Slippery Rock State Normal School, Fiftieth Year Reunion Booklet, 1967, p. 2.

[132] *Slippery Rock State Normal School Catalog*, 1910-11, p. 39.

[133] *Ibid*, pp. 39-42.

[134] *Ibid.*

[135] *Ibid.*, p. 39.

[136] *Ibid.*, pp. 45-46.

[137] *Ibid.*, p. 46.

[138] *Ibid.*

[139] *Ibid.*, p. 43.

[140] *Ibid.*, p. 39.

[141] *Slippery Rock State Normal School Catalog,*, 1912-13, no pagination.

[142] *Slippery Rock State Normal School Catalog*, 1913-14, pp. 34-38.

[143] *Butler Eagle*, (Butler, Pa.: Eagle Printery), February 21, 1916, p. 2.

[144] *Ibid.*

[145] *Ibid.*, February 19, 1916, p. 1.

[146] H. Adams, E.E. Abrams, J.A. Aiken, A.G. Black, Miss M.C. Bard, Miss Alice Bard, Mrs. J.E. Bard, J.S. Bingham, F.P. Bingham, Thomas Bingham, Miss M.C. Bingham, Mrs. J.S. Bingham, J.B. Buchanan, John W. Brown, O.K. Bingham, Mrs. H.E. Bard, Hugh Bard, J.H. Christley, C.I. Christley, Miss Mary Christley, A.W. Christley, John B. Campbell, Joseph L. Cooper, A.I. Cooper, George W. Cooper, Salina Cooper, Hattie Cooper, Frank Cooper, Clara Cooper, J.M. Covert, E.M. Cowan, Mrs. Jane Coulter, Mrs. Mary Covert, A.W. Davidson, Dr. Thomas Duff, Fred Doerr, L.M. Double, H.M. Gill, H.P. Griffith, W.R. Hockenberry, Jacob Hilgar, Mrs. Margie Hobaugh, W.M. Humphrey, C.R. Humphrey, C.P. Hawks, John Kelly, L.D. Kiester, J.S. Kiester, John C. Kerr, Jane Kauffman, Evaline Kauffman, George A. Lingerfelter, Thomas Logan, James P. McQuistion, C.C. McCarnes, Julia McCarnes, William McLaughlin, Henry McConnell, W.J. Morrison, A.E. Maltby, S.G. Morrison, John Morrison, J. Frank Miller, Mrs. J. Frank Miller, C.H. Mayberry, Mary E. Mayberry, Harriet Maltby, Mrs. R.J. Offut, Anna E. Pearson, Norman D. Patterson, Lewis C. Patterson, James R. Patterson, Effie Pearson, Benjamin Pearson, Jr., W.S. Ramsey, Jr., Robert Ralston, G.S. Rodgers, Thomas M. Rhoades, C.E. Reineke, J.C. Ricketts, C. Sanderson, P.M. Sowash, J.R. Showalter, J.E. Stoops, H.R. Smith, Mrs. H.R. Smith, B.P. Stillwagon, W. Uber, Mary A. Vincent, John N. Watson, Dane E. Walters, the Rev. S. Williams, J.S. Wilson, David Wilson, Caroline Wilson, R.A. Wilson, Margaret Wilson, Mrs. Roy A. Watson, Ray P. Wilson, A.L. Wilson, Earl Watson and Grover Watson, *Ibid.*, February 21, 1916, p. 2

[147] *Ibid.*

[148] Pi Gamma Mu Fraternity, *Thru Fifty Years of Normal School and Teachers College*, (Slippery Rock, Pa.: 1939), p. 32.

[149] *Ibid.*, pp. 30-31

[150] C. Hale Sipe, *History of Butler County, Pennsylvania*, Vol. I, (Topeka-Indianapolis: Historical Publishing Company, 1927), p. 646.

[151] Pi Gamma Mu Fraternity, *Thru Fifty Years of Normal School and Teachers College*, (Slippery Rock, Pa.: 1939), p. 33

[152] C. Hale Sipe, *History of Butler County, Pennsylvania*, Fol. I, (Topeka-Indianapolis: Historical Publishing Company, 1927), p. 647.

[153] Pi Gamma Mu Fraternity, *Thru Fifty Years of Normal School and Teachers College*, (Slippery Rock, Pa.: 1939), p. 35.

[154] *Ibid.*, p. 34.

[155] *Ibid.*, pp. 34-35.

[156] *Slippery Rock State Normal School Catalog*, Vol. 31, #1, June, 1919, p. 72.

[157] *Ibid.*

[158] Pi Gamma Mu Fraternity, *Thru Fifty Years of Normal School and Teachers College*, (Slippery Rock, Pa.: 1939), p. 35.

[159] *Slippery Rock State Normal School Catalog*, Vol. 30, #1, June, 1918, pp. 45-46.

[160] *Ibid.*, pp. 48-49.

[161] *Ibid.*, p. 48.

[162] *Ibid.*, p. 17.

[163] *Ibid.*

[164] *Ibid.*

[165] *Ibid.*

[166] *Slippery Rock State Normal School Catalog,* Vol. 30, #3, December, 1918, p. 1.

[167] *Slippery Rock State Normal School Catalog*, Vol. 30, #4, March, 1919, p. 8.

[168] *Slippery Rock State Normal School Catalog*, Vol. 31, #1, June, 1919, p. 37.

[169] *Ibid.*, pp. 37-39.

[170] Pi Gamma Mu Fraternity, *Thru Fifty Years of Normal School and Teachers College*, (Slippery Rock, Pa.: 1939), p. 61.

[171] *Slippery Rock State Normal School Catalog*, Vol. 31, #4, March, 1920, p. 7.

[172] *Ibid.*

[173] *Slippery Rock State Normal School Catalog*, Vol. 33, #1, June, 1921, p. 44.

[174] *Ibid.*

[175] *Slippery Rock State Normal School Catalog*, Vol. 31, #4, March, 1920, p. 8.

[176] *Ibid.*, pp. 9-10

[177] *Slippery Rock State Normal School Catalog*, Vol. 32, #1, June, 1920, p. 34.

[178] *Ibid.*

[179] *Ibid.*, pp. 34-35.

[180] *Slippery Rock State Normal School Catalog*, Vol. 34, #4, March, 1923, p. 12.

[181] *Slippery Rock State Normal School Catalog*, Vol. 36, #4, March, 1925, p. 26.

[182] *Ibid.*, pp. 26-27.

[183] *Slippery Rock State Normal School Catalog*, Vol. 38, #4, March, 1927, p. 26.

[184] *Slippery Rock State Normal School Catalog*, Vol. 37, #1, June, 1925, pp. 20-21.

[185] Application appearing in Board of Trustees *Minutes*, Slippery Rock State College, June 1, 1926, p. 20.

[186] *Ibid.*

[187] C. Hale Sipe, *History of Butler County, Pennsylvania*, Vol. I, (Topeka-Indianapolis: Historical Publishing Company, 1927), p. 648.

[188] *Ibid.*

[189] *Slippery Rock State Normal School Catalog*, Vol. 38, #1, June, 1926, p. 28.

[190] *Ibid.*

[191] *Ibid.*, pp. 35-44.

[192] Pi Gamma Mu Fraternity, *Thru Fifty Years of Normal School and Teachers College*, (Slippery Rock, Pa.: 1939), p. 64.

[193] *Ibid.*

[194] *Ibid.*

[195] *Slippery Rock State Normal School Catalog*, Vol. 38, #1, June, 1926, p. 29.

[196] *Ibid.*, p. 24.

[197] *Ibid.*, pp. 24-25.

[198] *Slippery Rock State Teachers College Catalog*, Vol. 44, #1, June, 1932, p. 23.

[199] *Ibid.*, p. 24.

[200] *Ibid.*

[201] *Slippery Rock State Normal School Catalog*, Vol. 31, #1, June, 1919, p. 72.

[202] *Minutes*, Board of Trustees, Slippery Rock State College, January 8, 1924, October 5, 1926 and October 7, 1929.

[203] *Ibid.*

[204] *Minutes*, Board of Trustees, Slippery Rock State College, July 6, 1926.

[205] *Slippery Rock State Teachers College Catalog*, Vol. 45, #1, June, 1933, p. 54.

[206] *Slippery Rock State Normal School Catalog*, Vol. 33, #1, June, 1921, p. 57.

[207] Application appearing in Board of Trustees *Minutes*, Slippery Rock State College, June 1, 1926, p. 20.

[208] *Minutes*, Board of Trustees, Slippery Rock State College, February 11, 1929.

[209] Pi Gamma Mu Fraternity, *Thru Fifty Years of Normal School and Teachers College*, (Slippery Rock, Pa.: 1939), p. 18.

[210] *Ibid.*

[211] *Ibid.*

[212] *Minutes*, Board of Trustees, Slippery Rock State College, July 14, 1930.

[213] Pi Gamma Mu Fraternity, *Thru Fifty Years of Normal School and Teachers College*, (Slippery Rock, Pa.: 1939), p. 17.

[214] *Ibid.*

[215] *Ibid.*

[216] *Ibid.*

[217] *Ibid.*

[218] *Ibid.*

[219] *Ibid.*

[220] *Minutes*, Board of Trustees, Slippery Rock State College, April 8, 1929.

[221] *Letter* received from Mrs. Catherine McLaine Fuller, Deltona, Florida, March 7, 1977.

[222] *Ibid.*

[223] *Ibid.*

[224] *Ibid.*

[225] *Minutes*, Board of Trustees, Slippery Rock State College, January 13, 1930.

[226] C. Hale Sipe, *History of Butler County, Pennsylvania*, Vol. I, (Topeka-Indianapolis: Historical Publishing Company, 1927), p. 649.

[227] Pi Gamma Mu Fraternity, *Thru Fifty Years of Normal School and Teachers College*, (Slippery Rock, Pa.: 1939), p. 67.

[228] C. Hale Sipe, *History of Butler County, Pennsylvania*, Vol. I, (Topeka-Indianapolis: Historical Publishing Company, 1927), p. 649.

[229] Pi Gamma Mu Fraternity, *Thru Fifty Years of Normal School and Teachers College*, (Slippery Rock, Pa.: 1939), p. 649.

[230] C. Hale Sipe, *History of Butler County, Pennsylvania*, Vol. I, (Topeka-Indianapolis: Historical Publishing Company, 1927), p. 649.

[231] *Ibid.*

[232] *Ibid.*

[233] *Slippery Rock State Normal School Catalog*, Vol. 31, #1, June, 1919, p. 57.

[234] C. Hale Sipe, *History of Butler County, Pennsylvania*, vol. I, (Topeka-Indianapolis: Historical Publishing Company, 1927), p. 650.

[235] *Ibid.*

[236] *Ibid.*

[237] *Slippery Rock State Normal School Catalog*, Vol. 30, #1, June, 1918, p. 57.

[238] C. Hale Sipe, *History of Butler County, Pennsylvania*, Vol. I, (Topeka-Indianapolis: Historical Publishing Company, 1927), p. 650.

[239] *Slippery Rock State Normal School Catalog*, Vol. 32, #1, June, 1920, p. 53.

[240] Pi Gamma Mu Fraternity, *Thru Fifty Years of Normal School and Teachers College*, (Slippery Rock, Pa.: 1939), p. 67.

[241] C. Hale Sipe, *History of Butler County, Pennsylvania*, Vol. I, (Topeka-Indianapolis: Historical Publishing Company, 1927), p. 650.

[242] *Ibid.*

[243] *Ibid.*

[244] *Ibid.*

[245] *The Slippery Rocket*, Vol. 5, #12, April 27, 1923, (student newspaper), Slippery Rock State Normal School, Slippery Rock, Pa.

[246] Pi Gamma Mu Fraternity, *Thru Fifty Years of Normal School and Teachers College*, (Slippery Rock, Pa.: 1939), p. 66.

[247] *Ibid.*

[248] *Ibid.*

[249] *Minutes*, Board of Trustees, Slippery Rock State College, June 1, 1934.

[250] *Minutes*, Board of Trustees, Slippery Rock State College, July 9, 1934.

[251] *Ibid*, July 16, 1934.

[252] Pi Gamma Mu Fraternity, *Thru Fifty Years of Normal School and Teachers College*, (Slippery Rock, Pa.: 1939), p. 36.

[253] *Ibid.*

[254] *Ibid.*

[255] *Ibid.*

[256] *Ibid.*

[257] In 1916, Dr. Miller married Ethel Boyard of McKeesport, whom he had met at Allegheny College and was a member of his class. Dr. and Mrs. Miller had five children: Charles Junior, Robert, Martha, William and Stephen. Charles Junior and Robert attended the junior-senior high school division of the Laboratory School during their father's presidency. *Ibid.*, p. 37.

[258] *Minutes*, Board of Trustees, Slippery Rock State College, November 12, 1936.

[259] *Ibid.*

[260] *Ibid.*

[261] *Ibid.*

[262] *Ibid.*

[263] *Ibid.*

[264] *Ibid.*, February 12, 1937.

[265] *Ibid.*

[266] *Ibid.*

[267] *Ibid.*

[268] *Ibid.*

[269] *Ibid.*, May 27, 1937.

[270] *The Slippery Rock Signal*, (Slippery Rock, Pa.), August 11, 1937.

[271] *Ibid.*

[272] *Ibid.*

[273] *Ibid.*

[274] *Minutes*, Board of Trustees, Slippery Rock State College, August 11, 1937.

[275] *Ibid.*, September 29, 1937.

[276] *Butler Eagle*, (Butler, Pennsylvania: Eagle Printery), October 16, 1937.

[277] *Ibid.*

[278] *Ibid.*

[279] *Ibid.*

[280] *Ibid.*, October 18, 1937.

[281] *Ibid.*

[282] *Ibid.*

[283] *Ibid.*

[284] *Minutes*, Board of Trustees, Slippery Rock State College, November 17, 1937.

[285] *The Rocket*, student newspaper, Slippery Rock State Teachers College, (Slippery Rock, Pa.), November 24, 1937.

[286] *Minutes*, Board of Trustees, Slippery Rock State College, January 19, 1938.

[287] Ground Breaking Ceremony Booklet, Wednesday afternoon, 2:00 p.m., January 19, 1938.

[288] *The Slippery Rock Signal*, (Slippery Rock, Pa.), January 20, 1938.

[289] Ground Breaking Ceremony Booklet, Wednesday afternoon, 2:00 p.m., January 19, 1938.

[290] *The Rocket*, student newspaper, Slippery Rock State Teachers College, (Slippery Rock, Pa.), January 19, 1938.

[291] General Contract: Weinstein Co., Akron, Ohio $349, 940 – Heating: Graham Pipe Co., Pittsburgh $39,000; Plumbing: W. M. Clark, New Castle $18,000; Electric: Hale Electric, Pittsburgh $26,313; Total $433,586; *Minutes*, Board of Trustees, Slippery Rock State College, January 19, 1938.

[292] General Contract: Spence Bros., Saginaw, Mi. $347,990; Plumbing: W.M. Clark, New Castle $22,000; Heating & Vent.: Graham Pipe Co., Pittsburgh $63,330; Electric Wiring: Marvin Electric Co., New Castle $89,226; Total $521,549; *The Rocket*, student newspaper, Slippery Rock State Teachers College, (Slippery Rock, Pa.), March 22, 1938.

[293] *Ibid.*

[294] *Minutes*, Board of Trustees, Slippery Rock State College, October 22, 1938.

[295] *The Rocket*, student newspaper, Slippery Rock State Teachers College, (Slippery Rock, Pa.), October 21, 1938.

[296] *The Rocket*, student newspaper, Slippery Rock State Teachers College, (Slippery Rock, Pa.), February 18, 1939.

[297] Pi Gamma Mu Fraternity, *Thru Fifty Years of Normal School and Teachers College*, (Slippery Rock, Pa.: 1939), pp. 21-25.

[298] *Ibid.*, p. 19.

[299] *Ibid.*, p. 19-25.

[300] Pi Gamma Mu Fraternity, *Thru Fifty Years of Normal School and Teachers College*, (Slippery Rock, Pa.: 1939), p. 37.

[301] *Slippery Rock State Teachers College Catalog*, Vol. 45, #1, June, 1933, pp. 24-25.

[302] *Slippery Rock State Teachers College Catalog*, Vol. 49, #1, March, 1937, pp. 23-24.

[303] *Ibid.*, p. 24.

[304] *Ibid.*, p. 26-29.

[305] *Ibid.*, p. 26-29.

[306] *Ibid.*

[307] *Ibid.*, p. 31.

[308] *Ibid.*

[309] *Ibid.*, pp. 26-35

[310] *Ibid.*, p. 29

[311] *Slippery Rock State Teachers College Catalog*, Vol. 50, #1, March, 1938, p. 21.

[312] *Ibid.*, p. 22-24.

[313] *Ibid.*, p. 25.

[314] *Ibid.*

[315] *Slippery Rock State Teachers College Catalog*, Vol. 51, #2, March, 1939, p. 27.

[316] *Ibid.*

[317] *Slippery Rock State Teachers College Catalog*, Vol. 38, #1, March, 1936, p. 62.

[318] *Slippery Rock State Teachers College Catalog*, Vol. 50, #2, March, 1938, p. 90.

[319] *Ibid.*

[320] *Ibid., p. 97.*

[321] *Ibid.*, p. 96

[322] *Slippery Rock State Teachers College Catalog*, Vol. 46, #1, June, 1934, pp. 43-45.

[323] I*bid.*

[324] *Ibid.*, p. 3.

[325] *Ibid.*, p. 39.

[326] *Ibid.*

[327] *Ibid.*

[328] *Ibid.*

[329] *Ibid.*, p. 40.

[330] *Slippery Rock State Teachers College Catalog*, Vol. 51, #2, March, 1939, p. 80.

[331] *Ibid.*

[332] *Ibid.*, p. 81.

[333] *Ibid.*, p. 82.

[334] *Minutes*, Board of Trustees, Slippery Rock State College, May 4, 1937.

[335] *Slippery Rock State Teachers College Catalog*, Vol. 51, #2, March 1939, pp. 83-84.

[336] *Ibid.*, p. 84.

[337] *Ibid.*

[338] *Ibid.*, pp. 84-88.

[339] *Ibid.*, pp. 88-89.

[340] *Minutes*, Board of Trustees, Slippery Rock State College, February 17, 1939.

[341] *Ibid.*

[342] *Ibid.*, January 8, 1940.

[343] *Ibid.*, January 17, 1940.

[344] *Ibid.*, June 7, 1940.

[345] *The Rocket*, student newspaper, Slippery Rock State Teachers College, (Slippery Rock, Pa.), April 10, 1940.

[346] *Minutes*, Board of Trustees, Slippery Rock State College, June 7, 1940.

[347] *Ibid.*

[348] *Ibid.*, July 8, 1940.

[349] *Ibid.*, July 23, 1940.

[350] *The Rocket*, student newspaper, Slippery Rock State Teachers College, (Slippery Rock, Pa.), September 25, 1940, p. 1.

[351] *Ibid.*

[352] *Ibid.*

[353] *Ibid.*

[354] *Ibid.*

[355] *Ibid.*

[356] *Ibid.*

[357] *Butler Eagle*, (Butler, Pennsylvania: Eagle Printery), November 4, 1941, p. 1.

[358] *The Rocket*, student newspaper, Slippery Rock State Teachers College, (Slippery Rock, Pa.), September 25, 1940, p. 1

[359] *The Rocket*, Slippery Rock State Teachers College, (Slippery Rock, Pa.), September 25, 1940.

[360] *Slippery Rock State Teachers College Catalog*, Vol. 53, #3, March, 9141, p. 106.

[361] *Slippery Rock State Teachers College Catalog*, Vol. 54, #4, April, 1942, p. 108.

[362] *Minutes*, Board of Trustees, Slippery Rock State College, February 26, 1941.

[363] *Slippery Rock State Teachers College Catalog*, Vol. 52, #4, June, 1940, pp. 37-38.

[364] *Saxigena*, Slippery Rock State College Yearbook, (Slippery Rock, Pennsylvania: Archives), 1941, no pagination.

[365] *Minutes*, Board of Trustees, Slippery Rock State College, February 26, 1941.

[366] *Butler Eagle*, (Butler, Pennsylvania: Eagle Printery), November 4, 1941, p. 1.

[367] *Ibid.*

[368] *Ibid.*

[369] *Ibid.*

[370] *Ibid.*

[371] *Minutes*, Board of Trustees, Slippery Rock State College, November 15, 1941.

[372] *Ibid.*

[373] *Ibid.*

[374] *Ibid.*

[375] *Ibid.*, December 6, 1941.

[376] *Ibid.*

[377] *Ibid.*

[378] *Ibid.*

[379] *Ibid.*, January 17, 1942.

[380] *Butler Eagle*, (Butler, Pennsylvania: Eagle Printery), January 17, 1942, p. 1.

[381] *Ibid.*

[382] *Saxigena*, Slippery Rock State College Yearbook, (Slippery Rock, Pennsylvania: Archives), 1943, no pagination.

[383] *Butler Eagle*, (Butler, Pennsylvania: Eagle Printery), January 17, 1942, p. 1.

[384] *Ibid.*

[385] *Ibid.*

[386] *Saxigena*, Slippery Rock State College Yearbook, (Slippery Rock, Pennsylvania: Archives), 1945, no pagination.

[387] *Ibid.*, 1943, no pagination.

[388] *Minutes*, Board of Trustees, Slipper Rock State College, October 20, 1945.

[389] *Ibid.*

[390] *The Rocket*, Slippery Rock State Teachers College, (Slippery Rock, Pa.), March 3, 1943, p. 1.

[391] *Ibid.*

[392] *Ibid.*, March 24, 1943, p. 1.

[393] *Ibid.*, April 14, 1943, p. 1.

[394] *Ibid.*

[395] *Ibid.*

[396] *Ibid.*, March 24, 1943, p. 1.

[397] *Ibid.*, April 14, 1943.

[398] *Ibid.*, March 24, 1943.

[399] *Ibid.*

[400] *Slippery Rock State Teachers College Catalog*, Vol. 55, #4, April, 1943, p. 64.

[401] *Slippery Rock State Teachers College Catalog*, Vol. 56, #3, April, 1944, p. 42.

[402] *The Rocket*, Slippery Rock State Teachers College, (Slippery Rock, Pa.), November 17, 1943.

[403] *Ibid.*

[404] *Ibid.*

[405] *Minutes*, Board of Trustees, Slippery Rock State College, March 18, 1944.

[406] *Ibid.*

[407] *Ibid.*

[408] *Ibid.*, July 1, 1944.

[409] *Ibid.*, October 20, 1945.

[410] *Ibid.*, July 1, 1944.

[411] *Ibid.*

[412] *Ibid.*

[413] *Ibid.*, June 16, 1945.

[414] *Ibid.*

[415] *Ibid.*, September 15, 1945.

[416] *Ibid.*, October 16, 1945.

[417] *Ibid., September 15, 1945.*

[418] *The Rocket*, Slippery Rock State Teachers College, (Slippery Rock, Pa.), October 16, 1945.

[419] *Ibid.*, October 16, 1945.

[420] *Minutes*, Board of Trustees, Slippery Rock State College, October 20, 1945.

[421] *Ibid.*, October 21, 1944.

[422] *The Rocket*, Slippery Rock State Teachers College, (Slippery Rock, Pa.), January 21, 1942.

[423] *Minutes*, Board of Trustees, Slippery Rock State College, September 15, 1945.

[424] *Ibid.*

[425] *Ibid.*

[426] *Ibid.*, March 16, 1946.

[427] *Ibid.*, October 20, 1945.

[428] *Ibid.*, November 24, 1945.

[429] *Butler Eagle*, (Butler, Pennsylvania: Eagle Printery), November 24, 1945, p. 1.

[430] *Ibid.*

[431] *Ibid.*

[432] *Ibid.*

[433] *Ibid.*

[434] *Ibid.*

[435] Dr. Houk, his wife, Ruth and two children, Beatty Jeanne and Glenn LeLand, arrived at Slippery Rock early in 1946. *Ibid.*

[436] *Undergraduate Enrollment Summary*, Office of the Registrar, Slippery Rock State Teachers College

[437] *Ibid.*

[438] *Ibid.*

[439] *Minutes*, Board of Trustees, Slippery Rock State College, January 19, 1946.

[440] *Slippery Rock State Teachers College Catalog*, Vol. 59, #1, March, 1947, p. 39.

[441] *Minutes*, Board of Trustees, Slippery Rock State College, July 15, 1950.

442 *Undergraduate Enrollment Summary*, Office of the Registrar, Slippery Rock State Teachers College, p. 1.
443 *Slippery Rock State Teachers College Catalog*, Vol. 64, January, 1954, p. 31.
444 *Minutes*, Board of Trustees, Slippery Rock State College, June 26, 1948.
445 *Slippery Rock State Teachers College Catalog*, Vol. 61, #1, January, 1950, p. 56.
446 *Slippery Rock State Teachers College Catalog*, Vol. 62, #1, January, 1951, p. 45.
447 *Ibid.*
448 *Ibid.*
449 *Ibid.*
450 *Ibid.*
451 *Ibid.*, p. 49.
452 *Ibid.*, p. 49.
453 *Ibid.*, p. 59.
454 *Slippery Rock State Teachers College Catalog*, vol. 63, #1, January, 1952, pp. 61-63.
455 *Ibid.*, pp. 62-63.
456 *Minutes*, Board of Trustees, Slippery Rock State College, January 25, 1949.
457 *Ibid.*, July 10, 1954.
458 *Ibid.*
459 *Undergraduate Enrollment Summary*, Office of the Registrar, Slippery Rock State Teachers College, p. 1.
460 *Ibid.*
461 *Ibid.*
462 *Minutes*, Board of Trustees, Sippery Rock State College, May 14, 1955.
463 *Ibid.*, March 12, 1955.
464 *Ibid.*, May 14, 1955.
465 *Ibid.*, May 5, 1956.
466 *Ibid.*
467 *Ibid.*, June 9, 1956.
468 *Ibid.*, July 16, 1956.
469 *Saxigena*, (Slippery Rock, Pennsylvania: Archives), 1960.
470 *Ibid.*
471 *Ibid.*
472 *Minutes*, Board of Trustees, Slippery Rock State College, July 16, 1956.
473 *Ibid.*, August 25, 1956.
474 *Ibid.*, March 21, 1957.
475 *Ibid.*
476 *Ibid.*
477 *Ibid.*
478 *Ibid.*
479 *Ibid.*
480 *Ibid.*
481 *Ibid.*, November 14, 1957.
482 *Ibid.*
483 *Ibid.*
484 *Ibid.*
485 *Ibid.*
486 *Ibid.*
487 *Ibid.*
488 *Ibid.*
489 *Butler Eagle*, (Butler, Pennsylvania: Eagle Printery), October 11, 1958, p. 2.
490 *Ibid.*
491 *Minutes*, Board of Trustees, Slippery Rock State College, December 6, 1956.
492 *Ibid.*
493 *Ibid.*
494 *Ibid.*, June 6, 1957
495 *Ibid.*, December 9, 1958.
496 *Ibid.*
497 *Ibid.*, March 25, 1959.
498 *Ibid.*
499 *Slippery Rock State College Catalog*, Vol. 67, #1, January, 1961, p. 15
500 *Minutes*, Board of Trustees, Slippery Rock State College, November 8, 1958.
501 *Ibid.*
502 *Ibid.*
503 *Ibid.*
504 *Ibid.*
505 *Slippery Rock State College Catalog*, Vol. 67, #1, January, 1961, p. 15.
506 *Ibid.*, p. 53.
507 *Ibid.*
508 *Ibid.*

509 *Slippery Rock State College Catalog*, Vol. 68, #3, 1964-65, p. 6.

510 *Ibid.*, pp. 4 and 14.

511 *Ibid.*, pp. 15-27.

512 *Ibid.*

513 *Slippery Rock State College Catalog*, Vol. 67, #2, August, 1962, p. 1.

514 *Ibid.*, p. 9

515 *Undergraduate Enrollment Summary*, Office of the Registrar, Slippery Rock State College, p. 1.

516 *Minutes*, Board of Trustees, Slippery Rock State College, November 6, 1963.

517 *Slippery Rock State College Catalog*, Vol. 69, #1, April, 1965, p. 75.

518 *Ibid.*

519 *Slippery Rock State College Catalog*, Vol. 68, #1, January, 1963, p. 71.

520 *Ibid.*, p. 72.

521 *Slippery Rock State College Catalog*, Vol. 69, #1, April, 1965, p. 95.

522 *Minutes*, Board of Trustees, Slippery Rock State College, August 17, 1960.

523 *Undergraduate Enrollment Summary*, Office of the Registrar, Slippery Rock State College, p. 1.

524 *Minutes*, Board of Trustees, Slippery Rock State College, November 9, 1960.

525 *Slippery Rock State Teachers College Catalog,* Vol. 65, January, 1957, p. 15.

526 *Ibid.*, p. 36

527 *Ibid.*

528 *Ibid.*, pp. 33-34.

529 *Slippery Rock State Teachers College Catalog*, Vol. 65, #1, January, 1957, pp. 46-47.

530 *Minutes*, Board of Trustees, Slippery Rock State College, June 10, 1959.

531 *Ibid.*

532 *Ibid.*

533 *Ibid.*

534 *Ibid.*

535 *Ibid.*, March 9, 1960

536 *Ibid.*, November 9, 1960

537 *Ibid.*

538 *Ibid.*

539 *Ibid.*

540 *Ibid.*

541 *Ibid.*, June 7, 1961.

542 *Ibid.*

543 *Ibid.*

544 *Ibid.*

545 *Ibid.*, November 1, 1961.

546 *Ibid.*

547 *Ibid.*, March 7, 1962.

548 *Ibid.*, March 6, 1963.

549 *Ibid.*, November 7, 1962.

550 *Ibid.*

551 *Ibid.*, March 25, 1959.

552 *Ibid.*

553 *Ibid.*

554 *Ibid.*

555 *Ibid.*, June 10, 1959.

556 *Ibid.*, April 25, 1960.

557 *Ibid.*, March 6, 1963.

558 *Ibid.*

559 *Ibid.*

560 *Ibid.*

561 *Ibid.*

562 *Ibid.*

563 *Ibid.*, June 19, 1963.

564 *Ibid.*, July 24, 1963.

565 *Slippery Rock State College Catalog*, Vol. 68, #1, January, 1963, pp. 16-17.

566 *Ibid.*

567 *Ibid.*, p. 40.

568 *Ibid.*

569 *Ibid.*, pp. 31-40.

570 *Ibid.*

571 *Minutes*, Board of Trustees, Slippery Rock State College, March 6, 1963.

572 *Ibid.*, November 6, 1963.

573 *Ibid.*

574 *Ibid.*, March 4, 1964.

575 *Ibid.*

[576] *Ibid.*, March 26, 1965.

[577] *Inauguration of Robert S. Carter*, April 13, 1966, Morrow Field House, Slippery Rock State College.

[578] *Minutes*, Board of Trustees, Slippery Rock State College, October 4, 1967.

[579] *Ibid.*, Mach 2, 1966.

[580] *Ibid.*

[581] *Ibid.*

[582] *Undergraduate Enrollment Summary*, Office of the Registrar, Slippery Rock State College, p. 2.

[583] *Ibid.*

[584] *Minutes*, Board of Trustees, Slippery Rock State College, June 16, 1965.

[585] *Ibid.*, March 2, 1966.

[586] *Ibid.*, June 1, 1966.

[587] *Inauguration of Robert S. Carter*, April 13, 1966, Morrow Field House, Slippery Rock State College.

[588] *Ibid.*

[589] *Butler Eagle*, (Butler, Pennsylvania: Eagle Printery), May 3, 1966, pp. 1-2.

[590] *Ibid.*

[591] *Ibid.*

[592] *Ibid.*

[593] *Ibid.*

[594] *Ibid.*, May 4, 1966, pp. 1-2.

[595] *Ibid.*

[596] *Ibid.*

[597] *Ibid.*

[598] *Ibid.*, May 5, 1966, p. 1.

[599] *Ibid.*

[600] *Ibid.*

[601] *Ibid.*

[602] *Slippery Rock State College Catalog*, Vol. 69, #1, April, 1965, p. 82.

[603] *Slippery Rock State College Catalog*, Vol. 69, #3, 1966, pp. 16-17.

[604] *Minutes*, Board of Trustees, Slippery Rock State College, November 10, 1965.

[605] *Slippery Rock State College Catalog*, Vol. 70, #1, June, 1966, pp. 67-73.

[606] *Ibid.*, p. 58.

[607] *Slippery Rock State College Catalog*, Vol. 71, #1, June, 1967, p. 86.

[608] *Ibid.*

[609] *Slippery Rock State College Catalog*, Vol. 71, #4, 1967, pp. 21-25.

[610] *Slippery Rock State Teachers College Catalog*, Vol. 63, January, 1952; pp. 61-63.

[611] *Minutes*, Board of Trustees, Slippery Rock State College, October 4, 1967.

[612] *Ibid.*, August 16, 1966.

[613] *Ibid.*

[614] *Ibid.*

[615] *Ibid.*, January 31, 1968.

[616] *Ibid.*

[617] *Ibid.*

[618] *Ibid.*, March 6, 1968.

[619] *Ibid.*

[620] *Ibid.*, March 9, 1968.

[621] *Ibid.*

[622] *Ibid.*, March 16, 1968.

[623] *Personal Interview with Robert A. Lowry*, January 17, 1978.

[624] *Minutes*, Board of Trustees, Slippery Rock State College, March 16, 1968.

[625] *Ibid.*, May 9, 1968.

[626] *Ibid.*

[627] *Ibid.*

[628] *Ibid.*

[629] *Ibid.*, June 10, 1968.

[630] *Ibid.*

[631] *Ibid.*, September, 1968.

[632] *Ibid.*, May 1, 1968.

[633] *Ibid.*, June 3, 1968.

[634] *Ibid.*, September 4, 1968.

[635] *Ibid.*, June 3, 1968.

[636] *Inauguration of Albert A. Watrel*, May 3, 1967, Morrow Field House, Slippery Rock State College, no pagination.

[637] *Ibid.*

[638] *Ibid.*

[639] *Ibid.*

[640] *Minutes*, Board of Trustees, Slippery Rock State College, September 4, 1968.

[641] *Ibid.*

[642] *Ibid.*, November 7, 1968.

[643] *Ibid.*, February 25, 1969.
[644] *Ibid.*, September 10, 1969.
[645] *Ibid.*
[646] *Undergraduate Enrollment Summary*, Office of the Registrar, Slippery Rock State College, p. 2.
[647] *Minutes*, Board of Trustees, Slippery Rock State College, December 4, 1968.
[648] *Ibid.*
[649] *Ibid.*, June 4, 1969.
[650] *Ibid.*, February 25, 1969.
[651] *Ibid.*
[652] *Ibid.*, December 4, 1969.
[653] *Ibid.*
[654] *Ibid.*, December 19, 1969.
[655] *Ibid.*
[656] *Ibid.*
[657] *Ibid.*, December 4, 1969.
[658] *Ibid.*
[659] *Ibid.*
[660] *Ibid.*
[661] *Ibid.*
[662] *Ibid.*, September 2, 1970.
[663] *Ibid.*
[664] *Ibid.*, March 25, 1970.
[665] *Ibid.*
[666] *Ibid.*
[667] *Ibid.*
[668] *Ibid.*, September 2, 1970.
[669] *Ibid.*
[670] *Ibid.*
[671] *Ibid.*, March 3, 1970.
[672] *Ibid.*, March 25, 1970.
[673] *Ibid.*, November 30, 1970.
[674] *Ibid.*
[675] *Ibid.*, June 9, 1971.
[676] *Ibid.*, Mach 3, 1971.
[677] *Ibid.*
[678] *Ibid.*
[679] *Ibid.*, March 25, 1970.
[680] *Ibid.*
[681] *Ibid.*
[682] *Ibid.*, June 9, 1971.
[683] *Ibid.*, December 1, 1971.
[684] *Ibid.*, March 25, 1970.
[685] *Ibid.*
[686] *Ibid.*
[687] *Ibid.*, September 2, 1970.
[688] *Ibid.*
[689] *Ibid.*
[690] *Ibid.*
[691] *Ibid.*
[692] *Ibid.*, June 9, 1971.
[693] *Ibid.*
[694] *Ibid.*
[695] *Ibid.*, September 2, 1970.
[696] *Ibid.*
[697] *Ibid.*, June 9, 1971.
[698] *Ibid.*, June 1, 1972.
[699] *Undergraduate Enrollment Summary*, Office of the Registrar, Slippery Rock State College, p. 2.
[700] *Minutes*, Board of Trustees, Slippery Rock State College, September 1, 1971.
[701] *Ibid.*, September 7, 1972.
[702] *Ibid.*
[703] *Ibid.*
[704] *Ibid.*, March 3, 1971.
[705] *Ibid.*
[706] *Ibid.*
[707] *Ibid.*
[708] *Ibid.*
[709] Telephone conversation with Mr. Daniel Dorritie, Director of Contract Implementation for APSCUF, Harrisburg, Pa., January 22, 1979.

[710] *Ibid.*

[711] *Ibid.*

[712] *Minutes*, Board of Trustees, Slippery Rock State College, December 21, 1972.

[713] *Ibid.*

[714] *Ibid.*, March 15, 1973.

[715] *Ibid.*

[716] *Ibid.*

[717] *Ibid.*, December 21, 1973.

[718] *Ibid.*, June 13, 1974.

[719] *Privacy Rights of Parents and Students*, Federal Register, Vol. 40, No. 3, Monday, January 6, 1975, Department of Health, Education and Welfare, Office of the Secretary, Washington, D.C., pp. 1208-1216.

[720] *Minutes*, Board of Trustees, Slippery Rock State College, September 7, 1972.

[721] *Ibid.*, June 21, 1973.

[722] *Ibid.*, September 28, 1973.

[723] *Ibid.*

[724] *Ibid.*, December 5, 1974.

[725] *Ibid.*

[726] *Ibid.*, March 18, 1976.

[727] *Bachelor of Science in Nursing Program Proposal*, April, 1974, Diana F. Ney, Slippery Rock State College.

[728] *Minutes*, Board of Trustees, Slippery Rock State College, March 21, 1974.

[729] *Bachelor of Science in Nursing Program Proposal*, April, 1974, Diana F. Ney, Slippery Rock State college

[730] *Undergraduate Enrollment Summary*, Office of the Registrar, Slippery Rock State College, p. 2.

[731] *Ibid.*

[732] *Slippery Rock State College Catalog*, 1974-76, p. 20.

[733] *Ibid.*, p. 28.

[734] *Minutes*, Board of Trustees, Slippery Rock State College, September 10, 1969.

[735] *Slippery Rock State College Catalog*, 1974-76, p. 29.

[736] *Ibid.*, p. 30.

[737] *Ibid.*

[738] *Slippery Rock State College Catalog*, 1974-76, p. 30.

[739] *Minutes*, Board of Trustees, Slippery Rock State College, December 11, 1975.

[740] *Ibid.*

[741] *Ibid.*, June 15, 1972.

[742] *Ibid.*, March 15, 1973.

[743] *Ibid.*, September 29, 1973.

[744] *Ibid.*, December 5, 1974.

[745] *Ibid.*

[746] *Ibid.*, September 12, 1974.

[747] *Ibid.*

[748] *Ibid.*, December 5, 1974.

[749] *Ibid.*

[750] *Ibid.*, September 11, 1975.

[751] *Ibid.*

[752] *Slippery Rock State College Catalog*, 1974-76, p. 21.

[753] *Minutes*, Board of Trustees, Slippery Rock State College, September 11, 1975.

[754] *Ibid.*

[755] *Butler Eagle*, (Butler, Pennsylvania: Eagle Printery), June 12, 1976, p. 1.

[756] *Ibid.*

[757] *Ibid.*, p. 2.

[758] *Ibid.*, pp. 1-2.

[759] *Ibid.*, p. 1.

[760] *Philadelphia Inquirer*, (Philadelphia, Pennsylvania), October 3, 1976, p. 1-B.

[761] *Ibid.*

[762] *Ibid.*

[763] SHAPP FIRES SRSC PRES. WATREL, *Butler Eagle*, June 12, 1976; SHAPP AXES PRESIDENT OF COLLEGE, *Pittsburgh Post Gazette*, June 12, 1976; DR. ROBERTS NAMED ACTING PREXY AT SRSC, *Slippery Rock Area News Shopper*, June 23, 1976; A COLLEGE FOR SCANDAL, *Philadelphia Inquirer*, October 3, 1976.

[764] *The Rocket*, student newspaper, Slippery Rock State College, (Slippery Rock, Pa.), June 17, 1976, p. 1.

[765] *Ibid.*

[766] *Minutes*, Board of Trustees, Slippery Rock State College, June 13, 1976.

[767] *Ibid.*

[768] *Ibid.*

[769] *Ibid.*

[770] *Ibid.*

[771] *Ibid.*

[772] *Ibid.*

[773] *Ibid.*

774 *Ibid.*, May 9, 1977.

775 *News Release*, Slippery Rock State College, "Interim President Named," August 30, 1977, no pagination.

776 *Ibid.*

777 *Ibid.*

778 *Ibid.*

779 *Minutes*, Board of Trustees, Slippery Rock State College, February 6, 1978.

780 *Ibid.*

781 *Ibid.*, September 16, 1976, December 2, 1976, March 17, 1977.

782 *Ibid.*, September 16, 1976, December 2, 1976.

783 *Ibid.*, September 16, 1976.

784 *Ibid.*, September 21, 1977.

785 *Ibid.*

786 *Ibid.*, March 17, 1977.

787 *Ibid.*, September 14, 1978.

788 *Undergraduate Enrollment Summary*, Office of the Registrar, Slippery Rock State College, p. 2.

789 John Carpenter, *interview*, February 5, 1979.

790 *Ibid.*

791 *Ibid.*

792 *Minutes*, Board of Trustees, Slippery Rock State College, March 15, 1978.

793 Dr. Cook, Treasurer of Allegheny County, Pennsylvania, and Professor of Political Science at the University of Pittsburgh; Dr. Guisti, Director of the Beaver Campus of the Pennsylvania State University; Dr. Krause, Provost and Vice President for Academic Affairs at the University of South Dakota; Dr. Reinhard, Assistant to the President at Florida A. and M. University; Dr. Roberts, Vice President for Academic Affairs at Slippery Rock State College; and Dr. Sandefur, Dean of the College of Education at Western Kentucky University. *Minutes*, Board of Trustees, Slippery Rock State College, February 8, 1979.

794 *Minutes*, Board of Trustees, Slippery Rock State College, February 8, 1979.

795 *Ibid.*, February 22, 1979.

796 *Ibid.*

797 *The Rocket*, Slippery Rock State College, (Slippery Rock, Pa.), February 16, 1979.

798 *Ibid.*, March 2, 1979.

799 *Ibid.*

800 *Ibid.*, March 9, 1979.

801 *Ibid.*

802 *Ibid.*, April 20, 1979.

803 *Ibid.*, May 18, 1979.

804 *Minutes*, Board of Trustees, Slippery Rock State College, May 8, 1979.

805 *Butler Eagle*, (Butler, Pennsylvania: Eagle Printery), July 17, 1981.

806 *Minutes*, Board of Trustees, Slippery Rock State College, June 5, 1979.

807 *Ibid.*, June 5, 1979.

808 *Ibid.*, September 11, 1979.

809 *Ibid.*

810 *Ibid.*, November 28, 1979.

811 *Ibid.*, September 11, 1979.

812 *Ibid.*

813 *Ibid.*, June 5, 1979.

814 *Ibid.*, April 11, 1980.

815 *Ibid.*

816 *Ibid.*

817 *Ibid.*, November 28, 1979.

818 *Ibid.*, April 11, 1980.

819 *Ibid.*

820 *Butler Eagle*, (Butler, Pennsylvania: Eagle Printery), May 5, 1980.

821 *Ibid.*, May 5, 1980.

822 *Ibid.*

823 *Minutes*, Board of Trustees, Slippery Rock State College, September 11, 1979.

824 *Ibid.*, June 28, 1980.

825 *Ibid.*, December 5, 1980.

826 *Ibid.*, June 28, 1980.

827 *Ibid.*, September 5, 1980.

828 *Ibid.*, December 5, 1980.

829 *Ibid.*

830 *Ibid.*

831 *Ibid.*, June 28, 1980.

832 *Ibid.*, June 4, 1981.

833 *Ibid.*, March 13, 1981.

834 *Ibid.*, June 4, 1981.

835 *Butler Eagle*, (Butler, Pennsylvania: Eagle Printery), July 17, 1981.

836 *Minutes*, Board of Trustees, Slippery Rock State College, June 4, 1981.

837 *Ibid.*, March 13, 1981.

838 *Ibid.*, September 17, 1981.

839 *Ibid.*, March 13, 1981.

840 *Ibid.*, September 17, 1981.

841 *Ibid.*

842 *Ibid.*

843 *Butler Eagle*, (Butler, Pennsylvania: Eagle Printery), July 17, 1981.

844 *Minutes*, Board of Trustees, Slippery Rock State College, September 17, 1981.

845 *Ibid.*

846 *Butler Eagle*, (Butler, Pennsylvania: Eagle Printery), July 17, 1981.

847 *Minutes,* Board of Trustees, Slippery Rock State College, December 4, 1981.

848 *Ibid.*

849 *Ibid.*

850 *Ibid.*

851 *Ibid.*

852 *Ibid.*, June 24, 1982.

853 *Ibid.*, March 5, 1982.

854 *Ibid.*, June 24, 1982.

855 *Ibid.*, March 5, 1982.

856 *Ibid.*, June 24, 1982.

857 *Ibid.*

858 *Ibid.*, December 3, 1982.

859 *Ibid.*, September 22, 1982.

860 *Ibid.*, December 3, 1982.

861 *Ibid.*, June 9, 1983.

862 *Ibid.*

863 *Ibid.*, June 30, 1983.

864 *Ibid.*

865 *Ibid.*, June 24, 1982.

866 *Minutes*, Council of Trustees, Slippery Rock University, December 2, 1983.

867 *Minutes*, Board of Trustees, Slippery Rock State College, June 30, 1983.

868 *Ibid.*, March 10, 1983.

869 *Minutes*, Council of Trustees, Slippery Rock University, September 12, 1983.

870 *Ibid.*, March 23, 1984.

871 *Ibid.*, December 2, 1983.

872 *Ibid.*

873 *Minutes*, Board of Trustees, Slippery Rock State College, December 3, 1982.

874 *Minutes*, Council of Trustees, Slippery Rock University, September 12, 1983.

875 *Minutes*, Board of Trustees, Slippery Rock State College, September 22, 1982.

876 *Ibid.*, December 3, 1982.

877 *Ibid.*, December 4, 1981.

878 *Minutes*, Council of Trustees, Slippery Rock University, December 2, 1983.

879 *Ibid.*, September 12, 1983.

880 *Ibid.*, March 23, 1984.

881 *Minutes*, Board of Trustees, Slippery Rock State College, June 9, 1983.

882 *Ibid.*, December 4, 1981.

883 *Minutes*, Council of Trustees, Slippery Rock University, December 2, 1983.

884 *Minutes*, Board of Trustees, Slippery Rock State College, December 4, 1981.

885 *Ibid.*, June 9, 1983.

886 *Ibid.*

887 *Ibid.*, September 22, 1982.

888 *Ibid.*, December 3, 1982.

889 *Ibid.*, June 9, 1983.

890 *Ibid.*, June 24, 1982.

891 *Minutes*, Council of Trustees, Slippery Rock University, September 12, 1983.

892 *Ibid.*

893 *Ibid.*, May 12, 1984.

894 *Ibid.*, June 8, 1984.

895 *Ibid.*

896 *Ibid.*, September 10, 1984.

897 *Ibid.*

898 *Ibid.*

899 *Ibid.*

900 *Ibid.*

901 *Ibid.*

902 *Ibid.*, October 4, 1984.

903 *Ibid.*

904 *Ibid.*

905 *Ibid.*
906 *Ibid.*
907 *Ibid.*
908 *Ibid.*
909 *Ibid.*
910 *Ibid.*
911 *Ibid.*
912 *Ibid.*
913 *Ibid.*
914 *Ibid.*
915 *Ibid.*
916 *Greensheet*, March 22, 1985, Vol. 7, No. 28, SRU.
917 *Ibid.*
918 *Ibid.*
919 *Minutes*, Council of Trustees, Slippery Rock University, February 11, 1985.
920 *Ibid.*
921 *Ibid.*
922 *Ibid.*
923 *Ibid.*, April 1, 1985.
924 *Ibid.*, June 3, 1985.
925 *Ibid.*
926 *Ibid.*, December 6, 1985.
927 *Ibid.*, September 19, 1985.
928 *Ibid.*
929 *Ibid.*
930 *Ibid.*
931 *Ibid.*
932 *Ibid.*
933 *Ibid.*
934 *Ibid.*
935 *Ibid.*, March 14, 1986.
936 *Ibid.*
937 *Ibid.*, December 6, 1985.
938 *Ibid.*
939 *Ibid.*, September 19, 1985.
940 *Ibid.*
941 *Ibid.*
942 *Ibid.*, December 6, 1985.
943 *Ibid.*
944 *Ibid.*
945 *Ibid.*, June 6, 1986.
946 *Ibid.*
947 *Ibid.*, December 6, 1985.
948 *Ibid.*, March 14, 1986.
949 *Ibid.*, June 16, 1986.
950 *Ibid.*
951 *Ibid.*
952 *Ibid.*, September 19, 1986.
953 *Ibid.*
954 *Ibid.*, June 16, 1986.
955 *Ibid.*
956 *Ibid.*, March 23, 1987.
957 *Ibid.*
958 *Ibid.*, December 5, 1986.
959 *Ibid.*
960 *Ibid.*, June 16, 1986.
961 *Ibid.*, March 23, 1987.
962 *Ibid.*
963 *Ibid.*
964 *Ibid.*, September 19, 1986.
965 *Ibid.*
966 *Ibid.*
967 *Ibid.*, March 23, 1987.
968 *Ibid.*
969 *Ibid.*, December 5, 1986.
970 *Ibid.*
971 *Ibid.*

[972] *Ibid.*, September 19, 1986.

[973] *Ibid.*, December 5, 1986.

[974] *Ibid.*, June 8, 1987.

[975] *Ibid.*

[976] *Ibid.*

[977] *Ibid.*, December 19, 1987.

[978] *Ibid.*

[979] *Ibid.*

[980] *Ibid.*, September 22, 1987.

[981] *Ibid.*

[982] *Ibid.*, June 8, 1987.

[983] *Ibid.*

[984] *Ibid.*, September 22, 1987.

[985] *Ibid.*

[986] *Ibid.*

[987] *Ibid.*

[988] *Ibid.*

[989] *Ibid.*

[990] *Ibid.*

[991] *Ibid.*

[992] *Ibid.*, December 19, 1987.

[993] *Ibid.*

[994] *Ibid.*, September 22, 1987.

[995] *Ibid.*, March 10, 1988.

[996] *Ibid.*

[997] *Ibid.*, December 4, 1987.

[998] *Ibid.*

[999] *Ibid.*, March 10, 1988.

[1000] *Ibid.*, June 8, 1987.

[1001] *Ibid.*, September 22, 1987.

[1002] *Ibid.*, March 30, 1990.

[1003] *Ibid.*

[1004] *Ibid.*, September 22, 1987.

[1005] *Ibid.*

[1006] *Ibid.*

[1007] *Ibid.*

[1008] *Ibid.*, December 19, 1987.

[1009] *Ibid.*

[1010] *Ibid.*, March 10, 1988.

[1011] *Ibid.*, December 19, 1987.

[1012] *Ibid.*, March 10, 1988.

[1013] *Ibid.*

[1014] *Ibid.*, June 13, 1988.

[1015] *Ibid.*

[1016] *Ibid.*, September 19, 1988.

[1017] *Ibid.*

[1018] *Ibid.*, June 13, 1988.

[1019] *Ibid.*, March 10, 1988.

[1020] *Ibid.*, September 19, 1988.

[1021] *Ibid.*

[1022] *Ibid.*, March 13, 1989.

[1023] *Ibid.*, December 12, 1988.

[1024] *Ibid.*, September 18, 1989.

[1025] *Ibid.*, December 12, 1988.

[1026] *Ibid.*

[1027] *Ibid.*

[1028] *Ibid.*

[1029] *Ibid.*, March 13, 1989.

[1030] *Ibid.*

[1031] *Ibid.*

[1032] Rev. George S. Bowden, ed., *Souvenir History of Slippery Rock, Pa.,* (Butler, Pa: The Ziegler Printing Company, Inc., 1925), p. 34.

[1033] *Minutes*, Council of Trustees, Slippery Rock University, March 13, 1989.

[1034] *Ibid.*, June 12, 1989.

[1035] *Ibid.*, June 13, 1988.

[1036] *Ibid.*, September 19, 1988.

[1037] *Ibid.*

[1038] *Ibid.*, December 12, 1988.

[1039] *Ibid.*
[1040] *Ibid.*, March 13, 1989.
[1041] *Ibid.*, December 11, 1989.
[1042] *Ibid.*, September 19, 1988.
[1043] *Ibid.*, March 13, 1989.
[1044] *Ibid.*
[1045] *Ibid.*, September 19, 1988.
[1046] *Ibid.*, September 18, 1989.
[1047] *Ibid.*, December 11, 1989.
[1048] *Ibid.*, March 13, 1989.
[1049] *Ibid.*
[1050] *Ibid.*, June 12, 1989.
[1051] *Ibid.*, March 13, 1989.
[1052] *Ibid.*
[1053] *Ibid.*, September 19, 1988.
[1054] *Ibid.*, March 13, 1989.
[1055] *Ibid.*
[1056] *Ibid.*, September 19, 1988.
[1057] *Ibid.*, March 13, 1989.
[1058] *Ibid.*, June 12, 1989.
[1059] *Ibid.*
[1060] *Ibid.*, September 19, 1988.
[1061] *Ibid.*, June 12, 1989.
[1062] *Ibid.* June 12, 1989.
[1063] *Ibid.*, September 18, 1989.
[1064] *Ibid.*, December 12, 1988.
[1065] *Ibid.*
[1066] *Ibid.*, March 13, 1989.
[1067] *Ibid.*
[1068] *Ibid.*, December 12, 1988.
[1069] *Ibid.*, September 18, 1989.
[1070] *Ibid.*, March 30, 1990.
[1071] *Ibid.*, September 14, 1992.
[1072] *Ibid.*, March 30, 1990.
[1073] *Ibid.*
[1074] *Ibid.*, December 9, 1991.
[1075] *Ibid.*, June 11, 1990.
[1076] *Ibid.*, March 11, 1991.
[1077] *Ibid.*
[1078] *Ibid.*, September 17, 1990.
[1079] *Ibid.*, May 31, 1991.
[1080] *Ibid.*, March 11, 1991.
[1081] *Ibid.*
[1082] *Ibid.*, September 17, 1990.
[1083] *Ibid.*
[1084] *Ibid.*
[1085] *Ibid.*
[1086] *Ibid.*, March 25, 1994.
[1087] *Pittsburgh Post Gazette*, March 18, 1991, p. 19.
[1088] *Minutes*, Council of Trustees, Slippery Rock University, March 11, 1991.
[1089] *Ibid.*, May 31, 1991.
[1090] *Ibid.*, December 9, 1991.
[1091] *Ibid.*, June 13, 1994.
[1092] *Ibid.*, March 11, 1991.
[1093] *Ibid.*, May 31, 1991.
[1094] *Ibid.*, March 11, 1991.
[1095] *Ibid.*, May 31, 1991.
[1096] *Ibid.*, June 11, 1990.
[1097] *Ibid.*
[1098] *Ibid.*, May 31, 1991.
[1099] *Ibid.*, September 23, 1991.
[1100] *Ibid.*, December 9, 1991.
[1101] *Ibid.*
[1102] *Ibid.*
[1103] *Ibid.*, March 16, 1992.
[1104] *Ibid.*, December 9, 1991.
[1105] *Ibid.*, September 14, 1992.

[1106] *Ibid.*
[1107] *Ibid.*, June 10, 1996.
[1108] *Ibid.*
[1109] *Ibid.*
[1110] *Ibid.*, September 17, 1990.
[1111] *Ibid.*
[1112] *Ibid.*
[1113] *Ibid.*, December 9, 1991.
[1114] *Ibid.*, March 16, 1992.
[1115] *Ibid.*, June 19, 1992.
[1116] *Ibid.*
[1117] *Ibid.*
[1118] *Ibid.*
[1119] *Ibid.*, June 14, 1993.
[1120] *Ibid.*
[1121] *Ibid.*, March 25, 1994.
[1122] *Ibid.*, June 14, 1993.
[1123] *Ibid.*
[1124] *Ibid.*, September 23, 1991.
[1125] *Ibid.*, March 30, 1990.
[1126] *Ibid.*, December 3, 1993.
[1127] *Ibid.*, June 14, 1993.
[1128] *Ibid.*
[1129] *Ibid.*, December 4, 1992.
[1130] *Ibid.*, September 10, 1993.
[1131] *Ibid.*
[1132] *Ibid.*, December 9, 1991.
[1133] *Ibid.*, June 14, 1993.
[1134] *Ibid.*
[1135] *Ibid.*, March 12, 1993.
[1136] *Ibid.*, September 10, 1993.
[1137] *Ibid.*
[1138] *Ibid.*, June 16, 1995.
[1139] *Ibid.*, December 3, 1993.
[1140] *Ibid.*
[1141] *Ibid.*, September 10, 1993.
[1142] *Ibid.*
[1143] *Ibid.*, June 13, 1994.
[1144] *Ibid.*
[1145] *Ibid.*
[1146] *Ibid.*, December 3, 1993.
[1147] *Ibid.*, September 16, 1994.
[1148] *Ibid.*
[1149] *Ibid.*, June 13, 1994.
[1150] *Ibid.*
[1151] *Ibid.*, September 10, 1993.
[1152] *Ibid.*, December 3, 1993.
[1153] *Ibid.*, March 25, 1994.
[1154] *Ibid.*
[1155] *Ibid.*
[1156] *Ibid.*
[1157] *Ibid.*, June 13, 1994.
[1158] *Ibid.*, March 25, 1994.
[1159] *Ibid.*
[1160] *Ibid.*, December 3, 1993.
[1161] *Ibid.*, March 25, 1994.
[1162] *Ibid.*, September 16, 1994.
[1163] *Ibid.*, December 2, 1994.
[1164] *Ibid.*
[1165] *Ibid.*
[1166] *Ibid.*, June 13, 1994.
[1167] *Ibid.*, March 15, 1996.
[1168] *Ibid.*, March 10, 1995.
[1169] *Ibid.*, March 3, 1997.
[1170] *Ibid.*, September 18, 1995.
[1171] *Ibid.*, June 16, 1995.
[1172] *Ibid.*, June 10, 1996.

1173 *Ibid.*, December 2, 1994.
1174 *Ibid.*, September 18, 1995.
1175 *Ibid.*, March 25, 1994.
1176 *Ibid.*, September 18, 1995.
1177 *Ibid.*, March 10, 1995.
1178 *Ibid.*, June 16, 1995.
1179 *Ibid.*, December 1, 1995.
1180 *Ibid.*, June 16, 1995.
1181 *Ibid.*, December 1, 1995.
1182 *Ibid.*, June 10, 1996.
1183 *Ibid.*, August 30, 1996.
1184 *Ibid.*, June 16, 1997.
1185 *Ibid.*, August 30, 1996.
1186 *Ibid.*, December 1, 1995.
1187 *Ibid.*, August 30, 1996.
1188 *Ibid.*, June 13, 1994.
1189 *Ibid.*, March 15, 1996.
1190 *Ibid.*, March 3, 1997.
1191 *Ibid.*, December 1, 1995.
1192 *Ibid.*, June 10, 1996.
1193 *Ibid.*, June 16, 1997.
1194 *Ibid.*, August 30, 1996.
1195 *Ibid.*, June 16, 1997.
1196 *Ibid.*, March 30, 1990.
1197 *Ibid.*, September 14, 1992.
1198 *Ibid.*
1199 *Ibid.*, December 2, 1994.
1200 *Ibid.*, June 10, 1996.
1201 *Ibid.*, March 3, 1997.
1202 *Ibid.*, August 30, 1996.
1203 *Ibid.*, March 3, 1997.
1204 *Ibid.*
1205 *Ibid.*, June 13, 1994.
1206 *Ibid.*, March 15, 1996.
1207 *Ibid.*, June 16, 1997.
1208 *Ibid.*, March 3, 1997.
1209 *Ibid.*, June 16, 1997.
1210 *Ibid.*, March 16, 1992.
1211 *Ibid.*, March 10, 1995.
1212 *Ibid.*, August 30, 1996.
1213 *Ibid.*
1214 *Ibid.*
1215 *Ibid.*, June 10, 1996.
1216 *Ibid.*
1217 *Ibid.*
1218 *Ibid.*, December 6, 1996.
1219 *Ibid.*
1220 *Ibid.*, March 3, 1997.
1221 *Ibid.*, June 16, 1997.
1222 *Ibid.*
1223 *Ibid.*, March 3, 1997.
1224 *Ibid.*
1225 *Ibid.*, September 27, 1997.
1226 *Ibid.*, March 20, 1998.
1227 *Ibid.*, December 5, 1997.
1228 *Ibid.*
1229 *Ibid.*
1230 *Ibid.*
1231 *Ibid.*, September 27, 1997.
1232 *Ibid.*
1233 *Ibid.*, March 20, 1998.
1234 *Ibid.*, June 17, 1998.
1235 *Ibid.*, December 5, 1997.
1236 *Ibid.*
1237 *Ibid.*, December 4, 1998.
1238 *Ibid.*, June 17, 1998.
1239 *Ibid.*, December 4, 1998.

[1240] *Ibid.*, June 17, 1998.
[1241] *Ibid.*
[1242] *Ibid.*
[1243] *Ibid.*, December 5, 1997.
[1244] *Ibid.*, June 17, 1998.
[1245] *Ibid.*, December 5, 1997.
[1246] *Ibid.*, June 17, 1998.
[1247] *Ibid.*, September 18, 1998.
[1248] *Ibid.*,
[1249] *Ibid.*,
[1250] *Ibid.*, December 5, 1997.
[1251] *Ibid.*
[1252] *Ibid.*, September 18, 1998.
[1253] *Ibid.*, September 24, 1999.
[1254] *Ibid.*
[1255] *Ibid.*, December 10, 1999.
[1256] *Ibid.*, March 23, 2001.
[1257] *Ibid.*, September 14, 2001.
[1258] *Ibid.*, December 4, 1998.
[1259] *Ibid.*, March 19, 1999.
[1260] *Ibid.*
[1261] *Ibid.*, June 18, 1999.
[1262] *Ibid.*, March 19, 1999.
[1263] *Ibid.*, June 18, 1999.
[1264] *Ibid.*
[1265] *Ibid.*, September 24, 1999.
[1266] *Ibid.*, June 18, 1999.
[1267] *Ibid.*
[1268] *Ibid.*, September 24, 1999.
[1269] *Ibid.*, December 10, 1999.
[1270] *Ibid.*, September 24, 1999.
[1271] *Ibid.*
[1272] *Ibid.*
[1273] *Ibid.*
[1274] *Ibid.*
[1275] *Ibid.*, December 10, 1999.
[1276] *Ibid.*, December 4, 1998.
[1277] *Ibid.*
[1278] *Ibid.*
[1279] *Ibid.*
[1280] *Ibid.*, September 24, 1999.
[1281] *Ibid.*, December 10, 1999.
[1282] *Ibid.*, September 24, 1999.
[1283] *Ibid.*, June 21, 2000.
[1284] *Ibid.*, September 24, 1999.
[1285] *Ibid.*, March 19, 1999.
[1286] *Ibid.*, March 10, 2000.
[1287] *Ibid.*
[1288] *Ibid.*, June 21, 2000.
[1289] *Ibid.*, December 8, 2000.
[1290] *Ibid.*, December 10, 1999.
[1291] *Ibid.*
[1292] *Ibid.*
[1293] *Ibid.*, March 10, 2000.
[1294] *Ibid.*, December 10, 1999.
[1295] *Ibid.*, September 15, 2000.
[1296] *Ibid.*, December 10, 1999.
[1297] *Ibid.*, March 10, 2000.
[1298] *Ibid.*
[1299] *Ibid.*, March 23, 2001.
[1300] *Ibid.*, March 10, 2000.
[1300] *Ibid.*, March 10, 2000.
[1301] *Ibid.*, June 21, 2000.
[1302] *Ibid.*
[1303] *Ibid.*
[1304] *Ibid.*, September 15, 2000.
[1305] *Ibid.*

[1306] *Ibid.*, June 21, 2000.
[1307] *Ibid.*, September 15, 2000.
[1308] *Ibid.*, December 10, 1999.
[1309] *Ibid.*, September 15, 2000.
[1310] *Ibid.*
[1311] *Ibid.*
[1312] *Ibid.*, September 14, 2001.
[1313] *Ibid.*, March 23, 2001.
[1314] *Ibid.*
[1315] *Ibid.*
[1316] *Ibid.*, June 8, 2001.
[1317] *Ibid.*, December 7, 2001.
[1318] *Ibid.*, June 8, 2001.
[1319] *Ibid.*, September 15, 2000.
[1320] *Ibid.*
[1321] *Ibid.*, December 10, 1999.
[1322] *Ibid.*, September 15, 2000.
[1323] *Ibid.*
[1324] *Ibid.*, December 8, 2000.
[1325] *Ibid.*, March 23, 2001.
[1326] *Ibid.*, December 7, 2001.
[1327] *Ibid.*
[1328] *Ibid.*, March 23, 2001.
[1329] *Ibid.*, December 8, 2000.
[1330] *Ibid.*
[1331] *Ibid.*
[1332] *Ibid.*, March 23, 2001.
[1333] *Ibid.*, September 14, 2001.
[1334] *Ibid.*, December 8, 2000.
[1335] *Ibid.*, March 23, 2001.
[1336] *Ibid.*, June 21, 2000.
[1337] *Ibid.*, December 8, 2000.
[1338] *Ibid.*, June 21, 2000.
[1339] *Ibid.*, March 23, 2001.
[1340] *Ibid.*
[1341] *Ibid.*, December 8, 2000.
[1342] *Ibid.*, March 23, 2001.
[1343] *Ibid.*, December 7, 2001.
[1344] *Ibid.*, June 8, 2001.
[1345] *Ibid.*
[1346] *Ibid.*
[1347] *Ibid.*
[1348] *Ibid.*, March 23, 2001.
[1349] *Ibid.*, March 15, 2002.
[1350] *Ibid.*, June 8, 2001.
[1351] *Ibid.*
[1352] *Ibid.*
[1353] *Ibid.*
[1354] *Ibid.*
[1355] *Ibid.*
[1356] *Ibid.*
[1357] *Ibid.*, September 14, 2001.
[1358] *Ibid.*, March 23, 2001.
[1359] *Ibid.*, June 8, 2001.
[1360] *Ibid.*, December 8, 2000.
[1361] *Ibid.*, June 8, 2001.
[1362] *Ibid.*
[1363] *Ibid.*, September 14, 2001.
[1364] *Ibid.*, December 7, 2001.
[1365] *Ibid.*, September 15, 2000.
[1366] *Ibid.*, December 7, 2001.
[1367] *Ibid.*
[1368] *Ibid.*
[1369] *Ibid.*
[1370] *Ibid.*
[1371] *Ibid.*, March 15, 2002.
[1372] *Ibid.*, December 7, 2001.

[1373] *Ibid.*, June 14, 2002.
[1374] *Ibid.*
[1375] *Ibid.*, December 7, 2001.
[1376] *Ibid.*
[1377] *Ibid.*
[1378] *Ibid.*, June 14, 2002.
[1379] *Ibid.*, September 13, 2002.
[1380] *Ibid.*, March 15, 2002.
[1381] *Ibid.*
[1382] *Ibid.*, December 7, 2001.
[1383] *Ibid.*, June 14, 2002.
[1384] *Ibid.*, March 15, 2002.
[1385] *Ibid.*
[1386] *Ibid.*, June 14, 2002.
[1387] *Ibid.*, December 7, 2001.
[1388] *Ibid.*, September 13, 2002.
[1389] *Ibid.*, June 14, 2002.
[1390] *Ibid.*, June 8, 2001.
[1391] *Ibid.*
[1392] *Ibid.*, June 14, 2002.
[1393] *Ibid.*
[1394] *Ibid.*, December 7, 2001.
[1395] *Ibid.*, September 13, 2002.
[1396] *Ibid.*
[1397] *Ibid.*
[1398] *Ibid.*, March 15, 2002.
[1399] *Ibid.*, June 14, 2002.
[1400] *Ibid.*, September 13, 2002.
[1401] *Ibid.*
[1402] *Ibid.*
[1403] *Pittsburgh Post Gazette*, December 10, 2002.
[1404] *Ibid.*
[1405] *Ibid.*
[1406] *Ibid.*
[1407] *Ibid.*, March 14, 2003.
[1408] *Ibid.*
[1409] *Ibid.*
[1410] *Ibid.*
[1411] *Ibid.*
[1412] *Ibid.*
[1413] *Ibid.*
[1414] *Ibid.*
[1415] *Ibid.*
[1416] *Ibid.*, September 12, 2003.
[1417] *Ibid.*, March 14, 2003.
[1418] *Ibid.*
[1419] *Ibid.*, December 5, 2003.
[1420] *Ibid.*, March 14, 2003.
[1421] *Ibid.*
[1422] *Ibid.*, June 13, 2003.
[1423] *Ibid.*
[1424] *Ibid.*, September 12, 2003.
[1425] *Ibid.*, June 13, 2003.
[1426] *Ibid.*
[1427] *Ibid.*, March 11, 2005.
[1428] *Ibid.*, March 14, 2003.
[1429] *Ibid.*, September 12, 2003.
[1430] *Ibid.*
[1431] *Ibid.*
[1432] *Ibid.*
[1433] *Ibid.*, June 13, 2003.
[1434] *Ibid.*, September 12, 2003.
[1435] *Ibid.*
[1436] *Ibid.*
[1437] *Ibid.*, December 5, 2003.
[1438] *Ibid.*
[1439] *Ibid.*

[1440] *Ibid.*
[1441] *Ibid.,* September 12, 2003.
[1442] *Ibid.*
[1443] *Ibid.*
[1444] *Ibid.*, December 5, 2003.
[1445] *Ibid.,* September 12, 2003.
[1446] *Ibid.*, December 5, 2003.
[1447] *Ibid.*
[1448] *Ibid.*
[1449] *Ibid.*, March 19, 2004.
[1450] *Ibid.*, December 5, 2003.
[1451] *Ibid.*, March 19, 2004.
[1452] *Ibid.*
[1453] *Ibid.*, June 11, 2004.
[1454] *Ibid.*, March 19, 2004.
[1455] *Ibid.*, June 11, 2004.
[1456] *Ibid.*
[1457] *Ibid.*, March 19, 2004.
[1458] *Ibid.*, June 11, 2004.
[1459] *Ibid.*, March 19, 2004.
[1460] *Ibid.*, June 11, 2004.
[1461] *Ibid.*
[1462] *Ibid.*, March 11, 2005.
[1463] *Ibid.*, June 11, 2004.
[1464] *Ibid.*, March 19, 2004.
[1465] *Ibid.*, June 11, 2004.
[1466] *Rockpride*, Volume 4, Issue 17, May 11, 2004.
[1467] *Minutes*, Council of Trustees, Slippery Rock University, June 11, 2004.
[1468] *Ibid.*
[1469] *Ibid.*
[1470] *Ibid.*, December 17, 2004.
[1471] *Ibid.*, June 11, 2004.
[1472] *Ibid.*, September 10, 2004.
[1473] *Ibid.*, June 11, 2004.
[1474] *Ibid.*, September 10, 2004.
[1475] *Ibid.*
[1476] *Ibid.*, June 11, 2004.
[1477] *Ibid.*, September 10, 2004.
[1478] *Ibid.*
[1479] *Ibid.*
[1480] *Ibid.*, December 17, 2004.
[1481] *Ibid.,* March 11, 2005.
[1482] *Ibid.*, December 17, 2004.
[1483] *Ibid.*
[1484] *Ibid.*
[1485] *Ibid.*
[1486] *Ibid.*, December 2, 2005.
[1487] *Ibid.*, December 17, 2004.
[1488] *Ibid.*
[1489] *Ibid.*, September 9, 2005.
[1490] *Ibid.*, December 17, 2004.
[1491] *Ibid.,* March 11, 2005.
[1492] *Ibid.*
[1493] *Ibid.*
[1494] *Ibid.*
[1495] *Ibid.*
[1496] *Ibid.*
[1497] *Ibid.*
[1498] *Ibid.*
[1499] *Ibid.*
[1500] *Ibid.*
[1501] *Ibid.*
[1502] *Ibid.*
[1503] *Ibid.*
[1504] *Ibid.*, June 6, 2005.
[1505] *Ibid.*, September 9, 2005.
[1506] *Ibid.*, June 6, 2005.

1507 *Ibid.*, September 9, 2005.
1508 *Ibid.*, June 6, 2005.
1509 *Ibid.*
1510 *Ibid.*
1511 *Ibid.*
1512 *Ibid.*, September 9, 2005.
1513 *Ibid.*
1514 *Ibid.*
1515 *Ibid.*, June 9, 2006.
1516 *Ibid.*, September 9, 2005.
1517 *Ibid.*
1518 *Ibid.*, December 2, 2005.
1519 *Ibid.*
1520 *Ibid.*
1521 *Ibid.*
1522 *Ibid.*, March 24, 2006.
1523 *Ibid.*, December 2, 2005.
1524 *Ibid.*, March 24, 2006.
1525 *Ibid.*
1526 *Ibid.*
1527 *Ibid.*
1528 "2 SRU Sports Return", Kris Miller, *Butler Eagle*, (Butler, Pennsylvania: Eagle Printery), July 30, 2006.
1529 "Comprehensive Settlement Reached in Title IX Lawsuit Against Slippery Rock University," *prnewswire.com*, April 10, 2007.
1530 *Minutes*, Council of Trustees, Slippery Rock University, March 24, 2006.
1531 *Ibid.*
1532 *Ibid.*
1533 *Ibid.*
1534 *Ibid.*
1535 *Ibid.*
1536 *Ibid.*
1537 *Ibid.*
1538 *Ibid.*
1539 *Ibid.*, June 9, 2006.
1540 *Ibid.*
1541 *Ibid.*
1542 *Ibid.*
1543 *Ibid.*, September 8, 2006.
1544 *Ibid.*
1545 *Ibid.*
1546 *Ibid.*
1547 *Ibid.*
1548 *Ibid.*
1549 *Ibid.*
1550 *Ibid.*
1551 *Ibid.*, December 15, 2006.
1552 *Ibid.*
1553 *Ibid.*
1554 *Ibid.*
1555 *Ibid.*
1556 *Ibid.*
1557 *Ibid.*
1558 *Ibid.*
1559 *Ibid.*
1560 *Ibid.*
1561 *Ibid.*
1562 *Ibid.*
1563 *Ibid.*
1564 *Ibid.*
1565 *Ibid.*
1566 *Ibid.*, March 9, 2007.
1567 *Ibid.*
1568 *Ibid.*
1569 *Ibid.*
1570 *Ibid.*
1571 *Ibid.*
1572 *Ibid.*
1573 *Ibid.*

[1574] *Ibid.*
[1575] *Ibid.*
[1576] *Ibid.*
[1577] *Ibid.*
[1578] *Ibid.*
[1579] *Ibid.*, June 15, 2007.
[1580] *Ibid.*
[1581] *Ibid.*
[1582] *Ibid.*
[1583] *Ibid.*
[1584] *Ibid.*
[1585] *Ibid.*
[1586] *Ibid.*
[1587] *Ibid.*
[1588] *Ibid.*
[1589] *Ibid.*
[1590] *Ibid.*, September 14, 2007.
[1591] *Ibid.*
[1592] *Ibid.*, December 14, 2007.
[1593] *Ibid.*, September 14, 2007.
[1594] *Ibid.*
[1595] *Ibid.*
[1596] *Ibid.*
[1597] *Ibid.*
[1598] *Ibid.*
[1599] *Ibid.*
[1600] *Ibid.*, December 14, 2007.
[1601] *Ibid.*
[1602] *Ibid.*
[1603] *Ibid.*
[1604] *Ibid.*
[1605] *Ibid.*
[1606] *Ibid.*
[1607] *Ibid.*
[1608] *Ibid.*, April 4, 2008.
[1609] *Ibid.*
[1610] *Ibid.*
[1611] *Ibid.*
[1612] *Ibid.*
[1613] *Ibid.*
[1614] *Ibid.*
[1615] *Ibid.*
[1616] *Ibid.*
[1617] *Ibid.*
[1618] *Ibid.*
[1619] *Ibid.*, June 6, 2008.
[1620] *Ibid.*
[1620] *Ibid.*
[1621] *Ibid.*
[1622] *Ibid.*
[1623] *Ibid.*
[1624] *Ibid.*
[1625] *Ibid.*
[1626] *Ibid.*, September 12, 2008
[1627] *Ibid.*
[1628] *Ibid.*
[1629] *Ibid.*
[1630] *Ibid.*
[1631] *Ibid.*
[1632] *Ibid.*, December 12, 2008
[1633] *Ibid.*
[1634] *Ibid.*
[1635] *Ibid.*
[1636] *Ibid.*
[1637] *Ibid.*
[1638] *Ibid.*
[1639] *Ibid.*

[1640] *Ibid.*
[1641] *Ibid.*
[1642] *Ibid.*
[1643] *Ibid.*
[1644] *Ibid.*
[1645] *Ibid.,* April 16, 2010.
[1646] *Ibid.,* February 20, 2009.
[1647] *Ibid.*
[1648] *Ibid.,* April 17, 2009.
[1649] *Ibid.*
[1650] *Ibid.*
[1651] *Ibid.*
[1652] *Ibid.*
[1653] *Ibid.*
[1654] *Ibid.*
[1655] *Ibid.,* June 19, 2009.
[1656] *Ibid.*
[1657] *Ibid.*
[1658] *Ibid.*
[1659] *Ibid.*
[1660] *Ibid.,* October 2, 2009.
[1661] *Ibid.*
[1662] *Ibid.*
[1663] *Ibid.*
[1664] *Ibid.*
[1665] *Ibid.*
[1666] *Ibid.*
[1667] *Ibid.,* December 4, 2009.
[1668] *Ibid.*
[1669] *Ibid.*
[1670] *Ibid.*
[1671] *Ibid.*
[1672] *Ibid.*
[1673] *Ibid.*
[1674] *Ibid.,* April 16, 2010.
[1675] *Ibid.*
[1676] *Ibid.*
[1677] *Ibid.*
[1678] *Ibid.*
[1679] *Ibid.*
[1680] *Ibid.*
[1681] *Ibid.*
[1682] *Ibid.*
[1683] *Ibid.*
[1684] *Ibid.,* October 1, 2010.
[1685] *Ibid.*
[1686] *Ibid.*
[1687] *Ibid.*
[1688] *Ibid.*
[1689] *Ibid.*
[1690] *Ibid.*
[1691] *Ibid.*
[1692] *Ibid.,* December 3, 2010.
[1693] *Ibid.*
[1694] *Ibid.*
[1695] *Ibid.*
[1696] *Ibid.*
[1697] *Ibid.*
[1698] *Ibid.*
[1699] *Ibid.,* March 18, 2011.
[1700] *Ibid.,* June 10, 2011.
[1701] *Ibid.,* March 18, 2011.
[1702] *Ibid.*
[1703] *Ibid.,* September 9, 2011.
[1704] *Ibid.*
[1705] *Ibid.,* March 18, 2011.
[1706] *Ibid.*

1707 *Ibid.*
1708 *Ibid.*
1709 *Ibid.*
1710 *Ibid.*
1711 *Ibid.,* June 10, 2011.
1712 *Ibid.*
1713 *Ibid.*
1714 *Ibid.*
1715 *Ibid.*
1716 *Ibid.*
1717 *Ibid.*
1718 *Ibid.*
1719 *Ibid.*
1720 *Ibid.*
1721 *Ibid.,* September 9, 2011.
1722 *Ibid.*
1723 *Ibid.*
1724 *Ibid.*
1725 *Ibid.*
1726 *Ibid.*
1727 *Ibid.*

BIBLIOGRAPHY

Archival Sources

Butler County, Pennsylvania, Sesqui-Centennial Association, Butler, Pennsylvania, 1950.

Catalogs, Slippery Rock University, Slippery Rock, Pennsylvania, 1983-2011.

Catalogs, Slippery Rock State College, Slippery Rock, Pennsylvania, 1960-1983.

Catalogs, Slippery Rock State Normal School, Slippery Rock, Pennsylvania, 1889-1927.

Catalogs, Slippery Rock State Teachers College, Slippery Rock, Pennsylvania, 1927-1960.

Centennial Souvenir of Butler and Butler County, Goodwin and Curry, Butler, Pennsylvania, 1900.

Fifty Year Reunion Booklet, Class of 1917, Slippery Rock State College, 1967.

Inauguration of Robert M. Smith, President of Slippery Rock University, Slippery Rock, Pennsylvania, November 5, 2004. (Program.)

Inauguration of G. Warren Smith, President of Slippery Rock University, Slippery Rock, Pennsylvania, December 19, 1998. (Program.)

Investiture of Robert N. Aebersold, President of Slippery Rock University, Slippery Rock, Pennsylvania, April 11, 1986. (Program.)

Inauguration of Herb. F. Reinhard Jr., President of Slippery Rock State College, Slippery Rock, Pennsylvania, May 3, 1980. Program.)

Inauguration of Albert A. Watrel, President of Slippery Rock State College, Slippery Rock, Pennsylvania, May 3, 1967. (Program.)

Minutes, Council of Trustees of Slippery Rock University, 1983-2011.

Minutes, Board of Trustees of Slippery Rock State College, 1960-1983.

Minutes, Board of Trustees of Slippery Rock State Normal School, 1889-1927.

Minutes, Board of Trustees of Slippery Rock State Normal School Association, 1888-1889.

Minutes, Board of Trustees of Slippery Rock State Teachers College, 1927-1960.

Pi Gamma Mu Fraternity, *Thru Fifty Years of Normal School and Teachers College*, State Teachers College, Slippery Rock, Pennsylvania. 1939.

Privacy Rights of Parents and Students, Federal Register, Vol. 40, No. 3, Department of Health, Education and Welfare, Washington, D. C., January 6, 1975.

Saxigena, Slippery Rock University, Slippery Rock, Pennsylvania, 1983-2007. (Yearbook.)

Saxigena, Slippery Rock State College, Slippery Rock, Pennsylvania, 1960-1983. (Yearbook.)

Saxigena, Slippery Rock State Teachers College, Slippery Rock, Pennsylvania, 1941-1960. (Yearbook.)

Sesquicentennial History, Slippery Rock, Pennsylvania, 1825-1975. Historical Committee, Slippery Rock, Pennsylvania, 1975.

Slippery Rock State College, *Bachelor of Science in Nursing Program, Proposed Program*, 1974.

Slippery Rock State College, "Interim President Named," August 30, 1977. (News Release.)

Slippery Rock State College, *The Rock*, 1975.

Slippery Rock State College, *The Slippery Rock State Historian*, Vol. 1, No. 1, Fall, 1969.

Slippery Rock State College, *Undergraduate Enrollment Summary*, 1924-1978.

Slippery Rock State Teachers College, *Ground Breaking Ceremony*, January 19, 1938. (Program.)

The Rocket, Slippery Rock University, Slippery Rock, Pennsylvania, 1983-2011.

The Rocket, Slippery Rock State College, Slippery Rock, Pennsylvania, 1960-1983.

The Rocket, Slippery Rock State Teachers College, Slippery Rock, Pennsylvania, 1937-1960.

The Slippery Rocket, Slippery Rock State Teachers College, Slippery Rock, Pennsylvania, 1923-1937.

Books

Bowden, Reverend George., ed. *Souvenir History of Slippery Rock, Pennsylvania,* Butler, Pennsylvania: Ziegler Printing Company, 1925.

Brandon, James Campbell, *A Concise History of Butler County, Pennsylvania, 1800-1950*. Butler, Pennsylvania: Butler Historical Society, 1962.

Brown, Robert C., ed. *History of Butler County, Pennsylvania*, Chicago: Robert C. Brown and Company, 1895.

Chicago. *History of Butler County, Pennsylvania*, Chicago: Waterman, Watkins and Company, 1883.

Counts, George S. *Education and American Civilization*, New York: Teachers College, Columbia University, 1952.

Dunaway, Wyland Fuller. *A History of Pennsylvania*. New York: Prentice-Hall, Inc., 1935.

Duncan, Robert D., Joseph Frazier, and Donald S. Kelly. *Focus on Historic Mid-Western Pennsylvania*, Slippery Rock, Pennsylvania. 1975.

Hofstadter, Richard and Smith, Wilson, eds. *American Higher Education: A Documentary History*. 2 volumes. Chicago: University of Chicago Press, 1961.

McGrath, G. D., James L. Jelinek, and Raymond E. Wochner. *Educational Research Methods*, New York: The Ronald Press Company, 1963.

Meyerhoff, Hans., ed. *The Philosophy of History in Our Time*. Garden City, New York: Doubleday and Company, Inc., 1959.

Ralston, Raymond and Ruby Ralston. *Life Along the Slippery Rock Creek*. Slippery Rock, Pennsylvania, 1967.

Sack, Saul. *History of Higher Education in Pennsylvania*. 2 volumes. Harrisburg; Pennsylvania Historical and Museum Commission, 1963.

Sipe, C. Hale. *History of Butler County, Pennsylvania*. Topeka-Indianapolis: Historical Publishing Company, 1927.

Watson, Robert J. *Slippery Rock State College The Legend Behind the Name*. Slippery Rock, Pennsylvania: The Slippery Rock State College Alumni Association, 1982.

Dissertations

Maszkiewicz, Ruth. "The Presbyterian Hospital of Pittsburgh: From Its Founding to Affiliation with the University of Pittsburgh." Ph.D. dissertation, University of Pittsburgh, 1977.

Merryman, John Edward. "Indiana University of Pennsylvania: From Private Normal School to Public University." Ph.D. dissertation, University of Pittsburgh, 1972.

Serinko, Regis Jerome. "California State College The People's College in the Monongahela Valley." Ph.D. dissertation, University of Pittsburgh, 1974.

Interviews

Carpenter, John. Slippery Rock, 5 February, 1979.

Dorritie, Daniel. Harrisburg, 22 January, 1979.

Headland, Howard. Grove City, 20-21 February, 1977.

Lowry, Robert A. Slippery Rock, 17 January, 1978.

Vincent, Leila. Slippery Rock, 16 January, 1979.

Letters

Fuller, Catherine McLaine Mrs., to the writer. Letter. March 7, 1977.

Newspapers

Butler Eagle. Butler. May 16, 1895, July 2, 1896, February 19, 21, 1916, October 16, 18, 1937, November 4, 1941, January 17, 1942, October 11, 1958, May 3, 4, 5, 1966, June 12, 13, 17, 1976.

News Shopper. Slippery Rock, June 23, 1976.

Philadelphia Inquirer. Philadelphia. October 3, 1976.

Pittsburgh Post-Gazette. Pittsburgh. June 12, 1976.

Pittsburgh Press. Pittsburgh. June 13, 1976.

Pittsburgh Sun-Telegraph. Pittsburgh. March 25, 1928.

Slippery Rock Signal. Slippery Rock. August 11. 1937, January 20, 1938.

Wall Street Journal. New York. September 11, 1975.

INDEX

445